GENTLEMEN OF UNCERTAIN FORTUNE

GENTLEMEN OF Uncertain Fortune

HOW YOUNGER SONS MADE THEIR
WAY IN JANE AUSTEN'S ENGLAND

RORY MUIR

YALE UNIVERSITY PRESS
NEW HAVEN AND LONDON

Published with assistance from the Annie Burr Lewis Fund.

For information about this and other Yale University Press publications, please contact:
U.S. Office: sales.press@yale.edu   yalebooks.com
Europe Office: sales@yaleup.co.uk   yalebooks.co.uk

Set in Van Dijck MT by IDSUK (DataConnection) Ltd
Printed in Great Britain by TJ International Ltd, Padstow, Cornwall

Library of Congress Control Number: 2019941049

ISBN 978-0-300-24431-1

A catalogue record for this book is available from the British Library.

10 9 8 7 6 5 4 3 2 1

CONTENTS

ILLUSTRATIONS

9. 'Fitting out Mastr Willm Blockhead', coloured aquatint by George Cruikshank, published by Thomas McLean (1835). National Maritime Museum, Greenwich, London.

10. 'Master B Finding Things Not Exactly What He Expected', coloured aquatint by George Cruikshank (1835). National Maritime Museum, Greenwich, London.

11. Ensign Johnny Newcome and his soldier servant eating breakfast on a roadside in Portugal, hand-coloured copperplate engraving drawn and etched by Thomas Rowlandson, from Colonel David Roberts' *The Military Adventures of Johnny Newcome* (1815). Florilegius / Alamy Stock Photo.

12. 'Ensign Johnny Newcome down with dysentery in his billet in Medina, Spain', hand-coloured copperplate engraving drawn and etched by Thomas Rowlandson, from Colonel David Roberts' *The Military Adventures of Johnny Newcome*. Florilegius / Alamy Stock Photo.

13. 'English Family at Table under a Punkah', coloured aquatint by Sir Charles D'Oyly, from his *The European in India* (1813). Chronicle / Alamy Stock Photo.

14. Detail of *The Market Place of Trichinopoly* by Philip Le Couteur (1800). © National Army Museum.

PREFACE

ANYONE WHO HAS READ *Pride and Prejudice* knows that the Bennets had a problem. Their five children were all girls and the family estate of Longbourn was entailed on the male line, so that when Mr Bennet died it would pass to a distant relative, the Rev. Mr Collins. The girls would each inherit a mere pittance, a thousand pounds of capital, which, safely invested, would scarcely yield enough to enable them to live in even the reduced circumstances of Miss Bates in *Emma*. Nor could they have much hope of improving their circumstances by working, for the only acceptable work for a woman of their class was as a governess, a companion or a schoolteacher, occupations that were notoriously underpaid. The obvious injustice of this arrangement has alerted modern readers to the plight of young women in Regency Britain who, if they lacked independent means, could only hope to obtain comfort and security through the lottery of marriage.

But suppose that the Bennets had five sons, not five daughters: the estate would pass to the eldest son – the male counterpart of the gentle Jane. The other four boys would still have to make their way in the world, for they would inherit no more than if they had been girls. Their father, and after his death, their eldest brother, might give them some help in establishing themselves in a career, but they would be expected to become independent and make enough money to be able to support a wife and family, before they could contemplate marriage. What would they do for a living? What careers were open to the younger sons of good families in Britain in the late eighteenth and early nineteenth centuries? How could a gentleman work for his living without ceasing to be a gentleman?

There were limited choices facing a young man: he might go into the Church, or practise medicine or the law; he might even go into banking or one of the other respectable branches of trade; he might join the navy or the army; he might go out to India or one of the other colonies, or he might secure a government position. Few other possibilities existed, and they were usually unattractive or limited to a handful of places. Indeed, each of these careers had its own characteristics that gave it an appeal to some, while making it unsuitable to others. The purpose of this book is to explore these possibilities, to consider the prospects of the young men who embarked on these careers, and to examine the ingredients that would contribute to their success or failure. In addition, I hope to convey a sense of the experiences they would encounter in their career: to view things from an individual as well as a collective perspective – how it felt, as well as how it worked.

The focus is on young men born in the second half of the eighteenth century, and in particular the generation who came of age around 1790, just before the long war with France broke out in 1793. This was the generation of the Duke of Wellington and of Jane Austen and her brothers; of George Canning and Lord Castlereagh; of Walter Scott and William Wordsworth – although I have drawn examples from across the half-century and very slightly beyond. These young gentlemen were just getting established in their careers when Jane Austen wrote the drafts of her early novels, and were mid-career when her six novels were published between 1811 and 1818. They lived through the alarms and difficulties of the war with Revolutionary France in the 1790s, the fear of invasion by Napoleon in the early 1800s, and then the growing improvement in the fortunes of the war with Wellington's campaigns in the Peninsula beginning in 1808. In 1815 Waterloo brought a lasting peace, but the next few years were just as difficult, as the economy faltered when the stimulus of war spending was withdrawn and foreign competition revived. After five turbulent years, prosperity and stability returned, just as the Regency was ending, and the comparatively tranquil reign of George IV began. These events helped to shape the careers of some young men of this generation – most obviously the soldiers and sailors among them – while having little direct influence on the careers of others, including most clergymen and lawyers. Some of these men helped shape the events of the time, but a great many more were swept along by the tide, with little control or even a sense of where they were going, and it is these ordinary young men who are the primary subject of this book.

Most of these young men were the sons of private gentlemen of independent means, or of men in the gentlemanly professions: clergymen, naval officers and the like; in other words the sons of men like Mr Bennet, or of the Rev. Mr Austen, Jane's father. However, the careers open to the younger sons of the aristocracy were generally much the same as those open to the sons of other gentlemen, and many of their experiences were very similar, so that the examples include the sons and brothers of earls and viscounts as well as of the gentry. This is not to deny that rank and fortune were very considerable advantages (although not as great as good connections within the profession) and we shall see how they were brought to bear, but the young men in any particular career were all running in the same race, even if some were given a head start.

Not all the men whose experiences are discussed were younger sons, for some eldest sons embarked on a profession either from necessity, if their father was not wealthy, or from choice, and once they entered the race the advantage of birth, by itself, counted for little. Equally, many members of all these professions were not the sons of gentlemen but came from 'the middling classes' – sons of shopkeepers and farmers, clerks and tradesmen, and they shared many of the same experiences as their colleagues. Nonetheless this is predominately a book about the well-born second son and his younger brothers: about the 'spares' who never became 'heirs'.

It is also a book overwhelmingly about men. The challenges women faced were equally formidable but quite different, and have been admirably explored in a number of scholarly works including, most notably, Amanda Vickery's *The Gentleman's Daughter*. Women appear here largely as mothers and sisters, lovers and wives, and occasionally as patrons such as Lady Catherine de Bourg, while some of Austen's other female characters also make appearances in order to shed light on social attitudes. But despite the relative absence of women from the text, I hope that the book illuminates the dilemmas they faced in marrying; what it meant to marry a young clergyman, naval officer or barrister; and also why there were so many young men of good family who were in no position to marry unless their intended had money of her own.

Finally, it is a book about a world that was already beginning to change dramatically two hundred years ago. Modern attitudes on many subjects – most obviously primogeniture and the place of women – are completely different from those even of the 1820s, let alone the 1780s. Readers do not need me to point this out constantly, and will, I hope, take for granted that when I write, for example, of 'good families' I am using the language of the time to convey the values of the time, not that this reflects my own outlook.

In writing this study I have been blessed by the abundance of entertaining and revealing accounts written at the time by the young men and members of their family, chiefly in the form of letters, diaries and memoirs, which shed light on the progress of their careers. I have also drawn on the fiction of the period – most notably Jane Austen's novels – which sometimes spell out with great clarity the underlying assumptions of the age. Austen's own family is also a particularly good source of evidence: whatever their private virtues and talents, her father and brothers were perfectly unremarkable in worldly terms; their successes and failures were typical of men of their class, and they represent thousands of men with similar careers who are completely forgotten simply because they failed to provide themselves with a sister who wrote some of the finest novels in the language.

I have also benefited from a great deal of excellent work by fellow historians on the social history of individual professions, and on Regency society as a whole. Each chapter rests on foundations built by specialist books and articles, as well as the experiences of individuals conveyed through biographies and their letters and journals. I am greatly indebted to the work of these historians and editors, and one of the pleasures of writing this book has been the discovery of so much good scholarship, often very well written, in fields that are new to me. It would be invidious to single out specific examples, but the references in the notes should be read as conveying a warm sense of appreciation and admiration for works both old and new.

But while individual professions have been studied with great care, there has been surprisingly little work comparing them. There are some good works on the rise of the professions that treat them primarily as corporate bodies and concentrate on their collective power rather than the individual experience of their members. These works are important, but they do not really explain the pros and cons of each career and the considerations that influenced a young man and his family in deciding which profession he should enter. In recent times there has been greater academic interest in the position of men in society and the history of masculinity, and the works of Henry French and Mark Rothery in particular concern the same period and touch on some of the subjects addressed in my work. However, there is less overlap between their work and mine than might be expected. I come to the subject from a different direction; I am interested in answering different questions, and I write in a different style. I respect their work, but I do not seek to emulate it, although I hope that together we all help to illuminate the subject.

By examining all the careers open to young men of good families in a single volume, I hope to give a better sense of the possibilities open to them and the implications of their choices. What was the right choice for the male equivalent of an Elizabeth, a Jane, a Mary, a Catherine or a Lydia Bennet as they considered how to make their way in the world? What would the world offer them, and what would it expect in return?

I have been working on British history of the late eighteenth and early nineteenth centuries for many years, and in that time have received an enormous amount of help from a great many people and institutions, and this assistance underpins this work even when the help was given long before this particular project was conceived. For example, the quotation from the unpublished journal of Henry Smith in Chapter 11 comes from some transcripts generously given to me years ago by Tim Rooth, when I was in the midst of studying Wellington's campaigns in the Peninsula. So I would like to begin my acknowledgements by thanking Tim, and everyone else who has helped me in years gone by, and who ensured that I did not start this project from scratch.

Throughout the period that I was writing this book I have continued to be a Visiting Research Fellow in the Department of History in the Faculty of Arts at the University of Adelaide, and I am very grateful to the university and in particular to the Barr Smith Library, with its rich resources, for the many ways in which it has enabled and facilitated my writing. I would also like to thank the organizers of the Immortal Austen conference at Flinders University in 2017 for creating such a successful event, with some excellent speakers and stimulating conversation on the sidelines, from which I learnt a great deal. This conference led to me giving a paper on the subject of younger sons to the Jane Austen Society of Adelaide, and I am appreciative of their kind reception and their informed comments, and I should particularly like to thank Barbara Baldock for her invitation. On a similar theme I would like to thank Ruth Williamson for the opportunity to contribute a short article on younger sons and their careers to the *Chronicle* of the Jane Austen Society of Australia.

Many people are involved in the publication of a book, and my thanks are due to my agent, Bill Hamilton of A. M. Heath; to all the staff at Yale University Press, in particular Julian Loose, Marika Lysandrou, Matt James, Rachael Lonsdale and Clarissa Sutherland. Jenny Rogers was the perfect copy editor and her comments and suggestions greatly improved the script and I greatly enjoyed our correspondence which made something that might have been a chore into a pleasure.

I would also like to thank Ron McGuigan, John Harding-Edgar, Anthony Gray, Bob Burnham and Roger Knight for answering questions on specific points that arose while I was writing. And I am grateful to Elaine Chalus for sharing some of her fascinating work on Betsey

Fremantle before it appeared in print and for reading and commenting on the two chapters of my book relating to the navy. More generally I would like to thank them and all my other correspondents, including Chris Woolgar, Mark Thompson, John Malcolm, Russ Foster and Zack White for their encouragement and support. I have always found other historians – inside and outside the academy – extremely generous, and there is a great sense of camaraderie both in direct contact and online, through the Napoleonic Discussion Forum and, more recently, through Twitter, which I joined after the text of this book was substantially finished. To everyone out there whom I follow, or who follows me, or whose tweets I see through others, thank you.

Two old friends, Charles Esdaile and Howie Muir, have remained steadfastly loyal and supportive even as my interests have veered away from the subjects which they find most rewarding, and have continued to provide good advice as well as much encouragement. And a more recent friend, Jacqueline Reiter, has done even more, reading the entire script and providing a wealth of pertinent and perceptive comments reflecting her expertise as a fine historian of the period.

My parents brought me up with a love of history and of books which has enriched my life immeasurably; while it was from watching my mother that I first discovered the joys and frustrations of research and writing. They also gave me an older sister and I am immensely grateful for all the love and support which Kathie, and her partner Anthony, have given me, as well as Kathie's comments on reading the draft of the early chapters of the book.

And finally to my wonderful and very much loved wife Robin, who was enthusiastic about this project from the outset, and who has championed it all along the way. I thank her for reading every word (often more than once), for her constant support, acute advice and great inspiration – and for much, much more besides.

A NOTE ON MONEY

BRITAIN ONLY INTRODUCED DECIMAL coinage in 1971. For more than a thousand years before that one pound was equal to 20 shillings, each of which was worth 12 pennies. The abbreviated Latin names were l. s. d. written as £, s. and d. So £1 19s. 6d. was sixpence less than two pounds.

For most of the eighteenth and nineteenth centuries Britain was on the gold standard, and banknotes could be exchanged for actual gold and silver coins, which had the effect of limiting inflation, although possibly also reducing economic growth. However, in 1797, when the long war with France was going badly, the government responded to a financial crisis by 'suspending cash payments' – Britain went off the gold standard. This led to considerable inflation during the war, followed by sharp deflation from 1815 as Britain prepared to return to the gold standard, which it did in 1821.

In the eighteenth century the principal British gold coin was the guinea, which was worth 21s. or £1 1s., and many prices were quoted in guineas: 100 guineas was £105. After the defeat of Napoleon, as part of the preparations for returning to the gold standard, new gold coins were issued, which were commonly known as sovereigns, and were worth one pound. Guinea coins became rare, but the term guineas continued to be used for many prices well into the twentieth century.

CHAPTER ONE

YOUNGER SONS AND THEIR FAMILIES

NOT ALL GENTLEMEN WERE rich; indeed, many had little money of their own and had to pursue a career. The eldest son would normally inherit the family estate, while the daughters and younger sons would receive no more than a start in life. The girls would be introduced into society where they might find a husband, and they would receive some money either as part of their marriage settlement or as capital on which they might contrive to live as a spinster. The younger sons would be helped in the first steps of their career, educated for the Church or the law, or found a place in the army or the navy, and they too would be given or inherit a little capital. Their father, and when he died their eldest brother, would continue to use whatever influence he possessed to help them along, but their success would largely depend on their own endeavours and their own good fortune.

This unequal treatment complicated relations between siblings, especially if their parents died while they were still young. George Gordon, 4th Earl of Aberdeen, inherited a vast estate in Scotland, which yielded an income of £16,000 or £17,000 a year, when he was only 17 years old. His five younger brothers and one sister each received £2,000. Not an *income* of two thousand pounds a year, but £2,000 in total, which, prudently invested, might give an income of £100 a year; and £100 a year was poverty for even a single man or woman if he or she had any pretensions to being a gentleman or a lady. To marry on such an income, without the certain expectation of its rapid increase, was to be almost insanely irresponsible.[1]

Not surprisingly, all of Aberdeen's brothers pursued careers. William and John went into the navy; Alexander and Charles went into the army; and Robert became a distinguished diplomat. Aberdeen assisted them with money and influence, but although they were all more or less successful, they found it very difficult to establish their financial independence. By the age of 27 Alexander Gordon had seen action on three continents, having taken part in the capture of Cape Town, Buenos Aires and Copenhagen. He had served in the Coruña campaign on the staff of Sir David Baird, who was second-in-command to Sir John Moore; and he had spent four more years in the Peninsula as one of Wellington's most trusted aides-de-camp. He wrote long, interesting letters home to Aberdeen, giving him the latest news from the Peninsula and intelligent comments on the way the campaign might unfold, which must have helped Aberdeen appear unusually well-informed as he mixed in the leading political circles in London. Aberdeen often replied, although his correspondence was less regular than that of his brother, and he did not hesitate to give Alexander commissions: could he please send home some good Spanish merino sheep, as other officers had done? Could he look out for some old silver plate and arrange for it to be smuggled into Britain, so as to avoid paying duty on it? What about a pipe of the true port wine, unadulterated with brandy? Alexander not only did his best to comply but looked out for things that might please his brother. Aberdeen was an enthusiastic classical scholar with highly developed aesthetic tastes, and Alexander suggested sending him home some Roman statues that he had seen and admired in Spain. The response was decided: 'Pray do not think of sending me those headless trunks you mention at Merida, or any mutilated things of the kind; they are never worth the carriage. An entire stature [statue] of good work is quite a different thing.' And when Alexander wrote home with a detailed account of the paintings that had delighted him in Madrid, Aberdeen's reply was rich in condescension:

I envy you very much the sight of the fine things at Madrid. Your observations are pretty judicious for so inexperienced a person with the exception of what you say about Mengs who is the most miserable dauber possible. A cartload of his works would sell for nothing in England. Most likely many of the Raphaels are false . . . Murillo, though a pleasing, is still a second rate painter . . .

Admittedly art was Aberdeen's field, not Alexander's, but not many men of 26 would appreciate this tone in a letter from their father, let alone a brother who was only two years their senior.[2]

Every now and then Alexander rebelled and wrote a furious letter home, usually complaining of his brother's slackness in writing, but invariably he went on to apologize within a few weeks. In part this was because he felt a genuine deference for Aberdeen as the head of the family and the hub through which the siblings maintained contact (for both their parents were dead). But Aberdeen also helped him financially, giving him an allowance of £250 a year, for even on active service Alexander could not live on his pay and allowances amounting to about £200 a year. His active and conspicuous position on Wellington's staff meant that he had to spend heavily on good horses and fine uniforms, and while the position came with extra pay, it was not enough. Given the vast sums – many thousands of pounds – that Aberdeen was spending at this time on renovations to Argyll House in London and improvements to his estate in Scotland, not to mention paintings, books, coins, antiquities and other luxuries which he bought in large quantities, it was unfortunate that he did not refrain from criticizing what he saw as his brother's extravagance in ordering an ornate scabbard for his sword. But that was the difference: Aberdeen was the eldest son, a peer of the realm, already a figure of note in the world of politics, and he was entitled to all the good things the earth had to offer; while Alexander was a younger son, a very promising officer who might even rise to greatness, but who needed to win his fortune before he could stop counting his pennies. Aberdeen eventually rose to be Prime Minister, while Alexander Gordon was killed at Waterloo.[3]

Although Alexander Gordon was hurt by his brother's arrogance and lack of tact, he does not seem ever to have questioned the inequality of their inheritance. Inequality of various kinds was universal and taken for granted, challenged only by the most radical and impractical of political philosophers and French republicans in the most extreme phase of their disastrous revolution. The hierarchical principle was supported both by the teachings of the Church and by the evidence of nature, which itself was God's creation. Loyalty to the King and government by Parliament was underpinned by an acceptance of authority that was inherently hierarchical, and parallels were often drawn between the position of a monarch in the nation and a father in his family. In theory, children were expected to respect, honour and obey their parents, and while the reality was always more complicated and human than such doctrines suggest, a much greater degree of deference was actually exacted than is common today. Society frowned on children – even adult children – who openly quarrelled with their parents, only sympathizing with them if the parent's behaviour clearly put them in the wrong. And when parents died before their children had grown up, the eldest son inherited a good deal of his father's authority and standing. By the standards of the day Aberdeen was a relatively caring and considerate brother, who did his best to advance the interests of his siblings and regarded them with real affection.

Younger sons of the late eighteenth and early nineteenth centuries usually accepted their inferior position and meagre inheritance without complaint. Two hundred years before, however, in late Tudor and early Stuart times, there were many more objections. Indeed, a plentiful literature of protest was written by and for younger sons in the decades preceding the English Civil War, in which their grievances were set forth with considerable vehemence. Their plight was pitiable: brought up and educated as gentlemen they were quite unable to maintain their station in life unless they had the good fortune to see their elder brother die without leaving an heir, or they chanced upon a pot of gold in some military or mercantile venture. Since then the position of younger sons had been alleviated by the rising wealth of the country, which meant that a handful of professions afforded the hope of a reasonable living and a respectable place in society. Literary protests died away along with any sense of younger sons being a distinct group with common interests. By Alexander Gordon's day younger sons were much more likely to regard each other as competitors for the limited rewards on offer than as fellow sufferers in an unjust society.[4]

The odds were stacked against them. Well-born families of this period averaged five or six children who survived to adulthood.[5] In a completely static society there would only be room for two of these children to take the place of the parents: the eldest son to inherit the family estate, and one of the daughters to marry as well as her mother. However, Britain in this period was growing richer quite rapidly, and while some of the additional room in the upper strata of society was being claimed by the *nouveau riche*, there was also space for more younger sons and daughters to hold their ground. So it might be that of six surviving children, three could live as well as their parents, and of these three, one would be the eldest son. The other three would slip down the social scale, usually only a few rungs, but the decline was unmistakable and often cumulative over the generations. Historians often write about 'social mobility' in Hanoverian England, but their focus is usually on the absorption of new blood and new money into the upper classes and the resistance it encountered. Much less attention has been paid to the simultaneous decline of the younger branches of almost every great family.[6]

This process can be seen clearly if we follow a single line of descent in a single family. Lady Jane Bertie was the daughter of the 2nd Duke of Ancaster. She married a soldier, General Edward Mathew, who played an important part in the American War of Independence and went on to be Commander-in-Chief of the Windward and Leeward Islands and Governor General of Grenada. He was a man of substance and distinction, but not a duke or even a peer. Their second daughter, Anne Mathew, at the late age of 32, married a young clergyman, James Austen (brother of the more famous Jane). James Austen had the prospect of inheriting a fortune from his maternal uncle, and would certainly inherit his father's living at Steventon in a few years time. But when he married he had only a meagre income, which General Mathew supplemented with an allow-ance of £100 a year. The granddaughter of a duke had become the wife of a country clergyman: she had a daughter, Anna, and then died in May 1795. James Austen prospered modestly as many clergymen of his gener-ation did, but he could never live on anything approaching the scale of General Mathew or the Duke of Ancaster. Anna fared less well. She did not much like her stepmother, and in 1814 she married Ben Lefroy, a member of a local family who were old friends of the Austens. Ben was a serious, religious young man, but it was only after a good deal of hesita-tion that he took holy orders in 1817 and succeeded to a family living a few years later. It looked as though Anna would maintain her station in society, not rising back towards the heights her mother and grandmother had inhabited as children, but not falling either. She and Ben had seven children in 12 years, but then Ben died at the age of only 38. Anna lost her husband, her home and her income, and had to bring up their chil-dren in genteel poverty in a variety of rented lodgings, staying with rela-tives and suffering the ignominy of being the poor relation. She never remarried or recovered her former prosperity in the 43 years she spent as a widow before her death in 1872.[7]

Anna Lefroy was descended from the Duke of Ancaster through a female line, but the same trajectory could just as easily have happened through a line of younger sons. The duke's second or third son might easily have become a soldier and would have done well to have distin-guished himself as much as General Mathew.[8] And *his* second or third son could readily have been a country clergyman, living a life very similar to that of James Austen. It is true that if Anna had been a boy, the death of her spouse would not have had such a disastrous effect on her finances, but there were many other ways in which a family's finances might be ruined, and many husbands faced both financial ruin and the death of their wife at the same time, even if the two were not directly connected.

If Anna Lefroy's life illustrates how bad luck and an unexpected death could force someone down the social scale, the life of her half-brother, James Edward Austen-Leigh, shows that good luck and a long anticipated death could have the reverse effect. Like his father James and like Ben

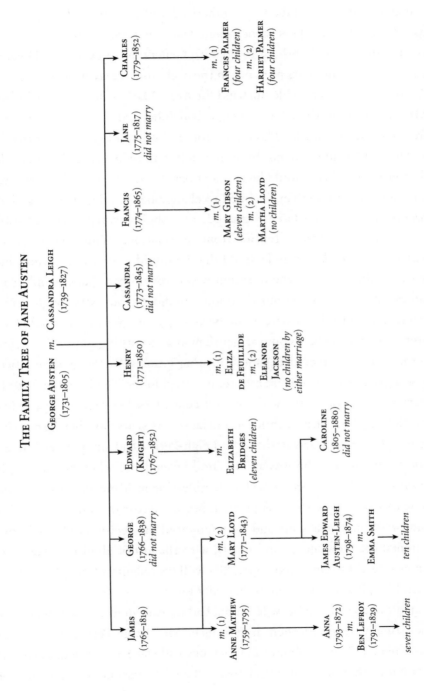

THE FAMILY TREE OF JANE AUSTEN

Lefroy, James Edward was a clergyman. But at the age of 38 – the same age at which Ben had died – he inherited a fortune from his great-aunt Mrs Leigh-Perrot.[9] This money came from his father's mother's side of the family – it had nothing to do with General Mathew or the Duke of Ancaster – although its presence in the background may have made James Austen a more acceptable husband for Anne Mathew many years before. Mrs Austen's brother, James Leigh, had inherited the fortune in 1751 from *his* maternal uncle, Thomas Perrot, and when it became clear that he and his wife would have no children he left it all to his wife, giving her the discretion as to who would be the next beneficiary. Mrs Leigh-Perrot was a rather difficult woman, inclined to change her mind and to make half promises which she later retracted, and she expected a considerable amount of deferential attention from her relations. While James Austen was alive it was always understood that he would inherit the fortune, but when he died in 1819 the question was thrown open. James's only son, James Edward, was the most obvious candidate, but Mrs Leigh-Perrot was displeased at his insistence on becoming a clergyman: she would have preferred that he be a country gentleman and nothing more. For a time her favour was directed at James's brother Francis Austen, a naval officer now apparently retired and ashore, but then Francis had the temerity to marry for a second time without first consulting her. (His first wife had died leaving him with 11 children and he was 54 years old when he married again.) It is not clear whether Mrs Leigh-Perrot had any personal objection to his bride (who was an old family friend), or whether she simply resented not having been asked for her blessing in advance, but her favour began to veer back towards James Edward. A year or two later and her mind was finally made up, and she announced the decision to Francis, but softened the blow most handsomely, with the gift of almost £10,000. As James Edward commented wryly, 'She will find plenty of people ready to offend her, if she pays them so liberally for it'.[10]

James Edward and his wife Emma had to wait another six years before they finally received their inheritance. Mrs Leigh-Perrot died on 13 November 1836 aged about 92. When her will was read a few days later it was found that she had left almost £30,000 to various relatives of her own or her husband, but the remainder of the estate went, as promised, to James Edward. Although the exact sum was not specified, it included her much loved country house of Scarlets and significant investments which made James Edward a wealthy man, and enabled him to provide for his 10 children.[11]

For a younger son, inheriting a fortune was undoubtedly the pleasantest preservative from want; however, there were fewer fortunes waiting to be inherited than there were deserving young men in need of them. Still, some were lucky, among them Jane Austen's brother Edward who attracted the notice of Thomas and Catherine Knight, the distant Kentish cousins whose family had already bestowed the Steventon living on Mr Austen. The Knights first met Edward when they called at Steventon soon after their marriage and took the bright-eyed 12-year-old with them on their tour for a week or two. They enjoyed his company and began to ask him to spend his holidays with them at Godmersham. At first, this may not have meant much, for the Knights may still have hoped to have children of their own, but their affection for him grew as their own nursery remained empty. It is not known exactly when they adopted him as their heir, although it was probably in 1783 when he turned 16 and they commissioned a portrait of him. They sent him on a grand tour of the Continent between 1786 and 1788, and there never seems to have been any thought to training him for a career, so some commitment had presumably been made which gave him an assured future. The choice of Edward originally depended on his character and charm, but it was also in accordance with the ideas of the day, for his eldest brother James had already the prospect of the Leigh-Perrot fortune as well as his father's living at Steventon; and the second brother George had failed to develop normally, and was cared for privately. Edward was therefore next in line, and it often was the second son who benefited from the bequest of an uncle or cousin.[12]

Thomas Knight died in 1794 when Edward was 27, and left his estate to his widow for her lifetime, after which it would go to Edward. Catherine lived on in the great house at Godmersham for a little while, but in 1797 she bought herself a house in Canterbury, retiring there, and retaining a handsome income of £2,000 a year for herself, while turning over the rest of the estate to Edward and his young family. She did not remarry and remained a benevolent figure in the Austen family circle – quite unlike Mrs Leigh-Perrot – until her death while still relatively young in 1812. (It is thought – although the evidence is fragmentary and uncertain – that she gave Jane a small private allowance, and certainly both Jane and Cassandra learnt to appreciate her sense and generosity.) When she died, Edward changed his name to Knight, and proved a good brother and son, providing a house at Chawton for his widowed mother and unmarried sisters, extending hospitality to all his siblings and their families at Godmersham, and even investing a substantial sum of money in Henry's bank. He was by far the wealthiest member of the family, and took over much of the role that would normally have been played by the eldest son, although he was too good-humoured and cheerful to cause offence by any presumption of authority.[13]

Such a legacy was no less welcome in an aristocratic family. Wellington's older brother William, the second of the five Wellesley boys, was similarly fortunate, inheriting a large estate from his cousin, and changing his name to William Wellesley-Pole. Although he was only 18 when his cousin died, he had already spent three years in the Royal Navy as a midshipman, which suggests that nothing was being taken for granted. The inheritance transformed his life, and before his 22nd birthday he had left the navy, become one of the largest landowners in Queen's County and a member of the Irish Parliament, and had married Katherine Forbes, who was both rich and beautiful. However, little of his prosperity rubbed off on his younger brothers, and Arthur, Gerald and Henry still had to make their own way in the world, continuing to look primarily to their eldest brother, Richard, Lord Mornington, for patronage and help in their careers.[14]

The prospect of such an inheritance was enough to quicken the pulse of any poor younger son, but the hopes excited were sometimes dashed or only fulfilled after painful suspense and long years of waiting. James Austen died without ever receiving the Leigh-Perrot estate, and Thomas Anthony Trollope, the father of the novelist, spent most of his life anticipating a large inheritance from his uncle, only for the uncle to remarry and start a family at the age of 64, following the death of his first wife.[15] Henry Hickey, whose brother William wrote one of the most frank and enjoyable memoirs in English literature, was taken to Dublin by a wealthy and childless merchant, an old friend of his father. He spent four years in Ireland learning the business. He did well and his patron then proposed making him his partner in the business and his eventual heir, but imposed two conditions: that Hickey marry his niece, and that he become a Catholic. Hickey had no objection to the niece, who was lovely, but although he was not a religious young man, his pride rebelled and he refused to renounce his father's Anglican faith. A quarrel ensued and Hickey was sent back to London, where he lived a very wild and dissipated life until his father – who was a remarkably patient and loving parent – finally despaired, and procured for him a cadetship in the Madras army. Within six months of arriving in India Henry Hickey died of a fever. Meanwhile, back in Dublin, both the merchant and his niece had died, and their whole fortune, some £200,000, was left to several charities.[16]

Hickey's story suggests another possible way of acquiring a fortune: marrying an heiress. But unfortunately there were far fewer wealthy young women than needy young gentlemen, and those young women who did have substantial fortunes had a regrettable tendency to marry men who were at least as rich as themselves. This was understandable: a young woman with a fortune of £10,000 was probably accustomed to living in a style that could not be sustained on £500 a year – the income her own capital would produce – even if her husband was not extravagant in his own tastes. She and her family were also likely to be wary of a suitor who had no fortune of his own, suspecting that he might not be motivated entirely by love and that, after marrying her, he might not treat her well. A wealthy husband might also behave badly, but there was, at least, less reason to suspect his motives at the outset. In any case, a poor younger son would make a more credible suitor if he had at least embarked on a career and so had some prospects of his own, so that a good marriage was more likely to rescue a young man from a career that he disliked than to allow him to avoid embarking on an occupation. Marrying an heiress was like inheriting a fortune from a wealthy uncle or aunt: very nice if you could get it, but both rare and an imperfect substitute for a career.[17]

But if a younger son might search in vain for a young lady of fortune to rescue him from the unfortunate necessity of earning his living, he still could not – with any sense of responsibility – ignore money and propose to the woman he loved if she had no capital of her own and he lacked a sufficient income to support them. 'Love in a cottage' was a fine fantasy, but its charms could not stand against the awful prospect of a rapid succession of pregnancies and the ill health of mother and children exacerbated by poor housing and lack of domestic help. Of course, some young couples were imprudent, and either lived to regret it or made good, possibly driven by necessity to strive harder than they would otherwise have done. Quite a few young men postponed their marriage: Alexander Gordon might have married if he had not been killed at Waterloo, and relied on his connection with Wellington to ensure that he obtained a position with sufficient income to support a family, but his brothers William, Charles, Robert and John Gordon all died unmarried, while Lord Aberdeen had two wives and fathered eight children. John Aitchison, a young ensign in the Guards, remained in the army after the war, and delayed marrying until he was no longer liable to be sent on active service: at which point he was 68 years old, but nonetheless he went on to have three children. Most men were not this restrained: all of Jane Austen's brothers, except the unfortunate George, married, and both Francis and especially Charles felt the pressure of growing families and small incomes, at least for a time.[18]

——⊷◆⊷——

For most younger sons there was neither prospect of an inheritance nor an heiress waiting in the wings to rescue them from the need to pursue a career. The range of occupations open to a well-born young man was not wide, and differed only a little whether he was the son of an earl or of a country clergyman. The Church was the first and most obvious refuge for a younger son: it was a relatively safe choice, although not one to excite the ambitious. There were a few rich plums, but a great mass of plain pudding, and life for most clergymen was humdrum in the extreme, and often quite frugal. The law offered better rewards for a young man who had the necessary confidence, energy and ability, but competition was fierce in its higher reaches, and it had a well-earned reputation for requiring a great deal of drudgery in the early years. An adventurous lad might be keen to go to sea, and the navy had the advantage of being an economical choice, for it took boys young (commonly at 13 or 14), sparing their father the expense of school or university, although a small allowance – £30 to £50 a year – was almost a necessity. The army was rather more expensive, for each commission (rank) an officer held had to be purchased, although this might be waived in wartime, as was frequently the case during the long war with France, if the young man was not seeking to join a particularly fashionable regiment. Nor was the pay of a junior officer enough for most young men: some supplementary allowance from home was generally required.

Family connections might provide other opportunities: banking, overseas trade and some other branches of commerce conducted on a large scale were relatively respectable, and offered a much better chance of making a substantial fortune than the other professions, but sons of gentlemen usually only began on such careers if they already had a relative or close family friend ready to open the door for them. Manufacturing and the retail trades were less acceptable: a man might make a fortune in these fields and then retire and become a gentleman (as did Sir William Lucas in *Pride and Prejudice* and Mr Weston in *Emma*), but the sons of gentlemen were generally reluctant to go into such businesses. The same was largely true of the medical profession. A country doctor might be fully the equal of a country attorney, but a fashionable doctor was not equal to a leading barrister, let alone a judge, and the status of medicine was at a low ebb compared to its past or future. Government service offered a variety of positions, some of them very well paid, ranging from those which required constant attendance and hard work, to pure sinecures. However, competition for the more desirable positions was naturally intense, and the day had yet to arrive when many well-born young men were prepared to enter the public service as mere clerks. For the less blessed, there was India and the other colonies, although as Henry Hickey found, only a minority of the young men who ventured forth returned as wealthy nabobs. This, indeed, was true of almost all these careers: most young men were lucky to survive and make enough money to marry and gain a respectable place in society; a few did exceptionally well, but many fell by the wayside, claimed by shipwreck, disease, enemy action or bankruptcy, and even more simply lived out their lives in relative poverty and obscurity.

The rewards of these professions were not only doubtful, they were also usually slow in coming. In most cases the parents of a young man would need to provide him with at least some financial support into his early twenties and even beyond, and this was a formidable barrier for boys from a humble background. Otherwise it is rather hard to see many common elements between these careers. Officers in the army and navy, and those working for the government, could say that they were serving the King, while even those who were employed by the East India Company could argue that their endeavours benefited the nation; but it was difficult to make the same case for lawyers or bankers. On the other hand, lawyers, bankers and merchants were more likely to be independent, answerable to no one but themselves – something one might have thought particularly appropriate for a gentleman – but the other professions were strongly hierarchical and an officer in the navy, for example, was constantly called to account by his superiors and was expected to show them considerable deference. Perhaps the most important characteristics in common were that no one would ask a member of any of these professions to perform any menial, degrading or dishonourable task, and that those pursuing these occupations were expected to have the manners and education of a gentleman. But these were ill-defined features, and even at their most generous would struggle to accommodate some of the rough diamonds who adorned the different professions. Still, these were occupations in which a well-born younger son would find his place in society respected; he would not lose caste by joining them, while a man whose antecedents were less secure would reinforce his claims to being a gentleman by belonging to them.

It was usually the parents who decided which career each of their younger sons would pursue, although most parents would give some weight to the boy's own wishes if he expressed any. Francis Austen, Jane's brother, was eager to join the navy, and his father agreed, arranging for him to go to the Naval Academy at Portsmouth shortly before his 12th birthday. The young Matthew Flinders was also keen to go to sea; his imagination had been fired by reading *Robinson Crusoe*, and he had a cousin who had seen action against the French during the American War. However, Flinders encountered opposition from his father, who wanted Matthew, who was his eldest son, to follow in his footsteps and become an apothecary. Still, by persevering in his determination, young Matthew got his way and went on to become a great navigator and explorer, if not a wealthy man. Perhaps more typical was the case of the young Arthur Wellesley, who had no wish to join the army, but who could not suggest an alternative when his mother and elder brother puzzled over what to do with him. He was no scholar, and so was ill-suited to the Church or the law, and had no obvious talent for anything. A commission in the army could be obtained quite readily, and so his mother concluded that he was 'food for [gun]powder and nothing more'. Even more decided was the reaction of Thomas Hood – an attorney, not the poet – when it was reported to him that his son showed no eagerness to study the law:

> What he can mean by liking or disliking anything . . . much more daring to speak out, is no small surprise to me. I shall expect him to like what I may think to prescribe to him when the proper time arrives . . . If he should ever defeat my good intentions to him in this pursuit he will forfeit for ever my friendship and affections to him as a parent.

However, most parents and their sons were able to settle the question with affection and goodwill, even if their choice sometimes proved ill-advised.[19]

Parents and children alike inevitably made the choice with limited and partial information. Few fathers had themselves pursued more than one profession – many had not pursued any – and their ideas of other occupations were shaped by the common preconceptions of the day. Campbell's *The London Tradesman*, published in 1747, might declare that 'The rule was that the eldest son entered the Church, the second the navy and the youngest was articled to a noted attorney', but in fact there was *no* rule, and each family chose pragmatically according to its own particular circumstances.[20] Parents naturally favoured careers they knew, and in which they could assist their son. Often this meant that the son would follow the father into the same occupation, for a successful attorney could easily arrange to have his son articled to a capable friend in the same profession, and subsequently the son might become his father's junior partner. In the same way a clergyman might employ his son as a curate – or have a clerical friend do so – and soldiers and sailors would have comrades well placed to take a useful interest in the young man. Thus Mr Austen employed his son James as his curate and, when he was ready to retire, ensured that James succeeded him to the living of Steventon. In other cases it was not the father but an uncle or family friend who proved a valuable early patron. Nelson's father was a clergyman, but his maternal uncle, Maurice Suckling, was a captain in the navy who went on to be appointed to the immensely distinguished position of Comptroller of the Navy just when his influence was most useful to Nelson's career. And Alexander Gordon's career in the army owed less to Aberdeen than to his uncle, Sir David Baird, who not only employed him on his staff in his first campaigns, but who recommended him to Arthur Wellesley after the Battle of Coruña, in which Baird's own active career had been brought to a close by the loss of his arm.[21]

William Hickey's father 'did not approve of having two sons in the same line of business', and while seldom making this an absolute rule, many parents were inclined to choose a variety of careers for their sons if they had a large family.[22] Alexander Gordon's brothers were divided between the army, the navy and diplomacy; while Jane Austen's brothers went into the Church, the navy and the militia. William Wellesley-Pole was in the navy before he inherited the Pole fortune; Arthur Wellesley went into the army, Gerald Wellesley into the Church and Henry Wellesley took to diplomacy after a brief spell in the army. Brothers in the same profession might be able to assist each other, but they were more likely to compete for the limited influence and patronage that their parents could mobilize, especially in the early stages of their careers. Francis and Charles Austen both went into the navy, but they soon looked to different patrons to secure promotion and active employment. Alexander Gordon served under Baird and Wellington, but his brother Charles was appointed aide-de-camp to Sir John Hope, the Commander-in-Chief in Ireland, who belonged to a quite separate but very influential patronage network with strong Scottish connections. Even in the Church, influence which might secure a comfortable position for one son might be stretched to provide for two and needed to be exceptionally fruitful if it was to sustain three careers; although the Archbishop of Canterbury was able to provide not only for all his sons, but also for numerous nephews, cousins and other family connections.[23]

Clearly the abilities and character of each boy were also important: a shy boy with a stammer might transform himself into a successful barrister or an officer of dragoons, but most parents would think him better suited to the Church or an attorney's office. A heedless young larrikin was more likely to be sent into the army, the navy or to India than into the Church or set to study the law, although many young lads who were found places in government offices, banks and other businesses, kicked at the traces in their teens before settling down in their early twenties.

The choice of career was not binding for life, although most men continued on the path on which they took their first steps. Henry Austen, the most charming, mercurial and possibly ablest of Jane's brothers, was one of the exceptions. He was originally sent to Oxford with the intention that he become a clergyman like his father and his eldest brother James. But the outbreak of war in 1793 led him to join the militia, and this in turn led him to set up in business as a regimental agent. From this he evolved into a banker, only to go bankrupt in early 1816 during the hard times that followed Waterloo. He then took holy orders and spent the last 33 years of his life as a clergyman, although he would probably have secured a better position in the Church if he had stuck to his original intention and taken advantage of the patronage that was open to him in the 1790s. In the aftermath of the long war with France many under-employed military and naval officers looked around for new occupations; some joined the Church, and many others went out to the colonies, especially Canada and Australia, while others lived as cheaply as they could on the Continent.

Attitudes to work in the late eighteenth and early nineteenth centuries were distinctly ambivalent. On the one hand there was the old aristocratic prejudice, dating back to Roman times and beyond, against those who needed to labour to support themselves. A classical education shaped the attitudes of the upper classes, and Cicero had declared that 'The cash that comes from selling your labour is vulgar and unacceptable for a gentleman . . . for wages are effectively the bonds of slavery'.[24] There was an idealized vision of the gentleman as a man of leisure, taking an interest in his estates and his local community and perhaps also in national affairs, but free also to pursue such country sports and more intellectual pursuits as his taste might dictate. Two of Jane Austen's finest heroes, Mr Darcy and Mr Knightley, both embody this ideal.

But there was also a counterargument – a widespread recognition that some form of work helped to give interest and purpose to life. In 1812 Lieutenant-Colonel Arthur Gore of the 33rd Foot advised one of his junior officers who was thinking of quitting the army: 'If you should feel that you have [the] wherewithal to live on independent of the Pay of the Army, you ought by all means to find out something that would occupy your time and keep you from absolute Idleness.' Twenty years earlier Lord Mornington had told William Pitt that his brother, William Wellesley-Pole, 'is grown tired of leading an idle life, and would be very happy to be employed in any way that would give him constant occupation. He says . . . that emolument is not his object – so little his object that he would be glad to be employed without any salary at all rather than to remain idle'. And William Hickey, who had known more of the pleasures of dissipation and good company than most men, wrote his *Memoirs* because when he retired 'from a very busy and laborious life, in India, to comparatively absolute idleness, in England, and having fixed my abode in a country village, with very limited society, I there experienced the truth of an observation that I had frequently heard, – viz. that want of employment is one of the greatest miseries that can be attached to a mind not altogether inactive.'[25]

Jane Austen, who concealed her rigorous creative application behind an appearance of ladylike idleness, had two of her characters argue for the importance of work. General Tilney told Catherine Morland:

I am sure your father, Miss Morland, would agree with me in thinking it expedient to give every young man some employment. The money is nothing, it is not an object, but employment is the thing. Even Frederick, my eldest son, you see, who will perhaps inherit as considerable a landed property as any private man in the county, has his profession.[26]

And Mrs Dashwood discussed the subject with Edward Ferrars:

'I think, Edward,' said Mrs Dashwood, as they were at breakfast the last morning, 'you would be a happier man if you had any profession to engage your time and give an interest to your plans and actions. Some inconvenience to your friends, indeed, might result from it – you would not be able to give them so much of your time. But' (with a smile) 'you would be materially benefited in one particular at least – you would know where to go when you left them.'

'I do assure you,' he replied, 'that I have long thought on this point as you think now. It has been, and is, and probably will always be a heavy misfortune to me, that I have had no necessary business to engage me, no profession to give me employment, or afford me any thing like independence. But unfortunately my own nicety, and the nicety of my friends, have made me what I am, an idle, helpless being. We never could agree in our choice of a profession. I always preferred the church, as I still do. But that was not smart enough for my family. They recommended the army. That was a great deal too smart for me. The law was allowed to be genteel enough; many young men, who had chambers in the Temple, made a very good appearance in the first circles, and drove about town in very knowing gigs. But I had no inclination for the law, even in this less abstruse study of it, which my family approved. As for the navy, it had fashion on its side, but I was too old when the subject was first started to enter it – and, at length, as there was no necessity for my having any profession at all, as I might be as dashing and expensive without a red coat on my back as with one, idleness was pronounced on the whole to be the most advantageous and honourable, and a young man of eighteen is not in general so earnestly bent on being busy as to resist the solicitations of his friends to do nothing. I was therefore entered at Oxford and have been properly idle ever since.'[27]

Edward Ferrars was an eldest son, with some money of his own and considerable expectations; most younger sons did not have the choice not to work, and many would have been happy to risk the miseries of affluent idleness in return for financial independence and a secure place in the world. But although their elder brothers were highly privileged, there were some disadvantages to being the first son and heir. There was the provisional nature of their position in their father's lifetime, especially if they did not pursue a profession. A young man might have been brought up to be the lord and master of the estate, but so long as his father lived, he was no more than the Prince of Wales, the monarch in waiting. His father would usually provide him with a handsome allowance, but if the father did not also die quite young, his son might spend the best decades of his life with neither authority nor occupation. Some young men would find a place in society as a Member of Parliament; others would travel or take an interest in agricultural improvements, but many were at risk of rotting on the vine, filling their lives with drinking, gambling and other dissipations, not just for a few years when they were young, but deep into middle age.

Eldest sons faced another danger. Brought up with the constantly re-inforced belief that they were the most important member of their gener-ation in the family, they could find it hard if one of their siblings outshone them. It was bad enough if their sister married a man of greater rank, wealth and position than they possessed; but, for many, it was even harder to be sincerely happy when a younger brother's achievements eclipsed their own. In this regard Richard Wellesley, Lord Mornington, later Marquess Wellesley, had a particularly heavy cross to bear, for he had been a young man of immense promise, fêted at school and university, the friend of Pitt and Grenville, plainly marked by the gods as destined for greatness. By most standards his career was a success: a conquering Governor-General of India, an influential Foreign Secretary, and two terms as Lord Lieutenant of Ireland, posts at the very summit of power and prestige. However, there were long periods in the wilderness between these positions; his achievements in India never received the recognition he believed they deserved; and his colleagues, much to his surprise, never begged him to become Prime Minister even though his talents were so obviously superior to their own. But above all there was the astonishing, unexpected and frankly unaccountable success of his brother Arthur, a very good sort of man in his way, a capable soldier and all that, but quite without the breadth of vision and real genius of a true statesman. For much of the middle decades of his life Richard Wellesley was consumed with jealousy, trying hard to convince himself that Arthur's success was entirely due to the help he had given him in the early years, and railing against the injustice and absurdity of fate. No, it was not always easy to be the privileged elder brother, although few elder brothers had quite as big a pill to swallow as Richard, Marquess Wellesley.[28]

——◆——

CHAPTER TWO

MONEY AND SOCIETY

YOUNGER SONS NEEDED TO work in order to secure an income and, in some cases, their position in society. Their success or failure was measured – at least in part – by money, and to appreciate it we need to get a sense of what an income of £500 or £1,000 a year actually meant. The natural starting point is to make a comparison with today's money, and as a rough but convenient guide we can try multiplying an early nineteenth-century income by one hundred to find its modern equivalent: so £500 becomes £50,000 and £1,000 becomes £100,000.[1] However, this is only a *very* rough approximation as the relative cost of goods and services has changed enormously, and household budgets today are dominated by items that were either entirely absent or much less prominent two hundred years ago, such as utility bills. We can get a much better sense of the value of money at the time by examining how people were actually able to live on particular incomes.

In *Sense and Sensibility* Jane Austen tells us that Mrs Dashwood and her three daughters, Elinor, Marianne and Margaret, were left, after Mr Dashwood's death, with an income of £500. This is treated as an income just sufficient for their place in society, but needing to be managed with some prudence. They retire to Devonshire where a cousin, Sir John Middleton, provides them with a very pleasant cottage on easy terms (no figure is mentioned, but we are told that the rent was 'uncommonly moderate'). They can afford three servants: two maids and a man. The wages of these servants would not have been high: Parson Woodforde (the famous diarist) paid his cook and his maid £5 5s each per year in 1799, and his total wages bill for five servants, including two men who worked on his farm, was only just over £30 for the whole year.[2] (Multiplying by one hundred clearly does not work for low incomes such as these.) However, the total cost of the Dashwoods' three servants would have been far greater than their wages, for their employer would pay for all their food, clothes and any extraordinaries such as visits from the doctor if they fell ill. Nonetheless, servants were very poorly paid, and many spent only a few years in service when they were in their teens, before marrying or finding a more lucrative line of work.

It was almost impossible to live as a lady or a gentleman without servants, and most of the tasks they performed are now done for us either by machinery or, outside the home, often by retailers. We do not have to kill, pluck and prepare a chicken: we buy chicken in pieces on polystyrene trays wrapped in plastic and kept in a refrigerated cabinet in the supermarket. But every time Parson Woodforde or the Dashwoods sat down to a roast fowl, their servants had done far more than simply cook it. The servants also carried the coal or chopped the wood for the stove and kept its fire going throughout the summer as well as the winter, pumped water for the household, and heated whatever hot water was needed: getting hot water from a tap in the bathroom was a technological miracle that had yet to arrive. There was, of course, no electric light, and candles were expensive and needed attention, while washing, drying and ironing clothes was a serious undertaking that would preoccupy a household for a full day or even longer. Even with three servants Mrs Dashwood probably spent many hours each day managing household affairs, and needed a good deal of practical knowledge if life above stairs was to proceed smoothly. However, if her income had been larger she might have employed a housekeeper who could have undertaken most of these responsibilities, and her supervisory role might have been greatly reduced.

The Dashwoods could afford three servants, but they could not afford a carriage. This was a serious restriction on their life, for it largely limited their social circle to the few families within walking distance, for Mrs Dashwood would not make a habit of borrowing Sir John's carriage. Willoughby offered to give Marianne a riding horse, but Elinor forced her sister to decline the gift, not – surprisingly – because it would create an obligation, but on the grounds of economy. If Marianne had a horse, they would need a groom, the groom would need his own horse in order to accompany Marianne on her rides, and they would have to build a stable to house the horses. Willoughby's well-intentioned generosity would result in a considerable strain on the household finances. Nor did Elinor think that they could afford to visit London, even though they could stay with their half-brother and his family. The expense of such a visit would arise less from the cost of travelling to and from the metropolis – although that would not be insignificant – than from the cost of the clothes they would need and the entertainments they would attend while they were there. Such a visit would not last less than a few weeks, for travel was both laborious and slow, and quick trips were only undertaken for urgent business. In this case Elinor's prudence was overruled by Marianne's eagerness and the two older girls accompanied Mrs Jennings to London in her carriage. They stayed with her for two months, but the difficulties of the return journey, which would take several days, gave Elinor some concern.[3]

Jane Austen had a clear understanding of the limitations imposed by an income of £500 a year, as this was roughly the income for the household at Chawton in which she lived the last years of her life with her widowed mother, her sister Cassandra and their friend Martha Lloyd. Mrs Austen had an income of £210 a year, and this was supplemented by £50 a year each from James, Henry and Francis, and £100 from the wealthy Edward, who was also providing the house. Cassandra had a little money of her own: her fiancé Tom Fowle had left her his little capital of £1,000 when he died in the West Indies in 1797, and this would have produced an income of about £50 a year.[4] (While interest rates varied from year to year, 5 per cent was regarded as a standard rate of return on safe investments.) Jane's novels gave her a welcome – although not large – income. Her first book, *Sense and Sensibility* yielded a profit of £140; she sold the copyright of *Pride and Prejudice* for £110 although she had hoped for £150; and the publisher John Murray offered £450 for the copyright of *Emma*, *Mansfield Park* and *Sense and Sensibility* – the last two having already been published – although the offer was declined. When *Persuasion* and *Northanger Abbey* were published posthumously together they made £500 which went to Cassandra. Some novelists, notably Sir Walter Scott, made much greater sums from their writing, but others made less; and even today there are literary novelists, not to mention historians, who would not be unhappy to receive £14,000 for their first book.[5]

It was only natural that the Dashwood girls should aspire to a more generous income than £500 a year, one which did not require such constant prudence. For Elinor, wealth was an income of £1,000, but her younger and more romantic sister was less easily satisfied, regarding £1,800 or £2,000 as necessary for an elegant sufficiency. '"And yet two thousand-a-year is a very moderate income," said Marianne. "A family cannot well be maintained on a smaller. I am sure I am not extravagant in my demands. A proper establishment of servants, a carriage, perhaps two, and hunters, cannot be supported on less."' The anonymous author of *A New System of Practical Domestic Economy*, published in the 1820s, shows that Marianne was accurate in her calculations, even if optimistic in her expectations. An income of £1,000, according to the *New System*, would support a gentleman, his wife and their three children in some comfort, with an establishment of three female servants, a coachman and a footman, a carriage and a pair of horses, while still saving £100 a year for unforeseen expenses. At £1,500 a year the same family could afford two additional servants (a maid and a groom), a gig or other small, light two-wheeler as well as a larger carriage, and a third horse. They would also eat better, with the annual budget for provisions increasing from £266 to £399, and save a little more. If their income was £2,000 a year the same family might have 10 servants, two carriages and five horses, and spend over £500 on provisions. On this budget, the gentleman would be spending £80 a year on clothes and his wife £100, and £240 was allowed for rent, taxes and repairs – which still left £200 set aside for contingencies.[6]

Certainly an income of £2,000 a year enabled a family to live on a larger scale and have more indulgences than was possible on half that sum. Mr Bennet, in *Pride and Prejudice*, had £2,000 a year, and his house-hold had a butler, a housekeeper and a cook, in addition to at least two housemaids, and probably other servants. The Bennets kept a carriage, although the horses were sometimes required for the farm, and at least one riding horse, both of which imply a coachman/groom and possibly a stable boy. Colonel Brandon, who ultimately wins Marianne's affections and her hand, also has an income of £2,000, and his home at Delaford is described by Mrs Jennings as

> . . . a nice place, I can tell you; exactly what I call a nice old fashioned place, full of comforts and conveniences; quite shut in with great garden walls that are covered with the best fruit trees in the country . . . Then, there is a dove-cote, some delightful stewponds, and a very pretty canal; and every thing, in short, that one could wish for . . .[7]

According to the early nineteenth-century statistician Patrick Colquhoun, the average income for knights and esquires who made up the great bulk of the landed classes was £1,500, while gentlemen of private means averaged around £700. Only the most successful younger sons could hope to accumulate a fortune of £40,000, which was the capital needed to produce an income of £2,000. This was the fortune that Major-General Sir Arthur Wellesley brought home after eight years in India, during which time he had held positions of great power and respon-sibility and led his army to victory against the Marathas. It was, he felt, enough to make him independent, so that he could choose whether or not to accept further employment when it was offered.[8]

But if £2,000 a year was enough to secure comfort and independence it was still only the foothills of real wealth, at least for eldest sons who inherited their father's estates. Mr Bingley, in *Pride and Prejudice*, is not yet 23 years old, but he has an income of £4,000 or £5,000, for he has inherited the fortune his father made in trade, amounting to almost £100,000. His sisters received only £20,000 each: still enough to give them an income of £1,000, and to remove any need for them to marry to secure their futures. Mr Bingley's friend Mr Darcy was reputed to be worth £10,000 a year from his estate in Derbyshire, while his sister had a fortune of £30,000 which would give her an income of £1,500. As Mrs Bennet was quick to appreciate, £10,000 a year enabled a family to have a house in London, carriages, jewels, and generous pin money (a private allowance) for the wife. It was also an unusually high income for a man of good family but no title, not even a baronetcy. Patrick Colquhoun tells us that the average income for a peer was £8,000, while baronets generally had about £3,000 a year, although there were huge variations within both groups.[9]

Some successful professional men could also earn high incomes: Samuel Romilly was one of the leading barristers in London in the early nineteenth century with an income of around £8,000 or £9,000 a year; much the same as that of John Scott (later Lord Eldon) when he held a similar position around 1790. Scott's income initially fell when he accepted political office, but he went on to make a very large fortune indeed (£700,000) while serving as Lord Chancellor for a quarter of a century. As this suggests, some public offices were very lucrative, although few men held them for as long as Scott. Sir Arthur Wellesley served for two years (1807–09) as Chief Secretary for Ireland without letting it prevent him taking part in the attack on Copenhagen in 1807 or leading an army to Portugal in 1808, and the salary for this civilian office was £6,566 a year. And Spencer Perceval, who became Prime Minister in 1809, had an income of £9,651 from a combination of offices, and might have had more, but he refused to take any salary as Chancellor of the Exchequer while he was simultaneously Prime Minister. Perceval also declined to bestow a valuable sinecure that fell vacant on one of his sons, giving it instead to Charles Yorke, a significant political figure and former minister who was otherwise dependent on his elder brother, Lord Hardwicke. When Perceval was assassinated in 1812, Parliament recognized that his large family (he had 12 children) was not well provided for, and settled £50,000 on the children and gave a pension of £2,000 to their widowed mother.[10]

Lord Aberdeen's income of £16,000 or £17,000 made him a very rich man; but others were even richer. Henry Lambton, Lord Durham, was much teased for his remark that 'he considered £40,000 a year a moderate income – such a one as a man *might jog on with*'. His own income was, notionally at least, much higher, but he had accumulated such vast debts – the figure of £900,000 was mentioned – that his affairs were tangled and embarrassed. A dozen or more members of the Commons between 1790 and 1820 had incomes over £50,000, including John Rolle, whose estates in Devon were worth £70,000 a year, and Sir Francis Baring, the merchant banker, who was worth £80,000 a year. In the 30 years between 1809 and 1839 probate records show that 881 people died leaving estates worth over £100,000, and these figures do not include the value of land, which would greatly increase both the number of individuals and the size of their estates. They included Sir Robert Peel, the father of the Prime Minister, whose estate was commonly estimated to be worth at least £1.5 million, and Nathan Meyer Rothschild who was worth more than £3.5 million, both as it happens, younger sons. (The growth of the economy means that multiplying by one hundred gives an inadequate notion of the size of these estates: Rothschild would have to be worth far more than £350 million in today's money to hold a similar position: perhaps £14 billion, a multiple of 4,000).[11]

Lord Durham was not the only extremely rich man in this period to accumulate enormous debts, and a careless disdain for financial prudence could ruin even the very wealthy. Building a new stately home could be devastatingly expensive. In 1788 Warren Hastings, having returned from India with a large but not gargantuan fortune, paid £8,221 for a 550-acre estate at Daylesford in the Cotswolds. The sale included a further £1,000 for the unfinished shell of a house on the site, £959 for the standing timber (trees were a valuable asset, not just an ornament), and two annuities of £300 each for the vendor's two daughters. In all the total was around £15,000 or £16,000: a large sum, but not more than Hastings could afford, or than was reasonable. Four years later he bought a further parcel of land: 56 acres adjoining the estate for which he paid £3,150: a significantly higher price per acre and one that he was told was 'nearly double what it was worth'. He proceeded to build a 'restrained house in Cotswold stone, much admired for its comfort and convenience, with an extremely high standard of interior decoration'. He had budgeted £10,000 for the building, but inevitably this proved inadequate and the final cost was at least £25,000. Even this might have been sustainable – although together with the land it probably amounted to more than half his capital – but there was also the simultaneous cost of landscaping the grounds. By 1795 Hastings thought that he had spent a total of £60,000 on Daylesford, and if his wife had not kept control of money of her own he would have been unable to afford to live in the house on which he had spent so much. (His circumstances were complicated by the enormous legal fees he incurred during his impeachment, although these were re-imbursed by the East India Company.) None of the money spent on Daylesford was a good investment: when the estate was sold in 1853 it was worth barely £30,000 and produced an income of less than £800.[12]

The more prudent – and those who had yet to decide where they would settle – might rent a country house and its park for a year or more while they got to know a district, as was done by Mr Bingley in *Pride and Prejudice*, and Admiral and Mrs Croft in *Persuasion*. Lord Chatham was out of office and without a large income at the end of the Napoleonic Wars. He had been forced to sell the little land he had inherited and could not afford to buy a country estate, but he rented Abington Hall, some eight miles from Cambridge: a small but comfortable house with 40 acres of good fowling land. He agreed to pay £300 a year for the property and the exclusive right to the shooting, fishing and hunting on it, while prom-ising to carry out various repairs and to modernize the servants' quar-ters.[13] A decade earlier the fashionable Mrs Calvert and her husband took a lease on 5 Albermarle Street in Mayfair for £350 a year, 'independent of taxes, coach houses or stables'. And in 1813, Captain John Orrok, having left the army, took a furnished house in London for 18 months. 'There are three parlours,' he proudly told his father-in-law, '2 Drawing Rooms, and six Bedrooms, Kitchen, Garden and *water closet*, all very handsomely furnished . . . and close to Regent's Park, which is a delightful situation for the children.' The address was 39 Upper Baker Street, and the house was of white stucco on the ground floor and naked brick above. The cost was £200 per annum. However, Orrok's fortunes did not flourish in London, and at the end of the 18 months he sought cheaper living abroad, along with many other officers and civilians. After some hesitation he settled on Brussels where he found handsome furnished lodgings for less than £60 a year. Nor was this the only saving: 'Provisions are very Cheap; in London, Beef and Mutton was 1 Shilling a pound, here it is 4 pence! Other articles are cheap in the same proportion.'[14]

Children's education was a considerable financial burden for those on limited incomes then, as it can be today. Matthew Flinders, the apothecary in Lincolnshire, thought the £18 18s a year he paid to send his son Matthew to Mr Shinglar's school in nearby Horbling, 'expensive'. Mr Shinglar was a clergyman who had seven pupils in his small school. Mr Austen, Jane's father, also took in a few boys, usually just three or four at a time, whom he brought up in the family and educated alongside his own sons. He was a good teacher whose pupils often went straight on to university, and he was able to charge their parents between £35 and £65 a year including their board. When John Orrok was living in London he sent his three daughters to a local school as 'day boarders' (a servant took them there each morning by 9.30 and collected them in the evening around 7 o'clock). This cost him £118 a year for the three. Previously, when he had still been in the army, they had been full boarders at a different school costing £204 or £68 each. Predictably the public schools were even more expensive, with Eton and Harrow charging anywhere between £175 and £250 per boy in the early nineteenth century. Given the large size of many families it is not surprising that many parents educated their children at home or only sent them to school for a few years.[15]

A single man could live much more cheaply than a married man with a family. If he was in the Church, the army or the navy, accommodation might come with the job, at least while he was actively employed. If he had leisure he could more easily make long visits to friends and relations; and he could have a base in relatively cheap and simple lodgings, using the servants provided by the landlady or landlord. He could travel by public stagecoach or on horseback, avoiding the expense of a private carriage, and would not be expected to return the hospitality he received, except, perhaps by hosting the occasional dinner for bachelor friends. Lieutenant-General Sir George Murray, who had served as Wellington's Quartermaster-General in the Peninsula, was not a wealthy man. He married in his early fifties and told his cousin a few years later:

I find myself obliged to look much more narrowly into my pecuniary affairs more than I have ever been accustomed to do. In a great part of my life I had, as a single man, no cause for anxiety on that head, because I could shape my expenses to my income without any difficulty, or any inclination to consult but my own – and I always made my way, by good luck, to some Professional Appointment of emolument. Now, however I cannot so easily curtail my expenses at pleasure on a moment's notice, and the sphere of employment is much more narrowed than it used to be. A most heavy and unavoidable expense for many months past has been doctors fees, and apothecaries bills. However by parting with servants, and by giving up Carriage Horses, I hope to bring matters into such a shape as to keep clear of incurring debt.[16]

A single man with £500 a year would generally do very well unless he had expensive tastes or was already in debt. John Willoughby in *Sense and Sensibility* was supposed to have £600 or £700 a year, but he had reasonable expectations of having a much greater income in due course, so it is not surprising that he was extravagant and outspent his income. Lord Fitzroy Somerset, the eighth son of the Duke of Beaufort, had to be content with rather less, having inherited only an annuity of £600 which would cease at his death. This made him a poor prospect when he proposed to Emily Wellesley-Pole in 1814, but his personal qualities and the certainty of Wellington's patronage meant that her father was delighted with the match.[17] Even half this sum – £300 a year – was a reasonable income for a bachelor who did not aspire to mix in the top flight of society. Colonel Brandon thought it sufficient for a single man, but had no idea that a sensible man would contemplate marrying with such limited resources. Even £400 a year would need great care and good management if it was to provide a genteel life for a family. Fanny Price's parents had an income of £400 a year and kept two servants, but their household in Portsmouth was neither elegant nor comfortable; and Elinor Dashwood and Edward Ferrars 'were neither of them quite enough in love to think that three hundred and fifty pounds a-year would supply them with the comforts of life'.[18]

It was very hard indeed for a family to maintain its claims to gentility on anything much below £300. The warm-hearted Mrs Jennings was alarmed when she thought that Edward would marry Lucy Steele with only £150 or £200 between them.

> Then they will have a child every year! and Lord help 'em! how poor they will be! – I must see what I can give them towards furnishing their house. Two maids and two men indeed! – as I talked of t'other day. – No, no, they must get a stout girl of all works. Betty's sister would never do for them *now*.[19]

A single man might keep up appearances on £150 or £200, although the struggle would be desperate if his income was as low as £100, and there were many men – curates, half-pay officers and unsuccessful barristers among them, younger sons of good families – whose income was less than £100 and yet who still considered themselves gentlemen.

As for the great majority of the population, their incomes were usually – but not always – much lower. The Industrial Revolution created sudden bottlenecks, allowing skilled operatives in one part of the production chain to receive very high wages for a year or more until new machinery made their skills obsolete or more hands were trained for the task. There were also many intermediate positions in trade and industry, prosperous shopkeepers, farmers, cattle-dealers, tailors and innkeepers whose incomes often comfortably exceeded £100. Patrick Colquhoun estimated that there were about 100,000 shopkeepers and tradesmen with average incomes of £150 and 160,000 farmers with an average of £120. Below them in his tables were clerks and shopmen who might average £75, and nearly half a million artisans and labourers earning about £55 a year. These averages conceal a small minority who did very well: Charles Lamb the essayist began working as a clerk at the age of 16 for a salary of just less than £30 a year. He hated the work but stuck at it and slowly his salary increased as he gained seniority until it reached £730; at this point he had just turned 50 and he decided to retire, whereupon he was given a pension of £450 for the rest of his life. This was unusual, but there must have been many men in subordinate but responsible positions who achieved incomes of £300, £400 or £500 without ever pretending to the status of a gentleman.[20]

Not everyone earned even £1 a week. Many agricultural labourers made less than £30 a year, although they could usually supplement this with food they grew in their own patch of garden and by keeping a pig. Servants, as we have seen, were paid even less, although they too had their perquisites which added to their nominal pay. And the daughter of a gentleman, forced to work as a governess, could expect only a pittance for her labour. In 1839 Anne Brontë accepted a position that paid just £25 a year, while her sister Charlotte took one for £20 from which £4 was deducted for the cost of her laundry. And this was the fate of many daughters of younger sons who did not succeed in making a fortune, but who nonetheless married and had a family.[21]

⟞⟐⟝

Money was very important but it was not the only thing that decided someone's place in society. At the very top of the tree we can see three distinct but overlapping hierarchies: birth, wealth and political power. The aristocracy dominated the ownership of land and still controlled a substantial share of the country's wealth, although the rapid growth of new industries, the colonial empire and overseas trade was diluting its pre-eminence. There were many self-made men of large fortune; and also quite a number of relatively poor peers. Of the eight men who left personal fortunes (excluding land) of more than £1million between

33

1809 and 1839, five were commoners: Richard Crawshay, an ironmaster in South Wales; Philip Rundell, a goldsmith and jeweller in the City of London; Sir Robert Peel, cotton manufacturer; William Hollond, who had made his fortune in India; and Nathan Meyer Rothschild, the great merchant banker. If landed estates were included in the figures, these commoners would be considerably outnumbered by members of the aristocracy. As it was, the richest peer to die in these three decades was George Leveson-Gower, 2nd Marquess of Stafford and 1st Duke of Sutherland, whose wealth, including his vast landed estates, was estimated to be worth some £7 million, twice that of Nathan Rothschild.[22] Contrast this with the Duke and Duchess of Richmond who were living in Brussels in 1815 for the same reason as John Orrok – to economize – although that did not stop the duchess from giving her famous ball three days before Waterloo. The Richmonds were relatively poor, but their social status was immense, one which Nathan Rothschild, William Hollond or even Sir Robert Peel could never dream of equalling, although their children or grandchildren might do so.

More than half the members of every British cabinet of the period sat in the House of Lords, and many of those who sat in the Commons were either sons of lords or would go on to be granted a peerage. Yet the obvious implication – that the aristocracy exercised a stranglehold over government – is misleading. Most of the titled men who governed Britain were first-, second- or at most third-generation peers, and they came from families that had risen recently through politics and acquired a title and an estate as a symbol of their success. Lord Liverpool was an important cabinet minister almost continuously from 1801 to 1827 and Prime Minister for 15 years (1812–27). His father had been born plain Charles Jenkinson, the son of a cadet branch of a family of Oxfordshire gentry, and he rose through hard work and skill as a political operator and administrator, being rewarded with a seat in Pitt's cabinet and by being made Baron Hawkesbury in 1786 and Earl of Liverpool a decade later. A similar pattern can be seen with Henry Dundas, 1st Viscount Melville, who was Pitt's right-hand man and who dominated Scotland for a generation, and who passed his patronage network on to his son, Robert Saunders Dundas, who served loyally under

Liverpool. They became peers because they were politically powerful; they were not politically powerful because they were peers.

Many politicians became wealthy. Lord Eldon's fortune has already been mentioned, and the 1st Earl of Liverpool left an estate worth £200,000. On the other hand Lord Chatham, the son of one great Prime Minister and the brother of another, who was also a long-serving cabinet minister in his own right, was constantly harassed by financial demands throughout his life, and had little private means beyond the emoluments of office. And George Canning, who spent his life at the forefront of British politics, felt guilty that his career had greatly depleted the substantial fortune his wife had brought him, leaving her poorer as a widow than she had been as a bride.[23]

The great aristocratic families mostly supported the Whigs, not Pitt and his successors, and with a few brief exceptions the Whigs were out of office from the early 1780s until 1830. This does not mean that a great Whig magnate such as the Duke of Devonshire had no political power: he would usually still be the Lord Lieutenant of the county in which he was the principal landowner, and be able to access considerable patronage at both a local and national level. His recommendation would carry weight with the Prime Minister or Lord Chancellor in appointing a clergyman to a living in their gift; and he would not find it difficult to secure a commission in the army for a protégé, although his influence would be much greater if his friends were in power.

Even being a simple Member of Parliament gave a man considerable social status and enabled him to oblige friends, family and others with letters of recommendation that might secure some of the commoner and less desirable fruit in the orchard of government patronage. It might also greatly assist the man in his own career, and many ambitious officers in the army and navy went into Parliament in the expectation that it would assist them in gaining their professional objectives. In 1813 Wellington told John Malcolm, his friend from India, that

[a]lthough I had long been in habits of friendship with the public men of the day, and had some professional claims to public notice when

I returned to England, I believe I should have been but little known, and should not be what I am, if I had not gone into Parliament. I would, therefore, advise you to go into Parliament if you can afford it, if you look to high public employment.[24]

Most younger sons never reached these illustrious heights. Birth and wealth remained very important in determining their place in society. It was a great recommendation for a young clergyman arriving in a distant part of the country if it was known that he belonged to a family of well-established gentry, and even better if he also had some connection to the aristocracy or the powerful. Still, if he was wise, he would play these cards discreetly, letting the information fall only when pressed, and alluding to it infrequently. A man who constantly proclaimed his connections, especially if he exaggerated their significance, was always liable to ridicule. Equally, wealth was most persuasive when it was neither secret nor proclaimed openly: friends, gossips and, if need be, servants could be relied upon to spread the word, and through such means the tale would often grow in the telling. Miss Augusta Hawkins, Mr Elton's bride, 'was in possession of an independent fortune, of so many thousands as would always be called ten; a point of some dignity, as well as some convenience'.[25]

Attendance at one of the great public schools did not confer as much prestige in this period as it would do later in the nineteenth century: too many young lords and gentlemen were privately educated and went to university while still very young. However, some of the boys who went to public schools made friendships and connections there that proved invaluable in later life. It was at Eton that Richard Wellesley became friends with William Grenville, and through him with Pitt the Younger, thus laying the foundations for his subsequent public career. But Arthur Wellesley's three years at Eton were an almost complete waste of time: he did not thrive intellectually and made no friends of lasting consequence. The Rev. Sydney Smith was at Winchester with William Howley, the future Archbishop of Canterbury, but the only benefit he derived from the connection was a good quip in one of his essays many years later. Still, it was important that a young man appeared educated, that his speech

and language were not totally unpolished, and that his general knowledge was not obviously deficient: for example that he knew that Paris was
in France, not France in Paris. The bar was not set particularly high, and
too much learning, displayed ostentatiously, was as bad as too little.[26]

Equally significant was the choice of career and the level of success in
it. A clergyman was always respectable, but a poor curate had a distinctly
lower social position than the Rev. Henry Tilney, Rector of Woodston
and son of General Tilney. A young country attorney might or might not
be regarded as a gentleman: his profession opened the possibility but did
not guarantee the result, although a barrister, while possibly poorer, had
a rather higher status. Military and naval officers had clear claims to
gentility, but those of a lieutenant of the marines or the militia were far
less persuasive than a captain in a fashionable regiment of light dragoons,
or a young post-captain in the navy. Sometimes, as Edward Ferrars found,
it was easier to do nothing, to be a fashionable young man of leisure, but
relatively few younger sons could afford this luxury.

A final ingredient remained that could greatly elevate or depress the
standing of a young man: his personal qualities, and particularly his appearance and manner. Did he look and behave like a gentleman? And, even if this
was not in doubt, was his presence agreeable? Ideally a gentleman's manners
should be easy and free from embarrassment, but without any hint of
vulgarity or overfamiliarity. To be agreeable he must not be cold or excessively reserved, or try too hard to please: Mr Collins's elaborate compli-
ments were not to his credit, and Mr John Knightley remarked of another
clergyman, 'I never in my life saw a man more intent on being agreeable
than Mr Elton. It is a downright labour to him where ladies are concerned.
With men he can be rational and unaffected, but when he has ladies to please
every feature works'. And Emma agreed that 'Mr Elton's manners are not
perfect', although she went on to argue that 'where there is a wish to
please, one ought to overlook, and one does overlook a great deal'. This
remark may have been barbed, for Mr John Knightley was sometimes deficient in the wish to please, indeed we are told that 'He was not an ill-
tempered man, not so often unreasonably cross as to deserve such a reproach;
but his temper was not his great perfection'.[27] Mr Collins, Mr Elton and

Mr John Knightley were all undoubtedly gentlemen, even if they were not all invariably agreeable. A man might be as foolish as Sir Walter Eliot, as offensive as young John Thorpe or as ridiculous as Sir William Lucas without raising doubts as to his gentility; indeed, if Jane Austen paints an accurate picture of society, England would have been remarkably short of gentlemen if such personal flaws resulted in disqualification.

Robert Martin, the young farmer who, to Emma's dismay, courted Harriet Smith, had no claims to being a gentleman, and Emma – who we understand is behaving very badly – points out the distinction with snobbish relish. 'He is very plain, undoubtedly – remarkably plain: – but that is nothing, compared to his entire want of gentility. I had no right to expect much; but I had no idea that he could be so very clownish, so totally without air. I had imagined him, I confess, a degree or two nearer gentility.' She goes on to be a little more specific, criticizing 'his awkward look and abrupt manner – and the uncouthness of a voice, which I heard to be wholly unmodulated as I stood here'. And she asks Harriet to compare him to Mr Weston or Mr Elton: 'Compare their manner of carrying themselves; of walking; of speaking; of being silent. You must see the difference.' These were the intangible markers of a gentleman that were sometimes given the misleading label of 'good breeding'. And here too an excess was as dangerous as a shortfall, and risked the damning verdict that the offender had 'the manners of a dancing master'.[28]

Emma's criticism of Robert Martin was clearly unjust, as she half acknowledged to herself when she read his letter proposing to Harriet:

She . . . was surprised. The style of the letter was much above her expectation. There were not merely no grammatical errors, but as a composition it would not have disgraced a gentleman; the language, though plain, was strong and unaffected, and the sentiments it conveyed very much to the credit of the writer. It was short, but expressed good sense, warm attachment, liberality, propriety, even delicacy of feeling.[29]

Mr Knightley on the other hand values Robert Martin's good sense, describing him as 'an excellent young man, both as a son and brother', as well as admiring his hard work and competence as one of his tenant farmers. Yet the social gulf still remains: at the end of the novel we know that Emma will visit Harriet after her marriage, and Mr Knightley will continue to discuss crops and stock with Robert, but the Martins will not be dining with them at Hartfield or Donwell. When Harriet first discusses Robert with Emma she is amazed that Emma does not know him by sight, only to have their relative social positions explained with brutal clarity:

I may have seen him fifty times, but without having any idea of his name. A young farmer, whether on horseback or on foot, is the very last sort of person to raise my curiosity. The yeomanry are precisely the order of people with whom I feel I can have nothing to do. A degree or two lower, and a creditable appearance might interest me; I might hope to be useful to their families in some way or other. But a farmer can need none of my help, and is therefore in one sense as much above my notice as in every other he is below it.[30]

If the tenant-farmers were beneath Emma's notice there was another class in Highbury, and every other town in England, large and small, who were closer to gentility but whose place in society remained doubtful. Mr Perry, the Highbury apothecary, 'was an intelligent, gentlemanlike man, whose frequent visits were one of the comforts of Mr Woodhouse's life'. But these were professional visits and Mr Perry did not dine with the Woodhouses or mix with the top tier of Highbury society; or at least he did not do so yet, for there was talk of him getting a carriage and it was possible that he may have come to be accepted more fully if he continued to prosper. The Coles were a little further along this road:

The Coles had been settled some years in Highbury, and were very good sort of people – friendly, liberal, and unpretending; but, on the other hand, they were of low origin, in trade, and only moderately genteel. On their first coming into the country, they had lived in proportion to their income, quietly, keeping little company, and that little unexpensively; but the last year or two had brought them a considerable increase of means – the house in town had yielded greater profits, and fortune in general had smiled on them. With their wealth, their views increased; their want of a larger house, their inclination for more company. They added to their house, to their number of servants, to their expenses of every sort; and by this time were, in fortune and style of living, second only to the family at Hartfield. Their love of society, and their new dining-room, prepared every body for their keeping dinner-company; and a few parties, chiefly among the single men, had already taken place.[31]

Emma has, at first, no intention of encouraging their pretensions, but when an invitation finally does arrive, it is conveyed with such attention and real thoughtfulness that she changes her mind, encouraged by the fact that all her friends already intend to go.

Outside the bounds of fiction, society in many towns was dominated by the Perrys, the Coles and their kind. Sometimes they chafed against the condescension of long-established gentry families, and this irritation could have both a religious and political dimension, for they were often Nonconformists who resented the legal privileges and position of the Church of England, and they might be politically liberal. The protracted nationwide campaign against slavery and the intermittent campaigns for parliamentary reform both drew a great deal of support from such sources, and in return these campaigns instilled confidence and a willingness to challenge long-entrenched interests and established hierarchies. While some members of this newly emboldened professional and commercial class were narrow-minded and dogmatic, others displayed great intellectual curiosity, and they were one of the driving forces behind the rise of literary and philosophical societies in many towns in the last decades of the eighteenth century. Such activities were sometimes viewed with either disdain or distrust by the local gentry, but more often the leading families in the district gave their support, recognizing a welcome addition to their confined, limited and even tedious social round.

Many young men from this sort of background – the sons of Mr Perry and Mr Cole – joined the gentlemanly professions. Here they competed with the younger sons of more established gentlemen, and hoped that the deficiencies of their background would be expunged by their success. And so it generally was, providing that they were successful, but in many professions the competition was fierce and success often proved elusive.

CHAPTER THREE

———◆———

THE CHURCH

IN THE SUMMER OF 1794 a new curate arrived in the little village of
Netheravon, halfway between Salisbury and Marlborough. It was a pretty
village on the River Avon, but it was surrounded by the wastes of
Salisbury Plain, and it was a dozen miles to the nearest market town,
somewhere which might offer for sale such exotic luxuries as lemons and
newspapers. The curate, who had just turned 23, would miss such things,
for he was already well on the way to becoming a *bon vivant*, an intellectual and a wit. His name was Sydney Smith and he had been ordained
deacon some months before, although he would not be made a priest of
the Church of England for another two years. He owed his appointment
to his father's friendship with Michael and Henrietta Hicks Beach who
owned Netheravon Park and much of the rest of the parish as well as a
larger estate in Gloucestershire. Like most rural parishes, Netheravon
was a small place with fewer than 50 families, mostly agricultural
labourers but with a handful of farmers and artisans. Henrietta Hicks
Beach was eager to improve the lives of the villagers who were mostly
very poor. The year before Smith arrived she had asked her steward,
Mr Verrey, to prepare an account of conditions in the village, and he
reported that two thirds of the families in the village were in difficulties.
Smith subsequently added details which give us a sense of what this

actually meant: for example, 'John Head has a wife and four children (one born before marriage) – a wretched family, neither sheet or blanket, and only a miserable straw bed for the children. Only straw to burn and very little of that; no linen to wear and very badly clothed. Children four years to four months'. Another family lived in a house which was 'in a most shattered condition both within and without; there is no [bed] chamber, & they are obliged to sleep on the Ground Floor'. 'On Sunday last,' Smith reported during the following winter, 'there were three or four children with their feet upon the cold stones without any shoes, and one came a perfect *sans culottes* – or at least only with some grinning remnants of that useful garment, just sufficient to show that he was so clad from necessity, and not from any ingenious theory he had taken up against such a useful invention.'[1]

There was no schoolmaster in the village when Smith arrived, but he soon established a Sunday school and was delighted with the regularity and diligence of the pupils. Mrs Hicks Beach paid the teacher and covered the other costs, and Smith was soon requesting a supply of prayer books 'which from the *really surprising* manner in which the children come on . . . there will soon be great need'. Encouraged by this success, the curate and his patron went on to establish a School of Industry for poor girls which taught them darning, sewing, knitting and spinning, as well as distributing charity directly to poor families. The villagers remained desperately poor, but their plight was not quite as hopeless as it had been before.[2]

The sense of doing good brought Smith some satisfaction, but life at Netheravon was rather too quiet for the young curate. He enjoyed dining at the Park with the Hicks Beaches when they were in residence, but that was seldom, and the vicar too was absent, which was why Smith was employed to act in his place. Smith began with the intention of using his leisure to study hard as 'My stock of theological doctrine . . . at present is most alarmingly small', and he hoped to encourage more of the villagers to come to church 'for really at present . . . my preaching is like the voice of one crying in the wilderness'. Nonetheless the lack of educated company, intellectual stimulation and news of the outside world proved depressing, and after almost a year watching the seasons come and go

Smith wrote, 'Nothing can equal the profound, the unmeasurable, the awful dullness of this place, in which I lie dead and buried, in the hopes of a joyful resurrection in the year 1796'. At the end of two years he returned to Oxford although he remained on good terms with the Hicks Beaches, who would prove useful patrons in the next stage of his career and who always treated him with real kindness.[3]

The absent vicar paid Sydney Smith £50 a year for his time at Netheravon, and this was typical pay for a curate. Smith received a further £50 as a Fellow of New College, Oxford, and £40 from his father, which together meant that he had a better income than many young men just beginning their career in the Church, but also that he was still short of funds. Inevitably, he overspent and accumulated some modest debts. An appeal to his father to increase his allowance to £65 in 1796 was sharply rejected: relations between father and son were not close and money was often a point of contention, with both resenting the fact that at the age of 25 Sydney was still not financially independent. Robert Smith, Sydney's father, had a strange, miserly attitude towards money and frequently suggested that he was in straitened circumstances. He had made a fortune in America in his youth, lost part of it when America became independent, but with his brother's help retrieved his position and had substantial investments including in the New River Company which supplied London with much of its drinking water. Not all his ventures prospered, but when he died in 1827 he was worth between £40,000 and £50,000, and it is hard to believe that there was ever a time in his life when he could not have afforded to be a little more generous to his children.[4]

Only a minority of the clergy in the late eighteenth and early nineteenth centuries came from the aristocracy or landed gentry: one expert on the subject estimates that these amounted to about one in five. A much larger number came from families already established in the gentlemanly professions: many clergymen were themselves the sons, grandsons and even great-grandsons of clergymen, while the fathers of others were lawyers, soldiers and sailors. There were also many who had their origin at a slightly lower social level: the sons of apothecaries, successful shopkeepers and farmers. On the whole they tended to come from small towns and the countryside rather than the cities, and commercial backgrounds, such as Sydney Smith's, were underrepresented. Only a few are known to have come from humble families, but one of these, John Moore, rose to be Archbishop of Canterbury (1783–1805), showing that it was possible for an outsider to rise to the very top of the hierarchy.[5]

Most clergymen probably went to grammar schools, but a good many were educated privately like Mr Austen's sons and the pupils he taught alongside them. Some went to the public schools, including Sydney Smith who hated his years at Winchester, even though his academic performance was excellent and he rose to be Prefect of Hall or head boy. In later life he denounced public schools, claiming that they forced boys to be tyrants or slaves and to bully younger boys mercilessly. He also criticized the curriculum for its heavy emphasis on the composition of verses in Latin. At 18 he went up to New College, Oxford, on a scholarship linked to his performance at Winchester, and which he exchanged for a Fellowship in his second year. He would retain this until he married nine years later, without being required to reside in Oxford or to teach. He took his BA in 1792 and his MA in 1796, but here too he chafed at the heavy emphasis on the classics and the lack of discussion of contemporary issues. 'A genuine Oxford tutor would shudder to hear his young men disputing upon moral and political truth, forming and pulling down theories, and indulging in all the boldness of youthful discussion. He would augur nothing from it, but impiety to God, and treason to Kings.' While never a radical, Sydney was already far more liberal than most of his contemporaries at Oxford.[6]

Roughly half of all the students at Oxford and Cambridge (the only two universities in England at the time) went on to be ordained as clergymen, and those appointed to college fellowships were expected to take holy orders. The number of students was not high: the combined total of the two universities averaged under four hundred between 1730 and 1800, although it increased considerably in the early decades of the nineteenth century. Many gentlemen, eldest sons with no need of a career, attended university for two or three years with no intention of taking a degree or seriously pursuing their studies. They made friendships with like-minded young men from other parts of the country, and were able to indulge in some youthful indiscretions without embarrassing their parents by doing so close to home. It was mostly from them that the sporting, idling, drinking set came, and they are greatly overemphasized in our idea of student life at the time. Students destined for the Church tended to be poorer, more studious and better behaved. But even these embryo clergymen would not be exposed to much theology or biblical criticism either at school or university. All graduates had to subscribe to the Thirty-Nine Articles of the Church of England (which effectively prevented Dissenting Protestants or Catholics from attending either university), but the actual doctrines of the Church received much less attention than the classics or the everyday morality and behaviour expected of a gentleman.[7]

Not all clergy had been to university. A substantial minority, particularly in Wales and some of the poorer and more remote parts of England, had attended grammar schools and then studied privately, often while earning their subsistence as teachers. Several bishops in these areas published reading lists to guide such pupils, and some did notably well in the Church despite generally coming from relatively poor families. However, this route became increasingly difficult and restricted in the years after 1800.[8]

Few formal qualifications were needed to become an Anglican clergyman. In 1804 Parliament imposed a minimum age of 23 for deacons and 24 for priests. Candidates would then be examined by a bishop who would expect them to produce testimonials from their university college, or from a clergyman who had known them for several years, stating that their character and behaviour made them suitable for holy orders. They were required to have some Latin and Greek: at least enough to translate short and familiar passages of scripture into English, although some bishops were considerably more demanding in this respect, and the standard required probably rose over the period. Candidates were not expected to have studied much theology, and most clergymen were better acquainted with Cicero, Caesar and other ancient pagan authors than with contemporary biblical criticism.[9]

Candidates for ordination had to be respectable, and bishops privately circulated the names of those who were flagrantly unsuitable, for example the young man who had stolen the college silver. A personal interview was important more to check that a candidate was presentable than to test his academic ability. When Henry Austen decided to take holy orders in 1816, following the failure of his bank, he took some pains to brush up the Latin and Greek that he had studied at Oxford 25 years before. However, the Bishop of Winchester with genuine but possibly misplaced kindness, conversed with him on general subjects for some minutes and then, putting his hand on the New Testament in Greek remarked, 'As for *this* book, Mr Austen, I dare say it is some years since either you or I looked into it'. Henry secured his ordination, but if family tradition is to be believed he had been rather proud of his studies and was disappointed not to be able to prove his proficiency.[10]

In theory, candidates were expected to have felt an inner calling to the Church, but apart from a few evangelicals, there was little emphasis on a sense of religious vocation. The Church was a career like any other, and just as a soldier was required to have courage, a clergyman needed to have faith, and in most circumstances both the courage and the faith could be taken for granted. The truths of revealed religion as interpreted by the Church of England were well established and needed to be expounded and explained to a congregation that already accepted them, not debated with sceptics. A clergyman was also meant to demonstrate religious virtues by the life he led, although in many cases this did not extend far beyond avoiding the most obvious vices and attending to some of the needs of his parishioners. Humility, poverty, self-sacrifice and temperance were not the characteristics most commonly associated with the clergy of the Church of England under the Georges.

According to a memoir written by his daughter, Sydney Smith had no great desire to become a clergyman and would have preferred to become a barrister, a career which would certainly have suited his acute intelligence and ready wit. However, his father refused to support this ambition. Sydney was the second of four sons: the eldest, Robert ('Bobus') Smith, was already training for the Bar, and the two youngest had been packed off to India where they would not cost their father a penny. Sydney should be able to support himself on his New College fellowship and would in time secure a living, while if he turned to the law he might fail and prove a perpetual drain on the family coffers. The decision added a further, understandable, layer of resentment to the relations between Sydney and his father, whose behaviour on financial matters was never generous and often extraordinary. But many fathers would have made a similar decision, not as in Smith senior's case from apparent perversity, but from financial necessity or a sense of fairness to their other children. And many young men, like Sydney Smith, would have bowed to necessity and become clergymen, if not with reluctance, at least without any great enthusiasm.[11]

Once he had been ordained, a young clergyman would look for a 'living' or 'benefice', that is, a permanent appointment to a parish which he would hold for the rest of his life unless he gave it up or was forced from office for gross misconduct. There were 10,500 parishes covering the entire length and breadth of England and Wales, although many of these produced only a small income for the clergyman who held the living. For example, Netheravon was worth approximately £115 a year to the vicar, Ralph Smith, who employed Sydney Smith as his curate (they do not seem to have been related). In the early nineteenth century, when the prosperous state of agriculture increased the value of livings, between one third and one half were still worth less than £150.[12]

This income came from the tithes on the agricultural produce of the land which were generally paid by the farmers, not the agricultural labourers or the landowners; and from the land attached to the living – the glebe – which the clergyman might either work himself or lease to a farmer. In many places the tithes were no longer paid in kind, and often took the form of a fixed sum either in perpetuity or for a few years when the sum would be renegotiated, just like a lease. Rectors were entitled to all the tithes; vicars to only some types of tithes, with the rest going to the owner of the living; while the third sort of incumbent clergyman, 'perpetual curates', received none of the tithes but a fixed and usually small income. In general rectors were better off than vicars, who in turn were better off than perpetual curates, but there was an enormous range and overlap between different parishes and much scope for a determined rector or vicar, intent on exacting his full legal entitlements, to increase the value of his living, sometimes very significantly. Even so, most clergymen were not wealthy. In 1830 the median income for clergy with livings was only £275 a year in England and £172 in Wales. Behind these modest figures lurked some startling variations. On the one side a mere 76 parish clergymen had incomes of more than £2,000 a year. Algernon Peyton, the Rector of Doddington, headed the list with an income of more than £7,000, but Doddington was one of the largest parishes in England, some 38,000 acres with a population of 7,500. He was followed by Gerald Wellesley, brother of the Duke of Wellington, who had an income of just over £5,000, although much of this came from his additional position as prebendary of Durham Cathedral. At the other end of the scale were the 1,222 clergymen whose income was no more than £100, that is, roughly one-sixth of all clergy who held benefices. However, many of these poorer clergy would have supplemented their incomes in other ways, so that the picture is not quite as bad as it appears. Nonetheless it is obvious that the Church of England was far from an egalitarian organization.[13]

Roughly one third of all clergymen held more than one living at the same time. As well as being Vicar of Netheravon, Ralph Smith was Rector of Oaksey between Malmesbury and Cirencester, some 40 miles away. This was where he usually resided, employing a curate such as Sydney Smith to perform the duty at Netheravon. Mr Austen, Jane's father, also had two livings: he was Rector of Steventon and also of the neighbouring parish of Deane, and for many years did the duties of both parishes until, in his early sixties, he employed his son James as curate of Deane. Such pluralism allowed the more fortunate among the clergy to bolster their income, although it also helped create an underclass of poorly paid curates. However, criticism of pluralism needs to be tempered with common sense. Most parishes were very small, just a few square miles, and not heavily populated. When Mr Austen arrived at Steventon in 1764 there were no more than 30 families in the parish and even fewer in Deane. It was not difficult to be a capable and effective clergyman, familiar with the affairs of all the parishioners in two neighbouring parishes, when they were on this scale.[14]

In more than half the parishes in England and Wales the incumbent clergyman did not reside there. There were a number of reasons for this, with pluralism being the most obvious. (Even Mr Austen could not live in both his parishes, however well he served them.) In many other cases – perhaps one quarter of all parishes – there was either no parsonage at all or it had been neglected and was now unfit for habitation. In these circumstances the clergyman might reside in a nearby town or village without neglecting the affairs of his parish, or he might build a new parsonage, as became common in this period. Old buildings, some no more than Tudor cottages, were replaced by substantial Georgian homes, suitable for a gentleman and his family, complete with a drawing-room, a dining-room, a study, four or five bedrooms, servants' quarters, stables and an outhouse. Then there were clergymen who had, in effect, retired. When he was 70 Mr Austen, his wife and two unmarried daughters moved to Bath where they remained, with holidays to the seaside and to visit relatives, for the last four years of his life. During these years Mr Austen remained Rector of Steventon and Deane, for the Church made no provision for retirement incomes for its clergy, while James Austen was curate in both parishes.[15]

Clergy were not appointed to livings by any central authority. The right to appoint the clergyman to serve a parish was known as an 'advowson', and roughly half of all advowsons were in private hands, passed down through the centuries from whoever originally endowed the church with land and paid for the construction of the building. The other half was divided between the colleges of Oxford and Cambridge; the bishops and cathedrals; and the Crown, whose patronage was exercised by the Prime Minister and the Lord Chancellor. In some cases the rector of a parish would have the right to appoint a perpetual curate whose living was only semi-independent of the parish church. Most patrons controlled only one, two or perhaps three livings, in parishes where they were the dominant landowner, but some great magnates had a whole portfolio of livings at their disposal. The Lowthers had accumulated no fewer than 31 livings in Cumberland and Westmorland, which both reflected and reinforced their domination of that part of the country. And as late as 1855 the Duke of Beaufort had 24 livings in his gift, ranging from the Vicarage of Llandenny in Monmouth, worth £50 a year, to the Rectory of Llangattock in Brecon which was worth £1,123.[16]

Advowsons were private property and could be sold either outright or merely for the next appointment. Jane Austen mentions this in two of her novels. In *Mansfield Park* young Tom Bertram's extravagance at Oxford obliges Sir Thomas to sell the right of the next presentation at Mansfield – which had been intended for Edmund – and Dr Grant becomes the new Rector of Mansfield. And so 'the younger brother must help to pay for the pleasures of the elder', something which troubled Sir Thomas considerably more than young Tom. John Dashwood, in *Sense and Sensibility*, is astonished at Colonel Brandon's generosity in presenting the living of Delaford to Edward Ferrars when they were not connected by blood or marriage:

> . . . for the next presentation to a living of that value – supposing the late incumbent to have been old and sickly, and likely to vacate it soon – he might have got I dare say – fourteen hundred pounds. And how came he not to have settled that matter before this person's death? *Now* indeed it would be too late to sell it.[17]

Too late, because while it was perfectly legal to sell the right of presentation, it was not legal to sell the office itself, for that constituted the ancient crime of simony which was punishable by the church courts. This meant that sales could only take place when there was an incumbent in occupation, and this added a rather macabre element of speculation to the transaction: the right of presentation to a living where the incumbent was relatively young and in good health was clearly not as desirable or valuable as one where the incumbent was old or ill.[18]

So long as the incumbent was alive, there was nothing shameful or underhand about the sale of an advowson. Advertisements regularly appeared in the press, such as this notice in *The Times* for 14 April 1817:

VALUABLE CHURCH PREFERMENT – To be SOLD by Private Contract, the RIGHT of the NEXT PRESENTATION to the

VICARAGE of St ANDREW, in the borough of Plymouth, in the county of Devon, with its appendages, of the annual value of £800 and upwards, upon the avoidance thereof of the present incumbent, who is nearly 80 years of age. Application for further particulars may be made at the office of Messrs Sandys, Horton Rourke, and Sandys, Crane court, Fleet Street, London . . .[19]

It is probable that this sale would have brought the vendor between £5,000 and £6,000 (seven times the annual value of the living was a good rule of thumb, a point at which to begin negotiations); which might be enough to pay off the eldest son's debts or provide the marriage portion for at least one daughter. To modern eyes this is all rather shocking, for we like to pretend that all appointments are, or at least should be, made entirely on merit, and that of all organizations the Church should be the least worldly. But people in the early nineteenth century were more realistic, and regarded it as quite sufficient if the person appointed was qualified and competent to perform the duties of the position. Assured of this, the claims of family, existing obligations, political advantage and personal preference might all be given their due weight.

Mr Austen benefited from the sale of an advowson. He had been given the living of Steventon by a second cousin, Thomas Knight (father of the Thomas Knight who adopted Edward), who owned extensive property in Hampshire and Kent. But he received the living of Deane from his uncle, Francis Austen, a prosperous solicitor in Sevenoaks, who had purchased right of presentation for the two neighbouring parishes of Ashe and Deane so that Mr Austen could receive whichever fell vacant first. Most private patronage was exercised in a similar manner: helping relatives, family friends or young protégés find a suitable situation where their conscientious discharge of their duties would reflect credit on their patrons. Friendships formed at university might also help a young clergyman find a living, and so might friendships formed elsewhere. James Austen, Mr Austen's eldest son, was given his first living by a contemporary, William Chute of the Vyne, a great house some 10 miles from Steventon. William Chute and James Austen were both enthusiastic sportsmen and often rode with the Kempshott Hunt, then patronized by the Prince of Wales who was living nearby. The friendship formed on the hunting field led Chute to give James Austen the living of Sherborne St John when it fell vacant in 1791, and after church on Sundays James would dine at the Vyne. The Austens were well known in the neighbourhood and the appointment would have been widely welcomed, while William Chute ensured the pleasure of his friend's company and had the satisfaction of seeing the parish in good hands.[20]

James Austen went on to hold four livings simultaneously: Sherborne St John in Hampshire, Cubbington and Honingham in Warwickshire, and, after his father's death in 1805, Steventon. He was presented to Cubbington and Honingham by his mother's Leigh relations, and always employed a curate to do the duty at both churches. The living of Steventon he received from his brother Edward Knight, in accordance with the will of Thomas Knight. So Mr Austen received his two livings from two different patrons, and James his four from three different patrons. All these patrons, except William Chute, were family connections, but only Edward Knight was immediate family. Extended family mattered in the England of Jane Austen far more than it does today, and cousins and uncles who were in a position to help often – but not always – felt an obligation to do so.[21]

Some fortunate young clergymen had a family living already waiting for them. In many cases they would have to wait until the incumbent died before they could assume their position, but if there had been a vacancy only a few years before, it might have been 'kept warm' for them by the appointment of a clergyman who agreed to surrender the living when they were ready to take it up. Such agreements were quite legal and common, although they could complicate family relations. For example, Edward Knight intended that his son William should follow James Austen at Steventon. But James died prematurely, aged only 54, in 1819, before William Knight was old enough to be ordained. Edward then turned to his other brother in the Church, Henry Austen, and asked him to serve as Rector of Steventon until William was able to do so. The death of one brother benefited the other, but Henry's interests were subordinated to those of his nephew. Lucky William Knight, for if his uncle James had lived to be 80, he might have had to wait 20 years for the rectory – although his father would probably have found him another.

But not all young clergymen had relatives with advowsons in their pockets or the means of acquiring them. If the young man was a fellow of his college at Oxford or Cambridge, and was not impatient to marry (which would require him to surrender his fellowship), he would probably succeed to a college living eventually. Most colleges owned a considerable number of advowsons which became available as the incumbents died. The vacant living would then be offered to the fellows in order of seniority, or the fellows who wished to be considered would put their name forward and the choice would be made by election. It is not hard to imagine the delicate calculations which would arise: the living currently vacant was less desirable than several others, but were any of those likely to become vacant soon, or were the incumbents determined to live on for many years? Was a senior or more popular fellow likely to put himself forward if one of these choice plums *did* fall vacant, or would he prefer to live out his days in the college. Was it worth taking the living that was immediately available and so be able to marry, if the income it brought was insufficient to maintain a wife and family? Securing a good college living usually required great patience. Edward Drax Free became a Fellow of St John's College, Oxford in 1784 when he was 19, and he remained there until 1808 when he was given the living of Sutton in Bedfordshire, which was worth £250 a year. He might have had to wait even longer if he had not proved so quarrelsome and obnoxious that his colleagues were eager to be rid of him, and would not have looked kindly on anyone who, by standing in his way, forced them to endure his company any longer.[22]

Bishops had considerable patronage but were usually hard pressed satisfying the demands of their extended family and close associates. Still, many an ambitious young clergyman found advancement by proving himself useful to his bishop, and if that bishop did well, translated to a larger and richer see or even to York or Canterbury, his followers would rise with him. Walter King, the Bishop of Rochester, spelled out the obligations he felt most keenly in a private letter:

> *Mr Venables* my nephew, has a small Vicarage in Somersetshire; and I must take the first opportunity for procuring for him by exchange, or otherwise, some additional preferment.
>
> *Mr Davies* my curate at Burnham. He is soon to marry a near Relation of mine, and I have long promised him the first Living of moderate value that I may have in my Gift.
>
> *Mr Buckland* formerly my College Tutor, now my Chaplain; In addition to a valuable Sinecure The Chancellor has just given him a good Living in my Neighbourhood. They are worth together 12 or 1300 a year. I am therefore no longer anxious about him, but he may hold another Living, & he has nephews in orders, and he will expect to have the disposal of something as opportunities may offer.
>
> *Mr Etherington.* About Twenty five years ago came out of Yorkshire, a poor self taught Scholar, and found his way to Mr Burke. I received him from Mr Burke; We got him into orders and he has ever since been a Fag of mine at Gray's Inn and on other occasions . . .
>
> *Dr Winstanley* the Principal of St Alban's Hall Oxford. He was unsuccessful in a Competition with me, for a Fellowship, soon after we entered at College . . . I was engaged with him in the early part of my life in several literary projects, and pursuits . . .[23]

The clerical sons and sons-in-law of bishops were naturally prominent among the beneficiaries of their patronage: two sons of John Moore, the Archbishop of Canterbury, were given livings in Kent worth £2,500 and £3,500, and James Croft, the son-in-law of Moore's successor, had one worth £3,300. Jane Austen knew George Moore, the archbishop's eldest son (whose living was worth £3,500), and it has been suggested that Dr Grant in *Mansfield Park* was to some degree modelled upon him.[24]

However, even the Archbishop of Canterbury's patronage was slight compared to that of the Crown, which was largely divided between the

Lord Chancellor and the Prime Minister. When he first took office as Lord Chancellor, Lord Eldon was warned by the Archbishop of Canterbury that church patronage would destroy his peace, and he soon found that the warning was justified, complaining that he was overwhelmed with applications. Faced with an impossible burden of work on something that was only a subsidiary aspect of his office, he adopted a brutally pragmatic approach. He would reply only to those to whom he intended to give preferment, consider only livings that were actually vacant, and ignore all claims based on promises made by his predecessors. He gave little weight to the pastoral or intellectual abilities of the men he appointed, although on at least one occasion he specified that a Welsh living required an incumbent who spoke Welsh. On the other hand he accepted that great landowners should influence appointments in their district, for example, that the wishes of the Earl of Warwick be taken into account for any living in Warwickshire. Cabinet colleagues and other influential politicians also had claims that needed to be considered, although they all tended to seek the most desirable positions, which meant that they could not all be accommodated at once. And all these claims could be trumped by the intervention of a member of the royal family, whose wishes Eldon always tried to satisfy. For example, Princess Mary requested a valuable cathedral appointment for a clergyman whose fiancée's mother had been 'unremitting in her attentions & kindness to both my sister and myself' when the two princesses had been staying at Weymouth. Eldon found all this 'provoking beyond endurance', not because he disapproved of such patronage, but because it hampered his ability to give the best positions to his own friends and family.[25]

Lord Liverpool, the Prime Minister, was much more conscientious in his clerical appointments, particularly in creating and moving bishops. Political considerations continued to have some weight, for the bishops were an active presence in the House of Lords and their support was important for any government. But Liverpool was determined to raise the tone of the Church generally, and looked to capable and active bishops to make their clergy more attentive to their duties. He also expected bishops to set a personal example, and held this line even when attacked with great determination by Wellington, who wanted to get his brother Gerald made a bishop. Liverpool objected that although Gerald Wellesley and his wife lived apart he refused to divorce her, and the world assumed that this was not from Christian forbearance but because some of his own behaviour would not stand public scrutiny. Wellington thought that it was ridiculous to be so precious about a man's private life, but although he was both the victor of Waterloo and one of the most important members of cabinet, Liverpool would not yield, and eventually a compromise was reached with Gerald receiving valuable preferment but not being made a bishop: he was the only one of the five Wellesley boys not to become a member of the House of Lords.[26]

But if standards on the episcopal bench were being raised, it remained normal for clergy and bishops to be unashamed and blatant in putting forward their claims for a living, a cathedral position, a bishopric or, once that was granted, translation to a richer and more desirable see. They would write to Liverpool directly, accost him in the Lords or on social occasions, and call upon their friends, relatives and old patrons to support their case. A clergyman who waited quietly for his good work to be recognized and rewarded was likely to wait in vain: at best his superiors would think that he was content in his position and had no wish to be disturbed; more commonly, they would not think of him at all.[27]

Roughly one in five of all clergymen never secured a living, and most lived as curates either assisting a resident incumbent – particularly in large, prosperous parishes – or taking the place of one who was absent. Their pay was generally low and their life hard, leading Sydney Smith to write in one of his essays, 'A Curate – there is something which excites compassion in the very name of a Curate'. A curate in charge of a parish would commonly be paid £50 a year or thereabouts, sometimes even less. He might be able to live in the parsonage, if there was one, and grow vegetables in its garden, but if he had no other income he would face real poverty. William Jones was the resident curate at Broxbourne for 19 years on a stipend that never exceeded £60. He complained that 'a journeyman in almost any trade or business, even a brick-layer's labourer or the turner of a razor grinder's wheel' was 'generally better paid than a stipendiary curate'. Despite keeping a small school to supplement his income – something which he hated – there was often not enough food for his family.[28]

Some curates bolstered their income by doing the duty of more than one parish: James Austen employed a single curate to look after both Cubbington and Honingham, paying him £45 for Cubbington and £25 for Honingham, where the living was only valued at £60. Such pluralism was common in Norfolk where there were a number of very small, poor parishes. The curate of Bittering Parva was paid only £7 10s a year, but as there were only two houses in the parish, his duties were probably not very onerous. Similarly the curate of Bylaugh received £12 12s for a parish of seven houses, and the curate of Fishley £10 10s for attending to the needs of the single remaining inhabited house in that parish. It is not clear whether these curates performed divine service in these parishes each week, less frequently or not at all. Even in other parts of the country the business was often light: the curate of Littleton in Hampshire reported that he performed, on average, one burial and one baptism a year, and that in the seven years he had been in the parish he had never read the marriage service. Mr Austen had, on average, about six burials, baptisms and marriages each year, with his busiest year producing 15 such events. This shortage of activity left the clergyman with ample leisure, but it was not good for his morale and sense of purpose and it also affected his income, for each service brought with it a small fee, which in a prosperous urban parish might amount to a considerable total over the course of a year.[29]

Curates were not only poorly paid, they had no job security. William Andrew obtained the curacy of Gimingham in Norfolk thanks to a chance meeting, but after four years the rector decided to reside and Andrew and his pregnant wife lost their home and their income. His friends found him the curacy of Great and Little Witchingham, but less than a year later the incumbent died, and his successor had no need for Andrew's services. Andrew and his wife then went to live with her mother until a fresh opportunity could arise.[30]

Some resident clergymen treated their curates very badly, even mocking them for their poverty, but equally not all curates were either

conscientious or popular. When Parson Woodforde's health was beginning to fail he employed a curate, Mr Cotman, who resided outside the
parish. Unfortunately the new curate proved unreliable, arriving to
perform the service at unpredictable times on a Sunday, so that few of the
congregation attended, and completely failing to appear at all on Good
Friday despite promising to do so. Woodforde commented sadly, 'Mr
Cotman is not liked at all by the Parish. I flattered myself with the hopes
of his giving Satisfaction to the Parish, when I engaged him. I now wish
that I had not taken him for my Curate.'[31]

Parliament attempted to improve the position of the poorest curates
in 1813 when it passed the Stipendiary Curates Act which fixed the
minimum pay for a resident curate at £50 a year or the full value of the
living if this was lower than £50. This also applied equally to neighbouring clergymen who sometimes performed the duty for an absent
incumbent, and it is thought to have discouraged pluralism by making
it less profitable. However, the balance of power remained firmly with
the incumbent offering employment, not the curate seeking it, and this
was made worse by the sharp increase in the numbers of young men
being ordained in the years after Waterloo, which was not matched
by any increase in the number of livings. Competition for good places
in the Church sharpened considerably after 1815, and this in turn
probably strengthened the hand of those inside and outside the Church
urging its reform.[32]

Faced with such dire prospects some clergymen looked for other ways
to make a living. Teaching was the most obvious, and throughout the
period a high proportion of teachers in boys' schools were in holy orders.
Unfortunately teaching was seldom well paid or highly regarded.
Courtesy might, at a stretch, regard a university fellow as a gentleman,
but a schoolteacher could have no such pretensions unless founded on
other grounds. Some clergymen succeeded in obtaining a position in the
colonies or went out as settlers resolving to start a new life in a new land,
although their background and experience were seldom very useful as
preparation for the demands of frontier life. Some tried to support themselves by writing – then and now a desperate remedy that usually ended

in disappointment. Mary Russell Mitford noted that her publisher employed no fewer than '*three* regularly bred Oxonians, who, rather than starve as curates, condescend to marshal commas and colons, and the little magical signs which make the twenty-four [sic] letters, as compositors'. While most clergymen secured at least a reasonable living, there was a good deal of misery among the less successful, whether they spent their lives as curates or tried their hands at other careers.[33]

———◆———

There was little risk of Sydney Smith, with his ability, background and self-confidence, sharing such a fate, but his road to preferment was not straightforward. He left Netheravon in the summer of 1796 and returned to Oxford, but continued to correspond with Michael and Henrietta Hicks Beach and visited them at Williamstrip, their estate in Gloucestershire. In 1798 they engaged him as a private tutor for their eldest son Michael, who had just left Eton. At first they proposed that the two young men spend a year or two travelling on the Continent and studying at a German or Swiss university, but the war with France made this appear dangerous and the destination was changed to Edinburgh, then at the height of its reputation as one of the intellectual centres of Europe. Smith remained in Edinburgh for the next five years, sharpening his wit and clarifying his ideas in the company of an extremely talented generation of young lawyers, philosophers, clergymen and budding politicians. He became part of a coterie of friends that included Francis Jeffrey, Henry Brougham, John Allen and Francis Horner, and made himself known to a wider audience by preaching at Charlotte Chapel in Rose Street and publishing his sermons. Nor did he neglect his pupil, and when the boy had completed his two years of studying and being polished (and he showed more taste for polish than for study, being greatly concerned with his appearance and manners), his parents asked Smith to repeat the process with their second son, William. Their terms were extremely generous: £500 a year for the elder boy, and, after some negotiation, £400 a year for the younger, with Smith permitted to take a second pupil at the same time on similar terms. This he did, so that his income from teaching in his third and fourth years in Edinburgh was no less than £800 a year.[34]

Many young clergymen became private tutors, although few were as well paid. The Duke of Rutland's tutor received only £300 a year, while in the 1820s Mr Henderson, Lord Verulam's tutor, was paid only £150. Even so, these were desirable positions, for almost all the tutor's expenses were paid and he got to travel in much greater comfort than he could afford for himself. If all went well he would probably receive a family living when one became vacant, and if his charge went into politics and became successful he might do even better. Pitt the Younger made his tutor, George Tomline, Bishop of Lincoln and later of Winchester; Addington's tutor became Bishop of Gloucester; the Duke of Rutland's tutor got the See of Ely; the Duke of Northumberland's tutor became the Bishop of Bangor, while the See of St Asaph was given to Dr Luxmore, who had been the tutor of the Duke of Buccleuch. Mr Ogilvie's reward was of a different character. He was appointed tutor to the young children of the Duke and Duchess of Leinster after the duke's death; and a romance blossomed between the widowed duchess and the tutor which led to marriage and three children of his own.[35]

Marriage was also on Sydney Smith's mind in his first years in Edinburgh. He had proposed to Catharine Pybus, a friend of his sister whom he had known for years, before the end of 1798, but they were not finally married until July 1800. Catharine's father was dead and her brother did not much approve of the young clergyman and thought that he might simply be after her money, for Catharine was quite wealthy, bringing with her a portion of £8,000, which would give the couple a steady income of £400 in addition to whatever Sydney could earn. Sydney responded by insisting on a settlement that was unusually rigorous in protecting Catharine's interests and limiting his rights, something which inevitably offended his father. Not that his father approved of Catharine at all, regarding her as ugly and ill-humoured, but it is clear that Sydney regarded her with great affection, describing her to a friend: 'she is three years younger than me, a very old friend of mine – a good figure, and *to me* an interesting countenance, of excellent disposition, extremely good sense, very fond of music, and me – a wise, amiable woman such as without imposing specious qualities will quietly for years and years make the happiness of her husband's life'. And indeed the marriage proved extremely happy on both sides; Catharine was well able to hold her own, both in intellect and character, with her husband, while her quiet humour was a good foil to his exuberant wit.[36]

At the age of 30 Sydney Smith, a younger son who had received an education but no capital from his family, was a clergyman still without a living, but with an income of well over £1,000 a year. In the winter of 1801–2 Smith, Jeffrey and Horner conceived the idea of establishing a literary and political journal, published quarterly, that would be progressive in its views and much more serious and substantial than any existing periodical. And so the *Edinburgh Review* was born to immediate acclaim, and although all the contributions were anonymous, its success made Smith and the other principals into figures of consequence, although its politics did not endear them to the government of the day. By early 1803 Smith was ambitious for success on a larger stage: he felt that this was his moment and that he needed to catch the tide at the flood if he was to secure a permanent position and so provide for his growing family. He left Edinburgh behind with considerable regret and moved to London where he was greeted with enthusiasm by several old friends who introduced him into their legal and intellectual circles. He became a frequent guest at Holland House and became well known to many leading Whig politicians. His first introduction to Lord and Lady Holland came through his brother, whose wife was related to Lord Lansdowne, but it was the *Edinburgh Review*, his growing reputation as a wit and his liberal views that endeared him to the Hollands and their circle. He refused to be intimidated by the grandness of his surroundings, or by Lady Holland's formidable personality, and responded firmly to any hint of condescension. On one occasion, when Lady Holland told him to ring the bell for the servants he replied 'Oh Yes! and shall I sweep the room?', warning her against treating him as a dependant. With that firmly established, the ground was laid to establish a lifelong friendship with both the Hollands.[37]

Smith sought opportunities to preach before fashionable audiences but found the competition much stiffer in London than in Edinburgh, with the incumbents reluctant to provide openings for such an obvious rival. He had much greater success with three series of public lectures on moral philosophy which he gave at the Royal Institution, and which proved immensely popular for a season. He received £90 for the first set of lectures, £150 for the second and probably the same for the third. He was also well paid for articles in the *Edinburgh Review* and had several other minor sources of income, including a preaching position at the Foundling Hospital, and he was an auditor of the New River Company, a sinecure which he surely owed – directly or indirectly – to his father. Nonetheless it is unlikely that his income in London equalled that of his last years in Edinburgh, but he was making his name as a leading liberal intellectual within the Church, a rare breed at that time. His reward came when, early in 1806, the ministers resigned following Pitt's death, and the Whigs took office as part of a broad coalition known as the Ministry of All the Talents. Lord and Lady Holland used their considerable influence on the Lord Chancellor, Lord Erskine, to find a good place for Smith, and he obliged with the living of Foston-le-Clay, a few miles outside York, which was worth £600 a year. According to one version of the story, when Sydney went to thank Erskine, the Lord Chancellor replied, 'Don't thank me, Mr Smith. I gave you the living because Lady Holland insisted on my doing so: and if she desired me to give it to the *devil*, he must have had it'.[38]

Archbishop Markham of York did not put any pressure on Smith to reside in his new parish and the duty was done, as it had long been done, by a curate who rode over to Foston on Sundays. However, when Markham died in 1807 his successor was uneasy that such a prominent clergyman should be an absentee when he did not have the excuse of other clerical duties to perform. This was by no means unreasonable, and Smith could not appear other than hypocritical if he personally benefited from abuses that were denounced with much feeling and eloquence in the *Edinburgh Review*. One possible solution was to exchange the living for another closer to London, but when this proved impossible Smith bowed to the inevitable and in June 1809 headed north with his family.[39]

No rector had lived at Foston for more than a century and Smith regarded the old rectory as uninhabitable. He gained permission from the archbishop to live at Heslington, on the outskirts of York. In 1813, when he had been living there for almost four years, he took the decision to build a new rectory at Foston, acknowledging that he was living too far away to do the duty properly and that if he were a bishop he would expect that a clergyman in Smith's position would build. By acting as his own architect he managed to increase significantly the cost of the building to around £4,000; the lease on the house at Heslington was running out, and bad weather delayed work on the rectory, but it was made habitable with just five days to spare, and the whole family moved in even before the last doors were hung or the final rooms plastered. Nonetheless they were all delighted with their new home, and Smith took great pleasure in everything from the amount of light in the rooms to a device he designed to keep the fire-irons neat and tidy. Like his father, Smith was inclined to cry poverty, and he complained that the cost of building 'will keep me a very poor man, a close prisoner here for my life, and render the education of my children a difficult exertion for me'. His position was worsened by a succession of bad harvests and the slump in agricultural prices that followed the end of the war, and which affected clerical incomes across the whole country. Yet Smith was still fortunate: his living was considerably more valuable than most, and the income from his wife's settlement added an important layer of comfort. By 1821 farming conditions had improved, and in that year he received an unexpected legacy from his aunt, consisting of three properties in London, the Guildhall Coffee House and Tavern and two nearby houses, which together were worth some £8,000. This was more than enough to remove any financial difficulties that he faced, and to leave him relatively prosperous.[40]

Sydney Smith was a most unusual clergyman, but in many respects his life at Foston was much like that of thousands of other parsons across England and Wales, only better documented. On Sunday he would perform either one or two services in the parish church: where there were both, Morning Prayer was generally attended by the gentry and others of 'the better sort' and was longer and more complex; Evensong was shorter and simpler, although some members of the congregation would go to both services if both were offered. Not all services would include a sermon, and Holy Communion was seldom celebrated more than once a month, and often only every few months. Baptisms, burials and marriages added the occasional variety, but they were often very simple.[41]

The clergyman also needed to keep an eye on the fabric of his church and in conjunction with the churchwardens arrange for any necessary repairs. The church at Foston was small and dilapidated, with a square wooden belfry painted white which was not as straight as its makers had intended. Inside there were 12 high-backed wooden pews, each fitted with pegs on which the parishioners could hang their hats. There were galleries on the west and north walls although the steps leading up to the western gallery were unsafe, and its floor was so low that the congregation below could reach up and touch it. The sounds and smells of rural life were seldom far away, and the parish clerk would sometimes have to shepherd the gaggle of ducks that lived in the churchyard away from the door when the service was about to begin.[42]

The parish of Foston had a population of between two and three hundred, so it was not hard for Smith to get to know them individually. He helped the poor and the sick by distributing milk and other supplies, just as he had done at Netheravon and as many clergymen did throughout the country. He gave practical help and advice, acted as arbiter in disputes, and could be turned to by a young person wanting a character reference or parents seeking news of a son who had joined the army or navy. He set aside part of his glebe for allotments which he let out to the villagers at a nominal rent, encouraging them to grow potatoes and to keep pigs. He had always had an interest in medicine and was assiduous in visiting the sick, taking copious notes of their condition and keeping supplies of common drugs – to which he gave cheerful names – ready to hand. He was also sensible of his own limitations in the doctoring line, and always called in the local apothecary for serious cases, while ensuring that his patients received the medicines and food that the apothecary prescribed, whether the cottager could pay for them or not.[43]

Foston had a large glebe, some 300 acres, and when Smith first visited the parish after being given the living he went to see James Horner, the farmer who rented 200 acres of it. After some discussion they agreed that the rent should double, from £250 a year to £500. This was not as unreasonable as it sounds, for the rent had been unchanged for a generation – since Smith's predecessor had first received the living – and in that time agriculture had done extremely well, and was continuing to boom in the wartime conditions. Smith farmed the remaining hundred acres himself, just as Mr Austen and many other parsons farmed land. He was not a countryman, and had no background in the subject, but he had ample enthusiasm and delighted in ingenious inventions such as a scratching post set at an oblique angle so that animals of all sizes could relieve their itches without damaging his gates and fences. Rather less admirable was his use of a telescope and speaking trumpet to supervise his labourers from the comfort of the rectory; but the annual dinners he gave to the local farmers to celebrate the harvest and the payment of the tithe were well arranged and evidently popular. Smith's correspondence with friends in London and Edinburgh was full of talk of crops and the seasons, not to mention the advantages of horses over oxen for ploughing. He even, with marked lack of self-awareness, affected to despise 'gentleman's farming nonsense', and looked down on mere amateurs. His wife was more realistic, declaring that 'he was very fond of farming, and understood it very well. I believe he made it answer as well as any gentleman ever does.'[44]

Like many clergymen Smith became a Justice of the Peace or local magistrate. This duplication of roles attracted a good deal of criticism from reformers, who argued that it was wrong for the one man to be sentencing prisoners on a weekday and preaching forgiveness on a Sunday. But one in six clergymen was a JP, and one quarter of all magistrates were clergymen, and they were often particularly useful as they were generally resident throughout the year, and had a good knowledge of the characters of people of all classes, not just in their parish, but throughout the district. Smith appears to have been both conscientious and humane as a magistrate, going out of his way to help the disadvantaged and the poor. The work was frequently informal: people would bring their disputes, grievances or problems to him at the rectory and be shown into his study, to the right of the front door, where he would listen to their case

and give help and advice or threaten punishment according to circumstances. Once a fortnight he heard cases with slightly more formality, the
proceedings being held at the local public house, the Lobster Inn. He
disliked inflicting heavy punishments and was notably slack in enforcing
the Game Laws against poaching. Strict legality often gave way to his
sense of justice, but he could also be firm and even – at least by modern
standards – harsh, as when he forced a young girl to stand all day on the
rectory lawn with a sign saying THIEF around her neck after she had
been caught stealing fruit from his orchard.[45]

For many clergymen the magistrates' bench was just one of the ways in
which they took their place in local society. They hunted and shot with
the local gentry, dined, played cards and went to balls. There was nothing
distinctive about their clothing – cassocks were not worn at that time, and
the dog collar not yet invented – and, when resident, they were often
active and sociable. They took the lead in the establishment of circulating
libraries, and could be counted upon to subscribe to any good cause or
assist in any harmless pleasure. In some districts the style of living of the
gentry might be beyond the means of even a prosperous clergyman like
Mr Collins in Kent, although in such cases agreeable society might often
be found among other clergy in the district and other local professionals.[46]

Sydney Smith had little in common with the other clergy and gentry
near Foston: he was essentially a liberal urban intellectual and made little
effort to conceal his disdain for their boorish country ways. Asked to
preach to a gathering of the local clergy soon after his arrival in the
district he insulted them by criticizing their recreations and asking, 'Is a
minister of God to lead the life of a gamekeeper, or a groom?' Evidently
pleased with the impression he had made he published the sermon a few
months later. Not surprisingly he made few friends of his own class in the
neighbourhood. Fortunately Smith had a strong network of friends and
correspondents in London, Edinburgh and across the country who filled
the void. Foston may have been a long way from the capital, but it was
close to York and the Great North Road, and he had many visitors who
would turn aside and spend a few nights or even longer in his comfortable
rectory. These included Lord and Lady Holland, Francis Jeffrey, Samuel

Rogers (the banker and poet), Henry Luttrell (Smith's rival as a wit whose idea of heaven – according to Smith – was eating pâté de foie gras to the sound of trumpets), and Sir Humphry Davy the chemist. The York Assizes were the high point of the social calendar and brought some of Smith's old legal friends, and also new ones such as the young Thomas Babington Macaulay. The *Edinburgh Review* and numerous other books and periodicals kept Smith in touch with the latest eddies and currents in the world of ideas and literature, while his correspondents ensured that he was *au fait* with the latest gossip of politics and society. He made annual visits to London, staying at Holland House, sometimes with his whole family, while when he became more prosperous in the 1820s there were several trips to the Continent – a luxury well beyond the means of most clergymen.[47]

Despite all this Sydney Smith suffered periods of depression and melancholy; and boredom, isolation and ennui were some of the greatest dangers in the life of a clergyman. Activity in local affairs, friendship with neighbours, delight in family life, enthusiasm for country sports or intellectual pursuits, were the best preservatives, but even so many parsons lived lives of quiet despair. Loneliness was a recurring theme in the private records left by clergymen, especially the less wealthy whose pleasures were restricted by necessary economy. Those with more money might fall into the trap of overindulgence, especially in food and drink. Mary Crawford declared that 'A clergyman has nothing to do but to be slovenly and selfish – read the newspaper, watch the weather, and quarrel with his wife. His curate does all the work, and his business of his life is to dine.' And she supports her case with the example of her own brother-in-law, Dr Grant, who

> though he is really a gentleman, and I dare say a good scholar and clever, and often preaches good sermons, and is very respectable, *I* see him to be an indolent selfish *bon vivant*, who must have his palate consulted in every thing, who will not stir a finger for the convenience of any one, and who, moreover, if the cook makes a blunder, is out of humour with his excellent wife.[48]

Sydney Smith himself wrote that

the most inveterate disease to which a clerical life is exposed, is that of indolence: we are apt to see admirable understandings dwindling away into absolute insignificance from the want of some adequate object, and men who at school or college held forth the fairest promise of distinction, lulled into the tamest mediocrity by the gradual effects of solitude and retirement.

His remedy was the pursuit of knowledge, and many clergy used their leisure for serious study and made important contributions in many fields as diverse as economics and theology. One historian has compiled a list of some of the most prominent:

Thomas Burnett in cosmology, William Derham in science, Stephen Hales in physiology, Gilbert White in natural history, William Buckland in geology, Richard Bentley and Richard Hurd in classics, George Berkeley in philosophy, Thomas Malthus, William Paley, C. J. Blomfield, J. B. Sumner, Edward Copleston, Richard Whately in political economy, William Wake, Edmund Gibson, White Kennett, and William Stukeley in history.

Others wrote county histories, published papers on archaeological discoveries they had made, and were at the forefront of the topographical and travel literature, with its interest in the picturesque that was such an important thread in the culture of the time.[49]

Still, such men were the exception rather than the norm, and the life of Mr Austen, Jane's father, was probably more typical. He performed the duties of his two parishes conscientiously and well, and supplemented his income by taking in three or four boys as boarders whom he educated alongside his sons. He farmed 200 acres at Cheesedown in his parish, working closely with his steward John Bond, in a way that may have proved the model for Mr Knightley and William Larkins in *Emma*. He did not hunt or shoot, although he had no objection to his sons doing so, and he was not a magistrate. He was a man of considerable taste and learning, with a love of the classics and an eye for a well-turned English sentence that helped inspire his daughter. He was interested in the news of the day, and spent a good deal of money on new books, including novels and plays, which the whole family were encouraged to enjoy. His life lacked drama or distinction, but was rich in the contentment built on a happy marriage and a close interest and delight in his children, to which must be added a naturally cheerful temperament, sincere religious faith, and – what Sydney Smith once described as 'the great secret of life' – a good digestion.[50]

Lord Chesterfield thought that the Church was a suitable choice for 'good, dull and decent' boys, and certainly it was ill-suited to a young man with a craving for adventure or high ambition. Provided that a man had a fair prospect of securing a living, either through family influence, purchase or his college, it was a relatively safe, prudent choice of career, but the chances of great advancement were slender, and even with the significant increase in the value of livings during this period, most clergymen had very modest incomes. Essentially it was a career which offered respectability and a degree of comfort and security, but small profits and slow returns, and with little in the way of excitement, glamour or danger. For many men this was quite sufficient, and it provided as good a route as any to happiness for those with the temperament to grasp it.[51]

CHAPTER FOUR

——⟫◆⟪——

MEDICINE

LIKE MANY CHILDREN AT the time, and not a few since, John Green Crosse did not enjoy his early education:

> . . . my first lessons of reading, arithmetic and writing were received from a master of whom I entertained the greatest horror, for the ferocity of his conduct and the severe discipline by which he drove into us the simplest fundamental knowledge. His stern brow, raucous voice and long cane are now livelily depicted to my mind. How much I owe him I am, even with a long life in retrospect, unable to tell, but I was glad when circumstances arose that relieved me from his tutorage.

Fortunately a new school opened, which offered an education which included at least a smattering of Latin and Greek, and John become one of its first pupils and appreciated the uninspired but easy-going methods of his new teacher.

Crosse was born on 6 September 1790, the second son of William Crosse, a yeoman farmer near Stowmarket in Suffolk. At the time of John's birth William had yet to inherit the family farm from his father and was, in his son's words, 'supporting his family by the most active industry'. However, in the decades that followed, William Crosse did well, benefiting from the prosperity of agriculture in East Anglia during the war, and he was able to support his younger son through many years of unprofitable study.

On Wednesday 3 April 1805 John Crosse suffered an accident that decided the course of his life:

> returning from my day school, in a feat of jumping I had the accident, I ought not perhaps to say misfortune, to break my leg . . . The respectable village surgeon attended me: he was one of the old school, of fine, soft, soothing manners, clean dressed with powdered head; rode slowly on a very well looking horse; in short he was a gentleman and commanded the respect of everyone when he entered the house; he was also a skilful and kind surgeon. What wonder that the idea should be awakened in my mind to be of the medical profession![1]

Crosse's father would have preferred him to be an attorney, and he spent a few weeks in a lawyer's office 'attending bankruptcy proceedings, and feasting at midnight at the expense of the already distracted creditors'. But when this experience did nothing to change John's mind, his father agreed to let him turn to medicine, and Mr Bayly, the surgeon who had treated him, consented to take him as his first and only pupil for a premium of £200. The articles were signed and his apprenticeship began on 8 August 1806, when Crosse was just about to turn 16.[2]

Thomas Bayly was a surgeon-apothecary, which was by far the most common form of medical practitioner in provincial England in the eighteenth century. Our best source, Simmons's *Medical Register* for 1783 (which is generally reliable but not quite complete), lists 3,166 practitioners outside London, of whom more than 80 per cent are listed as 'surgeon-apothecaries', although in everyday life they would often be referred to as just the 'surgeon' or the 'apothecary' according to circumstances. (Often the same practitioner would be called a surgeon by one patient and the apothecary by another, even if they were receiving similar treatment: the terms were not quite interchangeable, but there was a great deal of overlap.) The remaining practitioners listed in the *Register* were divided between some who were described as purely surgeons or purely apothecaries — about one hundred of each — and 363 physicians, who held a university degree and so were the only ones qualified for the title of 'doctor'. There were a further 960 practitioners in London, including another 148 physicians, making a total of barely 500 physicians in all England, while altogether there were more than 4,000 practitioners for a population of about eight million.[3]

Surgeon-apothecaries were the forerunner of the modern general practitioner, although this term did not come into use until the early nineteenth century, and the eighteenth-century surgeon-apothecary generally undertook a much broader range of activities, including making up and supplying his own medicines from ingredients purchased from wholesale druggists. Many also acted as obstetricians, or 'man-midwives' in the language of the day. Their training consisted of a five-year apprenticeship, usually followed by a year or more attached to one of the London or provincial hospitals, 'walking the wards', observing, learning from leading surgeons, and attending the many private medical schools that abounded in the capital in the later eighteenth century. There was no formal course or qualification, although students who wished to practise in London needed to gain admission (by examination) to the Company of Surgeons — the progenitor of the Royal College of Surgeons. This became increasingly common and important in the later decades of the eighteenth century, but Thomas Bayly later told his pupil, 'I did not pass my examination at Surgeons' Hall nor do I remember any one who meant to settle in the country that did so. At that time it (the examination at Surgeon's Hall) was little thought of.'[4]

John Crosse kept a careful record of his activities as an apprentice. At first he did nothing more interesting than make pills and other simple medicines, but Bayly was a good teacher and encouraged him, and soon Crosse was writing proudly, 'Did up a man's leg before Mr Bayly was up, for the first time', and 'Made a pledget [a dressing] and put it into a boy's ankle', as well as 'Made 38 pills in the afternoon'. Only five weeks after he began his apprenticeship Crosse recorded that he 'Drew a tooth this morning before breakfast, for the first time'. He studied medical texts, but also – presumably with Bayly's help and encouragement – read more widely and studied French, Italian, Latin and Greek. Between 1807 and 1811 (when he was 17 to 21) he wrote two volumes of 'Letters to a Friend' in which he gave an account of his reading with selections and discussions of passages that particularly struck him. Some of the letters are in French, others in Italian, and there are extensive quotations in Latin, while the books discussed range widely from the classics to works such as Knox's *Moral and Literary Essays*, Bacon's *On Studies*, *The Spectator*, and Chesterfield's *Letters to His Son*. The letters were written in beautiful clear handwriting and illustrated with pen and ink sketches and coloured drawings that show considerable ability. The 'Friend', designated only as 'M.', was almost certainly imaginary, and the whole project was a clever device to give shape and purpose to his reading.

As this suggests, Crosse was a serious, reflective young man, and in the middle of these years, when he was about 19, he was for a time intensely religious, carefully examining his thoughts and behaviour and expecting a high standard of conduct in every aspect of daily life. He berated himself for idleness and wasting time, although his journal suggests that these criticisms were ill-founded. Fortunately, however, he also had a lighter side, and the intensity of his religious scrutiny did not last. He enjoyed all the entertainment provided by fairs, elections, parties and dances, and was received warmly into Mr Bayly's family, which consisted of Mrs Bayly and four daughters ranging in age from eight to fifteen when he first joined them. They played draughts, backgammon, chess and card games, and John learnt the flute, the piano and the organ, and played while the girls danced or Mr Bayly sang.[5]

It is an attractive picture of a diligent, intelligent, rewarding apprentice who was fortunate to find a warm-hearted, appreciative and conscientious master. Not everyone – master or apprentice – was so lucky, and there are many stories of apprentices who were treated badly or who proved a burden or an encumbrance to their masters. Typical complaints by apprentices were that they were expected to spend their lives in the shop, washing bottles, making up medicines and sweeping the floor, being treated badly and taught nothing. They might not be admitted into the family, but were not supposed to make friends of the servants either, and were expected to spend their evenings in solitude studying their books. As one manual of advice to masters declared emphatically,

An apprentice or assistant has no manner of business in the kitchen . . . one who is too fond of the kitchen is no good for anything . . . [if] too great familiarity with the servants is manifest, THERE IS NO MORE GOOD TO BE EXPECTED . . . [and] if the servant is too fond of being in the shop, the best way for a master to do, is to get clear of both as soon as he can.[6]

The same authority gives a description of the duties of an apprentice:

Be in the shop not later than SEVEN o'clock every morning, summer and winter. If anything lies over from the previous day rise earlier . . . Set the shop to rights . . . sprinkle, sweep . . . if your bed is in the shop, turn it up . . . trim the lamps . . . let this be done early, so as to be perfectly ready to come in to your breakfast with the family when called; combed hair, cleaned hands, clean face and clean shoes . . . I have seen a young man make his first appearance in his employer's shop in a morning gown and red Morocco slippers; this foppishness . . . ought by no means to be suffered.

The apprentice needed to be ready, for business did not come in a smooth, steady flow, but in urgent rushes:

It is no time to be gathering up your stockings, tying the knees of your breeches, adjusting your neckcloth or hunting for your shoes when half a dozen messengers, one after another, are running into the shop breathless, to call you to a man that has fallen from a scaffold: to a child suddenly seized with alarming fits, a person apparently dead and just cut down or taken out of the water . . . besides it is highly disrespectful to your employer to come into breakfast with your stockings about your heels.[7]

According to this dyspeptic view, apprentices were all potentially troublesome and needed firm discipline and not too much kindness if they were to be kept in check. Potential masters were warned that if they left their apprentice in charge of the shop he might well 'do business on his own . . . using drugs in the shop and entering nothing in the book', or he could pocket the money if customers came in to pay their accounts 'without waiting for having them sent out as usual at the year's end'. Some apprentices would treat their masters with disrespect, dress in fashionable clothes unsuitable to their position or their duties, and hardly be willing to do any work at all, although it is likely that the author was exaggerating in order to catch his readers' attention.[8]

Surgeon-apothecaries were willing to take on an apprentice for several reasons: the premium was a useful sum of money, between £200 and £500 in London in the early nineteenth century, although less in the provinces or at an earlier date. The apprentice might also be extremely useful in a humble way, performing tedious jobs like making pills, answering the door, taking messages and fetching drugs the practitioner discovered that he needed while making his rounds. Against this there was the risk inherent of taking an unknown or little known adolescent boy into the business and the family in the hope that he would prove dutiful and reliable; and the danger that a good apprentice might subsequently set up as a rival in the same district. Partly to avoid this danger, but mostly for better motives, some masters went to considerable trouble to help their former apprentices get established, creating a network of patronage that sometimes extended across many counties.[9]

When John Crosse was 21, and had completed his five-year apprenticeship to Mr Bayly, he went up to London to study more advanced surgery in the hospitals there. An introduction to Charles Bell, the leading anatomist of the day, led to John being accepted as a pupil and living in his house for a time. Bell was running the Windmill School of Anatomy, one of the best of the private medical schools in London, and Crosse also attended lectures on surgery by John Abernethy at St Bartholomew's Hospital and by Astley Cooper at St Thomas's Hospital. He was greatly impressed by Cooper's lecture on aneurysms and went to as many of his lectures as he could, although he usually had to stand as they were so crowded. He also joined the Royal Institution and attended scientific and literary lectures there by Humphry Davy, Dr Roget and the poet Thomas Campbell among others. In April 1812 he enrolled as a student at St George's Hospital and was placed under the instruction of Mr Keate and filled his notebooks with detailed descriptions of the operations he observed; while in 1813 he acted for four months as a dresser to Sir Everard Home. In April 1813 he passed the examination and was admitted to the Royal College of Surgeons.[10]

Poyntz Adams was also a medical student in London at this time – he arrived just a year before Crosse – and he gives an outline of his weekly schedule in letters home to his uncle, a clergyman. His days began with classes on midwifery with Mr Haighton from 7.45 a.m. to 9 o'clock; and then, from 10 until 11 o'clock he studied medicine or chemistry with Drs Babbington, Curry, Marcet and Allen. In the afternoon he had lectures on anatomy by Henry Cline or Astley Cooper. On Monday and Wednesday evenings Mr Haighton lectured on physiology, followed by Cooper on surgery. Tuesdays and Friday evenings brought Dr Curry or Dr Cholmeley on the theory of medicine, with the added bonus on Tuesdays of a lecture by Mr Allen on experimental philosophy. Adams confirms that Cooper's lectures were especially popular, with up to 230 students in attendance, with admission by ticket only, with the tickets printed in coloured ink with appropriate Latin mottoes. Many of the lecturers were flamboyant, even eccentric in manner. Crosse says only that he went to 'a surgical lecture by that droll man Abernethy', but other sources tell us that the great man would generally enter the lecture room with 'his hands buried deep in his breeches pockets, his body bent slouchingly forward, blowing or whistling, his eyes twinkling beneath their arches and his lower jaw thrown considerably beneath his upper. Then he would cast himself into a chair, swing one of his legs over an arm of it and commence his lecture in the most *outré* manner.' The students regarded all this with amusement and called it 'Abernethy at Home'.[11]

A few years earlier, at the very beginning of the nineteenth century, another student, Hampton Weekes, wrote home regularly to his father, a surgeon-apothecary in Hurstpierpoint in Sussex. He describes the 'taking in' day when new patients were admitted to St Thomas's Hospital: 'Today has been our taking-in day. The number of patients taken in amounted to 63 men and women, it is my place to write down the medicine the physician prescribes. I have done it today, also to enter all their names—Mr Cline operates to-morrow.'

Weekes fainted at the first operation he attended, but he soon grew callous: 'I have seen several operations since I last wrote and mind *nothing* about it, the more the poor devils cry the more I laugh with the rest of them [the other medical students].' And 'As to fainting away, I have entirely done that away, I take no Brandy now', and he laughed at novices, '2, 3 or 4 young fellows who are uncommonly sick, obliged to leave the theatre'. The students also attended the local lying-in hospital, with half-a-dozen being present at a delivery, which they called 'the groanings'. It was necessary for surgeons to find a way to distance themselves from the sufferings of their patients in an age before anaesthetics, but Weekes's account also suggests an initiation into an exclusive professional fraternity.[12]

Despite the number of students, the medical world in London was relatively small, dominated by a handful of leading surgeons and physicians, whom the students might gradually get to know, not just as lecturers but on a more personal level, with Crosse recording friendly social contact and invitations to their houses for dinner or tea. Popular lecturers might gain a substantial income from teaching alone – one calculation suggests that Astley Cooper would have earned about £700 a term for his surgical lectures and more than £1,000 for his lectures and demonstrations of anatomy, although this may have been a gross sum from which some costs had to be deducted. The standard of medical education had risen sharply over the previous half-century and the students emerged with a strong sense of professional pride and confidence in their expertise.[13]

Having completed his training, the young surgeon-apothecary, who was by now usually in his early to mid twenties, had to decide where he would practise. If he was fortunate he might be able to return home and join his father or uncle in a practice which he would inherit when they died or retired; however, this depended upon their being sufficient work for them both, and the great majority of practitioners (88 per cent in 1783) worked by themselves. Another route was to purchase the goodwill of an existing practice from a man who wished to retire or from the widow of a recently deceased practitioner. In March 1802 the surgeon and apothecary Matthew Flinders advertised his business in the local Stamford newspaper:

TO THE FACULTY. M. FLINDERS, SURGEON, APOTHECARY, AMD MAN-MIDWIFE, after a Practice of more than thirty Years in his present situation, wishes to retire from business, and will treat with any Gentleman wanting a Situation, who is well qualified in the different Branches of the Profession, and who would industriously apply himself to Business, who would find the Situation a good one, and well worth his Attention – To prevent Trouble, a premium to the amount of One Years Income of the Business to the present possessor is expected, and the Drugs, fixtures &c relating to the Business, to be taken at an Appraisement. None need make Application who cannot comply with these Terms – Apply personally to M.F.; or if by letter *Post paid*, or they will not be answered. M.F. feels himself most impressed with the utmost gratitude to his many Friends for their Confidence and Favors for more than thirty Years.[14]

Most new practitioners, however, seem to have started on their own, choosing a district in which they had some personal contacts and preferably one where there was not too much competition. It was sometimes necessary to give up on one district and move on to another, for example John Blount who was one of three surgeon-apothecaries in Bromyard in Herefordshire in 1779; four years later he was in Birmingham where a new hospital had opened; he remained there until 1791 but did not secure a position at the hospital, and 1792 saw him in Warwick where he joined in a partnership with an established practitioner and remained for quite a few years, setting up his own private lunatic asylum. However, his travels were not over and he subsequently moved to Great Wigston in Leicestershire before finally returning to Birmingham. Such constant movement was unusual: most practitioners hoped to find a good district, settle into it and build a reputation and mass of grateful patients, while moving would require them to begin again from scratch.[15]

Erasmus Darwin advised that a young man arriving in a district should decorate his shop windows attractively with a fine display of coloured glass bottles, mix freely with the farmers and tradesmen on market days, and not miss the opportunities provided by card parties and dances to make himself known to a wide circle. He should avail himself of as many letters of introduction as he could, while money could not be better spent than on dressing well. Darwin himself had experience of the even greater difficulties of starting a practice as a physician rather than a surgeon-apothecary, having made his first attempt in Nottingham in 1756. When this did not prosper he moved to Lichfield in the following year, and then, in 1781 to his wife's property outside Derby, where an opportunity had arisen thanks to the departure of a well-established local physician Dr William Butter, who had just moved to London.[16]

John Crosse took a different route, but did not find the task any easier. In August 1813, a few months after being admitted to the Royal College of Surgeons, he was introduced to James Macartney, who had just been appointed Professor of Anatomy at Trinity College, Dublin. Thanks to a recommendation from Charles Bell, Macartney offered Crosse a position as demonstrator. On 1 November Macartney delivered his first lecture to an overflowing house, and Crosse gave daily demonstrations in the dissecting room. Crosse hoped to establish himself as a specialist in treating diseases of the eye, and he proposed opening an infirmary in Dublin. This required the permission of the Lord Lieutenant, which in turn meant that he had to become a Fellow of the College of Surgeons of Ireland, and here he encountered difficulties. He failed to pass the examination at the first attempt, and a second effort led to a public rebuff and humiliation. Exactly what lay behind this unfortunate event is not clear, but the excuse given – that his first master, Mr Bayly lacked formal qualifications – seems spurious.

Crosse was understandably depressed and mortified by this setback, and resigned his appointment and left Dublin, somewhat consoled by the warmth of the good wishes he received from Professor Macartney and a handsome testimonial from his students. He consulted his teachers in London and was given much well-meaning – if contradictory – advice, but went home to Stowmarket still uncertain how he would proceed. At Stowmarket he was introduced to Dr Rigby, one of the two senior members of the Norfolk and Norwich Hospital, who made a favourable impression on him. Crosse decided that he would settle in Norwich and endeavour to make his living as a surgeon working in the hospital there, but first he would spend a few months in Paris studying the latest French surgical advances. He spent the winter of 1814–15 in Paris, attending the leading French medical schools: this was during the interlude between Napoleon's first abdication and his escape from Elba and the Hundred Days. Crosse was very impressed by Blainville's lecture on anatomy, but less so by Baron Larrey, Napoleon's famous military surgeon. In general he thought that the facilities for students were decidedly inferior to those in London, but that a higher proportion of French students were well informed. He wrote a paper on the uses of turpentine to treat various types of worm (tapeworms and the like) which was delivered to the Société Médicale d'Emulation by Dr Buschet in February 1815; and when he returned to England he published his impressions as *Sketches of the Medical Schools of Paris.*

Back in Norwich he busied himself writing and dissecting, but his practice was meagre, and for some time he was very discontented with his position. He regretted that he did not volunteer to go out to Belgium and attend the wounded as some other surgeons did after the Battle of Waterloo, and he considered joining Lord Amherst's diplomatic mission to China which was preparing to sail. However, in June 1816 he married Dorothy Bayly, his old master's eldest daughter, and gradually his practice grew until he was 'occupied with work from morning to night'. This work, in these early years, included attending at many births: 63 in 1819, 93 the following year, and 125 in 1821. In 1819 he also helped treat an outbreak of smallpox in Norwich, and published an account of it in a pamphlet, and in 1822 he was appointed Assistant-Surgeon at the Norfolk and Norwich Hospital. Further official appointments and other honours came in due course, for he was a man of great energy and ability with a taste for public life, publication and official committees. He developed a particular interest and expertise in lithotomy (the surgical treatment of kidney, bladder and gallstones), and in later life his income was said to have amounted to some £3,600 a year, although the failure of a bank in the last years of his life caused him much distress and worry. He had a succession of apprentices — some 40 in all — while he and his wife had eight children. In 1848 his health began to fail and he died on 8 June 1850 aged only 59.[17]

⟫⟩◆⟨⟪

Unlike John Crosse, the majority of surgeon-apothecaries settled into country practice. The limitations of medicine in the eighteenth and early nineteenth centuries are obvious — the absence of antibiotics, anaesthetics and all the other advances of the past two hundred years — but most of the medicine practised by a provincial surgeon-apothecary like Thomas Bayly was relatively simple and moderately effective. A ledger kept by William Pulsford, a surgeon in the town of Wells in Somerset in 1757, gives us some details of his work. Much of his time was spent on minor injuries, boils, abscesses, in pulling teeth, and treating skin and eye complaints and chronic infections and ulcers, which might need to be regularly dressed for several months. Major operations such as amputations were rare even in provincial hospitals. For example, John Wright, the honorary surgeon to the Nottingham General Hospital, undertook only four major operations from the 152 surgical in-patients he treated between 1795 and 1797. As Irvine Loudon, the historian who has analysed Pulsford's ledger concludes:

> The common picture of the eighteenth-century surgeon frequently engaged in major operations should be modified. Instead, a picture should be substituted of a surgeon such as William Pulsford making his

rounds on horseback with two large saddlebags containing ointments, lotions, bandages, and plasters, as well as instruments. In the periods between urgent calls, his time would be spent on the tedious and often smelly business of draining pus from infected wounds and abscesses and dressing chronically infected and suppurating lesions . . .[18]

A contemporary guide agrees that the surgeon-apothecary's work was often far from glamorous:

Are you too fine a gentleman to think of contaminating your fingers by administering a clyster to a poor man, or a rich man, or a child dangerously ill when no nurse can be found that knows anything of the matter? This is a part of your profession that it is as necessary for you to know how to perform as it is to bleed or to dress a wound. Or are your olfactory nerves so delicate that you cannot avoid turning sick when dressing an old neglected ulcer; or when, in removing dressings, your nose is assailed with the effluvia from a carious bone? If you cannot bear these things, put Surgery out of your head and go and be apprentice to a Man Milliner or Perfumer.

It seems likely that the prospect of such experiences deterred some well-bred young men from contemplating a career in medicine, and rather lowered the standing of the whole profession.[19]

Country surgeon-apothecaries drew on most ranks of society for their patients, not just the wealthy, but farmers, artisans, shopkeepers, craftsmen and at least some of the poor. A householder would usually pay for the medical practitioner to treat his servants when they were ill, while the indigent frequently received free treatment paid for by the overseers of the poor. Later in the eighteenth century it became common for working men in towns and cities to join insurance clubs where small weekly fees would be used to pay for medical treatment when a member fell ill; while many other poor people were able to afford at least some treatment in an emergency, if only by borrowing. Some practitioners also treated poor patients gratis, for example Samuel Marshall, a surgeon in

Wakefield, who offered free advice for the poor between 10 a.m. and 1p.m. on Tuesdays and Thursdays. However, the sheer mass of unsatisfied demand forced practitioners to impose a brake on too much generosity of this kind.[20]

Richard Smith wrote of his fellow Bristol surgeon Thomas Baynton that he

> . . . had in the greatest possible perfection the art of 'talking over patients'. He usually began by alarming them: 'He did not know what to say exactly – he feared there was great reason to apprehend the worst – it was almost too late to undertake the case – but it was one of those cases to which he had turned his particular attention – he had seen a great many – had several now under his care – and if anyone could cure it, he was happy to say – *he was the man*.' He knew also the value of 'my good friend' and 'my dear Madam' even in the lowest classes, and turned all to advantage.

As this suggests, Smith had no great opinion of his colleague, and condemned him for 'catching eagerly at all new medicines or proposals . . . these *remedies*, as they were termed had of course their day and then sank into oblivion'. Nonetheless, Baynton had a large and successful practice for many years, and died a rich man, although much of his wealth came from some land he had bought which proved to have coal under it.[21]

Apart from those who attended hospitals or free clinics in cities and large towns, most patients appear to have been treated in their own homes, although surgeon-apothecaries generally still kept a shop from which drugs could be purchased and simple advice given, and some probably had a room in which they saw patients who came to them. Nonetheless, almost all country practitioners needed a good horse – not a well-bred showy beast, but a hard-working, patient, reliable animal that would carry them out in all weathers, day and night, at a good steady walk and bring them home again, even if they were nodding off in the saddle. As Walter Scott remarked in his story of a Scottish surgeon, 'there is no creature in Scotland that works harder and is more poorly requited than the country doctor, unless perhaps it may be his horse'.[22]

A well-established country doctor in the later part of the eighteenth century generally had an income in the region of £400 or £500, although many of his patients would expect long credit – bills were often settled only once a year, and sometimes then not in full. Much of this money came from the sale of drugs, which was extremely profitable, and the position of surgeon-apothecaries was placed under considerable pressure at the end of the century by the rise of retail dispensing chemists. Medicines were no less a part of the rising consumer culture of the time than clothes or furniture. Richard Smith was a young surgeon-apothecary in Bristol in the 1790s and recalled that he 'had a patient bequeathed to me by Mr Alland who frequently took day and night (for if he was awake he took a draught) six or seven bottles – my apprentice regularly made up and ready two or three packets'. Similarly the Greenly family from fashionable Clifton 'could not move without a regular supply of physic – they took with them to Weymouth 200 "tonic draughts" and one thousand pills of various descriptions' so that Smith's apprentice complained that he was 'sick to death of rolling them'. Some medicines, designed for wealthy patients such as the Greenlys, contained musk or oil of cinnamon and were charged at half a guinea – 10s 6d – of which 10 shillings were profit.[23]

While a number of leading London physicians made fortunes delivering the babies of wealthy society ladies, most rural practitioners found their role as a 'man-midwife' essential but quite poorly paid, considering the risks and uncertainty it involved. In the first year covered by his journal Matthew Flinders attended 43 births, including that of his own daughter: all the mothers survived and only one child died. This was probably an unusually fortunate result, but Flinders appears to have been a careful, hard-working man, with a serious interest in his profession and considerable competence. He kept meticulous financial records which show that his income quickly rose from only £72 in the first year of his practice in Donington, Lincolnshire to £200, and then more slowly for a decade before again accelerating in the late 1780s and reaching a peak of

£582 in 1798. He was careful never to spend as much as he earned and eventually saved and invested almost £3,000 out of his income. In early years he invested these savings in property – cottages, houses and land in the district – so that by 1792 he was receiving about £120 in rent. For example, in 1788 he bought a property of 30 acres with a farmhouse and outbuildings for £915, which brought in rent of £45 a year. Six years later he sold the property for £1,500. During the 1790s he shifted his capital increasingly into government stock, and when he died in 1802 his estate was valued at over £6,000.

Flinders was a typical country practitioner. He had served his apprenticeship to Richard Grindall, a London surgeon, and had attended lectures on midwifery by David Orme at St Saviour's in Southwark. He took over his practice from his father, John Flinders, although antagonism with his stepmother probably meant that he inherited little else. He lived in a substantial two-storey brick house in the centre of Donington facing the marketplace, with a small, single-storey annexe at one end for his apothecary's shop. He kept two servants: a maid and a boy, who were paid £3 and £2 10s a year respectively. In the 1790s he belonged to a local medical society consisting of six surgeon-apothecaries and two physicians, and he had no difficulty in consulting physicians about his more complicated cases. He always feared competition, knowing that the district was not rich enough to supply two practitioners with a good living, but seems to have been generally contented with his life, although his children had a variety of problems which caused him a good deal of anxiety. In 1796 he and his wife had a week-long holiday in London, looking at the sights, visiting Lackington's bookshop and going to the theatre. He took the opportunity to call on the druggists who supplied him, to see some members of his extended family, and to make some further investments. Reflecting on the trip a few months later he wrote that he and his wife agreed that 'this was the most agreeable jaunt we ever had, & hope sometime to repeat it'. Otherwise his chief recreation and only real indulgence was reading, and he regularly spent considerable sums on books and periodicals, mostly solid works of non-fiction, a few medical texts, and the occasional piece of relative frivolity like *The*

Beauties of England. He led a modest, thoroughly respectable but quiet life, apparently without the desire for anything more.[24]

⟫•⟪

Physicians were much more inclined to cut a dash than country surgeon-apothecaries. A satire in the *Lancet* in 1833 advised a young physician to keep a carriage with fine horses and colourful livery, that should be driven in a perpetual hurry to attract attention and create the impression that the physician was very busy and in great demand, something that would be aided by an abundance of loose papers and notes. 'The late Mr Heaviside always contended that his cream-coloured carriage picked out in sky-blue, and a pair of grey horses, hooked many a patient for him.' Nor was this satire lacking foundation, for when a vacancy occurred at the Worcester Infirmary in 1825 we are told that three young physicians, 'Hastings, Malden and Lewis . . . made a grand exhibition of gigs and highly decorated horses and footmen, driven with such rapidity through the streets that "merciless death was never before so closely pursued"'. The modern physician's fondness for a prestige car as a symbol of his or her success has a long history.[25]

Most of the physicians in England had been trained, not at Oxford or Cambridge, where the teaching of medicine was 'virtually moribund' in the eighteenth and early nineteenth centuries, but in Scotland. Edinburgh dominated the scene, producing almost half of the physicians listed by Simmons as practising in the English provinces in 1783, and a substantial, but lower proportion of those working in London. St Andrews and Aberdeen also contributed a significant number and there were still a few who had gone to Leiden, whose school had been pre-eminent earlier in the eighteenth century. Admission to the Royal College of Physicians was limited to graduates of Oxford, Cambridge and Trinity College, Dublin, but such was the popularity and success of physicians trained elsewhere that the college was forced to create a special category of licentiate in the hope of retaining some of its nominal authority over the profession (an authority which in any case was limited to London and its environs). Relations between the licentiates and the college remained poor, however, and this helped to prevent the college from taking the lead in any improvement in the training of physicians in this period.[26]

In theory, physicians kept themselves apart from surgeons and apothecaries: they undertook no manual operations, and scarcely touched their patients except to take their pulse; and they prescribed, but did not dispense, medicine. But in practice there was a great deal more common ground than this suggests. Some of the leading London physicians specialized in obstetrics, and although they characteristically preferred the pretentious term '*accoucheur*' to 'man-midwife' they still rolled up their sleeves and helped deliver babies. In addition to their university training, physicians were expected to spend some time apprenticed to a surgeon-apothecary and walking the wards of a hospital, and many felt that they had equal expertise in all branches of medicine. When John Barr arrived in Birmingham from Scotland in the 1780s with both a degree as a physician and training in surgery, he found that the town was over-supplied with physicians and so embarked on a very successful practice as a surgeon-apothecary. Conversely, Edward Jenner practised as a surgeon-apothecary for 20 years before growing weary of the labour involved. He then wrote off to the University of St Andrews, enclosing a modest sum of money and two testimonials from colleagues and promptly received his MD without ever having set foot in Scotland. With this qualification he proceeded to build up a practice as a physician and developed his theories on the use of cowpox to prevent smallpox.[27]

The leaders of the profession recognized the overlap between its branches. John Abernathy had told his students that 'A physician must be a surgeon and a surgeon a physician', and John Gregory had expounded the same doctrine with more argument a few years earlier:

If a surgeon or apothecary has had the education, and acquired the knowledge of a physician, he is a physician to all intents and purposes, whether he has a degree or not, and ought to be treated and respected accordingly. In Great Britain surgery is a liberal profession. In many parts of it, surgeons or apothecaries are the physicians in ordinary to most families, for which trust they are often well qualified by their education and knowledge; and a physician is only called in where a case is difficult, or attended with danger.[28]

Because physicians charged higher fees they were usually only consulted either in difficult, complicated cases, when they might be brought in by the surgeon-apothecary who treated the patient first, or by the wealthy who could afford to have them as their primary source of medical advice. This in turn meant that they found it much harder to establish themselves in practice, for who would spend large sums on the advice of a young, untried physician? When James Currie received his degree from the University of Glasgow in 1780, he initially hoped to obtain an appointment to a military expedition to Jamaica. Disappointed in this, he wrote to a relative, William Currie, who was one of the three physicians at the Chester Infirmary, and also to a friend, Richard Worthington, who was practising as a physician near Wrexham, asking for advice. Neither was eager for him to join them, and so encroach on their business, but William Currie pointed him in the direction of Liverpool and gave him valuable introductions to influential people there. Currie's first few months in Liverpool were not easy, with him writing ruefully that 'I get a little practice, but my patients seem to die out of spite'; however, he soon found a home in the radical and literary circles around William Roscoe, and secured his fortune at the beginning of 1783 by marrying Lucy Wallace, the daughter of a wealthy merchant.[29]

Currie was fortunate to fall on his feet, but not all physicians were so lucky. Erasmus Darwin was delighted that his son Robert 'had been concern'd for near fifty patients in the first six months' of his practice in Shrewsbury in 1786–87, and Sir George Lefevre declared that a young physician in London should expect to earn nothing in his first two years, and that even then many were forced 'to put their diplomas in their pockets and go into the country to practice as an apothecary'. Dr John Simpson of Bradford wrote in his diary in 1825 that the 'medical profession is quite overstocked'. There were far more physicians in his district than it could comfortably support – three in Bradford alone, another four in Halifax and five in Wakefield – and that 'medical men are ill paid here . . . If I had a son to bring up to a profession I certainly should make the choice of law.'[30]

Physicians had to cultivate their patients, courting the wealthy and influential, and attending them at their convenience. Erasmus Darwin eventually built up a large and successful practice among the intellectual and mercantile elite of the Midlands in the late eighteenth century, but this meant that he often had to travel long distances from one patient to another. The improvement in roads made such travel quicker and easier, but it was still not altogether safe, and at least one physician was held up by a highwayman who 'behaved with great insolence: broke the glass of the chaise with his pistol, and took, besides the watch and money, everything the Doctor had in his pocket, even his letters and papers'.[31]

An honorary appointment to a hospital, either in London or the provinces, would help a physician's career in its early stages by enhancing his reputation, but this was not as essential as it was for a specialist surgeon; and many physicians resigned their hospital positions once their private practice was well established. The support of a well-connected private patron could be equally beneficial: people liked to talk about their medical problems, and an enthusiastic personal recommendation could introduce a young physician to a wide circle of fashionable patients. Some patrons went even further: it is said that Lady Burlington was so impressed with Dr Robert Taylor's treatment of her husband that she made her own carriage available to transport patients to his consulting rooms, and looked around for invalids whom she could press upon him.[32]

Royal patronage was an even more powerful endorsement. Nor was it as exclusive as it sounds. Between 1762 and 1800 no fewer than 50 physicians and 35 surgeons held royal appointments; while there were also places for apothecaries, oculists, dentists, an aurist and even an 'anatomist to the household'. As the Queen and the Prince of Wales had their own independent (if smaller) establishments, it seems that a significant proportion of all the physicians in London at any time must have had some official connection to the royal family. However, at least in most cases, such appointments followed professional success rather than paved the way for it, and a young physician starting his career was unlikely to make his name by treating royalty.[33]

⟫•⟪

We have only scant evidence for the social origins of medical practitioners of the late eighteenth and early nineteenth centuries, but what we have suggests that very few came from the landed gentry or the aristocracy. Rather more than half appear to have had fathers in the gentlemanly professions or living on modest independent incomes, while a significant number came from the families of prosperous tradesmen, farmers (like John Green Crosse's father), schoolmasters and the like. A few, but only a few, came from even more humble backgrounds. The social origins of physicians was scarcely higher: of 135 members (fellows and licentiates) of the Royal College of Physicians for whom we have details, two were the sons of baronets and one the son of the Lord Chief Justice, then we descend into 'Esquires', 'Gentlemen', naval and army officers, barristers and even a historian, although by far the largest group, amounting to one third of the total, comprised the sons of medical practitioners. Dr Wells, himself a physician, was emphatic in comparing his fellows to members of the legal profession in a pamphlet published in 1799: 'Physicians in this country are almost universally taken from the middle ranks of men. They cannot therefore be expected to conduct themselves, as a body, in the same liberal manner as the members of the profession which contains a number of persons of high birth and large hereditary fortunes.'[34]

This is rather surprising given medicine's ancient recognition as one of the liberal professions along with the Church and the law, but its social standing was not particularly high at this time. A country surgeon-apothecary held a very similar position in society to a country attorney: he would struggle to be treated as an equal by the local landowners unless he had good connections or a particularly pleasing manner. Walter Scott praised his hero Gideon Gray for his 'enthusiasm, intelligence, humanity, courage and science' and paid generous tribute to the whole class of country practitioners: 'from whom Scotland reaps more benefit, and to whom she is perhaps more ungrateful than to any other class of men, excepting her schoolmasters'. Nonetheless he is clear that at the social highpoint of the year, when the county races were held in the burgh, and a ball attended by all the local gentry was given, Mr Gray and his apprentices would not be invited. Jane Austen confirmed the point in commenting on a story her niece had written: 'I have also scratched out the Introduction between Lord P. & his Brother & Mr Griffin. A Country Surgeon . . . would not be introduced to Men of their rank.' And in her own unfinished novel *The Watsons*, poor Sam Watson is thought to have little hope of marrying the wealthy Mary Evans, as he 'is only a Surgeon you know'.[35]

A physician had a higher status, thanks to tradition and his university education, and he would usually be admitted to country society in much the same way as a beneficed clergyman: his manners, his family, the extent of his prosperity, and the character of the local community determining the exact warmth and extent of the welcome he received. But the most successful physicians did not hold a place equal to the most successful lawyers, or soldiers or clergymen in Regency society. A few leading practitioners were given knighthoods and gained a place in fashionable circles: John Allen was the confidant of Lord and Lady Holland and acted as their librarian as well as their personal physician, while Sir William Knighton rose through the patronage of Lord Wellesley to be the Prince Regent's private secretary and general factotum, and was rather offended when the Prime Minister refused to admit him to the Privy Council. Yet the position of such men was distinctly subordinate rather than independent, and Knighton's profession counted against him, not in his favour. As Speaker of the House of Commons and then Prime Minister, Henry Addington was mocked because his father had been a physician, and of all the men who sat in the House of Commons at some point between 1790 and 1820 – more than two thousand in all – only nine were medical practitioners, compared to over one hundred naval officers and four hundred who had served or were serving in the army.[36]

An ambitious young man of good family would not choose to become either a physician or a surgeon unless he felt some particular calling towards medicine, and many other young men would be put off by the long hours, by squeamishness or by pride. Yet medicine offered a fairly reliable living, amounting to comfortable affluence in many cases, and was exposed to fewer risks and hardships than some of the careers more favoured by young gentlemen. There was also the satisfaction of being able to do clear and immediate good to many, to relieve suffering, cure some complaints and help others, of being welcomed in times of emergency and trouble and thanked for bringing loved ones back from the brink of death, and of healing the broken leg of a 15-year-old boy like John Crosse, inspiring him to follow in your footsteps, and enabling him to do so without a limp.

CHAPTER FIVE

———◆◆◆———

THE LAW
Barristers

IN 1830 AN ELDERLY lawyer recalled the excitement he had felt growing up in a provincial town when the judges and lawyers on circuit arrived for the assizes. 'It appeared to me that a barrister must be the happiest person in existence. I have heard of boys and men who panted for the red or the blue coat, but to be clad in a long and flowing robe of a counsel, and to have a wig curling over my shoulders, appeared to me this earth's supremest felicity.' The assizes were held twice a year, to hear serious cases, both criminal and civil, with less serious matters dealt with by amateur magistrates like Sydney Smith in the Quarter Sessions. There were six circuits in England and a seventh in Wales, with a whole train of judges and barristers travelling from town to town, spending a week in each. These two assize weeks were the highlight of the social calendar in most provincial towns. George Jackson, a young soldier and diplomat, was in Newcastle-upon-Tyne in 1808 and noted that

[t]he judges during the whole of their stay are entertained at the Mansion House, and open house is kept there, for which the mayor is allowed £100 per day. I dined there on Monday, on turtle and venison . . . We had two very good balls, both attended by all the families in the neighbourhood . . . On the intervening night we

bespoke a play, the 'School of Reform' . . . on Friday the judges left the town – the fair, too, is over – and Newcastle, after a week of great life and bustle, is again deserted.[1]

Half a century earlier John Scott, the future Lord Eldon, was a bright-eyed seven-year-old living with his family in Love Lane, Newcastle, and he would have been well aware of the excitement and bustle of the assizes, although at that age he was probably more interested in the fair. His father was a prosperous 'hoastman' – the intermediary between the owners of the coal mines and the shippers who took the coal to market in London. This made him a member of the commercial elite of the town, undoubtedly respectable and a figure of some consequence, although not exactly a gentleman. John had two elder brothers, William and Henry, and two sisters, Jane, the youngest in the family, and Barbara, William's twin. He was educated at the Royal Grammar School, Newcastle, where the Rev. Hugh Moises was establishing a reputation as an imaginative and enlightened teacher. Moises gave new life to the Latin classics by his enthusiasm and taste for drama, and rather than force all the boys to compose Latin verse, he allowed those who struggled to write English prose instead, provided that they paid scrupulous attention to their style. He also encouraged boys intended for holy orders to write sermons, telling them that their efforts 'will not be such, perhaps, as you will approve of in mature years, but they will give you such a habit of study and composition, as will be of essential advantage'. Under his guidance the school flourished and its pupils included many sons of the landed gentry from all over the north-east of England.

Mr Moises took great interest in both William and John Scott, recognizing their strong natural intelligence and their unusual diligence. This does not mean that they were spared the usual punishments of schoolboys of those days, and many years later Lord Eldon recalled, almost with pride and certainly without bitterness, 'I believe no boy was ever so much thrashed as I was'. He was flogged by both his teacher and his father – sometimes for the same offence – and also had many fights with local boys on his way to or from school, in which he was frequently worsted. None of this dented – it may even have enhanced – his considerable self-confidence.[2]

As John's schooldays drew towards their close his father had thoughts of taking him into his business, but his brother William, who was already a tutor at University College, Oxford, intervened, writing, 'Send Jack up to me. I can do better for him here'. And so in the late spring of 1766 the not quite 15-year-old John Scott travelled up to London by stage coach, on his own, a journey of three or four days and nights. His brother met him at the White Horse in Fetter Lane and took him off to the theatre in Drury Lane and showed him the sights of London before they went to Oxford, although in later life William admitted, 'I was quite ashamed of his appearance, he looked such a mere boy'.

Within a year John had gained a fellowship at University College which paid part of his expenses; his brother supervised his studies and ensured that he was not idle, although there is little reason to doubt that he also took part in the heavy drinking that was common at the time. He took his BA on 20 February 1770. 'An examination for a degree of Oxford,' he recalled years later, 'was a farce in my time. I was examined in Hebrew and History. "What is the Hebrew for the place of a skull?" – I replied, "Golgotha". – "Who founded University College?" – I stated (though, by the way, the point is sometimes doubted), that King Alfred founded it. – "Very well, sir," said the examiner, "you are competent for your degree."' Rather more impressive was his success in winning a recently instituted prize, worth £20, for the best composition in English prose, which he did with an essay on 'The Advantages and Disadvantages of Foreign Travel', much to the delight of his old teacher Mr Moises.[3]

Scott remained at Oxford studying for an MA, but he spent his holidays at home in Newcastle, and there he fell in love with Elizabeth Surtees, the daughter of a local banker. Her family discouraged him: Elizabeth was very young and Scott had no prospects of being able to support a wife and family for years to come. He confided his troubles to his brother, who was sympathetic and urged their father to make a marriage possible by purchasing the next presentation of a living for John as 'the most obvious way of giving him an early settlement'. But before anything could come of this idea the young couple took matters into their own hands. On the night of 18 November 1772 Elizabeth climbed out of her bedroom window and down a ladder into the arms of her lover, and they set off together for Scotland where they were married on the following morning by a Presbyterian minister.

Elizabeth had just turned 18, her husband was 21. A few weeks later he told a friend that their elopement

> was executed with some wonderful escapes, and exhibits, in my conduct, some very remarkable generalship: I eluded the vigilance of three watchmen, stationed in the neighbourhood, without the assistance of a bribe; and contrived to be sixty miles from Newcastle, before it was discovered that I had left the place. My wife is a perfect heroine, and behaved with a courage which astonished me . . .

After the excitement of running away came the anxiety of returning. The low point was at Morpeth where the inn was full and the young couple 'obtained their wedding-night's lodging only by the especial civility of Mr and Mrs Nelson the landlord and landlady, who gave up their own room'. Scott's funds were running low; they did not know how their parents had reacted to their escapade; and until they heard that they were forgiven they had no home to go to, so the first few days of their married life were anything but joyous. But then Scott's brother Henry appeared, bearing a kind message from his father, and an invitation to the couple to come and stay at Love Lane until everything was sorted out. Mr Surtees was slower to forgive his daughter but within a few weeks he had accepted the inevitable and each father contributed £2,000 to Elizabeth's marriage settlement. A second marriage ceremony took place on 19 January 1773 and John and Elizabeth set off for Oxford.[4]

By marrying Scott had forfeited his college fellowship. However, the rules gave him 12 months in which to resign, and if a college living fell vacant in that time he was still eligible for it, and intended to take any such opportunity that arose, for at this stage he still regarded the Church as his preferred career. But, as he could not rely on securing a living, he looked to the law as his best alternative, and began studying for it at once. He worked extremely hard, rising at four in the morning, eating frugally and drinking little in order to avoid drowsiness, and at night wrapped a wet towel around his head. His self-discipline was great, but it did not come easily, and he was not above making the most of his suffering, telling one friend that he was one 'whose every hour is dedicated to learned dullness, who plods with hagged brow o'er the black-lettered page from morning to evening, and who finds his temper grow crabbed as he find points more knotty'.

The year passed and no living came his way, so he renounced his fellowship on his first wedding anniversary; but he and Elizabeth continued to live near Oxford where they had some friends and cheap accommodation. Their first child was born on 8 March 1774 and two months later William wrote home that, 'Jack's wife has had a melancholy time, but is now, thank God, in a fair way. Jack behaved to her with infinite tenderness, and she really deserves it, for she is an excellent wife, and makes him very happy under the inconveniences of a scanty income'. William helped them financially with loans and the occasional piece of university work, but it is clear that John Scott felt under great pressure, telling a fellow law student, 'I have married rashly, and have neither house nor home to offer my wife; but it is my determination to work hard to provide for the woman I love, as soon as I can find the means of doing so.'[5]

Scott had enrolled in the Middle Temple in January 1773, soon after his marriage, and he visited London four times a year to keep his terms at the Inns of Court, but his study at this time was self-directed, with help from his brother and other academic lawyers at Oxford. By the end of 1775 he realized that he now needed to spend some time in the office of a conveyancer, and so the whole family moved to London. They took a little house in Cursitor Street which cost them £60 a year in rent and taxes, ar in later life the Lord Chancellor would recall that he would often run down to Fleet Market (where Farringdon Street now is) 'to get sixpenny-worth of sprats for supper'. He was delighted when Mr Duane, who had great connections in Newcastle and the north-east, not only agreed to take him on as a pupil, but waived the usual fee and gave him much friendly encouragement. Years later he was generous in his tribute:

'I was for six months in the office of Mr Duane the conveyancer. He was a Roman Catholic, a most worthy and excellent man . . . The knowledge I acquired of conveyancing in his office was of infinite service to me during a long life in the Court of Chancery.' Unlike many young lawyers in his position, Scott never studied with a special pleader or equity draftsman, but learnt all he could by copying everything he could lay his hands on, and greatly regretted the loss of two volumes of notes which he made at this time.

On 9 February 1776, only three months after moving to London, Scott was called to the Bar of the Middle Temple (that is, he became a barrister). He told his niece much later:

> When I was called to the Bar, Bessy and I thought all our troubles were over: business was to pour in, and we were to be almost rich immediately. So I made a bargain with her, that during the following year, all the money I should receive in the first eleven months should be mine, and whatever I should get in the twelfth month should be hers. What a stingy dog I must have been to make such a bargain! I would not have done so afterwards. But however, so it was: *that* was our agreement: and how do you think it turned out? In the twelfth month I received half a guinea; eighteen pence went for fees, and Bessy got nine shillings: in the other eleven months I got not one shilling.[6]

Towards the end of 1776 Scott's father died. He was a self-made man; none of his fortune was entailed, and unlike Sydney Smith's father he was a loving parent with no obvious mental quirks about money. He left his second son Henry £3,000, and John £1,000 in addition to the £2,000 he had already contributed to Elizabeth's marriage settlement. He gave each of his daughters, Barbara and Jane, £1,500, or half what he had given to his younger sons, even though neither of the daughters had yet married and this was insufficient to give them even a modest independence. But the greatest disproportion lay in the bequest to William, the eldest son, whose position at Oxford probably meant that he had less need of money than any of his siblings. Nonetheless William received properties and investments worth approximately £25,000, and no one seems to have thought this odd or unreasonable.

Despite the £1,000 bequest, which was probably added to capital or used to pay debts, John and Elizabeth Scott remained short of money. They moved from Cursitor Street to a small house in Carey Street which doubled as Scott's chambers. He continued to study hard, with Elizabeth quietly sitting up with him, keeping him company, deep into the night. For a time his health was precarious, but an alarming illness was followed by a full recovery. In his second year as a barrister he began to receive a little work. The Duke of Northumberland, who had received some attentions from Mr Surtees, repaid the kindness by retaining Scott in a case before the House of Lords, but pickings remained thin. He went on the Northern Circuit, and Mr Surtees procured for him a general retainer for the Corporation of Newcastle, but he did not make much impression, and his few briefs were hardly sufficient to cover his expenses. One year he did not go on the circuit at all, and on several other occasions was only able to do so thanks to loans from William. Three years after he had been called to the Bar, William told their brother Henry that 'Business is very dull with poor Jack, very dull indeed; and of consequence he is not very lively. I heartily wish that business may brisken a little, or he will be heartily sick of his profession. I do all I can to keep up his spirits, but he is very gloomy.'[7]

As his 30th birthday approached, Scott began to despair and to consider settling as a provincial counsel in Newcastle. He was offered the Recordership of Newcastle, and although it did not have a large salary he calculated that with the other local business he could obtain and the interest on their capital, there would be enough for a reasonably comfortable life. It would mean the end to any ambition, but after three or four fruitless years it seemed only sensible to admit defeat. He wrote home, accepting the position and asking his family to find him a house in Newcastle. Two cases turned the course of his life. The first was a disputed will, and he was engaged by one party for a simple fee of a single guinea to indicate their agreement with the terms of settlement proposed by one of the other parties to the case. It was a routine piece of business of no apparent interest, but having nothing better to do, Scott studied the precedents and came to the conclusion that his client was actually entitled to more than he would receive under the proposed arrangement. He argued this in court but lost; one of the other parties then took the case to appeal and this gave Scott another opportunity to make his argument, this time before Lord Chancellor Thurlow. 'Well, Thurlow took three days to consider, and then delivered his judgement in accordance with my speech, and that speech is in print, and has decided all similar questions ever since.' It made his name in legal circles and Thurlow, evidently impressed with the young man, treated him with great attention both in public and in private.

Even so he might still have returned to Newcastle if it had not been for a loud knocking on his front door early one spring morning in 1781. Four or five gentlemen were on the doorstep: the Clitheroe election petition was coming on in the House of Commons that morning, and they had just learnt that their counsel, Mr Cooper, had been detained in Oxford by illness, and that Mr Hardinge, the next counsel, would not lead the case because he had had no time to prepare. ' "Well, gentlemen," said I, "what do you expect me to do, that you are here?" They answered, "they did not know what to expect or to do, for the cause must come on at ten o'clock, and they were totally unprepared, and had been recommended to me, as a young and promising counsel." ' Scott replied that he could make a plain statement of the facts of the case, but nothing more, for there was no time to study the relevant law.

> They said that must do; so I begged they would go downstairs and let me get up, as fast as I could. Well, I did state the facts, and the cause went on for fifteen days. It found me poor enough, but I began to be rich before it was done: they left me fifty guineas at the beginning; then there were ten guineas every day, and five guineas every evening for a consultation – more money than I could count. But better still, the length of the cause gave me time to make myself thoroughly acquainted with the law.

The case was lost by a single vote in the committee, but Scott's career had been properly launched at last.[8]

Success on the circuit soon followed as attorneys and solicitors sought Scott out to give him their cases. One of his happiest moments was in a case of great importance to the coal trade where the judge had virtually told him that his case was hopeless at the outset, only to be ultimately persuaded by Scott's argument.

> When I went to the ball that evening, I was received with open arms by everyone. Oh! my fame was established; I really think I might have married half the pretty girls in the room that night. Never was a man so courted. It certainly was very flattering to be so received; but yet it was painful, too, to mark the contrast from the year before: – it certainly was not my fault that I had no cause to lead the year before.[9]

From here Scott's ascent was remarkably rapid: he was made a KC in 1783 on his 32nd birthday, just over seven years since he had been called to the Bar, and not quite 11 since he and Elizabeth had eloped. He was offered a seat in Parliament at the same time, which he accepted, and by 1785 he was earning almost £6,000 a year, which rose to over £9,000 four years later. In 1793 he was appointed Attorney-General in Pitt's government and held the post until 1799 when he was given a peerage as Baron Eldon and appointed Chief Justice of Common Pleas. Two years later, just before he turned 50, he was appointed Lord Chancellor, a position which he held – apart from the brief interlude of the Ministry of All the Talents – until the dissolution of Liverpool's government in the spring of 1827. Even then he remained a powerful figure in ultra-Tory circles, and was disappointed not to be offered a position (though not necessarily the Woolsack) in Wellington's cabinet in 1828. For all his conservatism and the dignified offices he held he never lost his robust, sometimes earthy, sense of humour; while his marriage to Elizabeth was truly happy, so that his elopement was both the most imprudent and the wisest action of his long life.

John Scott's success was remarkable, but there was much in the early stages of his career that would have been painfully familiar to other barristers of the period. The intense study as a student and a pupil, the dullness of the texts, the discouraging lack of success, month after month, both in London and on the circuit. Scott's triumph was founded on hard work and great ability, but equally important was sheer luck: the line between obscurity as a provincial barrister in Newcastle and the highest honours of the legal profession was barely the thickness of a single sheet of parchment.

The number of practising barristers in England and Wales rose sharply over the course of Scott's career: from fewer than 400 in 1785, to over 700 in 1810, and more than 1,100 in 1830: a rate of growth far greater than that of the population or the economy. Even so, there were far more students at the Inns of Court than is implied in these figures. Lincoln's Inn alone admitted some 1,400 students between 1780 and 1799 and the combined total for the four Inns was over 3,500. Clearly only a small proportion, somewhere between one in five and one in ten of these students, were actually ever called to the Bar (that is, completed their studies and became qualified barristers).[10] Part of the explanation is that many Irish law students came to London for a year or two (to study, and to make useful contacts) and were admitted to the Inns of Court, but returned to Dublin to be called to the Bar there rather than in England. There were also a considerable number of young men, often heirs to substantial properties, who were enrolled in the Inns of Court, but who never had any intention of practising as barristers. Some had no interest in their studies but, as Edward Ferrars told Mrs Dashwood, 'made a very good appearance in the best circles, and drove around town in very knowing gigs'. Others were more serious in their approach, but wanted just enough knowledge of the law to equip them as landowners and figures of consequence in their neighbourhood, so that they could under-stand the essential points of entails and marriage settlements, of prop-erty rights and enclosures, of turnpike trusts and canal companies, and of all the cases they would encounter when they took their place on the magistrates' bench as JPs. There were also a few young men, like George Canning, who studied for the Bar, but found the law irksome and abandoned it to pursue their ambitions in the House of Commons without ever qualifying as a barrister. And finally there was a group — probably quite a numerous group — who simply abandoned their studies and looked for some alternative career that required less study.[11]

Students were required to be enrolled in the Inns for at least five years unless they were university graduates, in which case the minimum term was reduced to three years, although only a few graduates took advantage of this concession. The Inns themselves provided very little in the way of teaching or supervision: it was up to the students themselves to find a barrister who would take them as a pupil for a fee, and in return guide their reading, give them access to books and allow them to copy endless manuscript precedents. Some students formed study and debating clubs and developed friendships that would stand them in good stead in later years, and they might also move from studying under one barrister to another to gain a thorough grounding in different branches of the law. Most found the experience dull, dreary and demanding great powers of concentration; however, James Stuart Wortley, writing home to his mother in the 1820s, strikes a more positive note:

> This life in a special pleader's office, does not appear to me near so bad as I had been led to expect. We sit (6 or 7 of us) in a tolerably comfortable room variously at different desks & tables, in reading cases [and] putting them in legal form. I am writing out all the different forms required by the law; we are in no way confined but at liberty to employ as many as four hours as we like between 10 in the morning & 10 at night. I find that the 6 hours which I have always proposed to myself will be considered good application. My companions, though not perhaps the most refined, are by no means deficient in intellect, & are very obliging and good humoured. The intervals of our labours are occupied with lively & tolerably agreeable conversation though frequently upon the merits of some case of the day.[12]

Quite a few successful barristers had initially trained, and even practised, as attorneys before overcoming the gulf that traditionally separated the two branches of the profession. Robert Gifford, the son of a 'dealer in a large way of business' in Exeter, began his career as an articled clerk in his home town and was called to the Bar in 1808 at the age of 29. His father's wide range of contacts helped bring him cases on the Western Circuit, while judges appreciated his technical competence, clear arguments, quick understanding and respectful demeanour. His townsman Sir Vicary Gibbs, the Attorney-General and later a judge, gave him encouragement and patronage, and in 1817 Gifford was made a KC and appointed Solicitor-General. Two years later he became the youngest Attorney-General for almost a century, and in 1824 he was made Master of the Rolls. By then he was widely regarded as a future Lord Chancellor, but he died of overwork and cholera on 4 September 1826 before he could attain this highest honour.[13]

The age at which barristers were called to the Bar was generally a little older than might be expected: fewer than one fifth of those who went on to be judges were under 24 years old when they began their career; half were between 24 and 29, and another fifth were 30 or older.[14] Once called to the Bar a newly minted barrister would find himself a set of chambers – not joining a well-established set as is the case today, but generally by himself, perhaps, as with Scott, in the house in which he lived with his family. Here he would wait for attorneys to send him briefs, and, as Scott found, the wait might be lengthy. Good legal connections were very useful at this point, for few attorneys would trust even a small case to a young man of whom they knew nothing, but they would find work for the son of a fellow attorney, or the nephew of a KC whom they sometimes consulted or the protégé of a judge. Still such connections only created opportunities; they did not ensure success. As John Campbell, the future Lord Chancellor, wrote soon after arriving in London in 1800:

> Practice at the English bar depends by no means so much upon family interest as at the Scotch [bar], and whoever distinguishes himself is sure of employment. Those who have powerful connections no doubt have a much better opportunity of displaying their talents, but if

they are dull or dissipated no interest however great can push them on. They must yield to those who, joining attention to talent, have shone into notice notwithstanding the seemingly impenetrable fog in which fate has enveloped them.[15]

This may have been a little sanguine, but the success of Campbell's own career, not to mention that of Scott, of Gifford and of dozens of others, shows that it was not entirely unrealistic. Of all careers in the late eighteenth and early nineteenth centuries, that of a barrister was probably the one most open to talent, provided that the ambitious aspirant had the financial and mental resources to survive years of study, followed by further years of thin pickings while he established himself.

As well as chambers, a barrister needed a clerk to handle his affairs and collect his fees. Not all clerks were figures of great weight or maturity as Campbell admitted to his brother soon after he first employed one in 1807:

I have for some days spoken almost perpetually of '*my clerk*'. Who do you think this object of my boasts may be? A scrubby boy nine years old, son of my washerwoman. He can scarcely read, far less write, but he blacks my shoes in the morning, brushes my coat, carries down my wig to Westminster, and goes errands for me to all parts of the town. The only use I have for a clerk is to keep the chambers open, and this he can do as well as if he had taken his degree at Oxford. When I am Attorney General he may perhaps, like Erskine's clerk, be worth £20,000, receiving 5 per cent on all his master's fees; but at present he is satisfied with being clothed from my old wardrobe and receiving 5*s*. a week.[16]

A new lawyer with time on his hands could earn a little by 'devilling' – that is, searching out precedents and doing other preparatory work for a busy barrister, but such work was poorly paid, demoralizing and not good for his reputation in a highly competitive profession. Almost all barristers struggled at first. Campbell admitted that 'During my first term I had not even a half-guinea motion', but he went on to put this in context, 'To be sure there were about thirty men called during the term, and of these only *one* had anything to do. So I have partners in misfortune.' He had already supported himself for several years in London as a journalist, and was able to supplement his income and gain a valuable connection by ghosting a book for a successful member of the Bar who lacked the time or the ability to write it himself.[17]

Most young barristers either relied on continued support from their families into their late twenties or supplemented their incomes in other ways. Some were fortunate enough to retain a university fellowship which might give them an income of £200 or £300 until they could afford to marry. Some provided private tutoring or coaching for younger law students, in London or at university. Campbell was not unusual in taking to journalism, with subjects ranging from court reports to literary and dramatic criticism and politics. There were also a number of part-time positions within the courts themselves that provided a valuable lifeline to a young barrister with more time than work, and these often helped make him known to more senior members of the profession.[18]

This supplementary income was all the more necessary as a young barrister faced considerable costs that were hard to minimize and impossible to avoid. In addition to the cost of chambers and a clerk – however young and poorly paid – was the cost of law books, which might easily run to £200 even for a beginner's library; while the six weeks spent on the circuit would probably cost a further £100, twice a year, for the circuit had certain rules designed to preserve the dignity of the profession that did much to increase the expense, for example, no barrister could travel by public stage coach or stay at an inn. This meant that a practising barrister needed an income of about £400 a year, even if he was unmarried and frugal; and very few barristers received briefs for even half this sum in their first few years at the Bar. It was a formidable obstacle for anyone without family resources or some other source of income, making it almost impossible for the son of poor parents, and difficult enough even for many sons of good but not rich families.[19]

Most barristers, at least until they approached the top of the profession, earned the bulk of their income on the assize circuit, and their success or failure was obvious and observed by all their colleagues. For beginners, as one young lawyer ruefully remarked, the circuit was likely to contain, 'more bugs than briefs, more fleas than fees'. Campbell records the potential for humiliation:

> When I arrived here no one had called for me . . . Men junior to me had got briefs and were inquiring for mine. I was in the deepest despair. Gloucester! my sessions town! where I had exhibited so often! which was to be the origin of all my success on the circuit! I fully anticipated the horror of going into court next morning without a single brief in my hand.

On this occasion he was spared by the arrival of several briefs, but most lawyers felt this mortification repeatedly in their early years on the circuit.[20]

Spencer Perceval was the seventh son of the Earl of Egmont, but when he began on the Midland Circuit in 1786 he was so short of money that he hired a horse instead of buying his own, and made a careful note of every shilling he spent on his dinner and the sixpenny tip for the chambermaid. Samuel Romilly, who began on Midland Circuit two years before Perceval, recalled that at the time it was dominated by a group of young barristers who were inclined to ridicule and bully anyone who differed from them. 'It is not easy to give an idea of . . . how very formidable that ridicule was . . .' Lawyers on circuit lived closely together, but it was not always a harmonious or friendly company. Fortunately the arrival of new faces on the circuit lessened the influence of this clique and Romilly and Perceval became close friends despite great differences in outlook and political opinions. They both went on to be distinguished lawyers and parliamentarians: Perceval as a courageous Prime Minister, Romilly as an eloquent and influential advocate of the reform of the criminal law from the opposition benches. Yet neither found success on the circuit easy or rapid. Perceval was too modest and perhaps too timid to make much of an impression, and was only able to persevere because his mother's family obtained the position of Deputy Recorder of Northampton for him –

which helped to cover his expenses. Eventually he made his name as junior counsel for the government in its prosecutions of Tom Paine in 1792 and Horne Tooke in 1794, and this led to further government work and a seat in Parliament. Romilly's rise was even slower, and came by attending the Quarter Sessions, where there were fewer barristers offering their services so that it was not hard to attract the notice of the attorneys and be given an opportunity to display his talent. Once he began to be successful, even in the lesser cases that were tried in the Quarter Sessions, he established a reputation and was soon given more important cases in the assizes.[21]

Romilly, Perceval, Campbell and Scott were all exceptional men whose careers progressed smoothly upwards once they were fairly started. But not all lawyers were so consistently successful and reputations fell as well as rose on the circuit, with every hint of ascent or descent observed by colleagues. John Coleridge (the nephew of the poet) was a young lawyer on the Western Circuit in 1824 and noted in his diary:

> The melancholy thing upon the circuit is to see the approaching fate of such really good men as Gaselee, Selwyn and Merewether, who are gradually declining, & will sink to cyphers probably; unless they should get elevation to the Bench. It would be well for the country if room was made for them – such a Judge as Burrough is really a disgrace to us.

And indeed later that year Stephen Gaselee was appointed as a Justice of the Court of Common Pleas. 'I rejoice in his elevation,' Coleridge wrote, 'though I do not think him a man of a large or cultivated mind; but he is an honest man, a good lawyer, & it *is an honest* appointment.'[22]

One of the leading lawyers on the Western Circuit at this time was Thomas Wilde, who had begun his career as an attorney and who had been called to the Bar in 1817 at the age of 34. He had no connection with the West Country, but joined the circuit when the appointment of Gifford as Solicitor-General, and the retirement of John Lens, opened the door to fresh talent. (Fourteen other barristers joined the Western

Circuit at the same time and for the same reason: competition was keen.) Coleridge did not think very highly of Wilde, writing that 'I very much question Wilde's long holding his lead if he is vigorously opposed, for he is very deficient in some of the most indispensable qualities of an advocate; he cannot examine or cross examine well, he wants temper, & though he speaks well, yet he does not speak winningly, and persuasively to a Jury'. Wilde's most frequent opponent, indeed the dominant barrister on the Western Circuit in these years, was Albert Pell who benefited most of all from the retirement of Lens and removal of Gifford, for in 1819 he was said to have had more than twice as many briefs as any other lawyer on the circuit. In 1822 Coleridge noted that

> Pell has maintained his superiority through the circuit – ignorant as he is, and really contemptible in many points, yet in the essential of getting a verdict for his client few can surpass him. He is very clear in his statements, and so commonplace in his remarks that the Jury always understand him, and delivered in a slow sententious way his commonplace remarks strike the Jury with effect. Then he has the good sense always to discover the main features of his case and to stick to them – never to call an unnecessary witness, or prove an unnecessary fact.

Nor was Coleridge any less critical of his own performance, noting that

> [t]oday I was in a long cause with Pell, which we won; I was exceedingly vexed to find my own unreadiness and inefficiency in the beginning of the case. I got hampered with my witness and afraid to ask questions from the fear of not asking legal ones, while he could put any thing, and extract any answers, which suited our purpose, without objections being made.

Pell retired from the circuit in 1825 due to ill-health, and Wilde dominated the circuit until 1835 when he concentrated on pursuing his career very successfully in London. Coleridge himself gradually prospered and in 1835 at the age of 44 he was appointed a Justice of the King's Bench.[23]

The Lord Chancellor presided over such judicial appointments with some involvement of the Prime Minister and, occasionally, the King. He was also very influential in the selection of the Crown law officers and the elevation of KCs, and he confirmed recommendations put forward by the Lords Lieutenant to the magistrates' bench in each of their counties. Lord Eldon was far more conscientious in the discharge of this legal patronage than he was in his ecclesiastical appointments, partly because this was his own field of expertise, and partly because a judge was a more senior position than a parish clergyman, and would not disappear into the provinces never to be heard of again. Personal advantage, political necessity and social prejudice all played their part in Eldon's judicial appointments – and completely dominated his thinking when it came to a number of lucrative sinecures – but legal ability was generally the most important consideration when it came to the appointment and promotion of judges. He also valued university education highly, so that this sometimes weighed as heavily as professional success in his choices; although its absence was no impediment to Robert Gifford's rapid rise.[24]

Judicial appointments were relatively rare, for there were remarkably few judges: 17 in all until 1813 when the number was increased to 18, including the Lord Chancellor himself. In the 30 years between 1790 and 1820 only 29 judges were appointed: most served for life, or until they chose to retire, but the Lord Chancellor might lose office with a change of government. County courts that formed an intermediary stage between the amateur magistrates of the Quarter Sessions and the assizes presided over by touring high court judges were an innovation of the 1840s, while even in 1875 there were fewer than 30 judges in all England. Apart from the Lord Chancellor, judges tended to be appointed to a junior position on the bench, and then sometimes promoted to a more senior position at the head of their particular branch of the courts. The more senior positions were much more lucrative, less thanks to their salary than to perquisites and fees which they received and the ability to appoint family members to valuable sinecures. The higher the office the greater the reward, and while Eldon's fortune was exceptional – reflecting his three decades at the very summit of his profession – most judges became rich men.[25]

Barristers who were not among the most successful might look to some lesser office as a refuge from life at the Bar: one young lawyer referred to 'the numerous posts of honour or retreat which our profession is well stored with'. There were many places in local government, attached to the courts and government departments in London, and with the handful of large organizations such as the East India Company and the Bank of England, that required legal training and which provided a comfortable income, which were too laborious and time-consuming to appeal to the ambitious. Such positions provided something of a safety net for a barrister who was struggling to establish himself on the circuit but who had the connections to secure the appointment. However, for many – perhaps most – of the young men called to the Bar in the early nineteenth century, even such consolation prizes proved elusive, and their years of hard study and persevering efforts on the circuit failed to find any adequate reward.[26]

Becoming a barrister was always something of a gamble: only a minority achieved even a modicum of professional success, and many quit the profession in disgust while relatively young men. The position worsened in the years after Waterloo when the size of the Bar expanded far more quickly than the demand for barristers – partly because the end of the war made alternative careers in the army and navy much less appealing. One of these 'briefless barristers' was Jane Austen's nephew Henry (the son of her brother Francis) who expressed their plight – and his underlying dislike of the law as a profession – in verse:

Law – always hateful – most so when it winds
Its tangled meshes round unwilling minds
I hate the law – and Equity's worse
More undefined, more arbitrary curse.

So I a briefless barrister
Am haunted by a busy clerk
Who every morning comes with, 'Sir,
I should be glad Sir, of some work.'[27]

Nonetheless for an ambitious young man, particularly of an earlier generation, the Bar was not necessarily a bad choice: it required great effort and considerable ability, luck and patience, while the rewards were far from certain; but it was relatively open to talent, and the rewards of success were great, not just in material terms, but in prestige and fame, and it could open a door into a career in politics as well as in the law.

——⊰•⊱——

CHAPTER SIX

THE LAW
Attorneys and Solicitors

SINCE THE MIDDLE AGES the English legal profession has been divided into two branches: barristers, who represent their clients in court, and attorneys and solicitors who deal directly with the client and cover a vast range of legal matters, including wills, property transfers and other affairs that usually do not need to be tested in court. Until the middle of the eighteenth century attorneys and solicitors were distinctly different types of lawyer, but acts of Parliament in 1729 and 1750 removed the barriers between them, and they gradually merged into a single profession. In the late eighteenth and early nineteenth centuries 'attorney' was the term more commonly used, but during Queen Victoria's reign 'solicitor' became the norm, and 'attorney' survived only in terms like 'power of attorney' and 'Attorney-General'. The terminology is quite different in the United States, where 'attorney' is in common use for both courtroom and other lawyers, and the division between the two is much less clear-cut.

Attorneys were much more numerous than barristers in Regency England. There are no precise numbers, but it is thought that there were between 4,000 and 6,000 attorneys in practice in England and Wales in 1800. Roughly one third of these were in London with the remainder widely scattered across the country, so that there was at least one attorney in every small town of any consequence. For example, the little town of Cockermouth in Cumberland, with a population of about 2,500, boasted no fewer than eight attorneys in 1780, including John Wordsworth, the poet's father. This was probably rather more than the town and surrounding district could support, for the number had fallen to four by 1800. Other examples include 22 attorneys in Salisbury in 1790, 15 in Colchester and 11 in Carlisle in 1800. Clearly attorneys were a very important element among the urban elite in such small towns, and they frequently dominated many civic positions in the local government.[1]

The social standing of attorneys relative to the gentry, the clergy and other genteel professions was open to doubt. They certainly lacked the prestige of barristers, and as late as 1870 an old-fashioned character in Anthony Trollope's novel *The Vicar of Bullhampton* 'always addressed an attorney by letter as Mister, raising up her eyebrows when appealed to on the matter and explaining that an attorney is not an esquire. She had an idea that the son of a gentleman, if he intended to maintain his rank as a gentleman, should earn his income as a clergyman, or as a barrister, or as a soldier, or as a sailor.' A century earlier, Dr Johnson had remarked that 'he did not care to speak ill of any man behind his back, but he believed that the gentleman was an *attorney*'.[2]

The most prominent lawyer in the novels of Jane Austen is Mr John Knightley who is almost certainly a barrister, although this is never specified. The most detailed portrait of an undoubted attorney is that of Robert Watson in the unfinished novel *The Watsons*.

Robert Watson was an attorney at Croydon in a good way of business; very well satisfied with himself for the same, and for having married the only daughter of the attorney to whom he had been clerk, with a fortune of six thousand pounds. Mrs Robert was not less pleased with herself for having had that six thousand pounds and for being now in possession of a very smart house in Croydon, where she gave genteel parties and wore fine clothes. In her person there was nothing remarkable; her manners were pert and conceited.

This was hardly a flattering picture, and the impression that attorneys were likely to be underbred is supported by the mature novels in which, while they never venture in front of the footlights, they can be glimpsed hurrying across the back of the stage or lurking in the wings. Young William Coxe is an attorney in Highbury and is invited to the ball at the Crown Inn, as is almost everyone with plausible claims to respectability, but Emma summarily dismisses him as a possible suitor for Harriet Smith: 'William Coxe – Oh! no, I could not endure William Coxe – a pert young lawyer'. And Mr Elton's bride, Miss Augusta Hawkins, had an uncle in Bristol 'in the law line – nothing more distinctly honourable was hazarded of him, than that he was in the law line; and . . . Emma guessed him to be the drudge of some attorney, and too stupid to rise'. Of course, Emma is being a frightful snob and Austen's touch is playful and ironic, but these passing references made sense to readers because they reflected the common assumptions or suspicions of the age.[3]

This all suggests that attorneys were little better than school-teachers or the better sort of shopkeeper: respectable enough in their way, but not a career for the younger sons of the gentry. However, a detailed study of 5,000 articled clerks (the group from which all attorneys came) between 1709 and 1792 shows that 61 per cent claimed to be the sons of gentlemen. The higher branches of the upper classes were barely represented: there were only 14 sons of baronets, 17 sons of knights, one son of a lady and one of a dame: 33 out of 5,000 shows beyond doubt that attorneys were not recruiting from the cream of county society. It is also likely that many of the claims of paternal gentility would have been summarily dismissed by Emma Woodhouse, for it was not uncommon for young men to show their respect for their fathers by elevating them up the social scale. Still, the 739 sons of esquires, 1,842 sons of gentlemen and even the 971 sons of widows would probably have included a good few who really were the younger sons of smaller landowners and of gentlemen of independent if not bountiful means, while many of the others would have had fathers who had prospered in one or other of the gentlemanly professions.[4]

One reason for this is simple: it was not cheap to become an attorney and, like all the gentlemanly professions, the financial rewards were deferred until a young man was well into his twenties at the earliest.

Attorneys learned their profession in the office of an existing attorney, in much the same manner as the apprentices of craftsmen. A boy would become an articled clerk, usually in his mid-teens, for a term of five years. His father would pay a substantial premium to obtain this opportunity for him: the most common figures for the years around 1800 were between £100 and £300, but £500 was not unknown, particularly for an attorney in London. Some fees were much lower (even less than £50), but in most of these instances the clerk was the attorney's son, nephew or other family connection, and the payment was purely nominal.[5]

In 1820 William Leigh, an attorney near Taunton, outlined his expectations of a prospective clerk:

> My clerks work very hard and we do not know the meaning of 'office hours'. All hours within which I want them are office hours . . . My articled clerks must look up to and respect my highly respectable managing clerk, Mr Rowcliffe, whom I have brought up and who has been with me upwards of 14 years. My writing clerk is as good a lad as can possibly be; we never hear of a dog or a gun. Business and study fill up the hours here. The situation and peculiar circumstances of my family prevent me taking any young gentleman who is not of the Established Church. My terms are 600 guineas, and my clerks pay for their washing out of the house, and I always stipulate . . . for obvious reasons that in the case of sickness the clerk should be provided with lodging and attendants as well as medical assistance by his father.[6]

The position does not sound very enviable although it is possible that Leigh was being unusually particular as he was unable to meet his prospective clerk, who lived on the other side of the country, and because he had just enrolled his own son as a clerk and was anxious to avoid any bad influence that might unsettle him. In the end an agreement was reached with Leigh lowering his terms to 500 guineas: still high for a country attorney, which suggests either that he had a particularly high reputation or that there was a keen demand for such places at the time.[7]

William Hickey's father was a successful London attorney with a wide practice: he already had two partners, his eldest son Joseph and Nathaniel Bayley, when he reluctantly gave up his hope that William would become a barrister. Although William was formally articled to Bayley it was his father who took the greatest interest in his studies and exerted some influence over him.

My father had all his life been a remarkably early riser, I, on the contrary, was a sluggard, and if allowed to pursue my own inclination, never left my bed before nine o'clock. It was therefore much against the grain that I was compelled to rise every morning by five, some-times earlier, my father calling me himself, and directing me to go to my books, using every argument in his power to persuade me to read hard. Over and over again would he say: – 'Now is your time, my dear William, for studying to advantage; read hard, read day and night. Until you are forty it will all prove beneficial, and you will retain it, but after that age reading becomes a mere amusement for the time, as the memory then begins to flag.' For two or three months I did obey my father's injunctions, and read a good deal, doubtless with consid-erable advantage to myself. Had I through life continued the same course I should at this day have been a very different sort of creature to what I am.[8]

The quality of training provided by attorneys for their clerks varied widely depending on their personality and circumstances. Some were assiduous, introducing their clerks to a wide variety of work, patiently explaining complexities, and encouraging them to study. Others paid them little attention and used them largely for copying documents and correspondence. A previous generation had even been expected to perform menial tasks better left to servants, but this had fallen out of favour with both clerks and attorneys by the second half of the eight-eenth century, for the pretensions of the profession as a whole were rising. Indeed, some attorneys went so far as to encourage their clerks to read widely beyond the law and acquire at least some elements of a liberal education so that they could converse with gentlemen as equals, although this remained relatively unusual.[9]

Most clerks complained that their lives were both dull and laborious, but some were relatively happy. The 17-year-old William Pattisson even injected a note of idealism into a letter home to his father:

> I think it my duty to endeavor [sic] to promote the happiness of society as far as possible & I know not in what manner I would more willingly undertake to do so than by studying the Law. The Law seems rather an abstruse Profession & it will undoubtedly require much time & study to become a Proficient in it. I must say I think I like it extremely & I hope custom will render the long confinement at my desk more & more consonant to my health, for now & then my head aches extremely.

But not all clerks were as dutiful as Pattisson sounds, and some made full use of whatever liberty they could obtain. As early as 1755 there were complaints that the attorneys' clerks in London were 'under no manner of government; before their times are out, they set up for gentlemen, they dress, they drink, they game, they frequent the playhouses, and intrigue with women; and it is a common thing with clerks to bully their masters and desert their service for whole days and nights whenever they see fit'.[10]

William Hickey tells us exactly how an intelligent and charming young man, with a warm heart and genuine respect for his father, could go badly astray through insufficient supervision and a love of good company. He had been an articled clerk for just over a year, and was employed almost as a messenger, taking documents to the different law offices, paying fees, obtaining writs and delivering briefs to barristers. He performed these duties extremely well, being popular with other clerks and more senior lawyers. 'My brother, who acted as cashier, was directed to furnish me with money for those purposes, and kept a book in which I was ordered to enter all receipts and disbursements.' Unfortunately, no one checked these accounts with any care: Mr Bayley would glance at them every few months but finding that the debtor and creditor totals balanced assumed that all was well. It wasn't.

> My error commenced in not keeping my pocket money distinct and separate from that belonging to the office. The consequence of not doing so was that I had unconsciously trespassed upon the latter before I was aware, and at the first discovery thereof was greatly alarmed. This proper feeling however soon subsided, and, like all those once commenced upon bad habits, I became by regular gradations, first uneasy, next indifferent, and by continued practice callous. Finding the balance every week considerably increasing against me, I endeavoured to counteract it by introducing sums I had never disbursed, entering others higher than I actually paid. True it is the old and faithful monitor conscience, frequently reminded me that such means were as dishonourable as unjustifiable, and upon discovery, which I knew must in the end take place, would bring me to disgrace and shame. Still, these internal upbraidings grew less and less, and I reconciled myself to making false entries by feeling that the cash I was thus purloining belonged to my father, and that plundering him was a different thing entirely to robbing a stranger.[11]

Hickey loved good company and spent money freely, drinking and whoring most of the night.

> Returning home from these intemperate scenes if my father was out of town, as he generally was, I went to bed for four or five hours, but if in town I went directly to my desk, where, laying my head down upon it, I soon fell asleep, in which state Mr Bayley would often find me, when, awaking me, he with a solemn face would say 'indeed, William, these are sad doings, and God only knows to what a life of such excess will lead you.'

Still neither Bayley nor anyone else wondered how he could afford to be so extravagant, and he continued to enjoy his wild life. He never took to gambling, and at times was bent on reform, for he always enjoyed rational intelligent company, but then would relapse, for he had little self-discipline and could not resist the appeal of a convivial time among friends. His peculations were discovered after about seven months; his father was shocked and astonished, while Hickey himself was sincerely ashamed and mortified. After a week of disgrace he appealed to his mother.

> At first she peremptorily refused, observing that I had behaved so uncommonly ill . . . that she had not a word to say in my behalf, nor dared she entertain a serious hope that I should ever forsake the evil courses I had so unfortunately fallen into, and, she was sorry to be obliged to add, against which I did not seem to make the slightest struggle. At this period however, I possessed the power of persuasion in a considerable degree, especially with those fond and partial as my mother was, and finally I prevailed.

William's father appears to have been equally susceptible, and probably welcomed the excuse to forgive him.

> Another tender, and to me, truly distressing scene took place between my father and me, at which I made a thousand protestations of altering my habits of life, and I can truly say I once more resolved rigidly to keep my word, and become a new man. My father assured me every thing that had passed should be buried in oblivion, and that no one should ever upbraid me respecting my late irregularities.[12]

His father was probably too generous, for London held too many temptations for William Hickey to resist for long, however genuine his repentance. He soon got into a fresh scrape and his father decided that he must be exiled to India and obtained for him a commission in the Madras army. This was just the beginning of Hickey's picaresque career – he did not like the look of Madras, and blithely sailed on to China and from thence back to England where his father forgave him yet again, and even then we are still in the first of the four volumes of his *Memoirs*! No one, not even Boswell, paints a better picture of the raffish life of a young man about town in eighteenth-century London.

⟫•⟪

Most country attorneys had good relations with a London attorney who regularly acted as their agent, and they would often send their clerks up to London towards the end of their five years in articles, to spend some months or even a year with the London attorney. Here they would gain wider experience and make useful contacts, while also no doubt tasting some of the less reputable pleasures readily offered by the capital.[13] Once his time in articles was completed, the clerk could be admitted to the profession. He would first be examined by a judge, but this was frequently no more than a formality. When William Hickey eventually completed his clerkship 'at least in point of time' (for a good part had been spent sailing to China and back), his father introduced him to Mr Justice Yates, one of the Judges of the Court of King's Bench, who asked him to come to breakfast the following day when he would examine him.

> At the time appointed I attended, and in a terrible fright I was at the ordeal I imagined I had to pass through, and the probable loss I might be at in answering some of the many questions I understood would be put to me upon points of practice. Being conducted into his parlour where the breakfast things were all arranged, in five minutes the Judge entered. We sat down, and he recommended his French rolls and muffins as of the best sort, but so predominant were my fears about the dreaded examination that I had no inclination to eat. Breakfast being over, he asked me how I liked the Law, how long I had been out of my clerkship, and two or three other questions equally unimportant, when a servant entered to announce the carriage being at the door, whereupon he desired his clerk to be called, upon whose appearance he enquired whether Mr Hickey's Certificate was ready. The clerk having it and the other papers in his hand, the Judge took it from him, and after perusal subscribed his name, and then said, 'Now

122

Mr Hickey, if you will be so good as to accompany me to Westminster Hall, I will get you sworn, and the business concluded.' . . . This being done the Judge ordered the oaths to be administered to me, after which, with my subscribing my name to each, I was entered upon the Roll as an Attorney, and making a respectful bow to the Bench and Bar, I retired, most agreeably relieved from my apprehensions respecting the various interrogations I had expected would be put to me on the subject of my qualifications.[14]

Of course, Mr Justice Yates knew Hickey's father as a respectable and successful attorney in London, and might have been more searching in his examination of an unknown clerk from the provinces, but there are still clear echoes of Henry Austen's ordination examination.

The next step in the budding attorney's career was much the hardest, and fewer than half of all clerks ever managed to make it. Setting up any business by yourself was difficult, but far more so when the ability to inspire trust in your potential clients was the first and most important requirement. 'The Generality of People,' one commentator remarked in the middle of the eighteenth century, 'not being over-fond of very young Attorneys.' The easiest solution was to join an existing firm as a junior partner, but most attorneys (80 per cent in London, and 90 per cent in the rest of the country) worked as sole practitioners with one or two clerks in the office. Where partnerships existed they were usually reserved for the attorney's son, or his son-in-law, and many an attorney's clerk courted his master's daughter hoping that personal and professional success would go hand in hand. If this was not possible, or did not appeal, a young attorney with money behind him might buy a practice, either from an elderly lawyer or from the widow of a lawyer. The latter situation was not uncommon, for most attorneys never made enough money to retire.[15]

The partnership agreement between Thomas Bollard of Leeds and John Atkinson made in 1792 sheds some light on the terms an established attorney might exact from his junior. Atkinson had first to produce £500, although it is not clear if this was paid to Bollard or represented working capital. For the first five years of the partnership Bollard would receive

75 per cent of the profits; for the next two years he would get two-thirds, and for the following seven years the profits would be divided evenly. Whether Bollard continued to practise during this time is uncertain, although it seems likely that he did, while gradually allowing Atkinson to take a greater share of the work.[16]

An attorney setting up in business on his own account, without an established partner, would need to have deep pockets both to keep afloat while waiting to build up a clientele and to cover the costs of the business he did conduct, for attorneys were generally not expected to charge their clients until a matter was concluded. There were also the costs of renting an office, stationery, furniture and perhaps a clerk, although that was not strictly necessary especially for a young attorney just beginning his business.[17] A young man might succeed if there was a shortage of capable attorneys in the district (not a common event), or if he had a network of contacts (often extended family) in the area who might be willing to entrust him with their affairs. He might find a niche as the agent for a large estate or have a second source of income — private means or some other business activity — that would help to support him, but it is clear that success was far from assured and seldom came easily or quickly.

We do not know with any precision what happened to all those clerks who never set up as attorneys in their own right, or to those who made the attempt but failed. Some remained working as clerks in the offices of attorneys for the rest of their working lives; some found a position in local government for which their training would often have been useful; some were probably employed by wealthy individuals or businesses as accountants; while others may have taken a completely new direction in their lives, joining the army or going out to India. It is possible that some young men were articled as clerks without any real intention that they should ever practise as attorneys: at least that is the suggestion made by Joseph Day in 1796, who complained that some parents and guardians placed their charges in an attorney's office, 'rather as a check on habits of dissipation than with the attempt or expectation that sufficient application would be given to attain a useful degree of professional knowledge'. There was a parallel here with young gentlemen reading for the Bar, and the high number of widows among the parents of eighteenth-century clerks in the study mentioned earlier (971 out of 5,000 is surely disproportionately high) suggests that there was at least some truth to this idea. Nonetheless it is clear that there was a marked oversupply of clerks qualified to practise as attorneys, and that the hopes of many parents, who paid quite a large sum to have their son articled thinking that this would lead to a secure and prosperous future for him, were quite often disappointed.[18]

The experiences of two country attorneys in the second half of the eighteenth century give some idea of what life had to offer for those lucky clerks who succeeded in becoming attorneys. Benjamin Smith was born in 1731 in St Peter's Eastgate in Lincoln. We know nothing of his family background: he may have been a tradesman's son, an illegitimate child of a member of the Brown family, or from a humble background; certainly he was not well born. Nor do we have any record of his early life or legal training, but he may have worked as a clerk (articled or not) for Matthias Brown, an attorney at Walcot in Lincolnshire, who was the agent for the Brown estates, and whose business Smith eventually took over. It is clear that by 1761 Smith was acting as an attorney, although he was not formally enrolled as such until 1767 – an irregularity which seems to have been unusual. His work seldom involved litigation; rather he prepared wills, mortgages and marriage settlements; did much conveyancing of land; and collected rents, prepared leases and presided over manorial courts for a number of landowning families in the country around Horbling, Walcot and Donington, south of Lincoln. Far from being tied to his desk he spent many hours on horseback, visiting clients, attending manorial courts, traversing all the country within 30 miles or so of his office at Horbling, and getting to know the land well. He corresponded with Robert Kelham, a solicitor in London who acted as his agent, obtaining counsel's opinion on difficult questions and also handling much business for Smith's clients.

However, Smith's most profitable activity – as it was for most country attorneys – was that of a money scrivener, acting as the middleman between those with money to lend and those needing to borrow. In such transactions he drew up the bonds and other legal documents and collected a brokerage fee for arranging the loan, but did not himself act as a principal in the transaction. Typically the lenders were widows, retired officers of the army or navy, retired tradesmen or farmers: people living on the income derived from a modest capital, who wished to lend part or all of it locally rather than putting it into government bonds, East India stock or other national investments, and who relied on their attorney's knowledge of local affairs for the security of their money. The borrowers were generally local landowners looking to raise money to pay off existing debts, to cover the cost of enclosing some of the land, to pay for election expenses or the marriage settlement of a daughter or daughter-in-law or establish one of their sons in a career. Local businessmen might also borrow money for commercial purposes, but this does not appear to have been as common, probably because their security was regarded as less reliable than that of the landowners.[19]

Many local attorneys played an important role as clerks of the Quarter Sessions, but there is no evidence that Smith did so. On the other hand he was heavily involved in the legal processes surrounding several enclosure acts affecting the district. Each enclosure required detailed planning, the appointment of commissioners, the agreement of the affected landowners including any clergyman, and precise listing of a mass of information ranging from the route of new roads to manorial rights, while the costs then had to be apportioned among the petitioners. Such work was perfectly suited to a country attorney, and it was well paid. In 1764 Smith became clerk of the Horbling Enclosure Commission; three years later he was appointed to a similar position on the Newton Enclosure Commission; in 1769 the parishes of Thurlby and Threckingham followed, with Helpingham coming in 1772 and Wilsford and Surfleet in 1775. The regularity with which new work arrived almost suggests that local landowners were willing to wait until he was free to undertake the task. He was equally enmeshed in a number of local turnpike trusts and projects to drain the Fens, notably the splendidly named Black Sluice Drainage Trust where he was clerk and managed most of the business. And he acted as clerk to several local charities, often established long before to provide funds for the needs of widows or the education of poor children, while he also served as clerk and treasurer of the Folkingham Association for Prosecuting Felons. All these activities made him a significant figure in the district and brought him into close contact with the gentry of the neighbourhood who, presumably, were impressed with his capacity for business.[20]

Benjamin Smith did well and by the time he died in 1807 he had taken two partners into his practice: his eldest son and namesake, and William Worth, formerly his clerk. In his will he left his widow an annuity of £100 and his sister £24 a year. His daughter Elizabeth received £7,000; his son Edward, who had gone to St John's, Cambridge and been ordained in 1807, £8,000. Another son, Francis, who became a grazier, received £2,500 but also properties that made his inheritance at least equal to Edward's, while Benjamin Smith Jnr inherited his father's share of the practice and also quite extensive property. In the following year the practice made a profit of just over £2,200 of which Benjamin Smith Jnr received £1,657 and William Worth £552. Figures for the next decade show that this was not untypical, although the profit varied quite sharply from year to year (that for 1809 being half that of 1808). The younger Benjamin Smith carried on his father's example of hard work and diligence, and reaped ample rewards, dying in 1857 worth approximately £140,000.[21]

If Benjamin Smith's success has echoes of a Victorian morality tale where the duller virtues were rewarded, William Yescombe's fate acts as the salutary lesson for those who were too impatient. Yescombe's grandfather was a country gentleman in Somerset around 1700, and his son Robert (William's father) was a successful attorney in Bath who married the daughter of a Bristol brewer and had three sons and three daughters. However, Robert died in 1750 at the age of only 44, before his children had been launched into the world. Five years later the eldest boy, another Robert, became an articled clerk to John Weston, an attorney in Olveston, Gloucestershire, and William, the second son, was articled to Thomas

Nash, an attorney in Bath. (The boys would have been 18 and 17 at the time, rather older than one would have expected, particularly for the sons of a widow.) The third son, Edward, went to Oxford and into the Church, becoming Vicar of Colerne and Rector of Rode before dying prematurely in 1773. After five years in articles Robert and William were enrolled as attorneys on the same day in November 1760 and promptly set up as practitioners in Bristol and Bath respectively, although Robert appears to have inherited a significant estate from his father and this, rather than his profession, was his principal source of income.[22]

William had received an inheritance of £400, presumably in addition to the cost of his training as an attorney; and two months before he had been enrolled he had married Sarah Collin, 'an agreeable young Lady, with a fortune of £6,000'. Part of this fortune consisted of an estate at Belton in Rutland, and £3,300 was placed in trust as part of her marriage settlement. The young couple could live on the income from her capital, but it was protected from William's creditors if his business did not prosper. They rented a house in Kingsmead Street which William also used as his office, and in 1764 moved to a better house in Monmouth Street which William purchased for £600. We know little of their private life, except that they had no children.

Fashionable Bath was a promising location for a young attorney in the middle of the eighteenth century, and William appears to have done well in his first few years in practice. There was regular bread-and-butter work drawing up wills, establishing trusts and conveying property, and he was also employed in more complicated matters, including the Highfield estate at Bitton in Gloucestershire where he acted for Benjamin Perrott, a tenant for life under an entail. William organized a private Act of Parliament (introduced by his brother Edward's brother-in-law, Sir Edward Bayntun, MP for Chippenham) to break the entail and allow the estate to be sold. He also acted as attorney to Charles Young, the heir of Richard 'Beau' Nash, who had done so much to establish Bath in the fashionable world, but who had died leaving considerably more debts than assets. The appointment was prestigious but soon proved more trouble than it was worth. Nash's mistress, Mrs Hill, presented a bond for £250 of dubious legitimacy, and Charles Young grew increasingly impatient, criticizing Yescombe for failing to keep him informed of progress and of being distracted by other business. There was further trouble over the estate of Thomas Chilcot, the late organist of Bath Abbey, whose heirs accused Yescombe of selling their father's assets to his own friends for below their true value, and for failing to invest the proceeds properly. This ultimately led to a suit in the Court of Chancery in which Yescombe admitted that he had used some of Chilcot's money for his own purposes, and he reimbursed it. The impression given is of muddle rather than fraud, and perhaps even that such muddles were commonplace.[23]

Alongside his legal work William took an active part in the booming property market in Bath. He began by acting as the agent for local builders in the sale of their houses, and this led him into the business of raising loans for the purchase of these houses, and then into lending money himself, and finally becoming a direct investor in the building of houses. The business was temptingly profitable, and by the early 1770s Yescombe owned a significant number of houses in Bath, most of them heavily mortgaged. Then, in 1772, the boom ended in a sharp credit crunch and crisis of confidence. Many provincial banks failed, and each bank failure precipitated a cascade of bankruptcies of individuals and other businesses in the district. In August of that year Thomas Creaser, a leading banker and businessman in Bath (he had begun as a draper only a decade before and ridden the boom without curb or bridle), failed with debts of £31,000 and assets whose value might be £30,000 (his own, optimistic, estimate) or only £10,000 (the estimate of his bankruptcy assignees). William Yescombe claimed to be a creditor for £550 and advertised that he would sell this for eight shillings in the pound (that is, £220). Creaser denied that the debt existed at all and the publicity around the affair raised questions as to Yescombe's own solvency. (In the end Creaser's creditors only received 4s 6d in the pound or 22.5 per cent.) By the end of 1773 Yescombe was in serious difficulties, with creditors wanting payment and debtors often unable to pay. He turned to his brother Robert, who helped cover a number of his debts, but was unable to keep him afloat. In January 1774 Yescombe's London agent brought an action against him in the Court of the King's Bench, and judgment was delivered against him on 21 March. Four days later he was dead, although there is no evidence whether he committed suicide or died of natural causes. He was 36 years old.[24]

All Yescombe's household goods were sold for the benefit of his creditors: his widow received nothing at all from his estate, although fortunately her marriage settlement ensured that she was not left destitute, and less than two years later she married a Bath apothecary. Robert Yescombe was seriously embarrassed by his attempts to save his younger brother – he had court orders totalling at least £6,500 against him and he had to come to an arrangement with his creditors, selling off some of the land near Wedmore that had been in the family for 150 years. This left him with little except his house in Bristol, but it was considerably better than the debtor's prison to which he might have been sent if he had been unable to satisfy the creditors. Evidently he had no surviving son, for his heir was his nephew Edward Bayntun Yescombe, who gave up any prospect of life as a country gentleman and obtained a position as captain of a Post Office mail ship in 1787 through the influence of his mother's family, and he prospered and eventually restored the family fortunes.[25]

Both the failure of William Yescombe and the success of Benjamin Smith were relatively common experiences in the eighteenth and early nineteenth centuries. The economy was growing rapidly but with many sharp depressions which the country banks and other local institutions often did not have the resources to survive. A man did not need to be imprudent himself to be ruined in a depression, for he could very readily be caught up in the ruin of others, as happened to Robert Yescombe. Luck, care and good judgment were all needed to survive, and it is not hard to e why attorneys began to cultivate an image of cautious, conserva ve, even stuffy respectability, or why they gradually withdrew from their role as money scriveners, despite its profitability. Even so, it was not really a career for a gentleman in this period. It required too much dry, detailed paperwork, and even Benjamin Smith clearly occupied a subordinate position when he acted as clerk to the landowners who sat on the local turnpike trust. Nonetheless, there was a good deal of inter-change between attorneys and the landowning families in a neighbour-hood. Mrs Bennet in *Pride and Prejudice* was the daughter of the Meryton attorney and her sister married his clerk, Uncle Phillips. Respectable, but not quite fit for a gentleman, it might do for a younger son at a pinch.

———◆———

CHAPTER SEVEN

BANKING AND COMMERCE

NEAR THE BEGINNING OF *Pride and Prejudice* we learn that Miss Bingley and her sister Mrs Hurst 'were of a respectable family in the north of England; a circumstance more deeply impressed on their memories than that their brother's fortune and their own had been acquired by trade'. A fortune derived from commerce, even if made in a previous generation, was not as prestigious as wealth that came from the ownership of land, especially an estate that had long been held by the same family. And yet *Pride and Prejudice* also gives us Mr and Mrs Gardiner, Elizabeth's uncle and aunt, who are – with Admiral and Mrs Croft – the most attractive example of a happily married couple in all Austen's work.

> Mr Gardiner was a sensible, gentlemanlike man, greatly superior to his sister [Mrs Bennet] as well by nature as education. The Netherfield ladies [Miss Bingley and Mrs Hurst] would have had difficulty in believing that a man who lived by trade, and within view of his own warehouses, could have been so well bred and agreeable. Mrs Gardiner . . . was an amiable, intelligent, elegant woman, and a great favourite with all her Longbourn nieces.

The very last paragraph of the novel is devoted to the Gardiners and their subsequent relations with the hero and heroine. 'With the Gardiners, they were always on the most intimate terms. Darcy, as well as Elizabeth, really loved them; and they were both ever sensible of the warmest gratitude towards the persons who, by bringing her into Derbyshire, had been the means of uniting them.' Austen both acknowledges the common prejudice against trade and points out its folly; and while none of her heroes is a merchant or a banker, she creates attractive secondary characters (Mr Weston, and even Mrs Jennings, as well as the Gardiners) with strong links to the world of commerce.[1]

Tensions between landed and commercial wealth had existed in Britain for centuries before Austen's day, often expressed as a conflict between the Country and the City, with the aristocracy and the upper flights of society generally associated with the country. London's astonishing growth was often resented even as it acted as a magnet for people – especially young people – of all classes. But while sharp contrasts made for good arguments and animated many plays and novels, the reality was usually more muddled and human. Throughout the sixteenth and seventeenth centuries younger sons of good families had often sought to make a fortune in trade of one kind or another. It was not uncommon for the younger son of a prosperous country gentleman to be apprenticed to a mercer, a draper or even a cheesemonger, either in a nearby town or in London if the family already had connections there. This gradually became less popular over the course of the eighteenth century as opportunities in the gentlemanly professions became more numerous and better rewarded. Some forms of trade were considered hardly acceptable for gentlemen: anything requiring manual skill, retail trade and small businesses were death to social pretension. The notion of a publisher, a bookseller or a goldsmith aspiring to be treated as a gentleman was challenging if not ridiculous, and they were probably the most acceptable of such occupations. But bankers and merchants who traded on a large scale, especially overseas, had a much greater social standing, especially if they were rich and had the manners of a gentleman. Lord Chesterfield, of all people, thought 'Trade' the equal of the more obvious careers for the son of a gentleman, recommending it for 'an acute, thinking and laborious [that is, hardworking]' boy.[2]

One indication of the social standing of merchants, bankers and other prominent businessmen is the significant number who were elected to Parliament in this period: no fewer than 360 out of the 2,143 MPs between 1790 and 1820. Almost half of these were bankers, although many of them had other commercial interests as well. There were 35 MPs engaged in the trade with the West Indies (including, up until 1807, the slave trade); 25 who traded with the East Indies; 10 who traded with the USA and Canada; 10 wine merchants who imported wine mostly from Portugal; and a dozen MPs who were primarily ship owners. Thirteen MPs were or had been directors of the Bank of England, and 32 were or had been directors of the East India Company. About 50 MPs were engaged in manufacturing or industrial concerns (including Sir Robert Peel, the father of the future Prime Minister); 30 derived a significant part of their income from coal mining; and 25 were brewers or distillers. Rather more than half of all these MPs were based in London, but others came from across the whole country, and they included both Irish and Scottish bankers. Most had made their own fortune, but there was a significant number who were the second, third or even fourth generation in their bank or business. And all these men, simply by being a Member of Parliament, had a strong claim to be regarded as gentlemen, unless they were exceptionally vulgar.[3]

Sir Peter Pole (1770–1850) is a fair example of a banker who sat in the Commons. His father, Sir Charles Pole, was the senior partner in a prosperous London mercantile and banking firm, Van Notten, and purchased an estate, Wolverton near Kingsclere, in Hampshire. (Charles Pole had been born Charles Van Notten, but had changed his name when he married Millicent, daughter and co-heir of Charles Pole of Holcroft, Lancashire.) Peter Pole and his younger brother both entered the firm and Peter succeeded his father as second baronet in 1813. In 1815 he extended his banking interests by becoming a sleeping partner in the firm of Down, Thornton and Free of Birchin Lane, adding his wealth to its capital in exchange for a share of the profits. Soon afterwards he began looking around for 'a quiet and peaceable seat' in Parliament 'with as few electors as possible'. This took a few years to find, but in 1819 he was elected for Yarmouth on the Isle of Wight. His partner in the bank, Peter Free, described Pole as 'a very shy man and perfectly unfit for anything like a popular election', but fortunately for him Yarmouth was a pocket borough with only 13 voters who took their orders from the borough's patron Sir Leonard Worsley Holmes.

Pole was no more interested in making a splash in the Commons than a stir in Yarmouth: his attendance was lax and in the six years he was an MP he made no speeches and never voted except in support of the government. Why then did he want to be an MP? For many bankers and merchants part of the answer lay in the prestige conferred by being a Member of Parliament and rubbing shoulders with the leading men of the day. Becoming a Member of Parliament proclaimed your success to the world: you had arrived. For others there were useful connections to be made with ministers in the government whose responsibilities were relevant to the member's business interests (for example, a merchant trading with the eastern Mediterranean would benefit from good relations with a Lord of the Admiralty or an undersecretary at the Foreign Office). Neither of these explanations quite explains Pole's decision to enter Parliament. More relevant was that it added an air of solid stability and security to the bank of which he was a partner. Banks were still small – private partnerships that relied on the wealth of the partners for their capital, for the joint-stock banks with thousands of shareholders still lay in the future. The public's confidence in a bank depended on the belief that the partners had very deep pockets: Pole's many assets and his estate in Hampshire were vital, and the seat in Parliament added to the impression. Lastly came a much smaller but still important motive: Members of Parliament could send and receive correspondence post-free, and this covered *all* their correspondence, including that of their bank or other business. As Peter Free explained, 'The fact is that as matters now are, a banking house, which has always had a Member in it, very often feels itself awkwardly situated without one. It is putting Parliament very low to talk of a seat in Parliament and eight pence for a letter. . .'[4]

Merchants and bankers played an equally important role in high society both in London and the country. In northern Hampshire Sir Peter Pole would have been regarded primarily as a significant local landowner and only secondarily as a banker. In 1825 his eldest son married a daughter of the Earl of Limerick, while a few years later one of his younger daughters married Viscount Turnour, the eldest son of the Earl of Winterton. Two of his other sons were officers in the army and one of his other daughters married a clergyman, while his eldest son became both a Deputy Lieutenant and High Sherriff of Warwickshire, the family giving every appearance of being typical members of the landed gentry. And Pole was not at all unusual in this respect, for many prominent figures in society had strong ties to the world of commerce. When Major Henry Percy arrived in London with the news of Waterloo he found the Prince Regent attending a fashionable ball at 16 St James's Square, the home of Mr Edmund Boehm, a wealthy West India merchant whose wife was cutting a figure in society.[5]

A commercial background might still invite sneers, for example the popular jingle that went the rounds when Robert Smith was created Lord Carrington:

Billy Pitt made him a peer,
And took the pen from behind his ear.

And when Sir Francis Baring's son Alexander (a partner in the firm) became a member of an important political dining group, the King of Clubs, Sydney Smith — who was also a member — remarked that it was 'upon the express promise that he lends £50 to any member of the Club when applied to'. Whether this was in jest or in earnest hardly matters. Nonetheless, a wealthy merchant or banker usually rated higher on the snobbery scale than a country clergyman or officer in the army or navy unless the latter had some special claim, such as good aristocratic connections or an independent fortune.[6]

Bankers and merchants came from a wide variety of backgrounds. The most socially assured usually belonged to the second or third generation: brought up in affluence and given at least part of a gentleman's education, but also knowing that they were expected to take their place in the firm. Men like Sir Peter Pole, Alexander Baring and Henry Thornton had one foot in the City and the other in Westminster and Mayfair. There were also a surprising number of Englishmen who had gone out to India as young men, made a fortune often while still young, and come home as wealthy nabobs who then invested their money as a partner in a bank. Given that they were already rich, they were unlikely to have been motivated primarily by financial gain, but by investing in a bank they gained a position in the social and commercial world that, as virtual strangers after years abroad, they might otherwise have struggled to find. It is also possible that they took to banking to keep boredom at bay: years of hard work in India was poor preparation for a life of idleness in England, and they were men who were confident of their ability in dealing with finance and business. No fewer than 13 such nabobs-turned-bankers took a further step and went into Parliament in the 30 years between 1790 and 1820.[7]

Many of the leading merchants in London in the early nineteenth century, especially those engaged in trade with continental Europe, had foreign origins. Men like Johann Friedrich and Johann Heinrich Schröder, the sons of a wealthy Hamburg merchant who flourished despite – or because – of the disruptions caused by the war; or Emanuel Henry Brandt, also from Hamburg, who became an important figure in trade with Russia. Sir Peter Pole's own father was either born in Holland or was of Dutch descent, and although the young Francis Baring came to London from Exeter to make his fortune, his wool-trading father had originally come from Bremen. British high society was somewhat less cosmopolitan or welcoming to foreigners than the commercial world, although much depended on personal qualities including manners, accent and whether a foreign-born merchant had any wish to be assimilated into the English upper classes. Where there were obstacles they were usually washed away in the next generation. The difficulties were greater for Jews: partly because it was genuinely harder to ignore the religious difference, and partly because of anti-Semitism, although this does not seem to have been as strong as it became later in the nineteenth century.[8]

Outside London many banks were begun by prosperous shopkeepers or other tradesmen of good repute offering to hold funds for their customers, paying them interest and providing other services such as transferring funds to London. Some attorneys also moved from their role as money scriveners to become bankers, not always with happy results. Similarly many merchants began trading in their local area and built up their business, sometimes rapidly seizing an opportunity and exploiting it to the full, sometimes slowly and steadily, and sometimes rising only to fall suddenly, for the economy was very volatile and commercial wealth was often fragile. Different roles frequently overlapped, as in the case of James Tappenden, a successful attorney and banker in Faversham, who held every public office of importance in the borough, including serving as town clerk for 36 years. His family were already prosperous when he was born in 1742, making their money in the coastal trade between Milton, near Sittingbourne, and London, carrying grain and hops in one direction and luxuries in the other. This led them to give credit to their customers and then into banking. One branch of the family settled in London and the other shifted from Milton to Faversham. James's father had married the daughter of one of the other leading merchants in Faversham and became mayor in 1743, but died two years later at the age of 38, leaving James just an infant. At the age of 16 James was articled to Thomas Buck, the leading attorney in Faversham, and went on to become his partner and later to succeed him as town clerk. In 1789 he established the Faversham Bank in partnership with William Bennett, a wealthy merchant in the town; and in 1801 Tappenden and two of his nephews paid £40,000 for a half share in the Abernant Iron Company in Wales, investing a further £30,000 over the next seven years building a tramway connecting the works to the Neath Canal. Tappenden was simultaneously an attorney, a town clerk, a banker, a merchant, an industrialist and a man of considerable consequence in the country around Faversham. Whether contemporaries would have regarded him as a gentleman is rather more doubtful, and might well have depended on their own social standing; but one of his daughters was married to the Dean of Westminster Abbey and the other to Lieutenant-Colonel William Samuel Currey of the 54th Foot.[9]

Success enabled bankers and merchants to become gentlemen, and gentlemen could also become bankers and merchants. The most obvious way was for a father to entrust one of his younger sons to his brother, brother-in-law or close friend who was already engaged in banking or trade. Such connections were not uncommon: Mr Bennet had Mr Gardiner, and, as we have seen, Henry Hickey was sent to Dublin to be trained in the business by an old friend of his father. Without such personal connections it was much harder for the father of a young man to find him a place in the commercial world, for there was no recognized career path as in the navy or the Church, but examples do exist, such as the two boys from County Durham whose parents each paid more than £600 to apprentice them to a London banker in 1755 after they had finished their time at Eton.[10]

Samuel Romilly's father was a successful, if financially imprudent, jeweller in London. He hoped that Samuel would become an attorney but gave way in the face of determined opposition, sparked by the boy's dislike of the only lawyer he knew. His next thought was that his son might pursue a career as a merchant, for he was on excellent terms with Sir Samuel Fludyer, who had risen by trade from poverty to riches, been made a baronet, had a seat in Parliament and became Lord Mayor of London. Samuel Fludyer was also Samuel Romilly's godfather,

> . . . and the humble situation of a clerk in his counting-house might, if I had pleased him with my conduct, have led to a very brilliant fortune. My father therefore determined to fit me for that situation, and it was resolved that I should learn the art, or science (I know not which it should be called) of keeping merchants' accounts. A master was accordingly provided for me. I was equipped with a set of journals, waste books, bill books, ledgers, and I know not what; and I passed some weeks in making careful entries of ideal transactions,

keeping a register of the times when fictitious bills of exchange would become due, and posting up imaginary accounts. I should have lost more time than I did in this ridiculous employment, if my instructor, Mr Johnson, as he was called (but whose name was perhaps as fictitious as those of my correspondents at Amsterdam, at Smyrna, and in both the Indies, and to whose merits my father had been introduced only by an advertisement in a newspaper) had not suddenly decamped to avoid his creditors.

Soon afterwards Sir Samuel Fludyer died 'and all the prospects of riches and honours, which we thought were opening upon me, were shut out for ever'. But while the world of commerce lost Romilly's very considerable abilities, they were gained – in due course and thanks to an unexpected legacy – by the law and Parliament.[11]

As well as private tutors of dubious background such as 'Mr Johnson', there were schools that claimed to specialize in training boys for jobs in the commercial world, although many young men appear to have begun as clerks with nothing more than a general education. William Jerdan, who was later to win some fame as a literary journalist, arrived in London from Scotland in the spring of 1801 about the time he turned 19. He was met by his uncle who introduced him to an acquaintance and townsman (such personal and local connections were important), John Robertson, who was a prosperous insurance broker. Robertson had no position to offer the boy himself, but soon found him a place with the merchants Samuel, Samuel and Turner, who traded with the West Indies, with an initial salary of £50 a year. Jerdan paints an attractive picture of life in the office. Much of the work was done by Mr Drew, 'a perfect example of the quiet, contented and sedulous London clerk . . . dressed in brown Quakerish garb, and ever most punctually attentive to his day-books and ledgers, his dinner-hour and all his other duties'. Mr Samuel Turner Jnr also worked as a clerk, presumably learning the business before being made a junior partner, while the senior members of the firm held meetings in the inner office. One of these partners, Mr Charles Turner, was standing for Parliament, and 'was, if I remember correctly, only an occasional aid in the counting-house'. Jerdan himself proved no great asset to the firm: 'I was, indeed, a bungling accountant, and unprofitable help even in letter copying or other routine employment'. But rather than dismissing him or making him unhappy, the partners treated him with great kindness, encouraged his literary tastes, took him home to dine with them and introduced him to 'the wealthy magnates of Antigua . . . and other persons of rank and station who formed [their] refined and social circle'. Samuel Turner Jnr was his best friend and 'seemed absolutely to enjoy my blunders and encourage my vagaries'. Jerdan was undoubtedly fortunate to find himself in such a friendly and hospitable environment, and he was wise enough not to outstay the generosity of his hosts, leaving Samuel, Samuel and Turner to pursue a career in journalism which proved precarious, but much better suited to his talents.[12]

A better sense of the work actually done in a merchant's office is given by a memorandum headed 'My Department in Business' drawn up by George Henry Gibbs, one of the partners in Antony Gibbs & Sons which played a very considerable part in the textile trade to Spain and Spanish America. It was not a large office: with three partners and five other staff, George's duties were many and various.

> *Letters.* Read the letters recd. and written & extract from them any thing worth notice.
>
> *Orders.* Give out all the orders received and see that they are properly executed & copied into the Inland & For[eign] Order Bk. Look frequently into Mr Wainwright's Shipping Book – see what good can be shipt & make enquiries of the Ship Brokers about Ships, Freights &c. When goods are ordered mark them in the order Book thus ✗ When the packing instructions are completely given add a stroke to the mark, thus ✗
>
> *Revise the Price Current every Saturday.*
>
> *Lloyds.* After sending the foreign letters go to Lloyds and extract from the Books & the Boards anything new. See Willis, and collect any news from him or others. On Post days go again to Lloyds before Change [Royal Exchange] & get the latest information. Generally go

every day to Lloyds about 3. See Lloyds List in the Reading room published twice a week, and the Cadiz Lists received.

Change. Go to the Change generally every day at 4. On Post days when any Bills to draw or take at ¼ past 3, & stay *patiently* till ½ past 4. See Brokers of all sorts, and make enquiries about Prices of Produce, Stock, in the market, &c &c. Pay particular attention to Wool.

Insurances. Attend to the execution of all Insurance orders, the recovery of Averages &c &c in short everything connected with Insurance Business.

Sales. Superintend the Sale of all Produce. Make out Account Sales.

Correspondence. Carry out the whole of the inland correspondence & part of the foreign. Be as particular as possible in giving every information wch. may be interesting to each correspondent, especially with regard to their orders, keeping them well informed of the state of forwardness in wch. they are, the prices at wch. we have contracted for them &c &c. The letters shd. be written as soon as possible in order that they may be copied in the Books from the originals, and that there may be no hurry in sending them to the Post. Keep a memorandum Book with each Correspondent's name in a separate page under wch. may be enter'd any thing that occurs to be said to each. Refer always to this Book before writing any letter. Also read the last letter written unless we have rec'd an answer to it, and recapitulate the important parts of it.[13]

Much of this work would have been routine and dull, but there would also have been considerable interest and even some excitement in the fluctuations of trade and the impact of wars and revolutions both in Europe and the Americas; while life would have been enlivened by both friendships and rivalries with other merchants.

<hr/>

There were approximately 8,500 businesses in the City of London in 1815, and a residential population of around 120,000 (and these totals were very much higher for the metropolis as a whole). Most merchants conducted their business with only a small staff, and banks were not much larger: Glyns, of the larger banks, had only 36 staff in 1815. Several of the insurance companies, the East India Company and above all the Bank of England were the most notable exceptions, with the Bank's staff tripling over the course of the war to a gargantuan total of some nine hundred clerks in 1813. It was the only bank whose stock could be owned by the public: all the others were private banks, with a maximum of six partners. It was easy to obtain a banking licence (renewable annually for £30 in 1815), which imposed no minimum capital requirement or proof of creditworthiness, but which allowed the holder to issue their own banknotes. (It was up to the public to decide whether or not to accept them, just as it was up to the public to decide whether or not to trust the bank with its deposits.) Small banks proliferated across the country: by 1800 there were 386 country banks; nine years later the total had reached 800. Evidently the opinion of a character in Austen's *Lady Susan* that 'when a Man has once got his name in a Banking House he rolls in money' was popular, but even in these relatively prosperous years there were numerous failures as well as successes among the banks.[14]

Country banks each had a connection with a bank in London which acted as their agent and would accept their bills, and these ties were sometimes reinforced when the sons of country bankers worked for a time in the London bank, even becoming a junior partner or marrying into the family. The leading London banks often specialized in one way or another. Coutts was the banker to royalty, high society and many leading politicians; Praed & Co. had strong contacts in the West Country and Cornwall; Child's had many Indian connections; Drummonds looked after army agents; Wright's was the banker of choice to the Catholic gentry; Herries assisted young men embarking on their Grand Tour; and Barings was deeply involved in foreign trade with loans to merchants and overseas governments. Across the country many Quakers were involved in banking, including in Lloyd's in Birmingham, Backhouse in Darlington and the Gurney family in Norwich. The Gurneys had close connections with the London firm of Overend, Gurney & Co. who were, for more than a generation, the largest bill discounter in the world, a banker's bank, who preserved many essentially sound businesses during the financial panic of 1825.[15]

The standing and creditworthiness of any bank or merchant house were highly dependent on the character and reputation of its principals, and the success of any bank or bill discounter depended on judging when and to whom it was safe to extend credit, and when and to whom such accommodation should be refused. A sense of how this worked in practice emerges in an extract from a character book kept by Barings Bank in the late 1820s:

C. A. Cordes. Formerly a Clerk in the House of J. H. Schröder & Co and entered into Business (about 1824) with a Mr Schroder of Hambro [Hamburg] under the Firm of Schroder & Cordes. Mr Schroder died shortly afterwards & he has been alone about 12 months, is doing a fair Commission Business in the Export trade, particularly in Sugar & Coffee to Germany. He has but little Capital, but is so cautious and prudent in what he does that the writer entertains the best opinion of him. In all his dealings he is scrupulously honest and there is not a Merchant in the City of London whose Character in every respect stands higher.

Lobeck, Strong & Co. Mr L failed in 1819 under the Firm of L & Kraft, traded until March last as L & Co, and since then under the present Firm. He can have no money but Mr S with whom he has connected himself is Nephew of the late Mr Rundell of Ludgate Hill; and it is said has brought into the Concern £10,000, so that they may be considered safe for what they do; but the writer has no confidence in Mr L's ultimate success in Life, thinking him by far too sanguine a man. Their business is executing Orders for the Shipment of Colonial Produce to the Continent, but their Connexions are not first rate.[16]

Banking and foreign trade were the core of the City's business in the early nineteenth century, but other financial services, including the Stock Exchange and insurance, were also important. Members of the Stock

Exchange lacked the social standing and respectability of established merchants and bankers, and their reputation was ambiguous at best. One contemporary authority bluntly warned that 'No person must ever expect, from a Jobbing Broker, fair and open advice when to buy or sell'. And there were a number of elaborate cases in which false reports were circulated in order to manipulate the market, including one in which the radical hero Admiral Lord Cochrane was – rightly or wrongly – implicated.[17] Nor did the boisterous high spirits displayed by the stockbrokers always endear them to outsiders. In 1812 the governing committee attempted to address the question by issuing the first formal set of rules and regulations, earnestly recommending '*order and decorum*' to the members, and discouraging 'as much as possible . . . those rude and trifling practices which have too long disgraced the Stock Exchange in the estimation of the public, [and] which would not be tolerated in any other place'. A member of the Exchange looked back on it fondly many years later:

We were only a few hundred strong then, and everybody knew everybody else. We had some fine games. At 2, Capel Court, Mendoza had a boxing booth, where, instead of knocking prices about, a member could go and knock somebody about or get knocked about himself, if things did not suit him inside. An old woman had a stall *inside* the House, close to Capel Court door, where those who had not quite outlived their earliest tastes could feed on buns, cakes, etc. A gallery ran round the old House; seats and desks were fitted up for clerks and members. It was very convenient, because if a man wanted a book he simply called up to his clerk, who would throw it over. Some of the funny ones used to drop things over on unsuspecting members.

Just *what* was dropped on unsuspecting members is a subject probably best avoided, while the school-boy behaviour of the members extended to mobbing and heckling unfortunate strangers who mistakenly ventured onto the floor of the Exchange.[18]

Banks, in marked contrast, cultivated an air of gentlemanly decorum, discretion and responsibility, enforcing good behaviour on their staff.

Each clerk at Glyn, Mills & Co. had to provide a fidelity bond of no less than £1,000 as security in case he should 'lose, embezzle, purloin, consume, misspend or unlawfully make away with, detain or keep any Money, Bond or Bonds, Bill or Bills, Note or Notes, Paper or Papers, Goods, Chattels, Effects or other Thing or Things whatsoever . . . or make any false or fraudulent Entry or Entries in any Book or Books of Account . . .'. Most of the clerks employed at Glyns between 1810 and 1840 regarded themselves as the sons of 'gentlemen', while others cited fathers who were farmers, surgeons, merchants and brokers. About one third came from London, the rest from all over the country. They were engaged when they were between the ages of 18 and 20, but usually put their names down a couple of years before, for there was a waiting list. Once they were engaged they served on probation for the first three months. Junior clerks lived on the premises, with one partner also always in residence. Most of the rest of the staff lived nearby. The working day began at nine o'clock, with the bank closing its doors at four o'clock, but the need to complete and balance the accounts meant that senior staff often did not get away until almost six o'clock and juniors even later. Saturday was a normal working day, and the clerks received one month's paid holiday – every four years. A fully qualified junior clerk received £70 a year until 1815 when it was increased to £75, and this pay was usually increased at a rate of £5 a year until it reached £100 with further increases depending on merit and responsibility. Senior clerks might earn £200 to £250, with heads of department getting £400, and all these figures would be significantly increased by a Christmas bonus paid for by the bank's customers (including the country banks). However, it was becoming rarer for a clerk, however senior, to leap the chasm and become a junior partner. There were many worse jobs in early nineteenth-century England than working as a bank clerk, but it was an occupation with few prospects.[19]

Life for the partners, at least in good times, was much less exacting. One partner was usually expected to reside at the bank or very close to it at any time, and this duty usually rotated unevenly, with senior partners spending as much time as they wished in the country. (Indeed, some senior partners, such as Sir Peter Pole, never played an active part in the business of the bank, their contribution being limited to their capital and the value of their name.) The partner in residence might need to take considerable responsibility when sudden demands were made upon the bank, but the most important decisions could usually be referred to one of the senior partners. The outbreak of war in 1793 was followed by a general tightening of credit and the partners at Hoare's Bank in Fleet Street, along with many others, decided to be cautious in granting new loans and pressing in their requests for the repayment of old ones. Soon customers such as the Earl of Thanet were receiving polite letters stating that 'We wish you in every respect to consult your own Convenience as to the time of replacing the Money overdrawn on your Account', or even – to the agent of Lord Rivers – 'we are extremely concerned that it will not be in our Power to advance the sum Lord Rivers requires'. This risked alienating old customers, but it also helped the bank's reputation for caution and stability, and, at least in this case, probably did more good than harm. Nonetheless such decisions could not have been taken lightly, and there were times when being the partner in a bank was the source of considerable anxiety.[20]

A country banker faced many of the same decisions, often with fewer resources and a much narrower range of potential clients. The career of Robert Barlow shows some of the qualities needed to weather the hard times as well as to flourish when the country as a whole was prospering. Barlow was born in 1780, the son of a wine merchant in Bolton in Lancashire who was also the local agent for the Royal Exchange Assurance, one of the large insurance companies. He went into his father's business and carried it on after his father died in 1803, and was quite successful, although getting supplies to Bolton was difficult enough in the best of times, and the disruption to trade caused by the war gave him 'more troubles than I care to recall'. Still the district was generally doing well thanks to the growth of the cotton industry, despite the periodic slumps of the trade cycle, and by the time Barlow was in his mid-thirties he was well established and had accumulated considerable quiet self-confidence. There was no bank in Bolton and people had to go to Manchester or Liverpool for this purpose. It seemed to me that the business of banking was one which I could readily carry on at my own premises since I was familiar with the bookkeeping necessary for such a project, provided I could get support from some of my more substantial friends to ensure the degree of confidence which is the first requisite.

He discussed the idea with a number of the leading businessmen in the town and two partners in a spinning firm, and two attorneys agreed to join him in the enterprise. They would each contribute £1,000 capital on which they were to receive a return of 5 per cent, while the cotton spinners were to add a further £2,000 each on which they would receive 3 per cent.

The bank, Hardcastle, Cross & Co., opened its doors on a fine day in August 1818, just as the postwar slump was beginning to ease. The guiding principle of all the partners, and Barlow in particular, was to proceed cautiously and not be in too much of a hurry. In the first six months the income was sufficient to pay all the costs and the agreed interest on the capital and leave a surplus profit of 10s 3d, but the business grew steadily if not rapidly, and the profit for 1821 was £741. At this point Barlow felt able to offer Thomas Appleton, his chief clerk, a salary of £180 a year with a bonus of £20 if the bank continued to make a satisfactory profit. 'He got the £20 each year and well deserved it'; while by 1847 Appleton was receiving £300 a year with a £40 bonus.

The bank survived the financial panic of 1825, but had its own trouble that year when thieves stole £1,860, or more than the entire profit for a whole year, 'and it was a long time before I got over it sufficiently to write it off the books'. Barlow bought a new iron safe, costing £30, and paid a clerk two shillings a week to sleep in the bank. The prudence with which the bank lent its money is shown by the fact that the crisis of 1825 resulted in loan defaults of no more than £1,000, at a time when it had some £70,000 in deposits. Against Barlow's wishes the bank followed the example of many other country banks and issued its own banknotes, but this did not prove profitable.

Barlow's son Robert joined the bank as a junior clerk on a starting salary of 16 shillings a week (just over £40 a year), rising steadily so that after six years he was earning £100 a year. Living was probably cheaper in Bolton than in London, but this was hardly lavish pay for 1834. Yet another junior clerk got even less: six shillings a week at first, and still less than a pound a week after five years, although at that point he had yet to turn 21. Such measured rewards did not satisfy this young man who 'did not take kindly to the humdrum routine of a bank clerk's life' and eventually 'decided to seek his fame and fortune in China'. Even Barlow's own son was sometimes reluctant 'to give that close attention to business as a matter of duty' that his father expected. 'We have, however, dealt very strictly with him, with the result that he has suffered deductions from his salary for absence even in the last few years.' (Barlow wrote his memoirs in 1849 when his son had been with the firm for more than 20 years.)

All the profits were re-invested in the business and by 1836 they had accumulated to just under £31,000, and some of the other partners were inclined to take their share, and Barlow agreed. They decided to distribute a dividend of 4 per cent of the accumulated profit each year, and still the accumulated profit increased, so that by 1849 the partners were dividing over £3,000 between them each year in addition to the steady return on their original investment. Barlow found this 'a pleasant increase on my salary' which had long been fixed at £500 a year, of which £100 was bonus dependent on profits. In his memoirs Barlow paid tribute to his partners. 'They have each had their own businesses to attend to and have left the management of the Bank entirely in my hands, though I have ever been able to call upon them, each with his own specialised knowledge, for help and advice when the need arose. Although we have not always agreed, we have had no serious differences . . .' He also felt that he had been 'well served by my small staff, who, having entered the Bank as young men, have stayed with me to this day', and in particular Thomas Appleton, 'the most faithful servant a man could have'. Barlow's success was founded on caution, prudence and patience, characteristics that became almost synonymous with banking in the second half of the nineteenth century and which lasted through the first and into the second half of the twentieth.[21]

———◆———

The career of Henry Austen, the novelist's brother, forms a marked contrast to that of Robert Barlow in many ways, while illustrating how a young gentleman with no family connection to the commercial world could find a profitable niche at the point where banking, the army, government service, high society and politics all intersected. Henry had originally been intended to follow his father and eldest brother James into the Church, and had gone to Oxford. He was 22 when the war with France broke out in 1793, still too young to be ordained, and he joined the militia, receiving his commission as a lieutenant in the Oxfordshire Regiment on 8 April 1793. The militia was a home defence force that would be disbanded when peace came, and no one knew in 1793 that the war would last for a generation, so it was not immediately a decisive shift from one career to another. Henry obtained sufficient leave to enable him to continue to keep his terms at Oxford so that in due course he would receive his MA, and in 1796 he made serious enquiries about the living at Chawton to which he might succeed if John Rawston Papillon (a distant relation, who had first claim on it under Thomas Knight's will), could be persuaded not to take it up. This led to some negotiations, but they came to nothing and Henry remained in the militia. In late 1794, through the patronage of the regiment's commander, Lord Charles Spencer, Henry had been appointed acting paymaster of the regiment, a position of considerable responsibility and some financial reward. Lord Charles was a generation older than Henry Austen, the younger son of the third Duke of Marlborough, and immensely well connected, including with ministers in Pitt's government such as the Duke of Portland (the Home Secretary and future Prime Minister) and Lord Spencer (the First Lord of the Admiralty).

Early in 1797 Henry was made adjutant of the regiment and given command of the colonel's company with the odd-sounding rank of captain-lieutenant. And on the last day of the year he married his cousin Eliza de Feuillide, the vivacious god-daughter of Warren Hastings and widow of a French count who had been sent to the guillotine four years before. At the time of his marriage Henry's pay and allowances amounted to just under £300, while Eliza had money of her own, probably amounting to £400 a year or even a little more. Eliza was a decade older than Henry, intelligent, smart, independent and sophisticated. He had first fallen in love with her when he was no more than a boy, and the marriage probably gave him more confidence and greater ambition. In 1798 he was promoted to captain and his long-standing appointment as acting paymaster was made permanent: evidently he was more than competent, for the auditor praised his record-keeping, declaring himself 'perfectly satisfied with the accounts, and wished he could always make as favourable a report'. Henry's position had given him a thorough under-standing of army finance and brought him into contact with many important men in the army, in banking and in Whig society. He was now in his late twenties, a married man, and as the end of the century approached, he felt that he had the opportunity and the need to move beyond the militia into a more rewarding career.[22]

On 24 January 1801 Henry Austen resigned his commission in the Oxfordshire Militia and soon afterwards opened business as an army agent in partnership with Henry Maunde who had served in the regiment with him. Austen & Co. had its office in Cleveland Court, a stone's throw from St James's Palace, while Henry and Eliza lived at 24 Upper Berkeley Street, off Portman Square in the West End. Each regiment of both the regular army and the militia appointed an army agent to receive and transmit the pay for the officers and men and handle other financial affairs relating to the regiment. Most agents went further, acting as bankers for the officers in the regiment, collecting and transmitting half-pay to retired officers, and procuring goods on commission for officers who were abroad or an active service. (If an officer wanted a new saddle, canteen or greatcoat he might ask the regimental agent to procure and send it to him, rather than bother a friend.) Agents were also heavily involved in arranging the sale and purchase of commissions in regiments in the regular army, which often required unofficial – indeed, technically illegal – payments above the official, regulation price. It was a role which required discretion, excellent contacts, an eye for detail, a nose for who should be trusted with credit and how much, and meticulous financial record keeping.[23]

The largest and most successful army agent was Cox & Greenwood, which had been founded in the middle of the eighteenth century by Richard Cox, who had begun his career as private secretary to Lord Ligonier, and who had benefited from Ligonier's rise to be Commander-in-Chief and Master-General of the Ordnance. The business proved very successful, with Cox reportedly making some £10,000 a year in profits and managing the business of considerably more than half the regiments in the British army. In 1793 Cox made his younger cousin Charles Greenwood, the son of a clergyman, a partner in the business, and Greenwood cultivated connections with the royal family, and in partic-ular the Duke of York, advancing the duke large sums of money. On one occasion the duke is said to have introduced him to the King with the remark that he was 'Mr Greenwood, the gentleman who keeps my money', whereupon Greenwood responded, 'I think it is rather his Royal Highness who keeps my money'. The comment delighted the King, who said, 'Do you hear that? Frederick, do you hear that? You are the gentleman who keeps Mr Greenwood's money.' Given the duke's long tenure as Commander-in-Chief of the British army (1795–1809, 1811–27) these large loans proved a remarkably good investment even though they were seldom if ever repaid. Richard Cox died in 1803, and the firm became Greenwood & Cox, for his grandson Richard Henry Cox had become a junior partner a couple of years before. The business naturally benefited from the long war with France, and by 1815 it had a staff of 100, mostly clerks, and it was in the process of building new premises in Craig's Court, which ultimately cost £16,000. Cox and Greenwood were formi-dable competitors for Henry Austen's new firm, but equally Austen would be well content with just a sliver of their business.[24]

Towards the end of 1801 Henry Austen and Henry Maunde formed a secret partnership with Charles James to engage in the sale of army commissions at above the regulation price, the proceeds to be divided into three equal parts. Charles James was a well-known writer on military affairs, the author of *Regimental Companion*, which served as an introduction to military affairs for many young officers, and a substantial *Military Dictionary*. More to the point he was also the confidential secretary and man of business to Francis Rawdon, Lord Moira, who had made his reputation as a soldier in the American War, and who was a close friend of the Prince of Wales. Moira was an influential figure in politics and the army, and in 1812 came within a whisker of becoming Prime Minister; but he was also extravagant, heavily in debt and constantly in need of money, largely because he never refused the Prince a 'loan' and never received any repayment. Austen & Co. had begun with nothing more than the agency for the Oxfordshire Militia, but with the help of Moira and James, fresh regiments were added to their books: the Nottinghamshire Militia, the North Devon Militia, the Derbyshire Militia and the 4th Garrison Battalion. However, Henry's attempt to secure the agency of the North Hampshire Militia by appealing to its colonel as a fellow Hampshire man, and promising unequalled 'promptness & precision' came to nothing. The business also diversified into naval agency, and Francis Austen, one of Henry's brothers in the navy, invested some of his prize money in the firm, becoming a partner, without relinquishing his naval career. The newly constituted firm was called Austen, Maunde & Austen.[25]

Henry Austen and his partners lent Lord Moira considerable sums of money, and Moira responded to requests conveyed by Charles James to use his influence in attempts (some successful, some not) to secure commands and promotions for both Francis and Charles Austen, Henry's two brothers in the navy. The connection between the loans and the influence was always left implicit, although they frequently happened in close parallel. Some loans were even repaid, although most were rolled over and any diminution of the overall size of the debt was short-lived. Whether Moira would ever be able to repay his debts to all his numerous creditors was debatable, for even by 1804 he owed at least £100,000 and all his existing assets were heavily mortgaged, but his friendship was worth the risk of some loss, and it was at least possible that he might yet gain a great windfall while acting in the public service. That possibility seemed likely to be realized in the spring of 1813 when he was appointed Governor-General of India, and this led Austen & Co. to give him another large loan (at least £3,400 and possibly as much as £6,000).[26]

In late 1806 Henry Austen moved into banking, becoming a partner in three country banks and the London correspondent for two others. The first of these banks was at Alton in Hampshire, not far from Steventon where he had grown up. His partners were William Gray, a local grocer, and Gray's uncle, William Vincent, who was also a partner in a bank at Newbury. The second was at Petersfield, also in Hampshire, and the third at Hythe in Kent, which had a large military presence at the time, which may have led to some mutual benefit for the army agency and the bank. In each of these cases the day-to-day business was managed by one of the other partners, while Henry provided the London connections and perhaps an air of sophistication. In March 1808 Austen & Co. occupied new premises at 10 Henrietta Street, Covent Garden, and this move can be interpreted as a shift in emphasis away from the army agency and more heavily towards banking. At the end of that year the firm lost the agency for the 4th Garrison Battalion when its new colonel preferred to give his business to one of their rivals. Nonetheless Henry's affairs were prospering and in January 1809 his sister Jane wrote that 'the progress of the Bank is a constant source of satisfaction. With such increasing profits . . . I hope he will not work poor High-diddle so hard as he used to'. (Whether 'High-diddle' was a clerk in the bank or a riding horse is anyone's guess.) A new partner, James Tilson, formerly of the Dorset & Co. Bank in New Bond Street, was added to the firm.[27]

Austen & Co. continued to do well over the next few years, and Henry seems to have enjoyed life, both in London and in the country. He kept a carriage and employed a French housekeeper, while enjoying long visits to his brother Edward's family at Godmersham, where he was excellent company, entertaining the children, going with enthusiasm to the races and taking part in country sports. He was equally happy to have his siblings, nephews and nieces to stay with him in London, where they would go to the theatre, shop and visit the dentist. He negotiated with publishers on Jane's behalf and was immensely proud of her work, and quite unable to preserve the secrecy of her authorship. Against this was the sadness of seeing his wife decline in a long and painful illness; they had always lived a good deal apart, but so far as we know the marriage was happy. Eliza died on 24 April at the age of only 51, and Henry composed an epitaph which paid generous tribute to her as 'a woman of brilliant generous and cultivated mind just disinterested and charitable'. But he was not in low spirits for long: a few months later Jane commented that Henry's 'Mind is not a Mind for affliction. He is too Busy, too active, too sanguine', and he had just been appointed to a responsible and potentially very lucrative position as Chief Receiver of Taxes for Oxfordshire, so he had plenty to distract him from his grief.[28]

He owed his new appointment not to his connection with Moira, but to his old patron Lord Charles Spencer, whose son John had been Henry's predecessor in the position but had got into considerable financial difficulties. It seems that Henry either took over £6,500 of John's existing debts or lent him the money outright, while he had also lent Lord Charles £2,000 a few months before, at the time his appointment was being arranged. (An earlier loan to Lord Charles may have been connected with Henry's appointment as Deputy-Receiver a couple of years before.) The Chief-Receiver was responsible for collecting the proceeds of the Land Tax and other assessed taxes from parish collectors and passing the proceeds on to the Treasury. For this he received two pence in the pound on the Land Tax (just under 1 per cent), and a penny ha'penny on the other taxes; but the real attraction of the post was that he held large sums of money interest free for a few months before transferring them to the Treasury – something that was especially valuable to a banker. However, the Chief Receiver was also responsible for the sums collected – if the money was lost or went astray he would be held personally liable – and before taking up the position he had to persuade three wealthy men to post guarantees that they would make up any shortfall if he defaulted. Edward Knight, James Leigh Perrot and Henry's uncle Thomas Hampson agreed to act as Henry's guarantors, posting bonds totalling £73,000 on 24 July 1813. That Henry was willing to ask, and that they were willing to agree, indicates the position was thought to be extremely lucrative, and that Henry was regarded not just as thoroughly honest, but also as reliable and competent.[29]

It was at about this time that Francis Austen retired from his partnership in the firm, a move which may have been associated with the fall of Napoleon and the coming of peace in the spring of 1814, which greatly diminished the chances of active employment for all army and naval officers. Among the many celebrations of the peace was a fashionable ball held at Burlington House and organized by the members of White's Club, attended by the Prince Regent, the Emperor of Russia and the King of Prussia, and which was said to have cost some £10,000. And Henry Austen, a charming, fashionable, 43-year-old widower and prosperous banker was one of the guests. His sister Jane reacted with a mixture of amusement and astonishment: 'Henry at White's! Oh, what a Henry'. It was the apogee of his career.[30]

The coming of peace led to the demobilization of the militia and a great reduction in the army agency business: the regimental payrolls handled by Austen & Co. fell from £112,000 in 1813 to only £34,000 in 1815 and would fall further in subsequent years. More seriously the country as a whole suffered a sharp and prolonged depression with falling prices, widespread unemployment and the failure of many businesses leading to a severe contraction of credit as confidence evaporated. Austen & Co. was not well placed to survive the crisis: it had expanded too rapidly, made too many loans that were unlikely to be repaid, and some of its subsidiary activities do not seem to have been well managed. Things were not helped when Henry fell seriously ill in October 1815. For a time his life was in danger but he recovered only to face a cascade of financial troubles that ended in complete ruin. The Alton bank failed on 27 November 1815. Henry had withdrawn from the partnership a few weeks before, and so was not liable for its debts, but Austen & Co. were owed almost £10,000. One of the local partners, Edward Gray, had seen the crash coming and had drawn off all the liquid assets and given them to his family and friends, which meant that there was far less left over to be distributed to other creditors, including Austen & Co. Thanks to a promissory note from Edward Knight for £10,000 Henry carried on, but in March 1816 the Treasury issued a demand for

£22,743 from the Oxfordshire Receivership. This could not be paid, and the bank closed its doors. Henry estimated his total debts at £58,000 and his assets at £52,000 although upon investigation these included a number of loans (such as those to Lord Moira) that were almost worthless and should have been written off – or at least written down in value – years before. The deficiency on the Oxfordshire tax receipts is harder to explain unless we assume that Henry used some of this money to try to prop up the rest of the business. The Crown called upon his guarantors to make up the short-fall and it appears that Edward Knight lost at least £20,000 and James Leigh Perrot at least £10,000. Other members of the family also suffered from the failure of the bank: Edward lost almost £500, Cassandra £132, Francis £292 and Jane £25. Mrs Austen and her daughters also suffered a diminu-tion in their income as Henry and apparently also Francis were unable to continue their annual contributions at this time.[31]

With no limited liability Henry lost everything, including almost all his personal possessions, and was left virtually penniless, but at least he received his Certificate of Discharge promptly, on 8 June 1816, and was free to begin a new life and was not at risk of being imprisoned for debt. (Bankruptcy was a possibility only for those engaged in trade; clergymen, gentlemen and even farmers could not avail themselves of it to put unpayable debts behind them, and were often imprisoned.) His niece, Caroline, recalled in her reminiscences that about a fortnight later 'he came to Steventon, *apparently* for it *truly* could not have been, in unbroken spirits', and a few months later Jane reported that he was 'in excellent looks' and as agreeable as ever. He had already decided to take holy orders, but not even his resilient temperament could wipe all bitterness and regret from his recollection of what had passed, and his later letters touching on the failure of the bank insist a little too much that it was anybody's and everybody's fault but his own.[32]

The intense anxiety and strain of the days in which a bank was in peril and at risk of failing are vividly caught in the letters written by Marianne

Thornton about her brother Henry's experiences in 1825. The Thorntons were a leading family of evangelical bankers and merchants, who played a prominent role in both commerce and politics. Henry Thornton Snr – Marianne's father – was born in 1760, the son of a wealthy merchant who traded with Russia, and himself one of the first generation of evangelicals. After working for some time in his father's business, Henry Snr became a partner in the banking house of Down, Thornton and Free, where he proved assiduous and scrupulously honest, disliking the habitual fudging of his partners. He constantly examined his own motives, once writing that 'the desire of money blinds the eyes and betrays into frauds which are unperceived'; and he believed that it was best in business as in the rest of life to concentrate on pleasing God, 'for be assured, that a man cannot be true to his gain, and true to his God also'. He was immensely generous, giving away six-sevenths of his income before his marriage, and one third of it thereafter, and he took a kindly interest in the welfare of the clerks who worked in the bank, rather against the wishes of his partners. For more than 30 years he was a scrupulous Member of Parliament and one of the leading opponents of slavery and the slave trade.[33]

Henry Thornton died in 1815 when his eldest son Henry was only 15. The younger Henry finished school and went to Cambridge, and then joined the bank as a clerk 'merely to *learn the trade*', on the understanding that he would then be admitted as a junior partner. The bank was now Pole, Thornton, Free, Down and Scott: with the senior, if inactive, partner being Sir Peter Pole, whose reluctant journey into Parliament was begun in consequence of the death of the elder Thornton. According to Marianne, there was some opposition to granting the partnership to young Henry 'from Pole . . . [who] did not like his share being diminished by Henry receiving some of the profits – and from Free who did not like being watched. However, for very shame's sake they admitted him.'[34]

The bank was doing well: it was regarded as one of the most stable and best connected houses in London, and was said to be making a profit of about £40,000 a year, but Henry was not happy with the way it was being run.

Down and Scott were perfect cyphers, Pole never came near them, Free governed supremely . . . There was a spirit of speculation, a love of concealing what he did, making the best of a story, which to Henry was intolerable, and they have had some lively disputes about things; on one occasion Henry set off in the night, and brought up Pole from Hampshire, to interfere by nine the next morning, because he could not make Free give up a plan which he did not think strictly honourable and *therefore* not prudent.

In late 1825 the speculative boom that had gripped the commercial world and extended far into wider society for over a year, finally burst. Numerous joint stock companies, promoting everything from commercial dairies to mines in Latin America, failed overnight and the rot soon spread to established companies in London and to the country banks. Henry was alarmed that Free was not keeping more cash in the bank, but relied 'on that credit which had never been shaken, and which would enable them to borrow whenever they pleased; he had really run things so near, that Henry had often remonstrated, especially as Pole's property is much of it in land, and cannot be turned into money the minute it is wanted'. On Thursday 1 and Friday 2 December 'there seemed to be something like a run upon them, and a difficulty in borrowing money which they had never felt before'. Worse was to follow.

On Saturday however – that dreadful Saturday I shall never forget – the run increased to a frightful degree, everybody came in to take *out* their balance, no one brought any in; one old steady customer, who had usually £30,000 there, drew it out without, as is usual, giving any warning, and in order to pay it the House was left literally empty. Henry went out to endeavour to borrow some but people made shuffling excuses – some said they would go and fetch some, and never returned – in short both he and Mr Free returned unsuccessful.

Free panicked and wanted to declare themselves bankrupt. 'Old Scott cried like a child of five years old, but could suggest nothing, Pole and Down were both out of Town. Henry saw it all lay upon him.'

Henry was convinced that the bank was still solvent: it just needed a little breathing space to turn solid assets into cash. At four o'clock on the Saturday, with an hour's trading to go and no reserves to speak of, he ordered the balances to be struck and found that before the close of business they would have to pay out £33,000 and would receive only £12,000. 'This was certain destruction, and he walked out, resolved to try one last resource.' He appealed to John Smith of the Carrington Smiths: the two firms had long been rivals, but John Smith had always been very kind to Henry and was a friend of his mother's family. Henry made no pretence, as bankers usually did, that his affairs were not in a critical state: if Smith refused to help, the bank must break. Smith asked for his word of honour that they were not insolvent and Henry assured him. Smith then agreed to help, but had to admit that he did not have quite enough cash on hand to cover the shortfall 'for they had been hard-pressed themselves that day'. Two chance deposits were just enough to fill the void, 'but never, he says shall he forget watching the clock to see when five would strike, and end their immediate terror – or whether any one would come in for more payments'. The clock struck, and the bank closed its doors, but Henry hardly felt that they would be able to open for business again on Monday morning.

John Smith had been greatly impressed with Henry's coolness and honesty, and he knew that if a bank of the reputation of Down, Free & Co. failed the immediate crisis would intensify and that no one would be safe. His own bank was not strong enough to save them, but he resolved to appeal to the Bank of England on Henry's behalf. Henry had little hope that this would achieve anything 'for the Bank had never been known to do such a thing', but he was naturally willing to try. He broke into the other partners' desks to get their books – telling them later that as they had left him to handle the crisis alone they had no right to complain – and sent off urgent messages to his uncle Robert Thornton and to Sir Peter Pole, while getting four confidential clerks to make a complete statement of their affairs. Meanwhile Smith organized a meeting with the directors of the Bank of England at eight o'clock on the Sunday morning.

Henry returned home at one in the morning,

> perfectly white and bloodless with the anxiety and exertion he had gone through, but so quiet and composed, I could scarcely believe it when he told me they must be proclaimed Bankrupts [on] Monday morning, but not to mind it for no one would lose anything by it; but he was certain the House was solvent, and he had rather break at once than go through such another day.

He was sorry that their failure would bring down 38 country banks but he had no hope. 'He next proceeded to do two or three things which almost broke my heart. He paid me and Nurse two or three pounds he owed us, for he said he shouldn't feel any was his own by Monday.'

He sat up through the night talking quietly to Marianne about the events of the day, for there was no hope of sleeping, and left again at six in the morning to John Smith's house. There he met all the directors of the Bank of England who were in town and a number of the other leading bankers in the City. John Smith began by saying that if the bank failed it would cause such widespread distress that he would regard it as a 'national misfortune', and that he had seen Henry handle the crisis and had confidence that it would be well managed in future if it could be saved now. He then asked Henry for his word that the bank was solvent. Henry then opened the books to everyone – 'those precious things which no Banker will ever let another catch a glimpse of, and which he begged they would examine thoroughly' and said he trusted that Sir Peter Pole would soon be there, who could give them an exact statement of his property – but he believed that after all the liabilities had been met there would be a very considerable residue. '"Well then," said the Governor and Deputy Governor of the Bank, "you shall have four hundred thousand pounds by eight tomorrow morning, which will I think float you." Henry said he could scarcely believe what he heard.'

The partners all had to give personal guarantees, and Henry Thornton was to report on the business of the bank to the Bank of England. Free was to go out, and Henry to choose a new working partner. 'But Sir

P. Pole's nerves have been so shaken that he seems anxious to be off, as he has now a very handsome fortune left, tho' Free has wickedly injured the enormous one with which he came in. So Henry begs that he will decamp and means to get a fresh Partner, just as rich and rather more wise.'

On Monday morning he went early to the Bank of England

> where he found the Governor and Deputy Governor who for the sake of secrecy had no clerks there, and they began counting out the Bills for him. 'I hope this won't overset you my young man', said one of them, 'to see the Governor and Deputy Governor of the Bank acting as your two clerks.' He went back to the Banking House £400,000 richer than he left it on Saturday. For the first hour there was a little run, but the rumours that the Bank of England had taken them under its Wing soon spread, and people brought back money as fast as they had taken it out on Saturday, and by night they were so full of cash that they might have done without assistance.[35]

However, this was not the end of the story and the reprieve proved short-lived. Too many of the country banks with whom Down, Free, Pole, Thornton, & Co. corresponded had failed, and if they borrowed more money it would simply drain away into satisfying the country creditors. The only honourable thing to do was to admit defeat, and pay out their own creditors. This was hard upon Sir Peter Pole, who was forced to make up the deficiency, but he was still left a wealthy man, and 'every one will be paid in full'. Henry's own reputation was enhanced by the crisis, and it is a shock to realize that he was still only 25 years old. 'Alexander Baring says there are two things he hates – an abolitionist and a saint – and yet he can't help liking young Thornton, in proof of which he very carelessl offered him £200,000 to begin with, if they were likely to want it.' Desp e the ruin Marianne told her friend, 'We find it quite impossible however to be very unhappy whilst he is amongst us – he says "if I had behaved like a rogue and ruined myself besides, you could but be so miserable; *now* I do think my character is rather the higher, and I believe the money is safe, so where is the use of being unhappy?"'[36]

Henry Thornton went on to be a partner in a new and successful bank which was notable for its conservative, prudent policies. In later life he was elected a Fellow of the Royal Society, and when he died, in 1881, his estate was valued at £330,000.[37]

Banking and commerce were risky activities in the early nineteenth century. Of the 13 nabobs who invested their Indian wealth in banks and sat in the Commons between 1790 and 1820, no fewer than five saw the bank fail and lost at least part of their fortune. It was this insecurity that helped underpin the social prejudice against trade. A landed gentlemen might prove a wastrel and ruin his estate, but most of his land was generally entailed, and even if it was not, his extravagance could be detected well before the final crash. But a merchant or a banker might appear prosperous and secure until, overnight, his fortune vanished or at least was severely reduced. Nor could his fall be softened except by the kindness of his friends. William Manning was one of the leading merchants in the City of London, a Governor and Deputy-Governor of the Bank of England, an MP for 36 years and one of the most respected figures in the commercial world, but ruin came in the winter of 1830–31, and his son went with him to the Guildhall, to appear before the Commissioner of Bankruptcy and lay down his gold watch, chain and seals. They were returned to him, as the custom was, but that was all. His house at Combe Bank was sold, and he was forced to rely on his relatives for his subsistence. Mr Boehm, whose wife had held the ball attended by the Prince Regent on the memorable night in 1815 when the news of Waterloo arrived, had made the same journey to the Guildhall for the same purpose in 1819, and Mrs Boehm lived out the last 23 years of her life in a grace-and-favour apartment at Hampton Court. The Faversham Bank in which James Tappenden was the senior partner collapsed in 1814, in part due to the unwise investment in the Welsh ironworks; and William Yescombe died a ruined man.

Commercial assets were never perfectly secure, and it is less surprising that many men, having made a fortune, chose to buy a country estate and rely on the rent of the estate's farms, or put their money into government bonds, than that so many men, already rich, would risk their all to accumulate even greater wealth.[38]

CHAPTER EIGHT

CIVIL OFFICE

AT THE BEGINNING OF March 1795 the 25-year-old Lieutenant-Colonel Arthur Wesley, the future Duke of Wellington, arrived in London from northern Germany. He had just served on his first campaign, and it had been a miserable failure. The British army had been forced to retreat across Holland in the depths of winter; it had run short of supplies and discipline had broken down, leading to scenes of suffering similar to those that would be played out in the retreat to Coruña 14 years later. Wesley's immediate reaction, when he got to England, was to seek an alternative career. He approached Lord Camden, the newly appointed Lord Lieutenant of Ireland, asking for an office in the Irish government. He had some reason to hope for success: he was a Member of the Irish Parliament and a loyal supporter of the government; he had been an ADC at Dublin Castle under successive Lords Lieutenant for the previous seven years, and had remained on particularly good terms with Lord Buckingham, who was the head of the influential Grenville family. More significantly, Wesley's brother Lord Mornington (the future Marquess Wellesley) was a close friend of the Prime Minister, William Pitt, and the Foreign Secretary, Lord Grenville, and a significant figure in the world of politics in both London and Dublin in his own right. But despite Mornington's warm support, Wesley's applications came to nothing.

Camden firmly rejected his request to be appointed undersecretary for military affairs in the Irish government, and refused to encourage Wesley's hope that he might be given a position on the Irish revenue or treasury boards when a vacancy arose. Wesley did not give up easily, he made repeated approaches to Camden over the course of six months, writing in a tone of deferential subservience that must have made him squirm. And it was all for nothing; neither his own standing nor his brother's influence was sufficient to secure a prize for which there was much competition, and in the autumn of 1795 he admitted defeat, reconciled himself to remaining in the army, and prepared to sail with his regiment on a new expedition abroad.[1]

Almost 20 years later in 1813 Wellington had just defeated the French army at Vitoria, driving King Joseph from Spain and raising the British army to a pinnacle of success it had not achieved since Marlborough. Earlier in the year he had been made a marquess (the dukedom was to come in 1814), and the Prince Regent rewarded the victory by making him a field marshal in the army. He had close personal connections with the ministers in London, and his fame, his glory and presumably his influence were unequalled. From these Olympian heights he deigned to ask Lord Whitworth, the newly installed Lord Lieutenant of Ireland, for a small favour. There was a young man in Dublin named Dickson or Dixon, aged about 20, the son of the wife of a shoemaker in whose house the young Arthur Wesley had lodged in the early 1790s. The boy had received a good education at Trinity College, Dublin, and was well qualified for a position in the Irish government. Wellington asked Whitworth to place the young man in a situation worth about £200 a year, with prospects for promotion if he proved able and deserving, 'to be put upon the ladder' was his phrase. There was no doubt in anyone's mind that young Dickson was Wellington's illegitimate son, and Whitworth was keen to oblige the man of the hour, and yet more than a year passed without any appointment being made.[2]

Wellington may not have been surprised, for he knew better than most the pressure on the Irish government for places. He had spent two years (1807–09) as Chief Secretary for Ireland, where dispensing patronage had been one of his principal duties. The Duke of Richmond had been made Lord Lieutenant at the same time, and as soon as their appointment was announced, both men were deluged with applications for positions and other favours. Irish peers wrote to remind the new government of the promises which had been made to them at the time of the crucial vote on the Act of Union six years before, and to suggest ways in which these might finally be honoured; gentlemen wrote asking that their son, nephew or grandson be granted a commission in the army or be promoted in the navy. Clergymen sought permission to exchange their living for one closer to friends and family or in a position better suited to their health; and impoverished ladies and gentlemen asked for a modest pension – as little as £20 a year – to enable them to maintain their respectability. Above all, people asked for jobs, for themselves and for their protégés. Wellesley's mother wrote enclosing three letters which she had received containing applications that she feared would be troublesome, but saw no alternative to forwarding. And his sister Anne suggested a candidate for the highly desirable position of the commander of the mailboat that ran from Dublin to England. This last produced a sharp retort: 'I think it may be expected that the Duke of Richmond or I, who have been all over the world, have naval friends of merit, but not rich, to whom we may be desirous of giving such a provision.' But such freedom of expression could only be used in writing to family or very close friends; other applications needed to be meet with bland courtesy even if there was no prospect of satisfying the claimant.[3]

In most cases neither Wellesley nor Richmond had a free hand. Much as they might have liked to help their friends, most of the patronage at their disposal had to be used to reinforce the standing of the Irish government by rewarding its supporters. In practice this meant that most positions were filled on the advice of local magnates sympathetic to the government, for whom this patronage was both a recognition of their support and a public affirmation of their importance. When Wellesley left Ireland in 1809 he prepared a memorandum for his successor which clearly explained the standing and claims of influential figures in each county in Ireland. For example, in County Antrim:

Mr McNaghten. Is brought in[to Parliament] principally by the influence of Lord Hertford. Attends well and is a steady friend. Government
are under an engagement to give him an office for life of £300 per
annum, which was made at the period of the Union, and has been
admitted by the Duke of Richmond. Lord Cornwallis was to have
given him an office of this description and value, and had made an
arrangement for it which was defeated by a trick of the late Lord
Avonmore. Lord Castlereagh knows the whole story. Mr McNaghten
has lately desired to have a pension for his life, of the value and instead
of this office, but by Lord Hawkesbury's desire I have refused it.

The Hon. John O'Neill [the other member of Parliament for County
Antrim] – is the brother of Lord O'Neill, supports Government and
attends tolerably. I believe he is a Lieut-Colonel of Dragoons. The
patronage of County Antrim should be distributed according to the
recommendation of Lord Hertford and Lord O'Neill. It must be
observed however that Lord Donegal will claim that of the town of
Belfast.[4]

Similarly the patronage of Queen's County was to be given to Mr Pole,
not because he was Arthur Wellesley's brother William Wellesley-Pole,
but because he was a member of the government and the leading supporter
of the ministry in the county. Politics only became irrelevant when there
was no shortage of places, for example commissions in the army late in
the war. When, as was usually the case, there were far fewer places than
needy and deserving applicants, it was generally necessary to reward the
government's supporters rather than appear magnanimously blind to
political differences. Fortunately the effect of this bias was much softened
by the fact that in most of the gentlemanly professions the government
was only one patron among many: a young naval officer looked mostly to
senior officers in the navy, not to politicians, for his promotion and
employment; an officer in the army could purchase his next step of rank,
and the Duke of York and Wellington both went out of their way to avoid
favouring officers according to their political allegiances. Most church
livings were not in the gift of the Crown, while Liverpool resisted giving

political claims too much weight in his appointment of bishops; Indian patronage was dispersed among the Directors of the East India Company, and success at the Bar or in commerce was a route to, not a product of, political influence.[5]

The Irish government was particularly hard pressed: its patronage had been diminished by the union with England, while there had been no reduction in the claims made upon it – quite the reverse if all the promises made to pass the Act of Union are taken into account. But even in England there were always far more applicants than positions open to be filled, and the first hint of a vacancy in any post was likely to bring a shower of letters, not just to whomever had the right to nominate a successor, but to anyone who might be able to influence them. John Wilson Croker was secretary to the Admiralty for more than 20 years (1809–30), and proved adept at playing the patronage game. His position gave him reason to correspond with naval officers all over the world, and he carefully ensured that these relations had a personal side to them. For example, he wrote to Admiral Penrose, the Commander-in-Chief in the Mediterranean in 1818, asking that he procure for him some marble or porphyry plinths suitable for the busts that Croker kept in his drawing room. This was a purely personal favour, and by asking Croker established an obligation to Penrose which would enable the admiral to ask a favour in return – perhaps the command of a ship for one of his protégés, or the transfer of another from one station to another. Penrose might not even need to make such a request: Croker would be keen to oblige him unprompted; while in time Croker might also ask Penrose for some further favour, for example a place on board his flagship for a worthy young man. In a similar way Croker would facilitate the passage of senior army officers, colonial officials and even well-connected private travellers on naval vessels: simultaneously bestowing a favour on them, and allowing the naval officer concerned to grant Croker a favour. In return officers might send Croker gifts or execute specific commissions, such as purchasing the plinths or looking for obscure pamphlets on the French Revolution which Croker collected; where appropriate Croker would pay for the purchase and any import duty, but still be much obliged to the officer for his trouble. All this was an unself-conscious extension of the normal forms of social exchange, courtesy and hospitality which flourished in the period, whether in the form of gifts of game, lending a box at the opera, or the hospitality that extended to prolonged country house visits. Only ignorant outsiders or fanatical moralists would have felt that there was anything improper about such attentions, let alone hint at the dreadful word 'corruption'.[6]

Croker also used his position to obtain jobs, usually in the naval administration rather than the navy, for many relatives and other protégés. These were not sinecures, and Croker insisted that 'I never will recommend any one who is not in my opinion *fit* for the situation in which he is to be placed'. Indeed, he went further, monitoring his appointees and threatening to cut off all further support, and even obtain their dismissal, if they disgraced him, either by being slack and inefficient or by failing to behave as gentlemen. In turn the fact that his nominees were known to perform well made it easier to place them.[7]

During the war entry-level positions in government departments were not particularly attractive: pay was low and promotion slow. In 1811 Croker warned a connection – Horatio Smith – whose business had failed, against applying for an Admiralty clerkship:

> The Clerks in all the public offices connected with the Naval Department come in young & their Sallaries [sic] rise slowly & gradually according to their length of Service. In the Adm[iralt]y Offices over which alone I have any patronage the established Clerks are, I believe, invariably chosen out of the number of supernumerary Clerks who drudge away at two guineas a Week and since I have held my present office not one vacancy in the Establishment has occurred nor do I indeed see any probability of one.
>
> Under all these considerations I cannot advise you to think of a Clerkship in any of our departments at least. Your talents would be miserably applied & meanly rewarded. Surely you can put them to some better use than any that inferior office can offer you. All attainable situations are too poor and all valuable situations too distant & no man shd I think come in to any dept at least older than 18 or 19.[8]

But in the years of austerity after Waterloo openings suitable for gentlemen became scarce and young men of good family became more than willing to take positions as clerks if they were given some reason to hope for advancement in due course. A change from promotion by strict seniority to one where 'merit' (as determined by departmental seniors) was rewarded may have encouraged this trend, for one man's 'merit' is often another man's nepotism. In 1824 Croker assured Lord Exmouth (a senior admiral and himself a skilled user of patronage networks) that a proffered position as an Admiralty clerk was not beneath his protégé:

> the last vacancy I gave to Barrow's eldest Son so that you may judge it is a fit and advantageous situation for a young gentleman – but he must be a good Clerk or must show a promise of becoming one & you know as well as I do the necessity in which I feel myself of appointing those only who are likely to do the public business well. As the place soon becomes one of great trust & confidence & is one of character & ultimate emolument – I look to have a *young gentleman* in it.[9]

As this suggests, there was no civil service in England in the early nineteenth century in the sense that later became commonly accepted: a large body of permanent, professional administrators, with standardized conditions of employment and promotion independent of their political masters. Even the term 'civil service' had yet to become current, and each individual office had its own traditions and peculiarities. Still, by the middle decades of the eighteenth century the state employed a large number of officials, and this number expanded greatly during the war with France. In 1797 by one calculation the total number, including those employed by the Irish government, amounted to 17,640 officials; and this then rose to just short of 25,000 by 1810, at which level it remained stable for a decade before falling slightly in the 1820s. Very few of these officials were employed in formulating policy. Excluding diplomats serving abroad, the Foreign Office had a permanent staff of only just over 20 including the Foreign Secretary at its head and the 'necessary woman' or house-keeper at the bottom, with most of those in between being clerks. Croker's Admiralty had fewer than 50 staff when he was first appointed, although this does not include the subordinate but larger Navy Office or the large civilian staff employed in the dockyards. The great majority of public officials – about five in every six – were employed in the departments charged with raising revenue, especially the Excise (6,580 in 1797 rising to 7,639 in 1815) and the Customs (6,380 in 1797, 10,807 in 1815 and 11,016 in 1829).[10]

The Excise and Customs departments were both organized in the same way, with a board of commissioners at the head, a substantial bureaucracy in London, and thousands of officers scattered across the country. Customs officers ensured that duties were paid on imports, and so were mostly based in the ports and scattered along the coast to attempt to prevent smuggling; while excise men collected taxes on locally produced goods and so operated throughout the country. Both departments were offshoots of the Treasury, and answered to the Chancellor of the Exchequer and the First Lord of the Treasury (the official title of the Prime Minister). There were also five smaller revenue boards, of which the most important was the Tax Office (which was responsible for administering the Land Tax and other direct taxes, such as the window tax, which were collectively known as the Assessed Taxes). The remaining four were the Stamp Office, the Salt Office, the Hackney Coach Office, and the Hawkers' and Pedlars' Office, each of which was responsible for collecting the revenue from a particular set of taxes or licences, although several had become stagnant backwaters by the end of the eighteenth century.[11]

A few rank and file revenue officers claimed to come from genteel backgrounds – a sample of excise men in 1820 found that one in ten described themselves as 'gentlemen' on entering the service, although it seems likely that this was using the word with considerable generosity. Those who really came from good families were commonly either black sheep or the victims of misfortune, and they usually struggled with their new subordinate status. Many positions, especially in the Excise, required considerable mathematical skills, and most new recruits appear to have come from a commercial background or to have worked as clerks, schoolmasters or accountants. Not all were young when they first joined the service, although the Customs Board limited its recruits to those between the ages of 21 and 45 for most of its positions. They were also never supposed to serve in their home district, for reasons that were spelled out with stark honesty as early as 1714:

> Can any one believe that a Coll[ector] or other officer, unless he has more integrity than . . . is usual in this Age, will detect his Brother, Uncle, or other Relation of any fraud committed to the prejudice of the Revenue, (at least I've never heard one instance of it,) On the contrary is it not rather to be apprehended that the officer and his trading Relation will agree to share the profit of such fraudulent Trade?

And for similar reasons they were forbidden to engage in any trade or private business of their own, although this rule seems to have been broken, or at least bent, quite often.[12]

Appointments were made through patronage: often the recommendation of a figure of some local consequence, and it was not unknown for this to be facilitated by the payment of money, even if this was not made directly to the prospective patron. The pay was respectable but not munificent: frequently under, though sometimes over, £100 a year, with some additional allowances and perquisites, but also varying deductions and other costs. The position gave the officers a certain status in the local district, similar to that of an established tradesman, although if they were not careful they might also become unpopular, especially in an area where smuggling was common or where a previous collector had taken a relaxed view of his duties and turned a blind eye to much evasion. The public reputation of revenue officers as a class was not high, with numerous stories of them abusing their powers by demanding favours (including sexual favours from the wives and daughters of victuallers, brewers and others in trades that were particularly vulnerable to pressure from the Excise). This probably exaggerated the extent of their misconduct – such stories spread far and wide – and most revenue officers preferred to live at peace with their neighbours rather than exploit them and run the risk of a nasty accident on a dark night. There was a good deal of camaraderie among the revenue officers themselves, and while some might boast of their exploits, the prevailing ethos was pride in steering a middle course between neglect of their duties and unreasonably rigidity in enforcing rules.[13]

The work of customs officers in particular was undermined by a lack of public support, and an assumption that gentlemen should not be inconvenienced by official rules and regulations. When George Murray and his elder brother Patrick set off on a tour of the Continent as teenagers in 1789 they were no sooner on board their ship than they

> had the honour of a visit from the customs house officers who came to see that we had nothing in our trunks which was prohibited to be carried out of the country. Upon putting half a guinea into their hands they took our word that our trunks contained nothing but wearing apparel, and then took their leave wishing us a pleasant voyage and making several low bows for their bribe.

When the brothers returned a year later a similar transaction smoothed the clearing of their luggage. In 1810 Lord Aberdeen asked his brother Alexander Gordon to purchase some old silver plate for him in Spain, adding 'You must keep the Plate with your own Baggage, unless you have any friend in a man of war to take it as the duties are so enormous'. In the event Alexander sent it home with his brother Charles, who failed to appreciate that it needed to be concealed, and as a result it was seized by the Customs, much to Aberdeen's annoyance. And in 1826 when Prince Pückler-Muskau arrived in England in search of a bride, he was able to secure the release of his luggage without delay: 'I found that the golden key, which rarely fails, had not lost its efficacy here, and saved me from long and tedious delays. Even a few dozen French gloves, which lay in all innocence open upon my linen, seemed to be rendered invisible; – nobody took any notice of them.'[14]

An occupation in which petty bribes were routinely offered and accepted was not suitable to anyone with pretensions to regard himself, or be treated by others, as a gentleman. It is not surprising that Sydney Smith reacted with outrage when, in 1836, Lord Melbourne's private secretary wrote that the government had nothing available for his scapegrace son Windham except a position as a land waiter (a junior officer) in the customs service.

> As to the Land Waiter's place I have too much real confidence in the proper feeling of Lord Melbourne & yourself to suppose for a moment that you are treating me with derision, & have therefore only to say plainly, that my situation in Life places me above the necessity of accepting such an offer, & *ought* perhaps to have guaranteed me from the pain of receiving it.

Clearly Melbourne's secretary had misjudged his man, but a position like this in the revenue service was exactly the sort of patronage which would be welcome slightly lower down the social scale, and which would be distributed through one of the local Members of Parliament or the dominant landowner in the county if he supported the government and was keen to maintain his local influence.[15]

The work of the revenue officers in the field, and of all the rest of government, was supported by a substantial central bureaucracy busy checking accounts, writing correspondence and making regulations. Apart from some specialists, like lawyers, these administrative officials were almost always appointed as young clerks and then rose through the ranks, usually within the one department. Responsibility for the appointment of new clerks varied, with some appointments being ordained from on high (the Prime Minister or, at least in theory, the King), some being made on the recommendation of the Commissioners, and others left to the senior official within the department. In the case of the Admiralty, Croker would make most of the appointments (probably sharing some with Barrow, the Second Secretary and his good friend); but the First Lord sometimes had a protégé, in which case his wishes would need to be accommodated. In many departments there was evidently also a class of supernumerary clerks who expected to be promoted in turn to a permanent position, and presumably most new arrivals began at the bottom of this group rather than leaping over them.[16]

By the early nineteenth century there was a small army of clerks in London, some working for government departments, some for great private institutions like the Bank of England, the East India Company or the large insurance companies, and some for smaller businesses and private banks. Most of these clerks came from respectable but not gentlemanly families: they were the sons of shopkeepers and tradesmen, schoolteachers and clerks, but there was also a scattering of sons of clergymen, attorneys, army and naval officers, and others in the lower reaches of the gentlemanly professions. At the end of *Mansfield Park* we are told that one of Fanny Price's younger brothers had obtained a position 'as a clerk in a public office in London', presumably with the help of Sir Thomas Bertram, who was a Member of Parliament. And both Nelson's uncle, William Suckling, and Nelson's brother Maurice, began their careers as clerks in government departments. Suckling was an able man who rose to the eminence of Deputy Collector of Inward Customs, one of the most senior positions in the customs service, which gave him both the prosperity and the connections to assist his nephew at several points in his career. In later life he lived in a substantial house in Kentish Town, which was then on the outskirts of London, and in his late fifties he married a Miss Rumsey of Hampstead. Maurice Nelson was also quite successful, although apparently less able. At the age of 15 he started his career in the Audit Office of the Excise, a position secured for him by his uncle, who also had him appointed purser on the *Swift*, which supplemented his income without requiring him to go to sea. Seven years later he was appointed one of the clerks in the Office of Bills and Accounts in the Navy Office, and was not required to pay the usual premium of £200 for his place. For this he received a salary of £60 a year and another £68 in fees and gratuities, and for four years he managed to combine this with his existing position without undue exertion. Despite being 'honest, dull and disorganized' he rose in the office and in 1801, when he was 48, he was appointed Chief Clerk in the Navy Office, a promotion which increased his income by £400 a year. Unfortunately he died suddenly a month later, leaving his brother to pay many of his debts and to provide a regular annuity of £100 a year to the woman with whom he lived, but whom he had not married. By the time they died both Suckling and Maurice Nelson were figures of some consequence in official circles in London, and although their social status was probably still rather ambiguous, their income, prospects and lifestyle would have been at least equal to most members of the gentlemanly professions. However, only a small minority of the young men who joined government offices as clerks achieved this level of success.[17]

The work performed by clerks, especially at the junior levels, was generally monotonous: literally copying letters in a fair hand and making a further copy to be kept on file, or in a bound register, or entering figures into ledgers, adding their totals and cross-checking other additions. Many government offices were in a poor state of repair and insalubrious, although that might not make them any worse than the rooms in which the clerks lived. The working day was not generally long: six hours was common, with the clerks in the Salt Office only working five; and holidays were frequent: 49 in the Salt Office, 52 in the Stamp Office and 45 in the Customs, although it is not clear whether Saturday was regarded as a normal working day, a half-day, or a full holiday.[18]

Many appointments were made without any formal process at all or with a simple interview with the chief clerk of the department to confirm a *fait accompli*. But other organizations had developed a procedure to ensure that new recruits were suitable, without greatly inhibiting the use of patronage. For example, applicants for a position as a clerk at the Bank of England would come with a recommendation either from one of the Directors of the Bank or from a well-regarded official within the Bank. Positions were never advertised. The candidate would be interviewed and subjected to a test by the chief accountant to assess his handwriting, his ability to handle money (which was not as simple as it sounds, given the

1. Jane Austen's brother Edward Knight was a younger son, but had the good fortune to be adopted by relatives and to inherit a valuable estate, becoming a landed gentleman while still in his twenties.

2. James Austen was the eldest of Jane Austen's brothers. He became a clergyman holding four livings, but did not survive long enough to inherit the Leigh-Perrot fortune.

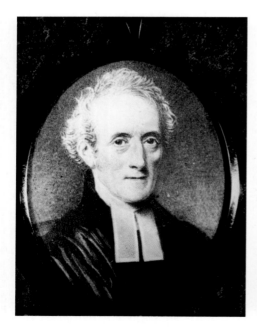

3. Henry Austen was a younger son who became an officer in the militia, then a regimental agent and a banker and finally, after his business failed, a clergyman.

4. Francis Austen became a successful naval officer but owed much of his later prosperity to a generous gift from Mrs Leigh-Perrot.

5. The Rev. Sydney Smith in comfortable middle age. A celebrated wit and intellectual, and one of the founders of the *Edinburgh Review*, Smith was hardly a typical clergyman, yet many of the challenges he faced in making his way in the world were common to young men entering the Church; and, like many clergymen, he battled isolation and depression in his rural living.

6. Detail of the 'lying-in' (or maternity) ward of Middlesex Hospital from Ackermann's *Microcosm of London* where medical students would learn by 'walking the wards', observing senior doctors practise and discuss their cases.

7. 'The Miseries of Human Life': Rowlandson's depiction of a court room scene where a barrister examines a witness. A career at the bar could be very lucrative, but success did not come easily – most young barristers struggled at first and many failed completely, sinking into obscurity.

8. The Court of Chancery from Ackermann's *Microcosm of London*. The court was presided over by the Lord Chancellor and considered contested estates, guardianships and other equity cases. Lord Eldon was the Lord Chancellor for many years.

9. The family of a boy who is about to join the Navy prepares his sea trunk. The first of a series of satirical prints by George Cruikshank tracing the career of a fictional naval officer, Master William Blockhead. Most boys were rather older than this – generally 13 or 14 and few younger than 11 – when they first went to sea.

10. The midshipmen's mess on a man-of-war was crowded, dark, smelly and noisy, and newcomers were often teased and bullied until they settled in to the unfamiliar world. Cruikshank shows the young boy's shock at the first sight of his new home.

11. A subaltern on campaign having breakfast prepared by his soldier servant. Provisions were often scarce even for junior officers, and they would quickly learn to be grateful and not to ask awkward questions if their soldier servant 'found' some extra food.

12. Illness killed many more officers and men than the enemy during the Napoleonic Wars. Arrangements for looking after sick officers on campaign were rudimentary.

13. In earlier decades many British officers and officials living in India had adopted local clothes and customs, but this fell out of favour by the late eighteenth century and there was a growing emphasis on recreating life at home in a new setting. Few of the young men who came out to India in this period returned home as wealthy nabobs, while many died of disease or became mired in debt.

14. The marketplace at Trichinopoly showing officers of the Madras Light Infantry (1800). This was a year after the death of Tipu Sultan and the fall of Seringapatam consolidated British domination of southern India.

great variety of coinage and notes in circulation), and his knowledge of accounts. Most candidates passed this test, although a few needed to make a second attempt; but this probably suggests that they did not take it until they were well prepared rather than that it was little more than a formality. Many had previous employment as clerks in other institutions, although most were young: the average age was just over 21, except for the sons of current or former clerks in the Bank who were significantly younger (18 and a half). All were asked about their financial position, although some debts and even a discharged bankruptcy do not appear to have disqualified them. None admitted to belonging to a political club of any sort – it is not clear whether this would have been an absolute bar or not – and a high proportion were members of the Church of England, although the Bank did employ many varieties of Dissenters. No Catholics were even considered: a rule against their employment was introduced in 1746 and was not abolished until 1829. Nor were any women employed as clerks at the Bank, although some appear to have worked as supernumerary clerks in some government offices, but not on the official establishment. Employment at the Bank was attractive: the pay was relatively good – a starting salary of £100 a year, paid quarterly in cash, and with prospects of incremental increases and bonuses – a high degree of job security, and a structure that allowed for promotion and advancement.[19]

Some government positions were still sold or, rather, the friends of a young man who was fortunate enough to be appointed were expected to pay a premium, in much the same way as they would if he were made a clerk to an attorney or an apprentice surgeon. In 1786 Sir Charles Middleton, the Comptroller of the Navy, estimated that he received more than £300 a year from the premiums on the appointment of clerks in the Navy Office. He did not regard this as an abuse, but an old-established practice that provided an important part of the income of the Comptroller. Nonetheless, the payment of premiums was strongly criticized by the administrative reformers of the 1780s and was largely abolished. This was part of a wider set of reforms, which saw the abolition or merger of many offices and an increased emphasis on economy and efficiency. There was also a reduction in the reliance on fees as a source of remuneration and the substitution of salaries as a more rational and frugal measure. However, this had the unintended consequence of removing one of the principal constraints on the growth of the bureaucracy (where fees provided a large part of the income, an increase in the number of staff led to a fall in the amount of money received by each official), and over the next 30 years the size of the central bureaucracy increased by one third, while the cost of salaries doubled.[20]

In some departments junior clerks were not paid until they had served for some time, although unlike modern interns they were almost guaranteed a job unless they performed very poorly. In others, like the Admiralty, they began as supernumerary clerks and sometimes took years to be placed on the Establishment. Even when they gained an official position they were generally paid no more than the £100 a year offered by the Bank of England, and sometimes rather less, but as they gained seniority or were promoted to more responsible positions, their income rose. The Chief Clerk in the Foreign Office was paid more than £1,000 a year, and those in the Home Office and the Treasury only a little less. In most cases the more senior officials also received other benefits that might very considerably increase their remuneration, including fees and bonuses, sinecure offices, free housing, the right to frank letters and newspapers for free postage, and even simple things like an allowance of coals and candles traditionally provided to the holder of particular offices. In purely prudential terms a position as a clerk in a government department was not a bad career for a younger son without good prospects. It was also one of the most gentlemanly of professions. However, its social status was considerably lower, and it required patience and a degree of subordination that did not suit most young gentlemen. Nor was it likely that a government clerk could afford to marry until early middle age at best.[21]

Clerks rose through a mixture of seniority and preferment, but unless their original patron was also a senior figure in the department – as Croker was – their connections, having secured them their initial position, counted for little subsequently. Able and hardworking clerks often introduced their sons or nephews into the same department, and during the eighteenth century there were a number of dynasties within the administration, such as the Lowndeses who provided no fewer than nine treasury officials between the 1680s and 1770s. Croker was certainly neither the first nor last official who favoured his relatives, but expected them to work diligently to justify the advantages they received. Some long-serving clerks developed considerable expertise in their field, and advised ministers on legislation and occasionally even wider policy, and in George Harrison, a lawyer who joined the Treasury and rose to be the most important permanent official of his generation, we see the first glimmer of the civil service mandarins of the future.[22]

The Customs and Excise departments had a well-established system of superannuation, which generally paid officers one third of their closing salary. Other departments granted pensions on an ad hoc basis, while some senior officials were given sinecures or appointed to boards requiring little work in the closing stages of their career. While no doubt there were individual cases of hardship, on the whole the government was generous: when two senior clerks were forced to retire from the Foreign Office in 1793 and 1794 due to ill-health they were each granted pensions equal to their full salary and other emoluments. Provisions were also often made for widows and other dependants: when James Hay died a few months after retiring as a senior clerk in 1806 the Foreign Secretary granted each of his unmarried sisters a pension of £75. However, this generosity was curtailed in later years by parliamentary pressure – led by the radicals – for economy in government and a reduction of 'abuses'.[23]

We have few first-hand accounts of the life of a clerk in a government office in the late eighteenth or early nineteenth centuries, but a short passage in the memoirs of Sir Herbert Taylor provides some interesting evidence, although he was far from a typical clerk. Taylor was born on 29 September 1775, the second son of a clergyman who unexpectedly inherited the family estate in Kent. The family had a respectable though not large income, and spent many years on the Continent living in Germany and travelling in Italy, where they mixed in good society including that of many other English travellers. Taylor tells us that 'My early inclination was for the military profession, but my father was opposed to it, and contemplated the law or some other civil profession for me'. One of their English acquaintances was Lord Camelford, and when his daughter married Lord Grenville, the Foreign Secretary, Camelford secured a position as a clerk at the Foreign Office for Taylor.

It was the summer of 1792, shortly before his 17th birthday, that Taylor arrived in London with his father. 'We were received very kindly by Lord and Lady Grenville, and I was on the same day introduced to the two Under Secretaries of State, Mr Burges and Mr A[ust], and was placed in the branch over which the former presided, to begin work in a few days after my father left London.' The season was over and the capital was quiet, but they dined with a few acquaintances including the Archbishop of Canterbury, who would have known Taylor's father, not just as a clergyman, but as a Kentish landowner. 'My father established me at a lodging in Bridge Street, Westminster, for which I paid a guinea a week (two good rooms) out of my allowance of £150 per annum, which he meant to continue until I should come on pay, the junior clerks not having then any salary.'

His father then left him and 'I found myself at seventeen, never having been a day separated from my family, living alone at a season when all with whom I had become acquainted abroad were absent from London, and having to make friends where I would'. Fortunately Mr Burges took Taylor under his wing both in the office and out of it, employing him in his room in the Foreign Office and inviting him home to dinner. He also dined occasionally with the Grenvilles and with the Archbishop, while his father's friend Mr Hallett also proved 'a kind-hearted and hospitable man'. Even so, 'I passed much of my time alone . . . and I then experienced the advantage of early habits of reading, and of the resources of drawing and music. I also engaged a person to read Latin with me.' For a naturally sociable young man, accustomed to good society abroad, it was a lonely life, at least at first.

In the office, Taylor's knowledge of languages was a great asset, but he was otherwise 'wholly unfitted for the duty. I wrote a bad hand, and was utterly ignorant of all official forms, to the extent even of not knowing how to fold and address a letter or note.' However, he was ambitious and keen to learn; and he shocked Lord Grenville's private secretary by saying that, although it was very unlikely, he hoped one day to be Foreign

Secretary himself. Not many Foreign Office clerks aimed so high, even those with good connections.

Taylor did not remain at the Foreign Office for long. In December of 1792 he was attached as secretary to Sir James Murray who was being sent on a mission to the Prussian headquarters at Frankfurt, and this opportunity led to others. He left the foreign service a year later, joined the army and attracted the attention of the Duke of York. This in turn led to his appointment, before he turned 30, as private secretary to George III, a position which he also held, many years later, under William IV, in both cases earning great respect for his efficiency and discretion. Lord Brougham, whose views on many subjects must have differed sharply from Taylor's, praised him as 'one of the ablest, indeed the most masterly men of business who ever filled any public employment'.[24]

<hr />

However, it was not a position as a clerk in a government office that Wellington sought for himself in 1795 or for his son in 1813. In addition to the permanent officials who rose through their department by steady progression, there was another class of office-holder: those who were appointed directly to positions of authority or emolument. These positions varied enormously and without any rationale, except historical accident. They ranged from some of the most responsible and demanding positions in the country such as the Prime Minister, to complete sinecures requiring no work, or with the duties of the office entirely delegated to others. And the rewards were equally diverse, with some hugely lucrative offices and others that yielded only petty change, without there being any correlation with the duties. In most cases there was no logical hierarchy or path for promotion: a man did not naturally progress from one office to another, and all the appointments were made through influence or patronage within government.

Some of the most senior and well-connected politicians of the age held valuable sinecures. Even men as little interested in enriching themselves as Pitt, Liverpool and Wellington accepted the office of Lord Warden of the Cinque Ports which brought with it the delightful residence of Walmer Castle on the Channel and, until 1817, an income of £3,000. This was handsome, especially as they were also well paid for the other offices they held, but it pales compared to some sinecures. The four Tellers of the Exchequer received a tiny percentage of all the money passing through the Treasury: this was pleasantly lucrative in the middle of the eighteenth century, but rose steeply during the American War to a peak of £7,000 a year to each Teller. In 1782, Parliament responded by capping the payment at £2,700 for future appointees, but it did not feel entitled to restrict the rights of those already holding the office. They included Lord Buckingham and Lord Camden, who had each been appointed to the office when young (Buckingham as a boy, Camden as a young man) when their fathers held high office: Buckingham's father, George Grenville, was Prime Minister and Camden's father was Lord Chancellor. The huge increase in government expenditure during the war with France swelled the value of the Tellerships, so that in 1808 Camden and Buckingham each received no less than £23,000 from this office, as well as the right to appoint deputies and other minor officials. In the face of parliamentary criticism in 1813 they agreed to voluntarily give up one third of this income, although Buckingham died before this sacrifice could take effect. Nor was this the only sinecure held by the Grenville family: Buckingham's brother Thomas Grenville, a bibliophile and good friend of Fox, was appointed Chief Justice of Eyre, south of the Trent, in 1800, a position that was worth just over £2,300 a year; while William, Lord Grenville, was first made Ranger of the Parks (£1,000 a year) in 1791, and then surrendered this when he was made Auditor of the Exchequer (£4,000) in 1794, although he did not accept the income while he was being well paid as Foreign Secretary in Pitt's government. Other members of the family also received valuable offices, although not all of these were sinecures.[25]

Many sinecures were granted in advance, or 'in reversion', when an incumbent was still in place. For example, Charles Greville, the diarist and grandson of the Duke of Portland, was given the reversion of the Secretaryship of Jamaica, when he was seven years old. It was 27 years before he succeeded to the position, and in the meantime his grandfather – who was twice Prime Minister and a long-serving Home Secretary – had him appointed Clerk Extraordinary to the Privy Council. This too was essentially a reversionary office, and when in 1821 one of the serving Clerks-in-Ordinary died, Greville succeeded to the position and received a salary of £2,000 which rose to £2,500 after three years. It was an office which placed him at the centre of the political world, while debarring him from taking any active personal role: the perfect position for a keen observer with a taste for gossip. When his predecessor as Secretary of Jamaica finally died in 1828, Greville immediately wrote to the Governor and Council of the island stating that his duties to the Privy Council would prevent his visiting them, and they responded by giving him permanent leave of absence. The position of Secretary was worth about £4,700 a year, but from this Greville had to pay a deputy to do the work and the costs of running an office, so that he probably cleared only about one third of the sum as profit. Nonetheless, when the position was challenged in 1834 he fought with determination to retain it and its emoluments and succeeded in doing so.

Thanks to these two offices Greville was able to lead a comfortable and self-indulgent life, combining his tastes for politics and the turf. Yet he had moments of intense dissatisfaction and self-criticism which he recorded in his diary, condemning himself for the time and money he wasted on racing and his failure to make more of his life.

I am . . . tormented with a sensation of self-reproach, of shame and remorse, which is exactly akin to what a drunkard feels in his sober intervals, without being able to shake off his pernicious habit. If this is the case why don't I give it [the turf] up anybody might ask. Because in spite of these feelings I like the amusement, the excitement; I like some of the habits it engenders and I have no sufficient temptation in any other quarter. I cannot find throughout the range of existence any other object *probably attainable* commensurate with the sacrifice. No path of ambition or honorable fame is open to me. I am neutralized in politics, and the habits of my mind sunk in indolence and inactivity, and my education (self-education I mean) miserably neglected, forbid me to aspire to any literary distinction.

And again, a few years later,

> I might have embraced any mode of life and have addicted myself to any society I pleased. I had ample opportunities of choosing between the best and the worst, but from indolence and procrastination, from having no fixed purpose and definite object, no ardent desires and determined will, I kept constantly vacillating between the two, cordially embracing and wholly rejecting neither, till I have at last brought myself to that unhappy pass that I am discontented and unhappy in both societies, ashamed of my associates in one, and ashamed of myself in the other.

Greville was in his forties when he wrote both these passages – they were not the posturing of a young man – and he clearly felt that in some respects his good fortune in being given a secure income from a young age had done him more harm than good. He may not have been right – many a man labouring over uncongenial work would have derided his regrets – but it is still a mistake to assume that all such sinecures brought their holders much joy.[26]

Valuable sinecures such as these were typically granted to successful politicians or their children, especially their eldest son: they were a reward of office, and while they might occasionally provide a secure place in the world for a younger son, they were not a career. Charles Greville's younger brother Algernon was forced to work for his living, obtaining a post as private secretary to the Duke of Wellington through his mother, who was the Duke's old friend and probably lover. Occasionally there are hints of other motives lying behind appointments, for example Lord Charles Spencer's use of his influence to grant Henry Austen the post of Collector of Taxes for Oxfordshire, after Austen had been extremely obliging in granting loans to Spencer and his son, but it is difficult to gauge whether such transactions were commonplace or exceptional.[27]

There were also numerous less lucrative sinecures – including around 150 in the customs department alone, and many more in the other revenue departments. Some of these were used to reward hard-working officials in the revenue and other government departments or provide for their retirement; but others were available to be granted as a political favour by the Prime Minister, the Chancellor of the Exchequer or, most commonly, by the Secretary to the Treasury, who had the task of keeping the government's supporters happy.[28]

It is impossible to draw a sharp line between sinecures and working positions, for many sinecures required the performance of some duties – either in person or by deputy – while the duties of some working offices were not particularly onerous. Members of Parliament were not paid and the demands of their position varied greatly, with the Members for some large, popular constituencies (such as Westminster, Liverpool or Yorkshire) being deluged with correspondence from their constituents, while many other members were able to actively pursue other careers, sometimes obtaining leave from attending the House for years on end if they were serving overseas. Most ministers and other senior figures in the government were well paid. As Lord Lieutenant of Ireland, Buckingham had received a salary of £20,000, although the costs of holding the office and living in state in Dublin meant that he is likely to have spent every penny of this, and perhaps more. When his brother, Lord Grenville, was serving as Foreign Secretary he netted between £5,000 and £5,600 a year from his office, while his undersecretaries received £1,000, a figure which had risen to £2,000 by 1822. Before leaving office in 1801 Grenville secured pensions of £600 a year for both his undersecretaries, while George Canning obtained the place of Receiver General of the Excise, worth £1,500 a year, for his undersecretary John Backhouse in 1827, on the understanding that he would not receive the income of both offices at the same time: the sinecure was to provide security for when he lost his position at the Foreign Office, which in the event was many years later.[29]

At the level below an undersecretary there were positions as junior Lords of the Treasury or the Admiralty, places in the Household, the Mint, the Ordnance or the Post Office, some of which required more work, others less. By 1800 the position of junior Lord of the Treasury was close to the borderline between an efficient office and a sinecure, with one of the secretaries to the Treasury dismissing them as 'mere signers of papers'. They attended twice weekly meetings of the Treasury Board, but the business done there was purely formal and all the real decisions were taken elsewhere by the Chancellor of the Exchequer. Nonetheless the junior Lords each received £1,600 a year, and it was sometimes used to give a promising young man a first taste of office. Like many such positions, it was a political appointment – the holders would lose their place in the event of a change of government – and was only open to a Member of Parliament who supported the ministry.[30]

Diplomatic appointments were not routinely changed with a change of government, although they were highly dependent on patronage and influence and a change of Foreign Secretary, even without a change of government, could make or mar a career. The most senior and desirable positions – such as ambassador to Paris – were generally reserved for noblemen, significant politicians needing a break from Westminster, or the close connections of the Foreign Secretary or other leading members of the government. In the early nineteenth century Castlereagh not only led important missions to the Continent in person while serving as Foreign Secretary, but employed his half-brother, Sir Charles Stewart, in a succession of posts for which he did not strike most observers as being temperamentally suited. Other important positions were held by Wellington's brother Sir Henry Wellesley, by Wellington himself, by Lord Aberdeen and by a senior if not very successful soldier Lord Cathcart. Less important positions were also often secured by the well connected: Lord Burghersh, the eldest son of Lord Westmorland (a long serving member of cabinet) and husband of Wellington's favourite niece, Priscilla, held a succession of highly desirable positions in the smaller states of northern Italy between 1814 and 1831. Even Francis and George Jackson, who appear the models of professional diplomats, relying on their skill and expertise, not their connections, for their appointments, were introduced into the service by the Marquess of Carmarthen (later Duke of Leeds), Pitt's Foreign Secretary from 1783 to 1791, who had been tutored by their father.[31]

The appeal of the diplomatic service rose in the years after Waterloo and its ranks became even more aristocratic, with more than half of the 391 British diplomats who have been identified as holding office between

1815 and 1860 being the grandsons of peers or baronets, while most of the remainder came from well-established gentry or gentlemanly families. Only 12 are known to have had a commercial background, while the proportion with blue blood increased noticeably in the higher reaches of the service: of the 23 men who rose to be ambassadors in this period, 20 came from aristocratic families. But as this statistic shows, the number of young men who found a career in the diplomatic service was not large, and it had been even smaller in the eighteenth century.[32]

Most younger sons of the well connected preferred to stay at home, and there were a number of offices open to them which were detached from the vicissitudes of party fortune. These senior administrative positions were seldom as well paid as political offices, but their tenure was much more secure, and they provided a comfortable income for their holders while requiring some work. For example, each of the revenue departments was headed by a board of commissioners, amounting, in 1800, to a total of 60 commissioners at any one time. These commissioners were paid quite well (£1,000 a year in the Customs, rather less on some of the other boards), and were virtually permanent positions: very rarely a commissioner was dismissed for misconduct, but they did not lose their position with a change of ministers. The excise and customs boards were the busiest, generally meeting each day except Sunday, while the other boards might meet only two or three times each week. Some commissioners did little more than attend board meetings, sign documents put in front of them, and occasionally claim a share of the patronage exercised by the board; but others were much more assiduous and exercised an effective supervision over their department. Indeed, the historian of the customs service in the eighteenth century roundly declares that 'Without exception, the [Customs] Boards throughout the period were conscientious, occasionally almost to a fault. . .'.[33]

The appointment of commissioners was a useful piece of patronage in the hands of the Treasury. Many commissioners were the younger sons or brothers of influential politicians or peers, for example Augustus Phipps, fourth son of the first Lord Mulgrave on the Excise Board; John Byng, second son of the 3rd Viscount Torrington, in the Stamp Office;

and John and Henry Fane, sons of the 8th Earl of Westmorland who found comfortable billets in the Tax and Salt Offices. It was a position as a commissioner on one of the Irish revenue boards that Wellington had sought in 1795, and his nephew Richard Wellesley ended his days as a commissioner of stamp duties in England. Because commissioners and their staff were barred from sitting in the Commons, active politicians did not usually compete for these jobs, opening the way for their younger brothers. Ministers and other politicians would also sometimes use these positions to reward other protégés: old tutors, private secretaries, party stalwarts who had fallen into financial difficulties and some royal servants. Lawyers and members of the gentry might be keen to secure such a position, although they would need considerable luck, or exceptionally good connections, to succeed. But many positions were given to experienced officials who had either risen up within the office or in one of the other departments of government (usually one of the departments under the Treasury). These were often treated as a provision for retirement, or semi-retirement, for undersecretaries or chief clerks who had already spent many years in service, although these men were also among the most active and efficient commissioners. The proportion of such 'professional' appointments rose at the end of the eighteenth century during Pitt the Younger's tenure of the Treasury, but there was always a mixture of well-connected and often young men and more experienced bureaucrats. The average age at which commissioners were appointed between 1754 and 1798 was 41 years old. And because their tenure was so secure, some commissioners made hard bargains in exchange for their resignation, in some cases trading it for other preferment for their son, or requiring their successor to pay them a part of his salary for a few years or so long as they lived. (This practice was officially discouraged, but remained quite widespread at all levels of the bureaucracy in 1800.)[34]

At a lower level there was a number of working offices in different branches of the administration, although some of them required specialist skills. For example, a young lawyer in London might, with a little influence, be appointed one of the 70 Commissioners in Bankruptcy, who worked in a crowded room in the Guildhall. The appointment was one of the many offices in the gift of the Lord Chancellor, and as it was unlikely to produce an income of more than £300 and required constant attendance, competition was less keen for the position than for many others. In the provinces, a lawyer – although usually a well-established attorney, not a beginner – might look to the office of Clerk of the Peace as a way of supplementing his income; although in many cases this office would be given to a dependant of the Lord Lieutenant, and an attorney would do the work as his deputy for a share of the fees.[35]

Another relatively modest office in the provinces was that of the Distributor of Stamps for a particular district. This has attracted more attention than most such positions, because one of the Distributors for many years was the poet William Wordsworth, and his experiences provide a good example of how such offices were filled and the work that they entailed.

Wordsworth was the second son of an attorney in Cockermouth on the edge of the Lake District. Early in 1812, when he was just over 40 years old, he recognized that his private income was insufficient to support and educate his family, and that his writing was not going to fill the gap. He had neither the qualifications nor aptitude for any particular profession, gentlemanly or otherwise, but he had the support of Sir George Beaumont, a well-known patron of the arts who had already given him a small property at Applethwaite, near Keswick, in 1803. Even more importantly he had the goodwill of Lord Lonsdale, the greatest magnate in the north-west of England. (Lonsdale had already made amends for the chicanery of his cousin and predecessor in the title, who had effectively defrauded the Wordsworth family of about £10,000, debts accumulated by Wordsworth's father when he was the older Lonsdale's agent.)

In February 1812 Wordsworth swallowed his pride and approached Lonsdale, asking for his assistance in securing a position, 'the duties of which would not call so largely upon my exertions as to prevent me from giving a considerable portion of time to study'. He justified this applica-tion by referring to Lonsdale's 'attachment to Literature and by the particular marks of kindness with which you have distinguished me', and it was supported (possibly without Wordsworth's knowledge) by a letter from Samuel Rogers the influential London poet and banker.[36]

Lonsdale replied that there were no suitable positions available at the moment, although it would probably have been more accurate if he had said that those positions which were vacant had already been promised to others. However, he assured Wordsworth that he would endeavour to find something for him and asked – very delicately and through Beaumont – if Wordsworth would be willing to accept £100 a year to help cover his immediate needs. Wordsworth was too proud or too shrewd to accept the pension – once granted, his claims to a job might never have reached the head of the queue – but he visited Lowther Castle and established cordial personal relations with Lonsdale. The peer was 13 years older than Wordsworth, and the tact and consideration with which he treated the poet were both commendable and rather surprising, especially as Wordsworth's own politics differed considerably from those of Lonsdale and the government.

Some months later, in the autumn of 1812 Lonsdale approached Lord Liverpool, the new Prime Minister, asking if the government might give Wordsworth a pension – something which Wordsworth would then have been willing to accept. However, the pension fund was already fully committed and Liverpool was unable to promise anything. Lonsdale soon found an alternative, and rather better, solution. The current Distributor of Stamps for Westmorland was growing old and incapacitated and was expected to retire soon: Lonsdale promised Wordsworth the post when it became vacant and renewed his offer of £100 a year in the meantime, and this time Wordsworth accepted. It is striking proof of the way government appointments were made that Lonsdale felt free to make such a promise when he had no official position in the Treasury, and his only relevant office was as Lord Lieutenant of Westmorland. He was, however, a strong supporter of the government and the dominant landowner in Westmorland, and so the patronage of the government to offices in the county passed through his hands – an arrangement that was so well understood that it did not produce comment or require explanation.

The old Distributor of Stamps retired in March 1813 but continued to receive £100 a year from his successor for the next few years as an unofficial pension. The office was no sinecure, although equally it was not a full-time position. As Distributor of Stamps, Wordsworth was responsible for collecting stamp duty on all legal papers, licences, pamphlets, newspapers, insurance policies and similar documents used in his district. The stamps were sold through sub-distributors scattered through the county – generally respectable shopkeepers in each of the market towns. Wordsworth's task was to supervise these sub-distributors and to tour his district, collecting the fees and forwarding them to London. Most distributors did this quarterly, but Wordsworth obtained permission to make a single annual collection. (The sub-distributors probably liked this, for it meant that they retained the government's money in hand for longer, but it increased the sums involved if they defaulted or absconded.) Wordsworth was required to keep precise and reliable accounts of all the transactions, and as this level of accounting was rather too demanding, he sensibly hired a trained clerk, John Carter, who acted as his secretary and accountant, while working in the garden at Rydal Mount in his spare time. Carter remained with the Wordsworths for 40 years, copying letters and poems as well as accounts, although his 'unprincipled conduct' in jilting one of the maids made him unpopular with Mary and Dorothy for some time.[37]

Wordsworth found that he quite enjoyed the work and responsibility of his office. He made his annual tour in November and delighted in the beauty of the countryside through which he travelled. He took care in selecting new sub-distributors, and on at least one occasion rejected a candidate proposed by Lonsdale's son on the not unreasonable grounds that enquiries showed that the man concerned had expensive habits and an unreliable character, leading Wordsworth to fear that he would not resist the temptation of helping himself to the public money that passed through his hands. Instead he appointed 'Mr Richardson the Tobacconist, who has property at Pooley Bridge, a regular and well-disposed man'. The ownership of property both suggested respectability and offered some security in case the man did defraud the government. There was also at least one case where a sub-distributor got into serious financial difficulties and was arrested for debt, and Wordsworth was forced to have all his possessions sold – a less enjoyable responsibility but not one which he could avoid. According to his biographer, he was 'strictly punctual; careful of the interests of his sub-distributors and of himself; quick to note any injustice arising out of the execution of wills; and very ready to combat official red tape. He urged on his "subs" the necessity for accuracy in their accounts, "even to farthings, as the board notice the most trivial errors".'[38]

The office was worth around £400 a year, a commission of 4 per cent on all the stamps sold. However, when the pension for Wordsworth's predecessor and John Carter's salary were deducted, Wordsworth probably only cleared half that sum. Still, £200 a year was a very significant and welcome addition to the family's income, and it increased when Wordsworth secured several neighbouring districts as well. The benefit of this additional work was reduced by two sharp cuts in the duties levied, the result of radical pressure in Parliament to reduce the size of government in the 1820s. Even more concerning was the campaign by Joseph Hume – one of the most active, if not the most talented or respected, of the radicals in Parliament – to award all positions such as Distributor of Stamps by public tender to the lowest bidder. Hume attacked Wordsworth by name in the Commons, accusing him of treating the office as a sinecure, and managed to procure a select committee to inquire into such appointments. The injustice of this attack, and the prospect of having to travel to London and give evidence to a hostile parliamentary committee, caused Wordsworth great anxiety and distress, and he presented Lonsdale with a detailed defence of his conduct, but Hume's attention soon wandered on to another outrageous instance of the waste of public funds, and the committee left Wordsworth alone, relieved but sore, and without the opportunity publicly to clear his name. He continued to perform his duties conscientiously until 1842 when he resigned his office in favour of his son, who had been sub-distributor at Carlisle for some years.[39]

A career in government service had many advantages for a younger son, especially if he could find an office as well suited to his tastes and habits as the Distributor of Stamps was to Wordsworth. But procuring such an office was not easy and almost invariably depended on a close connection to someone who was either the dominant local magnate or influential on the national stage. Most gentlemen had some connection – either by family or friendship – with a Member of Parliament or a peer, but this was not enough to give them a realistic chance of securing anything more than a clerk's position in a government office, if indeed it stretched that far. Wellington had failed to gain a civil office in Ireland in 1795 despite his brother's close friendship with the Prime Minister and the Foreign Secretary; and in 1813 he could not procure a position – even one worth only £200 a year – for his putative son, or at least not without waiting more than a year. Some politicians were more adept and successful at playing the patronage game than Wellington and Lord Wellesley – Buckingham was a master – but even so they faced far more claims than they could hope to satisfy, and had to make hard choices, disappointing more clients than they pleased. Most young gentlemen looking for a career were more inclined to seek an opening in the navy or the army rather than the civil side of government, especially during the long war with France, when opportunities were plentiful and glory was in the air.

CHAPTER NINE

THE NAVY

Young Gentlemen at Sea

FOR MANY BOYS GROWING up in England in the eighteenth century the Royal Navy was immensely glamorous, the object of intense fascination. Naval heroes such as Drake, Hawke, Anson and Rodney were widely celebrated in popular songs, cheap broadsheets, chapbooks, memorabilia and even pub signs. There was almost universal agreement that the navy was Britain's own particular strength, and that unlike the army, the navy defended the country and promoted trade without threatening traditional English liberties. Even in peacetime there were naval exploits to capture the imagination, such as Captain Cook's voyages of exploration, which made him a celebrity not only throughout Britain, but across all Europe. Boys were captivated by stories – fictional, semi-fictional and true – of life and adventure on the high seas, most notably by *Robinson Crusoe*, which found a wide and appreciative audience throughout the eighteenth and nineteenth centuries.

A career at sea, especially in the navy, appeared exciting, romantic and desirable; and there were numerous cases of young boys either running away to sea or demanding that their parents allow them to join the navy. Matthew Flinders and Lord Cochrane both overcame their father's opposition and joined the navy; while Francis Austen, William Light and Frederick Marryat successfully urged their parents or guardians to allow them to follow their inclination. Of course, not all boys joining the navy did so with eager enthusiasm, but of all the careers open to young gentlemen, this was clearly the most popular with the boys themselves, at least until Wellington's victories in the Peninsula allowed the army to claim a share of the limelight.[1]

Many parents favoured the navy as a career for their younger sons on more pragmatic grounds. It was traditional, patriotic and thoroughly respectable; it took boys when they were young – usually 13 or 14; and it was cheap, with no need to pay school fees or to purchase a commission, as in the army. The parents or friends of a young gentleman sent to sea would still normally give him an allowance, usually between £30 and £50 a year, although some young midshipmen were forced to live on nothing other than their pay and rations. This allowance might be a considerable drain on the resources of a poor clergyman or half-pay army officer with a large family, but it was still one of the most affordable ways of establishing a boy in a suitable career. It was also a particularly tempting solution for the parents of a wild or troublesome youth, who might hope that his high spirits and abundant energy could find a useful outlet aboard a man-of-war.[2]

Recent research by Evan Wilson has shown that only about one fifth of all naval officers came from the landed gentry and nobility; a second fifth had fathers who were themselves in the navy; and most of the remainder came either from the professions or from the world of commerce, although this last category ranged from small shopkeepers to wealthy merchants. As expected, very few came from humble backgrounds outside the navy and most of these remained stuck in the lowest ranks or were only given a commission at the very end of their career. In other words, naval officers were drawn from the same classes of society as clergymen and lawyers, although they had a rather higher proportion of fathers engaged in commerce than the clergy. Naval officers were also much less cosmopolitan than their crew: most came from England and especially southern England, with the southwest (Devon and Cornwall), Kent, Hampshire and London all being overrepresented, reflecting the location of the principal naval bases and the tradition of seafaring in these parts of the country.[3]

The most common way for a boy of good family to join the navy was as a 'servant' to the captain or, less frequently, to one of the other officers on board. Every captain was entitled to have four such servants for every hundred members of his crew – and a ship of the line might have a crew of seven or eight hundred. Some of these would actually be servants, older men with no expectation of promotion, but more than half were embryo officers who would remain under the captain's authority for at least six years. The official designation of these boys varied often with bewildering rapidity: any one might be a 'servant', a 'volunteer', a 'midshipman', a 'master's mate', or an 'able seaman', without this greatly affecting his role or life on board, although collectively they are best described as midshipmen. The captain was responsible for supervising their education and welfare and would, ideally at least, see that they gained a thorough knowledge of seamanship and navigation. He would also – again ideally – provide an example of how to manage the crew, maintaining authority with little resort to harsh discipline, and ensure that his midshipmen acquired the manners and general knowledge that befitted their future position as officers and gentlemen.[4]

The appointment of such boys was entirely at the discretion of the captain, and captains prized the privilege highly. Young relatives had an obvious claim on such patronage, and so did the protégés of patrons, senior officers and other men of influence. The connection could be quite tenuous: the young Matthew Flinders was introduced to Captain Thomas Pasley by his cousin Henrietta, who was governess to Pasley's children; while William Light found a place under Captain Charles Cunningham thanks to the recommendation of his guardian's son, who was the vicar of Hoxne in Suffolk, near Cunningham's home. Unlike most forms of apprenticeship captains did not charge the parents of boys a premium for taking their sons off their hands, although it is said that there were cases in which inconvenient tradesmen's bills, especially in dockyard towns, disappeared at the same time that the son or nephew of the tradesman was taken on board.[5]

A few boys entered the service through the Naval Academy at Portsmouth, which had been established in 1729 with the intention of providing better educated, more rounded, officers. The Academy had not been a great success – captains feared that it would encroach upon their patronage, and there were rumours of idleness, bullying and debauchery, although modern scholars have come to view these reports with considerable scepticism. Francis Austen joined the Academy in 1786 when he was just short of 12 years old, a small boy, full of energy, courage and liveliness, but also intelligent and with a warm heart. He was one of a dozen new pupils that year, although when his brother Charles followed in 1791, there were only three others in his class. Mr Austen paid £50 a year for each of his sons to attend the Academy, and it proved a useful way for a gentleman with no personal connections in the navy to get his sons into the service. Francis in particular thrived at the Academy, and won high praise for his aptitude, character and behaviour, so impressing Sir Henry Martin, its governor, that he became Francis's first patron.[6]

One great advantage of the Academy was that it softened the blow of parting for both parents and child: sending a son there was no worse than sending him to any other school, while if he went straight to sea it might be many months or even years before the parents would see him again – a time of real perils and immense change which the parents could only dimly imagine. Leaving home to go to sea the young boy would enter a completely foreign world. If he had not grown up near a port he might be unfamiliar with the sight of a warship. One officer wrote:

> never shall I forget the overwhelming and indefinable impression made on my mind upon reaching this wonderful and stupendous floating structure. The immensity of hull, height of the masts, and largeness of the sails, which had been loosened to dry, so far exceeded every anticipation I had formed, that I continued, unmindful of what was going on in the boat to gaze on her in dumb amazement, until awakened from my stupor by the coxswain, who now gruffly exclaimed, 'Come, master! come! mount a'reevo, 'less you mean to be boat-keeper'.[7]

Life on board lacked the restraint and decorum of a parsonage schoolroom or family parlour, and a new recruit was often disconcerted by his shipmates who were seldom interested in putting him at his ease. James Anthony Gardner recalled that

> I was shown down to the starboard wing berth. I had not been long seated before a rugged-muzzled midshipman came in, and having eyed me for a short time, he sang out with a voice of thunder: 'Blister my tripes – where the hell did you come from? I suppose you want to stick your grinders (for it was near dinner-time) into some of our à la mode beef'; and without waiting for a reply, he sat down . . .

While another young man recalled that at first he did not know if this new world was inhabited by devils or spirits, 'All seemed strange; different language and strange expressions of tongue, that I thought myself always asleep or in a dream, and never properly awake'.[8]

There is a detailed account of the experiences of a typical young midshipman in a burlesque poem, *The Adventures of Johnny Newcome in the Navy* by Alfred Burton, published just after the war in 1818 with 16 colour plates by Thomas Rowlandson. The poem begins with Johnny returning home from school. His father, a worthy clergyman, had always intended that he should go to university and study for either the Church or the law, but the local bank had recently failed, and the vicar had lost so heavily that he had been forced to sell the advowson that he had intended for his son in order to make some provision for Johnny's younger sisters. There was no longer even sufficient money to support Johnny while he went to university. Fortunately the local squire had some influence in the Admiralty and his nephew was a naval officer, Captain Dale of HMS *Capricorn*, and he offered Johnny a place on board. And so Johnny joins the navy, not from any hankering for glory or love of the sea, let alone patriotism, but on the purely pragmatic grounds of financial pressure and the ability of a local connection to help him onto the first step of the ladder. Many a gentleman's son began their career just like this, with their father gratefully seizing whatever opportunity came their way to settle their son.[9]

Johnny's father accompanies him to Sheerness and they meet Captain Dale, who impresses them with his good manners and air of calm authority.

Johnny then goes on board where the First Lieutenant hands him over to the Master's mate, with instructions to 'steer him clear of tricks and danger'. But the mate comments 'Boy! you're in my charge, a sort of prisoner at large, wid all your sorrows, all your care before you – like a young small Bear!'

The mate takes Johnny below where he is greeted with much mirth and raillery by 'a dozen men and boys, all full of mischief, glee and noise'. The scene was – or at least it appeared to Johnny – one of the utmost chaos and confusion. He is then summoned to take supper with the captain, and when he returns all appears quiet, with the other boys and young men feigning sleep while they watch him. Johnny undresses, puts his clothes on top of his chest, and, as he has done all his life, kneels down to say his prayers:

> The Sentry rubbed his eyes, and stared,
> And wondered so, he was half scared;
> The Mids, who watched him like a cat,
> Could not conceive what he was at;
> Thus to kneel down, beneath their gazes!
> They thought he must be mad as blazes!
> And softly from their hammocks stealing,
> Formed in a ring as he was kneeling;
> So mute, he never heard them tread,
> Nor saw them, till he raised his head.

They mocked and teased him, then leapt back into their hammocks – but when he attempted to follow suit, he naturally fell out:

> He flew clean over t'other side;
> And out he rolled, midst peals of laughter,
> With bed and bed-cloaths rolling after.

So he spreads his bedding on the deck and manages to fall asleep, whereupon his young messmates pull his mattress from under him, and in the process knock his head against a post. Seeing two midshipmen laughing at his plight he attacks them; one retreats, but the other 'who fancied John a chicken, stood out, and promised him a licking', but John emerges triumphant from the scuffle and is left alone for the rest of the night.[10]

Johnny wakes next morning to find that all his clothes and the key to his chest have disappeared, and to make matters worse orders have been given for the ship to prepare to sail. Amid all the bustle which ensued he eventually finds his clothes – shoved into the cook's unlit oven and fortunately undamaged – dresses in haste, and makes his way on deck where he very sensibly manages to keep out of the way. The ship makes sail and Johnny begins to feel queasy and then ill. He consults the doctor who, with a serious demeanour, advises him that the only cure is a combination of salt water and pork fat, which his fellow midshipmen prepare for him, with the inevitable result that he is violently sick.

> Johnny's exquisite distress
> Afforded fun for all the Mess.

He finally lies on the lockers, convinced that he is dying and wishing nothing more than that he could get off the ship. The captain's clerk suggests that he make a will – Johnny has nothing to leave, but is persuaded to dictate a dying letter, and only the laughter of all around makes him realize that he is being teased again.

The motion improves, Johnny recovers and slowly begins to gain his sea-legs and his confidence, feeling that although he had been a fool he will not be tricked again – but of course he is, repeatedly, until he slowly becomes more wary and his shipmates tire of the game.[11]

Such teasing was common, an initiation through which almost all young midshipmen were forced to pass, although its character, duration and severity varied considerably, both from ship to ship and according to the individual. Some boys were particularly vulnerable, and excited the cruelty of their tormentors. Others were better able to deflect attention and escaped relatively lightly. A good captain might do much to prevent teasing going too far, but even more important was the character of some of the petty officers and older midshipmen with whom the new recruit would spend every hour of his day. Frederick Marryat, who served in his youth on the *Impérieuse* under Lord Cochrane and who went on to write a series of successful novels with naval settings, was emphatic on the evils of bullying: 'At the period at which I entered the service, there was no species of tyranny, injustice, and persecution, to which we youngsters were not compelled to submit from those who were our superiors in bodily strength.' Marryat went on to praise William Napier, one of the senior midshipmen on board his ship, who was as benign as he was strong, and who did something to restrain bullying by others while commanding universal respect. Nonetheless,

> [i]n those times the ordeal of a midshipman's berth was severe, and too often the effect of its tyranny was demoralizing; for those who suffered when weak, waited with impatience for the development of that physical power which would enable them to tyrannise in their turns, and retaliate upon others the injustice to which they had been forced to submit. Might was right in the most extended sense of the phrase; and it was indeed rare to find one like Napier, who, with power to insure despotism, was so magnanimous as to refrain from exercising that power except in the cause of justice.[12]

Still, it must be said that most other accounts – including Burton's poem – do not paint quite such a dark picture. Unofficial but condoned violence there certainly was: Johnny Newcome was tied to the rigging until he promised the topsail men some grog which was regarded as their rightful privilege, and he was held down and beaten harshly when he inadvertently spoiled his messmates' dinner. These experiences left him sore and unhappy for a day or two, but they did not alienate him from his fellows for long, and he was not the target of sustained systematic bullying of the kind Marryat suggests was common. Indeed, Johnny gradually found his feet, made friends and learnt to enjoy his new life, and this was probably how most midshipmen fared after a rough beginning in which they longed for home and often wished that they had never been born.[13]

Despite the colourful phrase commonly attributed to Winston Churchill that equated the traditions of the Royal Navy with 'rum, sodomy and the lash', there is no reason to believe that Johnny or any other young midshipman was in much danger of being buggered on one of his Majesty's warships. Sodomy was almost universally regarded with abhorrence and was punished with great severity, whether the perpetrator was an officer or an ordinary seaman. Captain Henry Allen of H.M. Sloop *Rattler* was hanged from his own yardarm in 1797, despite his rank and excellent social connections. But detailed research in all the surviving records strongly suggests that it was also extremely rare: difficult to conceal and deeply unpopular with other members of the crew who were most unlikely to turn a blind eye. No doubt a few cases were successfully hushed up, and officers left the service under a cloud of suspicion, but such instances were very uncommon, and contemporaries would have been amazed at the idea of it being widespread, let alone a tradition.[14]

Some steps were taken to protect young midshipmen from the full harshness of life at sea. On ships of the line the junior midshipmen slept and messed in the gunroom under the supervision of the gunner, who was usually a steady, mature petty officer, who had enough authority to maintain order and – it was hoped – enough maturity not to abuse it. The gunroom was in the stern on the lower deck: it had windows which might, in particularly favourable weather, be opened, and so it was not quite as dark as most of the interior of the ship, although the air would seldom have been remotely fresh.[15]

When a midshipman had been aboard for a year or two and was about 14 years old he moved down to the after cockpit on the orlop deck, below the waterline forward of the mizzen mast. This was the main midshipmen's mess, shared with some other figures of ambiguous status including the schoolteacher, the captain's clerk and the assistant surgeons, and might be home to between 20 and 30 men and boys. It was a dank, dark, unwholesome place, reeking of tallow candles, bilge water, the smell of tobacco, the ooze from casks of food in the hold, wet clothes and the men themselves. In this tiny, crowded space the midshipmen ate, slept, boasted, quarrelled, wept and – in theory – studied, without peace or privacy, and with only the dignity they could summon up from within themselves. Not all midshipmen were youngsters, and there were mature men, perhaps in their forties, who lived in the after cockpit. In general these adults probably added a steadying influence and restrained the worst excesses of adolescent cruelty, but the authority they exercised was direct and not particularly gentle, while their manners may occasionally have lacked a little polish. On some ships the president of the mess – invariably an older man – would drive a fork into the table or a bulkhead when the first watch was set (about eight in the evening) as a signal for the young midshipmen to disappear, either to their hammocks or to some hidey-hole of their own, and to leave the mess and its conversation to the grown-ups. To be allowed to stay after 'the fork' was another step forward in the young midshipman's career, comparable to the move from the gunroom to the cockpit.[16]

The conditions in which midshipmen lived and the food they were issued were little different from those of the ordinary sailors. Edward Thompson, writing in the 1750s, declared that he and his fellows were 'bedded worse than hogs, and eat less delicacies'. In 1802 the young Basil Hall wrote home to his father (who was a baronet and an MP) that 'At breakfast we get tea and sea-cake: at dinner we have either [salt] beef, pork or pudding'. Many midshipmen filled letters home with pleas for hampers of food, with George James telling his mother that the failure of a hamper to arrive before his ship sailed was 'a most serious loss I can assure you upon honour'. Frequently the midshipmen clubbed together to purchase additional supplies of fresh food and even wine, and it was a dark day when these supplies were exhausted on a longish cruise and they were forced to rely entirely on their rations. Occasional invitations to dine at the captain's table, or with the lieutenants, were more than welcome, unless nervousness overcame appetite, in which case there was all too much to regret and the mockery of comrades to endure.[17]

The crew, including the midshipmen, were divided into two (occasionally three) watches, spending four hours on, four hours off, with two short two-hour shifts to break up the pattern. At sea, no one ever got a full night's sleep, and this, along with frequent cold and the constant dampness of salt water, was probably the greatest hardship of a sailor's life. The actual work on a man-of-war was considerably lighter than on a merchantman, which carried much smaller crews and where all possible space was kept for the cargo.

The crew of any ship shared the space with a large number of other living creatures: rats were always present and always hungry, and there were numerous insects and bugs depending on the climate. There were also the cattle, sheep, goats, hens, geese and even pigs that were carried on board to provide some fresh food, especially on longer voyages: and each animal required a supply of fodder, so that ships were often very crowded when they left port. Individual messes might purchase and bring on board ducks, hens and other smaller animals for the pot, and also pets including most commonly parrots and monkeys. The contribution of such animals to the sounds and smells of the ship in calm, cool weather would have been considerable, let alone in the tropics or in a gale.[18]

As the young midshipman became familiar with the new world in which he lived he would be expected to learn his trade and gradually take on responsibilities. Some lessons were simple and practical: how to tie knots and splice ropes, to climb aloft or take his station in action; others more academic, such as mathematics and navigation. Larger ships often, but not always, carried a schoolmaster, but he tended to be a despised figure, lacking the authority to command respect or even the attention of his pupils. Far more important were the officers and petty officers: the captain first and foremost, but also the lieutenants, the master and specialists like the boatswain and gunner who each had much to teach a midshipman. A great deal was learnt by doing and observing rather than by formal instruction: by supervising the setting, reefing or furling of the sails; attending small arms training and watching gun drills; patrolling below decks to ensure that there were no naked flames, and by assisting in casting the log and lead lines when the speed and location of the ship were regularly checked. Different ships brought out different qualities, and there were stereotypes that had at least some basis in fact: the midshipmen in ships of the line were thought to be sophisticated but hard-swearing; those in little sloops and brigs, slovenly and ill-bred; while those in frigates liked to regard themselves as an elite, smart, audacious and eager to seize every opportunity to distinguish themselves.[19]

During his years at sea every midshipman became familiar with the dangers and discomforts of bad weather. A storm might blow itself out in a few hours, but a succession of autumn or winter gales could last for days or even weeks. In these conditions the crew would have to put up with wet clothes and cold food, slippery decks and going aloft in high winds, while the masts swayed wildly and the rain and sleet pelted them and the ropes tore at their hands. It was difficult for the captain to take accurate observations when the sky was covered with clouds and the deck was constantly pitching, so that navigation became a matter of guesswork and the ship might stray many miles off course. Every year the navy lost ships that foundered in storms or were wrecked on the rocks, and often the entire crew perished with their vessel.

At the other extreme were the doldrums – extended periods of calm weather, usually close to the equator – where the ship could make no progress and might even be carried in the wrong direction by the current, while the captain anxiously calculated how long supplies of food and water would last. Boredom could become a real problem and the officers set about making work to occupy the crew in the hope of preserving morale, for idle hands soon led to murmuring and discontent. Here, even more than in the midst of a storm, a midshipman might feel intensely homesick and regret his vocation.[20]

Illness was another peril, with the Caribbean and East Indies notorious for exacting a high death toll, although even in the Mediterranean a midshipman was at some risk of yellow fever, the plague or malaria, while the disastrous Walcheren Expedition of 1809 showed that the Low Countries could be as dangerous as anywhere in the tropics.

A harsh or unsympathetic captain, or another officer with a personal animus, might easily make a midshipman's life miserable whether through undeserved punishments or simply with a sarcastic tongue. James Anthony Gardner's recollections are full of the portraits of such officers, for example the captain of the *Salisbury* who 'was a very good man at times, but often harsh and severe in his remarks. He once told me (and I have never forgotten it) I would never be fit for anything but the boatswain's storeroom.' And Alfred Burton's hero Johnny Newcome ends up quitting the navy when the good Captain Dale dies in the West Indies and his successor proves a tyrant who persecutes Newcome and finally disgusts him with the whole service.[21]

The most essential requirement for any midshipman or naval officer was courage in action, and this could be tested very early in his career. Lieutenant Paul Nicolas was a 16-year-old officer in the Royal Marines on his first voyage when his ship was heavily engaged at Trafalgar. During the approach to the enemy line under heavy fire,

[m]y two brother officers and myself were stationed, with about thirty men at small arms, on the poop, on the front of which I was now standing. The shot began to pass over us and gave us intimation of what we should in a few minutes undergo. An awful silence prevailed in the ship, only interrupted by the commanding voice of Captain Hargood, 'Steady! starboard a little! steady so!' echoed by the master directing the quartermasters at the wheel. A shriek soon followed, – a cry of agony was produced by the next shot, — and the loss of the head of a poor recruit was the effect of the succeeding, – and, as we advanced, destruction rapidly increased. A severe contusion in the breast now prostrated our Captain, but he soon resumed his station. Those only who have been in a similar situation to the one I am attempting to describe, can have a correct idea of such a scene. My eyes were horror-struck at the bloody corses [*sic*] around me, and my ears rang with the shrieks of the wounded and the moans of the dying.

At this moment seeing that almost everyone was lying down, I was half disposed to follow the example, and several times stooped for the purpose, but . . . a certain monitor seemed to whisper, 'Stand up and do not shrink from your duty!' Turning round, my much esteemed and gallant senior [Lieutenant John Owen] fixed my attention; the serenity of his countenance and the composure with which he paced the deck, drove more than half my terrors away; and joining him I became somewhat infused with his spirit, which cheered me on to act the part it became me.[22]

Once actively engaged with the enemy, 'Our energies became roused, and the mind diverted from its appalling condition'. Nicolas proved himself in his first battle, but young men whose courage faltered when put to the test were not irretrievably disgraced: they would lose some standing with their comrades and superiors, but they would generally have a second chance and often found this easier than the first. Only a habitual or extreme coward would be cast aside as worthless, but bravery in action was essential if a man was to gain a good reputation and make progress in his career in the navy.

Not all the time was spent at sea, indeed in the Seven Years' War ships of the Royal Navy were in harbour more often than not, although this would change in the Revolutionary and Napoleonic Wars with their close blockade of the French coast. The time spent in port was usually much more relaxed and pleasant than time spent at sea: there was still work to be done, for ships in port were generally being repaired, restocked and refitted for duty, but most of the crew could sleep through the night and the captain and other officers could relax their vigilance and their close eye on the weather. These interludes also gave midshipmen a better opportunity to pursue their more academic studies than when on the rolling ocean, although there were the temptations of the town to be resisted, not to mention the distractions of the comings and goings of other ships in the harbour. Recognizing this difficulty, it became quite common for a midshipman who had spent two or three years at sea to be sent to a proper school specializing in mathematics for a year or even longer, while nominally remaining part of the crew of a ship that stayed in harbour as a guardship or one that was being refitted.[23]

A young man would seldom spend his entire career as a midshipman in the same ship or under the same captain. Sometimes a ship would be taken out of service for repairs or to be broken up and the crew would be paid off, and sometimes the midshipman would request a transfer to another ship, either because he disliked the captain or another officer or objected to the duty on board. James Anthony Gardner made several such voluntary transfers in order to avoid serving in the West Indies, even though he knew that such wilfulness did not help his career.

I was recommended to Captain Hutt, commanding the *Queen*, 98, fitting in Portsmouth Harbour, by my late friend Admiral Bourmaster, and joined her early in 1793 . . . The *Queen* being ordered to the West Indies, I made (like a fool) application to Captain Bourmaster to get me removed to the *Berwick*, 74, commanded, by Sir John Collins, Knight, fitting for the Mediterranean, to which place I wished much to go. After long consideration he agreed to my request; at the same time observing that I stood in my own light and that I would lose promotion taking such a step. This I well knew; but the hatred I had for the West Indies made me blind to my own interest. When I saw Captain Hutt I found it no easy matter to bring him to my way of thinking, and it was a long time before he would give his consent . . . However, he gave me my discharge and a very good certificate, shook hands with me and wished me success.[24]

A promising young midshipman might be moved from ship to ship in order to give him a range of useful experience or to take part in an interesting voyage, as when Nelson's uncle ensured that he was sent on a voyage of arctic exploration in 1773 at the age of 16. At the other extreme there were some midshipmen whom any captain was glad to palm off onto another ship, such as 'thick-headed, unfeeling, unprofitable Dick Musgrove' who, we are told, spent no more than six months under the command of Frederick Wentworth.[25]

Many captains, and even admirals, followed with interest the careers of 'their' midshipmen even when they were no longer under their immediate command, giving advice, patronage and support, and in return expected that the midshipmen would reflect credit on them by doing well. Late in his career Nelson wrote to Charles Connor, one of his young men,

Dear Charles, As Captain Hillyar has been so good as to say he would rate you as Mid., I sincerely hope that your conduct will ever continue to deserve his kind notice, and protection, by a strict and very active attention to your duty. If you deserve well, you are sure of my assistance . . . And as you from this day start in the world as a man, I trust that your future conduct in life will prove you both an Officer and a Gentleman. Recollect that you must be a Seaman to be an Officer; and also that you cannot be a good Officer without being a Gentleman.[26]

There was more to being an 'Officer and a Gentleman' than seaman-ship, naval tactics and the handling of the crew. Nelson advised the father of one of his midshipmen that 'Dancing is an accomplishment that prob-ably a Sea Officer may require. You will see almost the necessity of it, when employed in Foreign Countries.' And he added, 'French is abso-lutely necessary', although it was a language which he never fully mastered himself. At Naples he arranged for his midshipmen, including the young William Hoste, to visit the King's museum and the ruins at Herculaneum, and introduced them to Lady Hamilton. Nor was this concern for the wider education of his protégés unique to Nelson. In the East Indies Admiral Peter Rainier advised his nephew and namesake to take full advantage of the opportunity to mix in company with Lady William Bentinck, the wife of the Governor of Madras, to improve his manners and address, so as to avoid the 'clownish awkwardness . . . [to] which Young Gentlemen of our profession are so particularly liable' on first being introduced into the 'enlivening society' of ladies. And he, too, urged the necessity of knowing how to dance, and recommended that his nephew read Chesterfield's letters, the *Spectator* and 'other popular authors of good fame' so that he acquired 'a competent knowledge of the English Language and a facility for expressing yourself with propriety in writing and in conversation'. At a more prosaic level, William Cathcart, a well-born midshipman on the *Alcmène* in 1798, urged his brother to pay attention to writing and arithmetic before joining him, but added,

[t]here are also some other trivial things, which seem very trifling to you, but without which you will appear ridiculous; such as carving meat. How ridiculous it is to see a man, in the character of a gentleman, who, if he is required to cut up a fowl, cannot do it; and what unnec-essary confusion it gives him to excuse himself![27]

Some midshipmen gained the disapprobation of their superiors on more substantial grounds than their inability to carve a roast chicken. In 1785 Captain Cuthbert Collingwood, who went on to be one of the finest and most careful officers in the service, wrote: 'The boy Pennyman is quite a plague, a dirty lad without one good quality to set against a great many bad ones. He is the dirtiest, laziest boy in the ship, gets drunk, neglects his duty, learns no one thing, and has been in every mess in the ship and has been turned out of them all'. Nelson himself complained that of some of the boys from aristocratic families that he had on board, 'Honourables will always do as they please. Orders are not for them – at least I never knew yet one who obeyed.' And Lord St Vincent told George III – who had sent his own son William to sea as a midshipman years earlier – that 'this vast overflow of young nobility in the Service makes rapid strides to the decay of Seamanship, as well as subordination'. At the other end of the chain of command, the seamen on board greatly resented some midshipmen who presumed too much upon their authority or who were incompetent. In one case a group of seamen protested against a 15-year-old who had struck them with a rattan cane, telling him firmly that 'we would not be treated in such a manner by a boy'; while in another the 'stoborness' of a midshipman in ignoring the advice of more experienced sailors led to the loss of four lives when his jolly boat was capsized.[28]

But the greater number of midshipmen gained maturity as well as experience from their years of service. The sister of two naval officers, who had seen them both grow from boys to young men, gives us a warmly affectionate picture of a fine young midshipman visiting his family on leave.

William was often called on by his uncle to be the talker [at dinner]. His recitals were amusing in themselves, but the chief object in seeking them, was to understand the recitor, to know the young man by his histories; and he listened to his clear, simple, spirited details with full satisfaction – seeing in them, the proof of good principles, professional knowledge, energy, courage and cheerfulness – everything that could deserve or promise well. Young as he was, William had already seen a great deal. He had been in the Mediterranean – in the West Indies – in the Mediterranean again – had been often taken on shore by the favour of his Captain, and in the course of seven years had known every variety of danger, which sea and war together could offer. With such means in his power he had a right to be listened to . . .

[Listening to William, Henry Crawford] longed to have been at sea, and seen and done and suffered as much. His heart was warmed, his fancy fired, and he felt the highest respect for a lad who, before he was twenty, had gone through such bodily hardships, and given such proofs of mind. The glory of heroism, of usefulness, of exertion, of endurance, made his own habits of selfish indulgence appear in shameful contrast; and he wished he had been a William Price, distinguishing himself and working his way to fortune and consequence with so much self-respect and happy ardour, instead of what he was![29]

CHAPTER TEN

THE NAVY
Promotion and Employment

FRANCIS AUSTEN, WHO WAS at least in part the model for William Price in *Mansfield Park*, left the Portsmouth Naval Academy at the end of 1788, when he was still just 14 years old. He was an active and highly intelligent boy, small for his age and slightly built with dark eyes and curly dark hair. In later life he was known for never hurrying his speech and for his great precision, but in his teens he radiated great energy held in check by even greater self-discipline. The two and a half years he had spent at the Academy had given him a good grounding in the academic side of his profession, together with some practical knowledge, but it was time that he experienced life at sea. He was fortunate in being appointed to the frigate *Perseverance* (36 guns) under Captain Isaac Smith, who had sailed with Cook on two of his great voyages of exploration, studied navigation on board the *Endeavour* and the *Resolution*, and been the first European to set foot in Botany Bay. Smith was an excellent officer who valued Francis's education at the Academy and encouraged him to develop a wide range of skills – not just practical seamanship and fitting in with the other members of the crew, but also nautical drawing, navigation and hydrography, which were to prove useful to Francis in his later career, when he made charts and sketches of the South China Sea.

In early February 1789, a few weeks after Francis joined the ship, the *Perseverance* sailed for India as part of a small squadron under Commodore William Cornwallis. It would be almost five years before Francis returned to England or saw any member of his family, and before he sailed Mr Austen gave him a long, humane and intelligent letter of advice, which Francis kept with him for the rest of his life. The voyage to India took seven months with brief calls at Madeira and Tenerife and three weeks at Rio de Janeiro. An accident at Ramsgate had cost the squadron its consignment of sauerkraut and as a result the crews suffered a good deal from scurvy, while some of the salt pork and beef was in poor condition, having been in barrels for five or six years, being left over from the American War. It was an age of austerity, and public money could not be wasted.[1]

A few months after the squadron reached India, war broke out with Tipu Sultan of Mysore, and the Royal Navy imposed a blockade on the Malabar Coast in order to prevent any French ships arriving with arms and military supplies. The squadron divided its year between Madras, on the east coast, and Bombay, on the west coast, to reduce the danger posed by the monsoons and other bad weather. Francis also took part in surveys of the Indian coast, the Andaman Islands and the Malay Peninsula, making several voyages across the Bay of Bengal. A good deal of time was spent ashore and Francis recalled that he saw 'a great variety of places', and that Smith kindly introduced him to many important people – the Austen family had close connections to Warren Hastings which would have opened many doors in India at this time.[2]

In November 1791 Francis Austen was transferred from the *Perseverance* to Commodore Cornwallis's flagship the *Minerva*. This was a very promising step for a midshipman who (including his time at the Academy) was beginning to approach the six years which was the minimum time he must serve before he could be considered for promotion to lieutenant. Serving under the immediate eye of a superior officer – the commodore or admiral commanding on a foreign station – gave a talented young man the chance he needed to impress. Cornwallis believed that India presented particular dangers to young men, complaining that 'nothing is heard of but [the] *making of money*'. He strongly opposed the prevailing corruption in the supply of provisions to his ships, and his intolerance of abuses may have influenced Francis, who developed a rather stern, unbending integrity which, combined with strong religious faith and an earnest, evangelical outlook, made him somewhat stiff and not especially popular.

After serving on Cornwallis's flagship for just over a year, Francis passed his examination at the very end of 1792, and a few days later he was formally made a lieutenant by being given a position on the armed brig *Dispatch* (12 guns) under Captain John Whitby. He was still only 18 years old, well under the minimum age of 20, although his was not the only case in which the rule was either circumvented or ignored. Such rapid elevation for a young man without any significant naval patrons is strong evidence of the favourable impression Francis had made upon Smith, Cornwallis and the other officers under whom he had served. His elevation was probably not viewed with unalloyed joy by his fellow midshipmen on Cornwallis's ship, for they were all engaged in a race for promotion, and an advantage to one was a disadvantage to all the others. Still, Francis recalled that they summoned up the good grace to congratulate him with every appearance of cordiality and sincerity – something which he felt reflected equally well on them and on himself.[3]

Gaining the rank of lieutenant was a crucial step in the career of any naval officer: it was the culmination of all their previous service and indeed of their adolescence, marking a coming of age professionally as well as personally.[4] The historian Charles Consolvo has made a detailed study of the careers of a group of 225 naval officers who passed their lieutenant's exam in 1790: of these, most were aged between 20 and 23 at the time; only a few were below the minimum age, and a small minority (just over 10 per cent) were over the age of 25. There were two stages to promotion: an examination by three senior officers, and then employment. At the examination the candidate was expected to produce certificates from the captains under whom he had served testifying to his professional skill, diligence, sobriety and obedience. He would take with him his personal logbooks for the ships in which he had sailed, and evidence of both his age and the length of his service in each rating. His examiners might test his knowledge on the different methods of fixing longitude, on holding course in the face of shifting winds, on how to handle the ship in a storm, or in areas with strong currents or tides, and how to handle misfortunes such as the loss of a rudder or a mast. They might also ask about the calculation of high water in an unfamiliar port, how to prepare a ship for action, or details of gunnery. Some examiners were thorough, asking difficult, detailed questions, others were more relaxed, and occasionally candidates were given only the most superficial test before being passed, but this was usually a much more rigorous test than those in other parts of society in the eighteenth century.[5]

Passing the examination did not in itself secure promotion to the rank of lieutenant: that depended upon being given a lieutenant's position on a ship or some other command reserved for an officer of that rank. Francis Austen was extremely fortunate that he received his position – and with it his commission as lieutenant – within a few days of his examination. Of the officers in Consolvo's study a sizeable number received their commission within months, and more than half got it within two years of passing their exam, but about one third waited more than three years, with one unfortunate (or perhaps unworthy) man waiting eight years as a senior midshipman. These were officers who were examined several years before the war with France broke out, and waiting periods probably fell in the early years of the war as the number of positions available in the navy grew rapidly as it mobilized and then expanded. However, the supply of experienced midshipmen soon exceeded the demand for new lieutenants again: captains were unrestrained in the number of boys they took on board, the wastage rate (whether from death or disenchantment) was not sufficient, and the navy began to have a considerable glut of qualified men impatient to be given a lieutenant's command. No solution for this was ever found, and the problem grew worse as the war went on. By 1813 there were almost 2,000 midshipmen who had passed their exam but who had yet to receive their promotion because there was no vacant position in which to employ them. This was William Price's predicament until Henry Crawford intervened and secured his employment and commission through the influence of his uncle Admiral Crawford.[6]

In the eighteenth century it was not uncommon for midshipmen who had passed their lieutenant's exam but not received their commission, or for lieutenants who had no current naval employment, to spend some time on a merchant vessel to gain experience and their livelihood. The Admiralty disapproved of naval captains doing so, and thought that lieutenants should not look lower than a position as mate on an East Indiaman, but otherwise made no objection. George Elphinstone served in the navy from 1761 to 1766 when he took a position as third mate on the *Triton* East Indiaman, commanded by his brother – and he rose, as Admiral Lord Keith, to hold some of the most senior and important commands at sea in the later years of the war against Napoleon. Even more remarkably, James Burney, brother of the novelist Frances Burney, sailed on an East Indiaman in 1770 as an ordinary seaman, but taking some goods with him in the hope of trading them at a profit. This did not impede his subsequent career, and within weeks of his return to England he was dining with his father and the First Lord of the Admiralty together with Captain Cook and Sir Joseph Banks, and succeeded in securing a place on Cook's next voyage of exploration. Social barriers appear to have become rather less permeable during and after the war, but there were more numerous opportunities in the service of the Crown for unemployed naval officers, including the Transport Board, the Sea Fencibles (a naval equivalent of the militia), the Impress Service and commanding prison and hospital ships, although these sometimes proved to be a cul-de-sac from which an officer might struggle to escape.[7]

Lieutenants on a ship of the line experienced much better conditions than the midshipmen in the cockpit. They lived in the wardroom, a space measuring about 35 feet long by 18 feet wide with little compartments on each side made out of deal or canvas that gave a degree of privacy, although an officer usually had to share his cabin with a large, heavy cannon. Still, there was room to swing a hammock which one officer praised warmly: 'a more luxurious bed cannot be conceived . . . snugness is consulted in its dimensions; and, by its swinging with the ship's motion, sleep is promoted'. The wardroom was at the stern, which in a sailing ship was always an advantage, under the captain's cabin (although in a three decker, an admiral might have his quarters on the intervening floor). When the ship was primed for action, all the partitions would be pulled down and the guns made ready, but for most of the time a lieutenant had at least the semblance of a room of his own.

In the centre of the wardroom ran a long narrow dining table. There might be six lieutenants on a 74-gun ship of the line, and they would share the wardroom with the captain of marines, his two lieutenants, the master, the surgeon, the purser and the chaplain, although these last four were only warrant officers. There were not sufficient cabins for all of these in the wardroom; the purser and surgeon would sleep down in the depths of the orlop deck, while the others had small cabins below or beside the wardroom. Considerable ceremony was observed at dinnertime, with each officer attended by a boy servant (or, in the case of the officers of the marines, by a private marine), and the food was purchased from a mess fund to which all the officers subscribed. In one instance this cost £60 a year: the food was quite good, but the officer (a chaplain) who gives us these details resented the cost of the wine, which was of poor quality. He thought most of his fellow officers only agreed to the expense from a sense of what was generally acceptable, and he led the resistance when a lieutenant with private means suggested raising the ration to a pint a day from half a pint. Most of his fellow officers were not well off and they ended up agreeing with the chaplain that it was not worth it 'to expend at least £40 for the nauseous purpose of swilling six glasses of sloe-juice mixed with sugar-of-lead'.[8]

The first lieutenant presided over the mess table, and there were frequent quarrels between officers which sometimes led to duels (always fought ashore, when they were fought at all). One captain advised his officers to abstain from any discussion of shipboard questions at the dinner table in an attempt to avoid disputes, but it was a forlorn hope to think that quarrels could be prevented between young men forced to live and work together in such close proximity. Sometimes more junior figures – midshipmen or master's mates – were invited to dine in the wardroom, invitations which were accepted with alacrity; while on special occasions the captain might be invited, although these meals tended to be rather stiff and formal unless the captain was particularly good at setting everyone at their ease.[9]

——✦——

Francis Austen served as a lieutenant for just over six years. He was only aboard the *Dispatch* for just over a month before she was laid up for repairs and he was transferred back to the *Minerva* as a supernumerary lieutenant for a few months, and was then allowed to return home to England as a passenger on an Indiaman. He landed at Southampton on 13 November 1793 and the following day was at Steventon, no doubt receiving a warm and excited welcome, not least from his 17-year-old sister Jane, whose feelings may have resembled those which she gave to Fanny Price in *Mansfield Park*. The long war with Revolutionary France had begun that February, but it seems that Francis was able to spend Christmas at home with his family, and did not receive a new appointment until the following spring. He was made first lieutenant aboard a 16-gun sloop, the *Lark*, which was employed in patrols in the Channel and North Sea, carrying messages and acting as a reconnaissance vessel. It was not a particularly exciting position, and Francis was soon eager for a change. A succession of brief postings followed: the *Andromeda*, a 32-gun frigate in May 1795, and then two large ships of the line, the *Prince George* (98 guns) and the *Glory* (98 guns) before the end of that year. In the spring of 1796 he was appointed third lieutenant on the *Shannon*, another frigate, but he detested his captain, Alexander Frazer, and spent the summer ashore and on half-pay rather than continue serving under him. That autumn he was appointed to the *Triton* (32 guns) under Captain John Gore who had been lieutenant on the *Perseverance* and whose ship was a happy one. Francis remained on the *Triton* for just over a year, while it was attached to the Channel Fleet, and took part in the capture of five French privateers and some other small vessels – none of which was of any great value. He was then transferred again – this time possibly without any request being made – to the *Seahorse* (38 guns) which was sailing to the Mediterranean, where he was shifted to Admiral Lord St Vincent's flagship the *London* as first lieutenant, and in line for promotion.[10]

Most officers in the navy struggled to rise above the rank of lieutenant, but all hoped to do so, first gaining the rank of commander and being employed in command of troopships or small warships such as the *Lark*, and then that of post captain, which opened the door to employment in command of a smart frigate or a mighty ship of the line. Such promotion depended on opportunities at sea and influence, both with the Admiralty in London and with the admiral commanding their fleet or squadron. A few officers gained these crucial steps with almost indecent haste. Charles Paget joined the navy in 1797 when he was 12 and spent his six years at sea before being made a lieutenant, but it was then only four months before he was made a post captain at the age of 19, having been a commander, as well as a lieutenant, in the meantime. Nelson too had a full six-year apprenticeship before passing his lieutenant's examination at the age of 18 and being given a commission on the following day. A little more than two years later he was a post captain, even though his main patron, his uncle Captain Maurice Suckling, had died in the interim – something which suggests that real merit was as important as influence in his rapid ascent. An even more striking, and rather less justifiable, example was Thomas Cochrane, who went to sea at the age of seven in his father's ship, and who was not only made a lieutenant in 1805 at the age of 16, but was made commander and then post captain within a year.[11]

These examples of rapid promotion, and others equally remarkable, were well known to ambitious lieutenants, and naturally made them discontented when they were forced to spend long years of service before they secured even the hope of their next step. In *Mansfield Park* Jane Austen tells us that the newly promoted William Price was proud of his fine lieutenant's uniform, and greatly regretted the regulations that prevented him wearing it at Mansfield, but Edmund Bertram conjectured that

> before Fanny had the chance of seeing it, all its own freshness, and all the freshness of its wearer's feelings, must be worn away. It would be sunk into a badge of disgrace; for what can be more unbecoming, or more worthless, than the uniform of a lieutenant, who has been a lieutenant a year or two, and sees others made commanders before him?

It would not be unreasonable to suppose that these feelings reflected those of Jane's own brothers, and many other naval officers.[12]

However, the careers of Paget, Nelson, Cochrane and others were a misleading guide to the prospects for most lieutenants. Consolvo's study shows that a more typical officer had to wait eight years for promotion to the rank of commander, of which two years might be spent unemployed on half pay, even though this was the decade of the war with Revolutionary France, when the navy was extremely busy and opportunities for winning glory were unusually abundant. A further two years would elapse before a typical officer would be promoted to the rank of captain, by which time he was probably in his early to mid-thirties. By this standard, Francis Austen did better than most, although still not as well as some of his contemporaries, for he was made a commander at 24 and a captain at 26.[13]

In 1794 when Francis was aboard the *Lark* he had no real grounds to expect immediate promotion, but to improve his prospects he wanted to move to another ship where he might have a better chance of distinguishing himself. It was not uncommon to seek such a transfer, and the official process was well established: Francis would submit a formal letter applying for the transfer to his captain, who would then decide whether or not to forward it to the officer commanding the squadron or fleet. The senior officer would usually decide whether or not to grant the application, subject to the approval of the Admiralty, although he would sometimes leave the decision up to the Admiralty itself, perhaps including some observations of his own. The officer might also bypass his superiors and directly present the First Lord of the Admiralty with a formal memorial, outlining his own services and explaining what he wanted. There was no impropriety in such an approach, and some officers made regular applications direct to the First Lord.[14]

Any application to a senior officer or to the Admiralty was more likely to succeed if supported by someone of influence. The most valuable patrons at this point were generally senior naval officers who all existed in an intricate web of mutual obligations and favours, and who took for granted the virtues of assisting their friends' protégés. Admiral Pellew was unnecessarily explicit when he wrote to his friend Admiral Markham, a member of the Admiralty Board, 'Do me all the kindness for my son you can; I may live to return it to one of yours, for you see the wheel goes round and round'. Nelson took care to promote the grandson of the officer who had, many years before, promoted *him*, and within the service this was generally regarded as the right and proper thing to do: anything less would be ingratitude and neglect, provided that the young man receiving the favour was moderately competent. If he was not competent, Nelson would try to make some other, more suitable, provision for him; but in the last resort, it was better to give an unprepossessing officer the benefit of the doubt than to neglect an obligation, for if he proved really incapable he might be safely put ashore on half-pay. Admiral Collingwood, one of the most honourable men in the service, made Charles Haultain a lieutenant in 1806, even though he recognized that Haultain was 'as dull a lad as I ever saw', whose captain could not wait to be rid of him. Collingwood was not happy with the idea of advancing such a man, but in the end found that he could not refuse the request of old Admiral Roddam, even though 'my conscience reproved me when I promoted him'.[15]

The families and connections of successive First Lords of the Admiralty and of the Secretaries to the Admiralty naturally did extremely well, and while Admiral Lord St Vincent complained vehemently of Lord Spencer's abuses when Spencer was First Lord, his own conduct in the office was every bit as bad. But the value of political influence fell sharply with distance from the Admiralty. Lord Sydney was a member of the cabinet and father-in-law of Lord Chatham, the First Lord from 1788 to 1794, yet in 1793 he complained that

[t]he getting a Lieutenant on board a Flag Ship is by no means an easy thing, and it is an object, which as yet I have never been able to attain, though I have been in pursuit of it frequently . . . Lord Chatham has uniformly refused me on that head, though I have every reason to believe, that he wished to oblige me.

Ordinary Members of Parliament or peers of the realm carried little weight in the Admiralty unless they had some patronage of their own

with which they could reciprocate any favour granted; and it is significant that William Price owes his promotion, not to Sir Thomas Bertram
MP, but to Admiral Crawford who had approached the Secretary to the
Admiralty through a mutual friend 'whom the Admiral had set to work
in the business'.[16]

When Francis Austen wanted to transfer from the *Lark* in 1794 he had
no senior naval patron to whom he could apply to support his application. But he was not totally without connections: his father wrote to
Warren Hastings, and Hastings wrote to Admiral Affleck, whom he had
known well in India and who was now one of the Lords of the Admiralty
working with Chatham. Affleck replied, saying that the final decision
rested with Chatham, but that he would put in a good word when he
could; however, before this could result in anything, Chatham was moved
from the Admiralty and Affleck lost his influence.[17]

A decade later, in 1805, when Francis was already a captain, he made
another attempt to employ outside influence, on this occasion in order to
be given a frigate with a roving commission which might enable him to
capture some valuable prizes. Through his brother Henry he secured a
letter from Lord Moira to Admiral Nelson asking him to further Francis's
views, although Nelson's reply was not encouraging, suggesting as it
did that Francis should have been thinking more of defeating the
French and less of capturing prizes. The letter also represents some of
the murkier waters of patronage and influence, for Moira was receiving
considerable loans from Austen & Maude at the time he was writing
the letter, and Francis was not just Henry's brother but also his partner,
having invested in the bank. None of the persons involved would ever
have made any explicit connection between these several facts – the pride
and self-esteem of them all benefited from the pretence that there was no
link whatever between the loans and the letter – but the line separating
favours between friends and outright corruption was sometimes more
than a little blurred.[18]

Moira's influence had been more useful on an earlier occasion, when a
series of letters from him to two successive First Lords of the Admiralty
(St Vincent and Melville), may have been responsible for Charles Austen's

promotion from lieutenant to commander and receiving the command of a sloop on the Bermuda station.[19]

But what any ambitious officer most needed was the support of a senior naval officer, especially one with influence with the Admiralty. Francis Austen was extremely fortunate when, in 1795, he was introduced to Captain James Gambier, the nephew of Admiral Sir Charles Middleton, Pitt's favourite naval administrator. Gambier himself was just beginning the first of three stints as one of the Lords of the Admiralty, and would go on to hold several important commands including the Channel Fleet from 1808 to 1811. He was also an evangelical and this formed a tie to Francis which strengthened their friendship. Francis later wrote that Gambier 'soon became his warm friend, and never lost sight of his Interest, nor neglected any opportunity of forwarding it to the utmost of his power'. It was due to Gambier that Francis had moved so frequently from ship to ship in the 1790s as they looked for a path to promote Francis; and when Francis finally sailed for the Mediterranean in the *Seahorse* in 1797, he carried a letter from Gambier to Admiral Lord St Vincent recommending him. St Vincent responded by appointing Francis first lieutenant on his flagship the *London* (98 guns), and at the end of 1798 he was promoted commander and given his own ship, a 24-gun sloop, the *Peterel*, with a crew of 121. Jane Austen reacted to the news by telling Cassandra, 'There! – I may now finish my letter, & go hang myself, for I am sure I can neither write nor do anything which will not appear insipid to you after this'.[20]

All senior officers in the navy developed a following of junior officers to whom they gave their patronage. Some of the advantages they received in return were intangible: there was real satisfaction in finding and assisting in the rise of an able young man, and in seeing the service and the country benefit as a result. It was flattering and creditable to be – even partly – responsible for making a Nelson, a St Vincent or a Pellew, while the promotion of protégés has always been a favoured means of demonstrating power in large organizations. And if the protégé proved to be successful he might be able to return the favour in years to come for a fresh generation of young men.

There was one way that an officer without influence could obtain rapid promotion (and which would also assist any officer): this was to distinguish himself in action, especially in a great battle or in the capture of a superior enemy ship. Even being present at a battle accelerated an officer's ascent up the promotion ladder, but young men dreamed of the chance of outstanding services that were recognized with immediate promotion. In 1813 Provo Wallis was second lieutenant of the *Shannon* when she had her famous engagement with the *Chesapeake*. The first lieutenant was killed and Captain Broke badly wounded, so that Wallis was left in command and brought the captured American ship safely to harbour in Halifax. For this he was immediately promoted to the rank of commander, and despite the general slowdown of promotion in the years after the war, he was made captain in 1819, and ultimately rose – thanks to longevity rather than favour or even ability – to become Admiral of the Fleet in 1877, and survived until 1892.[21]

The problem with such 'hero' promotions was that they usually happened only once in an officer's career, and so their beneficiary, if he lacked influence, might still get stuck, only at one rung higher on the ladder than if he had not distinguished himself. Take the example of John Hindmarsh who, in 1798, was a 14-year-old midshipman on the *Bellerophon* at the Battle of the Nile. The *Bellerophon* was anchored close to the massive French flagship *L'Orient* and suffered severely under her broadsides while fighting back furiously. Soon the *Bellerophon* was dismasted and had sustained heavy casualties while Hindmarsh was left the only officer on the quarterdeck when Captain Darby was wounded and taken below. He observed that *L'Orient* had caught fire, and on his own initiative ordered that the cable be cut, set the spritsail, and got the *Bellerophon* away shortly before *L'Orient* blew up. Captain Darby gave Hindmarsh full credit for saving the ship and all her crew, introducing him to Nelson and St Vincent. He was too young to be promoted immediately, but in August 1803, when still only 18, he received his lieutenant's commission and a desirable posting to the frigate *Phoebe*, on which he was present at Trafalgar. But despite years of capable service his career stalled, for Hindmarsh had no influence – his father was nothing more than a gunner on the *Bellerophon* – and he was only promoted commander in 1815, and did not receive a ship of his own (the 18-gun *Scylla*) until 1830. Even so Hindmarsh's exploit in 1798 counted for something, and may have helped him secure his appointment as the first Governor of South Australia in 1836, and Lieutenant-Governor of Heligoland in 1840, at a time when there was keen competition even for such desolate positions.[22]

For those unfortunate officers who lacked influence to assist their rise and who never had the opportunity to distinguish themselves in battle, the prospects were bleak: such men in Consolvo's sample took between 20 and 30 years to attain the rank of commander, and in many cases this was only granted as an immediate prelude to retirement. Those who survived and remained on the active list waited a further 10 or 15 years to be made captains, by which stage they were long past being usefully employed at sea. Some of these men were probably excellent officers, but influence and merit were not totally separate. A promising young officer like Francis Austen found a patron at least in part because he appeared capable and likely to reflect credit on Gambier, if Gambier helped him. The use of influence and patronage in promotion was not as blind or partial as it appears – rather it delegated informal power to large numbers of officers across the navy to select and encourage young men of ability, as well as those who had other – possibly less worthy – claims to advancement. And certainly the record of the navy throughout the Revolutionary and Napoleonic Wars does not suggest that able men struggled to rise to prominence or that the most important positions were reserved for those with political, family or other claims, but who were incapable of commanding at sea.[23]

The 20 months that Francis Austen commanded the *Peterel* in the Mediterranean were among the happiest and most successful of his whole career. He captured or destroyed 40, mostly small, French and Spanish vessels, accumulating a fair sum in prize money, and was particularly proud of his success against a group of three French ships: *La Ligurienne*, *Le Cerf* and *Le Joillet* on 21 March 1800 – he captured the first and drove the other two ashore, without losing a single man, and despite the fire of French shore batteries. He took part in the blockade of Genoa and received the thanks of Lord Keith for maintaining his post less than three miles off the mole head despite difficult weather. He was present, but not engaged, when Keith captured three French frigates and two brigs that had escaped destruction of their fleet at the Nile and were attempting to make their way back to France. And he subsequently joined Admiral Sir Sidney Smith off the coast of Egypt where he prevented the French from taking possession of a Turkish ship of the line that had run aground – an action which the Turks recognized by presenting him with a handsome sabre. He also carried dispatches from St Vincent to Nelson, and acted as a scout ship for the main fleet. Then, on 20 October 1800, putting into Rhodes, Francis learned that he had been promoted the previous May to the rank of captain, and so was superseded. Two days later he left the *Peterel* and returned to England in the New Year and helped his parents and sisters move from Steventon to Bath.[24]

The rank of commander, which Francis held while he was on the *Peterel*, had only been instituted in 1794 and was generally reserved for officers commanding small ships – sloops, brigs and the like – or troopships. On board they were always referred to as the captain, for they were the captain of the ship, even though they did not yet hold the rank of captain in the navy. During the course of the long war the first lieutenants on larger ships began to be given the rank of commander as well, reflecting the navy's inability to find employment in appropriate positions for all the capable and deserving officers in the service. Between 1795 and 1812 commanders wore a single epaulette, on the left shoulder; in 1812 they were allowed two epaulettes and lieutenants gained one, on the right shoulder.[25]

Franc 's next concern, after having returned home, was to gain further e iployment without spending too long on half-pay. This was a problem that increased with rank: in 1810 just 60 per cent of the lieutenants in the navy were employed on active service, but that compared favourably to 44 per cent of commanders and only 41 per cent of post captains.[26] Even allowing for some who were too old or ill to serve, that left a great many more captains than commands open to them. Fortunately Francis was not left languishing for too long ashore: before the summer was out Gambier had again come to his aid, appointing Francis as his flag-captain on the *Neptune*, the large, 98-gun battleship, from which Gambier commanded one squadron of the Channel Fleet. This appointment lasted until the Peace of Amiens, just over a year later, led to another period on half-pay ashore. With the renewal of the war in 1803 Francis received only the rather undesirable command of a body of Sea Fencibles at Ramsgate: it is probably significant that Gambier was out of the country at the time, having been appointed Governor of Newfoundland in 1802. The one consolation of this disappointing episode in his life was that it was in Ramsgate, in February 1804, that Francis met his first wife, Mary Gibson. This may have signalled a change in fortune, for in May 1804 Francis was appointed flag-captain to Rear-Admiral Sir Thomas Louis on the *Leopard* (50 guns) off Boulogne. The *Leopard* was an obsolete, unhandy, ship, and Francis was probably glad to move from her to the *Canopus* (80 guns) to which he and Louis transferred in the spring of 1805. The *Canopus* was a modern French ship that had been captured at the Battle of the Nile, and the move was the result of Louis – and Francis – being detached to join Nelson and the Mediterranean fleet. They took part in the pursuit of Admiral Villeneuve to the West Indies and back, but were not present at Trafalgar, having been detached to get fresh water and supplies at Gibraltar.

Missing Trafalgar was the greatest disappointment of Francis's career, and he was quite open in explaining his reasons in a letter to Mary Gibson (by then his fiancée). Writing before the battle had taken place, he expressed his anxiety at the possibility of not being able to take part.

As I have no doubt but the event would be highly honorable to our arms, and be at the same time productive of some good Prizes, I shall have to lament our absence on such an occasion on a double account, the loss of pecuniary advantage as well as professional credit. After having been so many months in peril of constant and unremitting fag, to be at last cut out by a parcel of folks just come from their homes, where some of them were sitting at their ease the greater part of *last* war, and the whole of *this*, till just now, is particularly hard and annoying.

And when the news of the battle arrived he added:

Alas! my dearest Mary, all my fears are but too fully justified. The Fleets have met and after a very severe contest, a most decisive Victory has been gained . . . Seventeen of their Ships are taken and one is burnt, but I am truly sorry to add that this splendid affair has cost us many lives, and amongst them a most invaluable one to the Nation, that of our gallant and ever to be regretted Commander-in-Chief, Lord Nelson, who was mortally wounded by a Musket shot, and only lived long enough to know his Fleet was successful . . . there is not an Admiral on the list so eminently calculated to command a Fleet as he was; I never heard of his equal, nor do I expect again to see such a man – to the soundest judgment he united prompt decision, and speedy execution of his plans and he possessed in a superior degree the happy talent of making every class of persons pleased with their situation and eager to exert themselves in forwarding the public service.

Returning to his own position he continued, 'I cannot help feeling how very unfortunate we have been to be away at such a moment . . . to lose all share in the glory of a day, which surpasses all which ever went before, is what I cannot think of with any degree of patience . . .'. He recognized that Mary might not entirely sympathize with him on this, but could not restrain his feelings:

You perhaps may not feel this quite so forcibly as I do, and in your satisfaction at my having avoided the danger of battle, may not much regret my losing the credit of having contributed to gain a Victory; not so, myself; I do not profess to like fighting for its own sake, but . . . I shall ever consider the day on which I sailed from the Squadron as the most inauspicious one of my life.

Taking part in the great triumph would have brought promotion, prize money and opportunities for better employment: these were real, practical benefits which Francis valued and regretted, but more significant was the loss of fame and glory, together with the sense that, having put in months and years of the hard work which laid the foundations for the victory, he had missed out on the bloody but memorable consummation.[27]

Francis got a taste of battle a few months after Trafalgar when the *Canopus* took part in the destruction of a French squadron at St Domingo in the West Indies on 6 February 1806. Of the five French ships of the line present, three were captured and two others driven ashore and burnt, while the British suffered lightly, losing no ships and fewer than four hundred casualties in the whole squadron. The victory was marked by the thanks of Parliament, a small gold medal and a memorial vase from the Patriotic Society of Lloyds: it was some consolation, but not much – St Domingo was not Trafalgar and Admiral Duckworth was no Nelson.

Francis also missed out on his other great wish: to be given a frigate and a roving commission. Although Nelson had not encouraged his hopes, he had written to the Admiralty recommending Francis, and the letter had been favourably considered, which was not surprising as the First Lord at this time was Sir Charles Middleton, now Lord Barham, Gambier's uncle. Orders were issued that Francis be given the *Acasta* as part of a complicated sequence of moves, but the opportunity to implement these orders never arose and Francis remained on the *Canopus* until June 1806, by which time there had been a change of government, Barham had left office, and Gambier was temporarily without influence. Francis then spent some months ashore and without a command, but may not have been unhappy to do so as it gave him the opportunity to marry Mary Gibson on 24 July 1806.[28]

After nearly a year ashore Francis received a new command. It is quite likely that this was the result of Moira's influence, for he was a member of the cabinet at the time, and Jane Austen had told Cassandra only a month before that the First Lord (Thomas Grenville) had promised Moira that 'Capt. A. should have the first good Frigate that was vacant' – although she then added that as he 'has since given away two or three fine ones, [Francis] has no particular reason to expect an appointment now'. Nor was the new command the frigate Francis wanted, but rather the *St Albans* (64 guns), a ship more than 40 years old and now obsolete, neither fast enough to keep pace with a frigate nor powerful enough to take its place in the line of battle. Still, there were many such ships in the navy, performing necessary if unglamorous tasks including guarding convoys of merchantmen and troop transports. Francis spent three years as captain of the *St Albans*, escorting convoys as far as St Helena and the Cape of Good Hope on their way to India and bringing homeward bound Indiamen back again, protecting the troopships that carried vital reinforcements to Sir Arthur Wellesley that reached him in Portugal just in time for the first British victory of the Peninsular War at Vimeiro in 1808, and – a few months later – helping to evacuate the tattered remains of Sir John Moore's fine army after it had been almost destroyed in the Coruña campaign. In the spring of 1809 the *St Albans* sailed for China, escorting merchantmen, arriving in Canton on 18 September and remaining there until the following March, while putting the interval to good use in preparing charts of the vicinity and approaches. On the return voyage, Francis was responsible for the safety of 13 Indiamen whose combined cargo was said to be worth nearly £2 million, and the East India Company expressed its gratitude for the success of the voyage with a bonus of just over £2,000. Other rewards for these voyages included four Egyptian-style candlesticks given to Francis by the captains of the merchantmen belonging to another convoy in thanks for 'his gentleman-like conduct to themselves' as well as his care and attention to the convoy – recognition that he clearly valued, regarding the candlesticks as an heirloom.[29]

In the autumn of 1810 Francis Austen left the *St Albans* at his own request to have a couple of months at home with his family before taking up a new, plum appointment which Gambier had secured for him. This was the position of flag-captain on the *Caledonia* (120 guns), the largest and most admired ship of the line in the navy, only two years old, and the pride of the Channel Fleet. Unfortunately in May 1811 Gambier was superseded in command of the Channel Fleet by Sir Edward Pellew, and the command of the *Caledonia* was too valuable a piece of patronage to be left unaltered by the change. For a moment it looked as if Francis might be sacrificed completely, but he was soon given a new ship, the *Elephant* (74 guns) which had been Nelson's flagship at Copenhagen in 1801, and had since been refurbished. This was a good command, and Francis remained in her until the end of the war. His first year in the *Elephant* was spent in the North Sea, blockading the Dutch coast and forming part of the fleet that was watching the naval squadron Napoleon was building at Antwerp and in the Scheldt. In late 1812 he was given a more enjoyable task, as commodore commanding a small squadron (the *Elephant*, the frigate *Phoebe* and the sloop *Hermes*) which was ordered to sail off the Azores and look out for American privateers. They had some success, capturing the American *Swordfish* after a hundred-mile chase, and Francis then spent a few months ashore, before the *Elephant* was ordered to the Baltic to escort convoys. He had trouble with his crew, finding them disobedient, drunken and neglectful, and had to resort to numerous floggings to maintain discipline, something which appears to have damaged his reputation both with his immediate superior and the Admiralty. This may have been the reason why Francis quickly withdrew his application for a further command when he signed off the *Elephant* in May 1814 at the end of the war.[30]

Francis Austen had just turned 40 when he came ashore in 1814, and he spent the next 30 years unemployed, living on half-pay and the income from his investments. His wife Mary died in 1823 leaving him with 11 children, and five years later he married Martha Lloyd who had long been a close friend of his sisters. His official services were recognized by a CB in 1815 and a KCB in 1837, while he continued to gain seniority in the navy, becoming a rear-admiral in 1830 and a vice-admiral in 1838. In 1844, the year after Martha died, he was appointed Commander-in-Chief of the North American and West Indies Station, raising his flag in the *Vindictive* (74 guns). This command lasted four years with Francis dividing his time between Halifax, Bermuda and the Caribbean, avoiding both the West Indian hurricanes and the worst of the northern winter. He returned to England in 1848 and was promoted Admiral of the Red. He died on

10 August 1865 at the age of 91, having two years before reached the most senior rank in the navy, Admiral of the Fleet.

—————

The life of a captain at sea, especially aboard a ship of the line, was markedly different from those of junior officers. While they were all crowded together, lacking any solitude or real privacy, the captain might be quite lonely, isolated from his officers by the dignity of his position. He generally dined alone, while even when he dined with his officers – perhaps once or twice a week – such meals were usually rather formal and stately occasions, with everyone on their best behaviour. When he walked on the quarterdeck, everyone who was not fully engaged in necessary work would move to the other side (port or starboard) to give him space, and if he left the ship for any reason, in port or to go aboard another vessel, the event would be marked with considerable ceremony, as would his return. No one would ever open a conversation with him unless he first invited them to do so, and everyone would remove their hat before speaking to him. These customs deliberately enhanced his authority, and it required a touch of Nelson's genius to simultaneously maintain this dignity and gain the affection of the crew, both officers and men.[31]

The captain's cabin was spacious even on a frigate. It was at the aft end of the quarter-deck, under the poop-deck, so that he had only to leave his quarters to be immediately beside the ship's wheel with the compass binnacle in front of him: this was the post from which he commanded the ship, whether in action, in bad weather or feeling her way through unknown and difficult waters. His quarters usually included a dining-room, a drawing-room, and one or more sleeping cabins, with the great windows to the stern giving plenty of light; some captains went to considerable expense fitting out these quarters with good furniture and extensive collections of books or scientific instruments. Sometimes his wife or daughter sailed with him. When Francis Austen sailed to Bermuda on the *Vindictive* in 1844 he was accompanied by his two unmarried daughters, Cassandra and Fanny, who acted as his hostesses when he was entertaining as Commander-in-Chief in the West Indies and North America. The elder Miss Austen, then aged 30, was not popular on board, with one officer commenting that 'She is the Mistress of the Ship, influences the Ad[mira]l. in every way, and in fact, I *imagine* will soon be Commander-in-Chief'.[32]

That was in peacetime, but naval wives sometimes accompanied their husbands even during the war, although this was most commonly when moving from station to station rather than on all their voyages. Still, Mrs Croft was exceptional in the extent of her travels with her husband:

in the fifteen years of my marriage . . . I have crossed the Atlantic four times, and have been once to the East Indies, and back again; and only once, besides being in different places about home – Cork, and Lisbon, and Gibraltar. But I never went beyond the Streights [sic] – and never was in the West Indies. We do not call Bermuda or Bahama, you know, the West Indies.

She was also famously robust in her defence of the life she lived on board:

nothing can exceed the accommodations of a man of war; I speak, you know, of the higher rates. When you come to a frigate, of course, you are more confined – though any reasonable woman may be perfectly happy in one of them; and I can safely say, that the happiest part of my life has been spent on board a ship. While we were together, you know, there was nothing to be feared.

However, Admiral and Mrs Croft had no children, while Francis and Mary Austen had 11, of whom the first five were born between 1807 and 1814. However spacious the quarters, they were hardly ideal for a nursery on a ship of the line on active service.[33]

A captain's pay depended on the size of the ship he was commanding, but it was never high, although it did rise over the course of the war. In 1793 the captain of a sixth-rate ship (the lowest class of frigate) was paid eight guineas per lunar month or just over £109 a year: a figure which had doubled by 1815. The captain of a first-rate ship of the line such as the *Caledonia* – a class which was rare in the navy – was paid £28 per lunar month in 1793 and £32 4s in 1815: or £364 and £418 respectively a year. So by the end of the war most naval captains would have been paid something like £300 a year while they were actively employed. This was supplemented by significant allowances, but reduced by tax and some deductions. In 1814 *Steel's List of the Royal Navy* published a table calculating the sums an officer might expect to actually receive, with the pay of a captain ranging from £255 to £721 per annum, a commander £225 to £245 and a lieutenant between £100 and £120. Admirals did rather better, but their pay was still far from generous: including allowances a rear-admiral received gross pay of £823 a year, a vice-admiral £1,226 and a full admiral £1,670.[34]

These figures only applied to officers who were employed, and most naval officers spent a substantial part of their career ashore and on half-pay even during the war, while such fallow periods were naturally much more common and longer during the peace that began in 1815. Naval half-pay amounted to rather more than half the nominal pay of a serving officer, but did not include the same allowances: in 1815 captains received between £191 and £269 per year according to seniority, commanders £155 to £191 and lieutenants £91 to £127. It is noticeable that while the half-pay of a naval lieutenant was little enough to live upon, it amounted to very nearly as much as his full pay, and that the ratio dropped as the rank increased. The Admiralty also promoted large numbers of junior officers immediately before placing them on half-pay at the end of the war, in a quiet but very practical act of compassion that encountered far less opposition than any attempt to increase half-pay or introduce a retirement pension. Even an admiral could only afford to live modestly if he was entirely dependent upon his half-pay, which ranged from £456 for a rear-admiral to £766 for a full admiral. And while Jane Austen paints a most attractive picture of the happiness of Captain Harville's home in a lodging house at Lyme Regis during the winter, it is clear that the accommodation was confined and not of the best quality, and that it was not a household in which much extravagance could be contemplated except with alarm.[35]

No one grew rich on naval pay, but many hearts beat faster with the hope of making a fortune through prize money. George Perceval was 11 years old and had been at sea for just over a year including being present at Trafalgar when he wrote to his mother, Lady Arden, urging that his brother John follow him to sea: 'Tell him I think he had much better come and be a sailor [than join the army]. Tell him to look and see what Prize money I should get for that glorious day.' And many years later in his autobiography Thomas Cochrane, Lord Dundonald, wrote that 'The streets abounded with seamen eager to share in anticipated prize-money – for whatever may be the ideas of modern statesmen on this subject, prize-money formed then, as it will ever form, the principal motive of seamen to encounter the perils of war'. A few spectacular examples kept these hopes alive. In the very first year of the war, 1793, a Spanish galleon, the *San Iago*, had been captured carrying almost £1 million in silver, which led to awards of £30,000 to each of the four captains present and £50,000 to Admiral Lord Hood. (The case was complicated by the fact that Britain and Spain were not at war, but the *San Iago* had already been captured by a French privateer and was heading for a French port, an explanation which did not entirely satisfy the Spanish government.) A few years later, when Britain and Spain were at war, two more Spanish treasure ships were captured off Cape Finisterre: the admiral got £81,000, the captains (again there were four present) £40,000 each, masters and lieutenants received over £5,000 each, midshipmen and petty officers £790, and even ordinary seamen received £182. These distributions were in proportions laid down by law in 1708, but this was modified in 1808 to increase the share going to the seamen and junior officers. The rule was that all those ships within sight of the action had a share of the prize; disputes were common and in the case of smaller prizes prolonged proceedings in the prize-courts often consumed a substantial part of the value of the prize.[36]

As these examples suggest, those who benefited most from the prize system were a handful of admirals employed on particular stations who received a generous cut from the success of any officer serving under them. Admiral Lord Keith is said to have made £64,000 in less than two years in command in South Africa and India, and £177,000 between 1803 and 1806 when he commanded the North Sea fleet – and these were only two episodes in an exceptionally lucrative career. Sir Edward Pellew, another officer with a Midas touch, is said to have made a total of over £300,000 during the war, from a combination of prize money, convoying and other bonuses. And when Admiral Sir Peter Rainier died in 1808, he left one tenth of his fortune of £250,000 as a contribution towards the reduction of the National Debt, in gratitude for the opportunities he had been given commanding in the East Indies, where he 'acquired the principal part of the fortune I now have which has far exceeded my merits and pretensions'. But not all admirals in senior positions benefited to this extent: Collingwood commanded in the Mediterranean for four and a half years, ruining his health with the strain of an exceptionally demanding position, and he gained only about £28,000 in this period.[37]

Naval battles also brought material benefits both in prize money and in other rewards. Lloyds, the great insurer, made a collection among its members after each great victory, producing considerable sums to be distributed to the officers and men of the fleet: £21,000 for the Glorious First of June, £52,000 for Camperdown, £38,500 for the Nile, and £15,000 for Nelson's victory at Copenhagen. The East India Company also granted Nelson £10,000 after the Battle of the Nile, while Parliament recognized the exceptional importance of Trafalgar by voting a grant of £320,000, even though most of the enemy ships captured in the battle subsequently sank. Captains received about £3,300 each, while Nelson's brother – an obscure clergyman – was made an earl and granted £90,000 to purchase an estate and given an annuity of £5,000 to support the title.[38]

However, such successes were exceptional: fewer than half the surviving officers in Consolvo's sample took part in the capture of any ships or ports that yielded any prize money at all, while the average merchantman taken as a prize was worth only £2,500. (Privateers were even less valuable, barely half that sum, although their capture was much more beneficial to the nation.) It is not clear exactly how much prize money Francis Austen received in the course of his career: Brian Southam estimates that he received 'no more than a few hundred pounds', but if this is correct it is difficult to see how he could afford to become a partner in Henry's business in 1807, so the true figure may be considerably higher. Still, it is clear that only a tiny minority of officers in the navy made their fortune, whether through prize money or any other means, and that most ended the war with only modest savings with which to supplement their half-pay.[39]

If the rewards of service were generally meagre, the perils were considerable. Almost one in four of the officers in Consolvo's sample died within 10 years of being made a lieutenant, and four in ten died before the end of the war in 1815, with a mean age of 35. This is, as Consolvo acknowledges, rather higher than other estimates, but there is no doubt that being a naval officer was a dangerous occupation. Disease, accident and shipwreck, not enemy action, were the great killers, as was true of all wars until the advances of modern science and technology brought about a more satisfactory situation in the twentieth century.[40]

Once an officer was made a captain he rose effortlessly by seniority, so that if, like Francis Austen, he survived long enough he would become Admiral of the Fleet. However, most officers remained stuck in the lower ranks of the profession, waiting long years for promotion. In 1848 there were still some 3,500 officers in the navy who had served in the war, and only 254 of these were rear-admirals or above. Even this was far in excess of the navy's needs, and after 1815 it required exceptional influence at the Admiralty for a senior officer to be employed at all, whatever his ability, however distinguished his record, and however great his need for employment.[41]

At the conclusion of his study, Charles Consolvo outlines the career of a typical officer who was commissioned as a lieutenant in 1790. He would have been born in 1767 and entered the navy at the age of 13 during the American War as an officer's servant. He spent eight and a half years as a young gentlemen, or about one third of all the time he would spend at sea. He moved between ships quite frequently: serving on nine ships in this period, for an average of 11 months on each. He passed his lieutenant's exam in 1788 at the age of 22, but did not receive his commission until 1790 when he was 24. He spent six of the next eight years on full pay as a lieutenant, and was then promoted to commander, where he might spend another two years on active service; with a little good fortune he would be promoted captain in 1800. His subsequent career would probably include only seven years at sea and on full pay, so that even during the war he would spend half his time as captain ashore on half pay. He had a rather better than even chance of surviving the war (three in five did so), and a less than even chance of taking part in a major fleet action or even gaining prize money. Only one in three of the sample married – the same proportion that lived to be made an admiral (although of those who were married the proportion who were made admirals was two in three). He died in 1836 at the age of 69 having spent nearly two-thirds of his time in the navy on half-pay.[42]

By this standard Francis Austen did well, gaining his promotions more quickly than was to be expected, and being employed for a much higher proportion of the war years than most of his generation. However, it is natural for an ambitious man – and Francis was certainly ambitious – to compare himself, not to the average, but to the most privileged and successful of his contemporaries, and it is clear that Francis himself felt that his career had not been quite as successful as he had hoped, or felt that he deserved. The long years ashore after 1814 were probably quite happy, but it is noteworthy that his ultimate prosperity arose less from his naval service than the generosity of his aunt, with her gift of £10,000 when she decided to make his nephew James Edward, not Francis, her heir.

Francis owed his success as a naval officer in part to his own ability and in part to the influence of James Gambier, who was a far more effective patron than has sometimes been recognized. But even more important than Gambier was the simple, crucial fact that Francis was born in 1774 and entered the navy in 1786. Francis, like the officers in Consolvo's sample, was already well on his way when the long war with France broke out in 1793. This meant that he was promoted commander and then captain in the middle of the war, with years of active service ahead of him before the fall of Napoleon and the arrival of peace brought down the curtain. His service in these years was better than average, but not exceptional: he missed Trafalgar, but did take part in a major action; he took some prizes, but none of enormous value; and he spent much time on the dull, routine convoy work, but did receive a reasonable amount of recognition for it, and it was preferable to kicking his heels ashore. He was never shipwrecked or seriously ill, and he survived the war with his eyes and limbs intact, although his temper may have become a little brusque thanks to his years on the quarterdeck.

The prospects were much bleaker for the officers of a younger generation. A young lieutenant in 1813, such as William Price, might find employment for a couple of years until after the end of the war of 1812 and Napoleon's final abdication following Waterloo, but he would then most likely be placed upon half-pay, with an income far below what he needed, and little ability to improve his lot except by leaving the navy and choosing another career. The reduction of the navy after the war was drastic: on 1 January 1814 there were 713 ships in commission, four years later the number was 121, and yet even in 1814 there had been employment for barely half the officers on the active list. No one at the time knew, of course, that the peace would last for almost 40 years; and many young men held on in the hope that some fresh conflict would arise when their country would be grateful for their services. In the meantime they lived as economically as possible, which often meant with their extended family or on the Continent, and contemplated the possibility of making a new life in the colonies. Constant application to the Admiralty might result in a few years at sea on full pay, but as the years passed they grew old in their rank, and the Admiralty was aware of the need to introduce some new blood into the system to prevent the navy atrophying completely.

Men in their position could not afford to marry unless they or their prospective wife had considerable money of their own, or they were prepared to sacrifice all claims to gentility for themselves and their children. Some made careers in the merchant navy, others in the service of foreign powers including Egypt and the new nations of South America, while a few others became engineers and inventors of note. Many more found employment in the Customs Service, while others took to writing, with Frederick Marryat becoming one of the most successful and highly paid novelists of the day. More typical than Marryat was Lieutenant Francis Swaine Price who saw a good deal of service, being wounded three times including the serious wound he suffered at Trafalgar. That led to his promotion to lieutenant, but he lacked the influence to gain any further advancement, and in the 1820s he found a position as agent and manager of a small china clay railway that ran from St Austell to the coast at Pentewan, while remaining on the 'active' list and drawing his half-pay until he became a retired commander in 1839, having been a lieutenant for 33 years, 32 of them ashore.[43]

So much for an officer without influence, but even one with the best possible connections struggled to make rapid progress in the post-war navy. Richard Saunders Dundas was the second son of the 2nd Lord Melville, who in turn was First Lord of the Admiralty from 1812 to 1827 and again from 1828 to 1830. Born in 1802, Richard Dundas graduated from the Royal Naval College (as it had become) in 1817, and was promoted captain in 1824, and had far more than his fair share of time at sea and opportunities to take part in whatever operations the navy was undertaking, including experiencing some action in the First Opium War. Nonetheless he did not gain flag rank until 1853, when he was 51 and already older than Nelson had been at Trafalgar, and yet he was among the first of the post-war officers to be made an admiral.[44]

On the whole the navy was not a particularly rewarding career for most officers, even for the men of Francis Austen's generation. Life at sea, especially for a midshipman, was harsh, uncomfortable and dangerous, while there was only a slim chance of making a fortune or even of becoming sufficiently prosperous to be able to marry and support a family in the style of a gentleman unless they had some private means of their own. Yet some men found it extremely satisfying, relishing their time at sea while also enjoying enforced periods of leisure at home with their families. This was largely a matter of taste and temperament rather than patronage or connections: there were plenty of men of all ages and ranks for whom the sight of a proud man-of-war setting sail lifted their hearts and made them thank fate – or their parents – for preserving them from a life of tedium and dullness behind a lawyer's desk or in a counting house. Patriotism, the pursuit of glory and, at least during the war, the sense of performing an essential service, provided intangible rewards, while a naval officer had a respected place in British society which long continued to regard the navy as central to its identity.

CHAPTER ELEVEN

THE ARMY

YOUNG MEN LEFT HOME to join the army as well as the navy. They were older – usually in their late, not their early, teens – but the parting could be just as painful. Harry Smith wrote many years later:

When I first parted from my mother to join my Regiment, the French Army was assembled at Boulogne, and every day was full of news that the French were coming. We dined early that day, I and my father, who was kindly to accompany me to Brabourne Lees, in Kent. At dinner I held up manfully. Then I ran to the stable to part with a beautiful little horse I had reared almost from a foal – he was thorough-bred, and carried me hunting in such a style that no one could beat me. I threw my arms round Jack's neck, and had a good cry. I saw my poor mother observed what I had been doing, and a smile of approbation curled upon her placid lip. The awful moment now approached: the buggy was at the door. I parted with my dear brothers and sisters (five boys and five girls) tolerably well, my poor mother glad to observe in me a force of character which *she hoped* in greater and more eventful scenes I might evince. It came next to her turn. She seized me in her arms, and wept awfully. Suddenly, with an effort I shall never forget, her tears were dried, she held me at arm's length, and, gazing at me most intently, said, 'I have two favours to ask of you: one is that you never enter a public billiard-room; the next – our country is at war – if ever you meet your enemy, remember you are born a true Englishman. Now, God bless and preserve you, which I hope He will, and listen to the constant, the fervent prayers, I will offer up for your welfare.' I exclaimed, 'Dear mother, I promise!' God knows the first request I have honestly fulfilled, the latter I hope I have – at least, my superiors and comrades ever gave me credit for a bold and courageous bearing. I returned to her beloved embrace after South America, and got a commission for my brother Tom, and again to her nearly naked and a skeleton after the retreat to Coruña. I was covered with vermin and had no clothes but those on my back. *To her alone* did I impart what, although I felt no disgrace, I did not want to be known. She dressed me, and put me in a hot bath, and we preserved our secret mutually inviolate. I soon again left her for Talavera, restored to health, by her care, never to see her again, but our intercourse by letters was constant . . .[1]

Harry Smith shows us the son's perspective, but Frances Calvert gives us a glimpse of the mother's feelings in the successive entries in her journal:

3 January 1808: 'Felix dressed himself in his regimentals today for me, and really looked very handsome.'

6 January 1808: 'My beloved Felix sets off this evening in the mail, to join his Regiment. I am very low.'

7 January 1808: 'Mr. C., Felix, and I dined together. At half-past six the dear boy took his leave of us. I shed many tears, and his own eyes were far from dry. I was low and wretched all evening. God Almighty protect him, and spare him to us.'

8 January 1808: 'I have received a letter from my Felix to say he was arrived safe at Deal – had been to call on his commanding officer, Major Arbuthnot, and had been introduced to twenty brother officers.'

10 January 1808: 'Doctor Knighton has ordered me to be bled tomorrow, and keep very quiet for a few days.'

19 April 1808: 'A letter from General Calvert with the unwelcome news that my beloved Felix is ordered upon immediate service, under the command of Sir John Moore. It is a great shock to me, but God's will be done. Their destination is Sweden.

Sir John Moore kindly gave leave to Felix to come up and see us for a day or two. He arrived by the night coach, looking remarkably well. He delights in going this expedition, the only drawback to his happiness is my not liking it. He says I was his first thought when he heard of it. Dear boy, he is everything I can wish. He went yesterday with James Knox to [George] Englehart, the painter, as he is getting his picture [a miniature] done for me.'

25 April 1808: 'My spirits are much depressed at my beloved boy's going . . . I have not seen him this morning, as he went at nine o'clock to Englehart about his picture. I hope it will be like. It will be such a comfort to me in his absence.'

27 April 1808: 'Yesterday was indeed a most dismal day to me, as I parted with my beloved Felix. He brought me his picture which is the very image of him. We dined at half past four, as he was to set off at six. A most dismal dinner it was indeed. I will not dwell on that, or our leave taking – indeed, words could not express what I felt.

We talked of nothing but him yesterday evening, and agreed that there never was a boy so improved in every respect. His picture was under my pillow last night. I must take it to Englehart to be finished. I hope he will not keep it long, for it is my greatest comfort, and I look at it five hundred times a day.'

29 April 1808: 'I continued very melancholy all Wednesday, and indeed I am not over and above gay now though everyone says it is a most desirable expedition, attended with hardly any risk. Never was any thing like my dear husband's attention and affection to me.'[2]

Apart from two short interludes of peace, Britain was at war from early 1793 to the summer of 1815 and countless mothers, fathers, brothers and sisters saw their sons and brothers head off to the war with a mixture of apprehension, pride and misery. Before the war, during most of the eighteenth century, the officers of the army had commonly come from military families, often serving together in the same regiment, with a steady but modest addition of new blood from the adventurous sons of fathers in the other gentlemanly professions. But the expansion of the army during the war exhausted these traditional sources and opened the door for an influx of such men from other parts of society. In 1792, the last year of peace, there were 3,107 officers in the army; by 1814 there were 10,590 on full pay, excluding those in foreign regiments and veteran battalions, and the army needed to find between five hundred and one thousand new men every year to replace those who died or quit the service, and to take up positions in newly created units.[3]

Army commissions, up to and including the rank of lieutenant-colonel, were available for sale. A young man wishing to join the army as an officer would purchase – or his father or friends would purchase on his behalf – a commission as a junior officer: an ensign in most infantry regiments, a cornet in the cavalry. He might subsequently purchase a higher rank and would only have to pay the difference between his old and new commission, the old one being sold to help fund the purchase of the next step. Commissions were not cheap: the official regulation price for an ensigncy in a line regiment was £400, while it cost £735 to be made a cornet in the dragoons, and in the Life Guards the price was £1,600; nor was any refund given if the officer was unfortunate enough to die (although in some cases, if he was killed in battle, the army might permit the sale of his commission for the benefit of his widow and family). Officers might also agree to exchange between regiments, perhaps to move into one that was about to go on active service, or out of one that was going to be sent to an unhealthy colonial posting. Some regiments were very fashionable, and a commission in them commanded an unofficial premium well above the regulation price; while it was not always easy to find a buyer for a commission in an undistinguished regiment in an undesirable location.[4]

However, the demand for new officers was so great during the war that commissions could readily be obtained without purchase, provided that the young man was not seeking to join a regiment that was in particular demand. Only one in five of the first commissions gained during the course of the Peninsular War (1808–14) was purchased, while even in the cavalry and the Guards, half of all new commissions were granted without purchase. Two examples give a sense of how easily this worked in practice. Harry Smith was the second son of a surgeon in Whittlesey, Cambridgeshire, who ensured that he got a thorough education. In 1804 he joined the local Yeomanry Cavalry and in the following year acted as orderly when Brigadier-General William Stewart reviewed the unit. Stewart liked the boy and said: '"Young gentleman, would you like to be an officer?" "Of all things," was my answer. "Well, I will make you a Rifleman, a green jacket," says the General, "and very smart."' The Brigadier-General kept his word and on 8 May 1805 Smith was gazetted second lieutenant in the 95th Rifles. (Stewart had great influence in the 95th, having played a pivotal role in their formation and training.) Peter Le Mesurier was the son of a good family in Guernsey whose sons had often joined the army and in one case risen to be Commissary General. His father was respectable but not wealthy, and his older brother, Abraham, was established in trade. He was granted an ensigncy in the 9th Foot on 13 August 1808 through the recommendation of Lord Pembroke, the Governor of Guernsey at the time and a lieutenant-general in the army.[5]

There were few formal qualifications needed to become an officer. The Commander-in-Chief, the Duke of York, imposed a minimum age of 16, although even after this was established, a significant number of 15 year olds received commissions, while half of all first commissions were bestowed on youths under the age of 18. A prospective officer also needed a letter of recommendation from a person of some standing, such as an army officer of the rank of major or above, or an MP, testifying to his 'character, education and bodily health', along with his willingness to serve. Beyond this, all that was required were his name and address, although if he was wise he would ensure that the recommendation was for a specific regiment, otherwise he might be sent to one of the West

India regiments or other colonial corps that always struggled to find sufficient officers.[6]

When John Orrok, a captain in the 33rd Foot then serving in India, secured a commission in the regiment for his young brother-in-law, he wrote to the young man's father about the education he would need:

> Let me entreat of you, my good friend, not to cram Thomas's head with Greek or Latin, they are of no use in his profession; but pray teach him to read, write and *spell* English gramatically, [*sic*] those are the most essential points and I am sorry to say they are very little attended to in Scotland. We have some Officers so very deficient in that respect that they are the ridicule of the others; so for his own Sake allow me to recommend his unremited [*sic*] attention to spelling in particular.

And when Peter Le Mesurier joined the 9th Foot he found that one of the rules of the officers' mess was a prohibition on using three or more words of Latin under any circumstances. Very few army officers had been to university, and while there were many highly intelligent men in the army, intellectuals were uncommon.[7]

A tiny minority – around 4 per cent – of new officers had attended the Royal Military College, which had room for only 100 cadets, of whom 20 were nominated by the East India Company and destined to serve in its army. Thirty of the remaining places were reserved for the sons of officers who had died or been maimed on service, and they received their education, board and clothing free; while 20 more places were kept for the sons of serving officers who paid a discounted fee of £40 a year. Most cadets were aged from 13 to 15 and had to pass a test intended to show that they had a grounding in grammar and arithmetic. One student, who went to the college from Eton, said that the 'beds are good and very clean. Our food very good and plain', and that the 'hardships are *nothing*', but that he still thought it a 'very disagreeable place' because 'one has no time to oneself . . . hardly anything but *study*'. However, another student at the time – the young Roderick Murchison, who went on to become a famous

Victorian geologist – admitted that he was a poor student, bad at arithmetic and even worse at geometry, but delighted in boisterous mischief and practical jokes of which there was no shortage.[8]

A much more common route into the army was through the militia. Commissions were granted by the Lord Lieutenant of the county, without purchase, and although there was a property qualification it appears to have been widely ignored, so that any gentleman whose character was not notorious might readily obtain a commission for himself or his son. Each regiment of militia had an official complement of 24 officers: a colonel, a lieutenant-colonel, a major, five captains, eight lieutenants and eight ensigns, together with 480 men divided into eight companies. The service was not onerous: as a home defence force the militia could not be sent abroad, and in winter up to two thirds of the officers in a regiment might be away on leave at any time. The quality of regiments, and their officers, seems to have varied quite widely: some were well disciplined, given extensive training and kept close to full strength, while others were less efficient and often less happy. Once the invasion scare of 1803–05 had passed, their main function was to act as a 'feeder' for the army, training men and officers who would then volunteer to join the regulars. Such volunteers had several motives: life in the militia was safe but tedious, and offered no prospect of adventure or wealth, or even any great sense of serving the country. When peace came the militia would be disbanded and almost all the officers left without employment, and there was no half-pay for militia officers. Moreover, if a militia officer could persuade a number of his men to volunteer into the same regiment of the regular army at the same time he did so, he would receive his initial commission for free (although, as we have seen, he would not find it hard to do so anyway). By the time of Wellington's campaigns in the Peninsula, one fifth of all the officers joining the army did so from the militia.[9]

In 1796 Henry Austen considered transferring from the militia to the regulars, hoping to become a lieutenant and the adjutant in a newly raised regiment, the 86th, which he was confident would be sent to the Cape of Good Hope. His sister sharply commented that 'I heartily hope that he will, as usual, be disappointed in this scheme', and so it proved, for he stayed home and married Eliza in the following year instead. Jane's dislike of the prospect of his service in the regulars proved well founded. The 86th was indeed sent to Cape Town, but then, three years later, to India where it saw much hard service and suffered heavy losses of officers and men, not returning to England for 20 years. If he had joined the 86th Henry Austen would have been lucky to see his family again unless he had transferred to another regiment or left the army.[10]

An officer who joined the army from the militia, or from the Royal Military College, had at least received some training, but most of the rest were complete novices. John Cooke, who had served in the militia for several years, recorded that,

> [w]hen an officer entered this corps it was the custom to send him to drill with a squad composed of peasant[s] from the plough tail and other raw recruits, to learn the facings, marching, and companies' evolutions. That being completed, he put on cross belts and pouch and learned the firelock exercise, again marching with the same. When it was considered that the whole were perfect, with and without arms, they began to skirmish in extended files. Last of all they learned the duties of a sentry, and to fire ball cartridge at a target. The officer was not considered clear of the adjutant until he could put a company through the evolutions by word of command, which he had practised in the ranks. It generally took him six months in summer at four times a day, an hour at each period, to perfect all he had to learn. The drill was never kept more than an hour under arms when, to a minute, the time beater tolled his drum, the only one in the corps (the light infantry regiments using bugles), and the recruits were instantly dismissed.[11]

However, Cooke was serving in the 43rd Light Infantry, one of the best regiments in the British army, which went on to form part of the famous Light Division under Wellington in the Peninsula, and training in other regiments was not always taken quite so seriously. Ralph Heathcote joined the 1st or Royal Dragoons in 1806 and describes how

> [at] about nine o'clock the trumpets sound for foot parade, when the different troops being formed before the stable doors march towards the centre of the barrack yard, and after having being formed in line are examined by the Major (viz. their dress and arms are inspected); . . . then the Sergeant Major exercises the regiment, with which we have nothing to do. At ten o'clock I breakfast with some others in the mess-room, many officers preferring to breakfast in their own rooms. At eleven all the subaltern officers . . . are to go to the riding school, but if you don't go, no notice is taken of it, excepting you were perhaps to stay away for weeks together, and at twelve the same subaltern officers have to attend foot drill, and then your business is done for the day.[12]

And he adds that

> [t]he Sergeant-Major brought me a list of the words of command for the manual exercise. I wished to learn it myself before I was to command the men. He told me I need not give myself the trouble; if I only gave the words of command, the men would know what they meant. I need not add (I hope) that I nevertheless had it shown to me for half an hour . . .[13]

Thomas Bunbury admits that although he had been an ensign in the 3rd Foot (the Buffs) for two years, and had seen action at Oporto and Talavera, he was ignorant of drill when he joined the Portuguese army, and had to study hard so that he could teach them. Captain Gronow wrote that

> I joined [the First Foot Guards] in February 1813, and cannot but recollect with astonishment how limited and imperfect was the instruction which an officer received at that time; he absolutely entered the army without any military education whatever. We were so defective in

our drill, even after we had passed out of the hands of the sergeant, that the excellence of our non-commissioned officers alone prevented us from meeting the most fatal disasters in the face of the enemy.

And within a month of Peter Le Mesurier's commission in the 9th Foot being gazetted he found himself on a troopship bound for Portugal and active service, so that he can hardly have received any training at all. As this suggests, there was enormous variation both between regiments and between the officers within a single regiment, although it is fair to add that the prospect of active service spurred most officers to improve their grasp of their role in battle.[14]

New officers had much to learn about army life that could not be taught on the drill square: the niceties of rank, entitlements, regimental traditions and the correct ways of interacting with civilians all contained pitfalls for the inexperienced. Each regiment had its own particular character: some were more fashionable than others, some full of experience, some had many other young men freshly joined. There was a ready market for books of advice and instruction for novices, including Charles James's *Regimental Companion* which went through a number of editions and was published by Thomas Egerton, who also – through Henry's influence – published Jane Austen's first novels.

The adjustment to life in the army was not always easy or happy. Having served for a few months in the Peninsula, Peter Le Mesurier returned to England in early 1809, but admitted to his brother that he did not much enjoy regimental life:

When the Officers are together the conversation is generally about the success they had the night previous to it in getting (*de bonnes aventures* [*sic*]). I have heard some of those Esprits forts say the Bible was a parcel of Stupid Stuff, unintelligible to their understandings. Plaguing young Officers, which do not exactly agree with them on

these points, is their greatest delight. I had some altercation this
morning with one of ours for making some observations on me because
I did not go out with them on their nocturnal expeditions. I do not
like their morals. They are dissolute in general yet I hope to find some
in the Reg': with whom I shall take pleasure to associate.[15]

Seven months later he still felt isolated: 'I do not enjoy the company of
our Officers. Their conversation is very different from that I have been
accustomed to hear. I am obliged to stay in my room the greatest part of
the day or be in their company. R is nearly as bad as the Rest. He begins
to follow P's example to laugh at Religion.' And the following week he
admitted that he spent most of his time in his room and amused himself
'in reading or looking over my Algebra'.[16]

Le Mesurier agreed with his brother that 'The army . . . are very
Licentious' and added,

I belive [sic] all Reg'ts: are alike. I think if the heads were to show a
good example they might check such conversations as are not fit to be
heard by Gentlemen at the Mess Tables, but on the contrary they
seem to encourage them. I have heard Officers go on with shocking
conversations before the men. No wonder they do not pay them the
respect they ought to do.

And his opinion finds some support in a letter from George Hennell, who
served in the 43rd a little later in the war:

I do not suppose there was ever a person in the army more quizzed
than I have been. The officers of the army are none of them half characters. They do not content themselves with a little swearing &
joking about serious things but they are generally openly profane &
coolly & deliberately take the seat of the scorner. My Bible has been
attacked in every way & the more impious the quotation the louder
the laugh. Indeed such a pitch has it arrived that what would shock
you would not raise a laugh here.[17]

When Thomas Bunbury first joined the 2nd battalion of the Buffs at Cirencester in 1807 he found that 'practical jokes were the order of the day'. Officers who accidently left their rooms unlocked would return to find their possessions scattered and in the greatest disarray, if not actually removed or spoilt. Their boots would be smeared with pomatum and then powdered, while the blacking bottle might be emptied into their hair powder. 'As an instrument in the hands of older sinners I was very mischievous' and persecuted a studious officer who had graduated from the Military College and served in the regiment for a considerable time.

As a matter of course, he was voted a great bore and a stupid fellow; and on these assumptions, we took delight in smoking the old fox as he was termed, and in order to drive him from his burrow, I was hoisted upon the roof of his barrack room, and supplied with a convenient board, which was carefully placed over the aperture of the chimney.

Generally Bunbury managed to get down before the poor victim emerged, when the perpetrators would be all mock innocence and helpful suggestions.[18]

Such bullying might be even worse in regiments on active service. Cheerful Johnny Kincaid of the 95th Rifles tells us:

I don't know how it was, nor do I know whether we differed from other regiments in the same respect, but our first and most uncharitable aim was to discover the weak points of every fresh arrival, and to attack him through them. If he had redeeming qualities, he, of course, came out scathless, but, if not, he was dealt with most unmercifully. Poor Tommy [Dangerfield] had none such – he was weak on all sides, and therefore went to the wall.

And in the Royal Dragoons a brash young officer of the name of Avarne was regaled with so many stories of 'stabbing, wounding and killing' that he came down with severe diarrhoea and begged to be sent to the rear. Here an experienced officer, his junior, saw 'yellow fever in Mr Avarne's eyes', and played upon his feelings until Avarne resigned from the regiment, thus assisting the junior officer's promotion by one step. Much of this teasing was simply young men behaving badly in a way that young men have always behaved badly, but it was not totally pointless. In battle, and on active service more generally, the regiment's success – the very survival of its officers and men – might depend on a junior officer such as Tommy Dangerfield keeping a cool head and not giving his men any reason to panic. His strength of character mattered, and the bullying formed a crude test of whether he would prove reliable under stress. And there is another, less practical but equally understandable, influence at play: a regiment like the 95th had seen a great deal of action and many officers had been killed, wounded or died of disease by the time fresh-faced Tommy Dangerfield arrived to fill the shoes of his predecessor. It is not surprising that the surviving officers should view any new arrival as somewhat presumptuous, and should wish to make him earn his place with a little suffering before they admitted him as their equal. Camaraderie and esprit-de-corps have their darker side, and a new officer joining a proud, experienced regiment was very much on probation.[19]

<hr />

Most ordinary regimental officers – the vast majority of all the officers in the army – came from the lower reaches of the landed gentry, the gentlemanly professions or respectable families engaged in trade, commerce or farming. Some members of the aristocracy served in the army, but they were concentrated in the Guards and a few extremely fashionable regiments such as the 12th and 15th Hussars, although as the war in the Peninsula went on, a few also sought commissions in the 95th Rifles and the other regiments in the Light Division. It was rare, although not unknown, for an officer with a title or the younger son of a peer to serve for any length of time in one of the ordinary regiments of the line. Nor is it always easy to tell the social class from which an officer came. Thomas Bradford and his brother Henry Hollis Bradford both served with distinction in the Peninsula: Thomas commanding an independent

Portuguese brigade and Henry serving on the staff of the Fourth and Sixth Divisions. By 1815 Thomas was a major-general and Henry was a lieutenant-colonel in the 1st Foot Guards, and both had received KCBs. Their father appears in reference books and their obituaries as Thomas Bradford of Woodlands near Doncaster and Ashdown Park, Sussex, which suggests that he was a well-established member of the landed gentry. And so he was, but he had begun his career in trade as an upholsterer (and probably furniture maker and retailer), who had gone bankrupt and recovered to make a fortune out of real estate development and land speculation, and then retired from business around 1799.[20]

Relatively few officers had been to one of the great public schools: only 127 old Etonians held full-pay regimental commissions in 1809 and this was double the number from Westminster, while Harrow and Rugby were even less well represented. It was much more common for officers to have received their education at local grammar schools, and they were not always the best or most attentive students. Nonetheless there was a general assumption that to be an officer in the army *was* to be a gentleman, and that this was not primarily a matter of birth. In 1840 Sir John Macdonald, the Adjutant-General of the Army, told a parliamentary committee that 'It is the proud characteristic of the British Army that its officers are gentlemen by education, manners and habits', while the Duke of Wellington declared that 'There is no greater mistake than to suppose that the Service performed by the British Army could be carried on by any other description of Man except one educated as is an English Gentleman!' Neither Macdonald nor Wellington explained exactly what this education meant, but it was certainly not academic achievement. To be an officer and a gentleman was rather to have a certain confidence and air of authority that ensured that soldiers would not question orders in battle, a willingness to accept responsibility, and a disinclination to keep 'low' society: a British officer should not allow his men to be too familiar or to treat him as their equal in any situation.[21]

Nonetheless some men leapt the gulf separating the other ranks from officers in the army: just over one in twenty officers had served as a private soldier. Most of these men were given commissions as reward for long and meritorious service, sometimes as a way of recognizing the exceptional performance of their regiment in battle or of individual acts of outstanding gallantry. They were much older than their fellow subalterns and usually had no private means other than their pay, so that they were often appointed adjutant, which both gave them some additional pay and authority, and utilized their thorough knowledge of drill, discipline and regulations. Officers promoted from the ranks were almost always given their commission in another regiment, and the Horse Guards had a tendency to make these commissions in unfashionable regiments serving in unhealthy colonies. Colonel Torrens, the Military Secretary to the Commander-in-Chief, explained in 1810, 'Unless there are some circumstances in the case of a Non Com[missione]d Officer of a very favourable nature when recommended for a Commission, the Com[mande]r in Chief generally attaches him to a W[est] I[ndia] Regiment as it is scarcely fair upon Officers in a regular Corps to send such people at once into their Society'. In these circumstances, such promotion might amount to a death sentence, while even if this fate was avoided, it was not necessarily better to be a junior and déclassé officer rather than a senior and respected NCO.[22]

Fortunately the anecdotal evidence of memoirs suggests that not all regiments were as prejudiced as Colonel Torrens and the Horse Guards. Some officers promoted from the ranks appear to have been readily accepted, although others were poorly treated, at least at first. John Shipp came from the humblest background – he had been raised in a poorhouse – and was granted a commission for his outstanding bravery in leading the storming party at the unsuccessful siege of Bhurtpore in 1805. He was apprehensive how he would be received when he joined his new regiment; however, 'All the officers of the corps flocked around me, and greeted me in the most handsome and friendly manner . . . Had I been the son of a duke my reception could not have been more flattering or friendly.' Against this there is the story of a new officer who is said to have asked to revert to his former status as none of the other officers in his regiment would associate with him, until the Duke of York walked arm in arm with him in front of the regiment on parade, and so broke the taboo. And when Sergeant-Major Buffet of the 28th was made an ensign his wife did not join in the party to celebrate the occasion, preferring to sit in the kitchen and smoke her pipe, declaring that although the King could make her husband a gentleman, not even the Sultan of the Indies could make her into a lady![23]

In general the army was more relaxed and open to outsiders during the war with France than before or afterwards, and even during the war regiments on active service were more flexible than those in garrison, especially at home. Commissions were also given to 'volunteers' – young men who joined a regiment on active service without a commission but in the hope of receiving one when illness or battle created a vacancy. These volunteers fought in the ranks and carried a musket but were permitted to mess and associate with the officers. The best known example is George Hennell, the son of a Coventry ribbon manufacturer, who went out to the Peninsula in 1812 with nothing more than a letter of introduction to General Picton. The general attached him to the 94th Foot as a volunteer and two days later Hennell took part in the storming of Badajoz and distinguished himself. Picton recommended him, and six weeks later he received a commission in the 43rd Light Infantry where he served for the rest of the war. Not all volunteers were as valuable as Hennell, and Charles Crowe, a lieutenant in the 27th Foot in the Peninsula, was decided in his opinion: 'Generally speaking they were not gentlemanly in appearance, or manners. Some associated with the private soldiers; others, dismayed by the hardships they had to encounter, left in disgust. If the numbers who came out and the few who obtained rank were recorded, the disproportion would be very surprising.' And this comment gains credibility as Crowe and a fellow officer took pity on one volunteer – much superior to the rest – and treated him with kindness until he was killed in the siege of San Sebastian.[24]

Most of the officers in the army were English, but Scots were over-represented compared to their proportion of the total population, reflecting a tradition of military service among the Highland gentry that stretched back a century or more. Irish Protestants were also overrepresented, while a sizeable number of officers were born outside the UK, including both loyalist Americans such as Samuel Auchmuty and William Delancey, and some French royalist exiles: a son of the Duc d'Orleans, Captain Paul St Pol, died while serving with the Royal Fusiliers at Badajoz. The right of Catholics to hold commissions in the army was complicated and at times controversial, but in practice there were seldom any real obstacles, at least up to the rank of lieutenant-colonel, although they were certainly underrepresented. Not all British officers were white, although there was a growing prejudice against non-white officers, especially when serving in India. William Light, who had a distinguished career in the Peninsula in the 4th Dragoons, as a liaison officer with the Spanish army and as a reconnaissance officer, had either a Eurasian or Malay mother, and while this was unusual it was not unique, and did not attract much comment.[25]

Officers in the army were not well paid. An ensign in an infantry regiment nominally received 5s 3d per day, or just under £100 a year, but considerable deductions were made from this, and it did not cover the cost of his meals, wine, washing and other unavoidable expenses, which absorbed every available penny. Lieutenants were not much better off, with pay of just under £120 a year unless they had served in that rank for seven years, in which event they were to be pitied despite receiving an extra shilling a day (just over an additional £18 a year). A captain's pay of £191 was more respectable but still far from sufficient, while majors received £292 and lieutenant-colonels £310. Pay was significantly higher in the cavalry and the Guards, but so were the necessary expenses, and a poor officer would be much better off in a line regiment than in the Guards.[26]

Few officers lived entirely upon their pay, at least in their first years in the army. In 1804 Sir John Moore told the father of a young man who was about to join the 52nd Light Infantry:

it is difficult in these times for a Subaltern to live upon his pay, there are some few who do it, but it requires a degree of economy and attention which few young men, at starting, are equal to. If you can do it conveniently I should recommend an allowance of not less than £50, – nor above £100. This will put him upon a par with most of his comrades and still oblige him to pay attention to economy which I have always considered a military virtue.

That might be sufficient for an officer in a line regiment, but a cornet in the 15th Light Dragoons – a particularly smart and expensive cavalry regiment – was said to need a private income of almost £400 in addition to his pay if he was to hold his own. Expensive uniforms, good horses and high mess bills put some regiments out of the reach of the average officer, while encouraging the fashionable beaux of the army to congregate together, to the great benefit of their tailors.[27]

Peter Le Mesurier tried to make ends meet, for example making his uniform last: both his coat and hat were 'turned' and worn long after they had begun to look shabby. Nonetheless he was forced on several occasions to draw on his father for £10, always doing so with great reluctance, for he knew that this was money that could not easily be spared. In the spring of 1811 he told his sister,

Do you know, I shall be inclined to join the Opp[ositio][n]: shortly if Ministers do not releive [sic] our wants. You see that our pay has only been encreased [sic] 3*d* or 4*d* since the year 1614, two hundred years ago, and they will not encrease our Pay, tho the necessaries of Life have more than trebled, ay, even are Ten times dearer than they were then.[28]

And William Grattan remarked that

[t]he life of a subaltern . . . is a perpetual scene of irritating calculation from the 24th of one month to the 24th of the next. No matter what circumstances, or in what corner of the globe the subaltern is placed, his *first* thought points towards that powerful magnet the *twenty-fourth* . . .

The 24th has scarcely passed when the same routine is pursued, every hour increasing in interest according to the immediate wants of the calculator; and time rolls on, either rapidly or slowly, in the exact ratio with the strength or weakness of his purse. The moment he receives his pay he discharges his bills, and by the time he has got about halfway into the first week of the next month, he has little occasion for a knowledge of Cocker to enable him to calculate his money.[29]

The initial cost of the uniform and other equipment for a young officer was considerable even in an infantry regiment, and much worse in the cavalry or the Guards. When Charles Booth joined the 52nd he paid £57 18s 6d for his uniform, sword, telescope and compass. Robert Knowles retained his militia coat – suitably modified – but his father still had to pay £43 15s, while in a cavalry regiment the initial outfit, including a horse or two of his own, would easily run to £300 and might exceed £500. Officers embarked on active service for the first time would often spend considerable sums at a military warehouse and outfitter in London where they would buy ingenious but often impractical devices to ensure their comfort and health when campaigning. And yet when the government increased the pay of officers in 1813 Captain R. M. Cairnes of the Royal Artillery was far from happy:

After the service of the Peninsula, let those who are judged deserving of it, be thus rewarded, but whilst that service is going on, let us take our chance of the only *honourable* reward we can or ought to seek, that of Rank & Command. Let money come afterwards, but don't let us in the very midst of fighting & of everything that incites to Fame & Military Character, be at once palsied by a shopkeeping reward of Pounds, Shillings & Pence.[30]

Once an officer was in the army there were several ways in which he might be promoted. He could purchase his next step, or rise by seniority, or be promoted for an exceptional act of gallantry, or for bringing home a dispatch announcing a victory. During the years of the Peninsular War, purchase only accounted for about one in five promotions; although the figure was much higher in fashionable regiments and was even higher after the war when the army stagnated. Seniority accounted for the great majority of wartime promotions, with a bare 10 per cent being due to distinguished conduct in action or official patronage. Purchasing rank was not cheap. A lieutenancy in a line regiment cost £550, although an officer who had purchased his ensigncy had only to pay the difference (£150), the rest of the cost being recouped by the seller from the sale of the other commission. Similarly to become a captain a lieutenant had to pay £1,500 (less £550 if he had bought his lieutenancy), £2,600 to become a major (less the £1,500), and £3,500 (less £2,600) to become a lieutenant-colonel. The figures were considerably higher in the cavalry (nearly £5,000 for a lieutenant-colonelcy) and higher again in the Foot Guards (£3,500 for a captain, £6,700 for a lieutenant-colonel). Sometimes it was difficult to find a buyer for the old commission, although in some particularly sought-after regiments commissions were sold at above the official rate.[31]

The Duke of York as Commander-in-Chief laid down rules stating that officers must serve a minimum length of time in one rank before being eligible for promotion – even by purchase – to the next superior rank. No officer could be made a captain until he had spent two years as a subaltern, or a major until he had spent six years as a commissioned officer. In 1809 these rules were tightened: officers then had to serve three years before being eligible to be promoted captain, seven years before they could become a major including at least two as a captain, and nine years in the army before they could be made a lieutenant-colonel. While these rules were designed to prevent rich young dilettantes from buying their way to a senior position which they were not competent to fill, they also slowed the rise of talented young men just as the army was embarking on its most sustained period of Continental operations for a century. It was not entirely beneficial to stipulate that a young captain in 1809 could not be made a lieutenant-colonel in 1814 if he had fought his way from Talavera to Toulouse. Nor was any flexibility shown in the enforcement of the rule: on several occasions Wellington sent home aides-de-camp like Alexander Gordon with dispatches announcing a victory, only for them to be ruled ineligible for the customary promotion until they had waited out their time.[32]

Wellington's own generation had greatly benefited from the absence of such rules: he had joined the army in March 1787 a little short of his 18th birthday. At first his promotion was slow: after four years in the army (much of it spent at Dublin Castle as an aide-de-camp to the Lord Lieutenant of Ireland) he was still a lieutenant. It was not until the outbreak of war in 1793 that he set about getting himself promoted with any urgency, but then it only took five months for him to rise from captain to lieutenant-colonel: ranks purchased with loans from his brother. Others rose even more rapidly. Edward Paget rose from cornet in the Life Guards to lieutenant-colonel of the 28th Foot in the space of two years, taking command of the regiment when he was still only 18, and, it needs to be added, proving an able and popular officer. Not all the officers who gained rapid promotion in the first years of the war when the army was being expanded rapidly proved as effective as Wellington and Paget, while those who lacked the resources or the ambition to make haste in 1793–95 were at a permanent disadvantage when a more orderly approach was imposed with the arrival of the Duke of York at the Horse Guards.

Once an officer reached the rank of lieutenant-colonel his further promotion was entirely a matter of seniority, and tended to be quite slow. Wellington became a major-general in 1802 almost nine years after being promoted lieutenant-colonel, and it was another six before he was made a lieutenant-general: 15 years in which Britain was at war and in which he was engaged in operations ranging from Belgium and Holland to India and back to the north of Germany and Denmark. He commanded large armies in India, proved exceptionally successful in the field, and won the confidence of the members of the cabinet at home; and yet in both 1808 and 1809 the King expressed the view that he was too junior an officer to command a large army, and that the position should be given to a more senior officer.[33]

The issue of seniority was very important because no British general could serve under his junior, even if he wished to do so. Wellington's success sidelined all the generals who were senior to him, until 1813 when he was promoted to the rank of field marshal, and so leapfrogged almost all his superiors, enabling them to join his army. (Promotion to field marshal was the one exception to the seniority rule, but it was very rare, except for members of the royal family.) Henry William Paget, who was Wellington's second-in-command in the Waterloo campaign, was one of these officers senior to Wellington, and he had recognized that this might be a problem as early as 1808, when he commented to his father, 'I feel it to be a real misfortune to me, as a soldier, that I am above him on the list, for I think there is a good chance of its cutting me off from all service'. This proved unduly pessimistic: Paget served in both the Coruña and Walcheren campaigns before Waterloo (operations commanded by more senior generals), but it is true that if he had been promoted a little more slowly, and so had been junior to Wellington, he might have seen a great deal more action in the Peninsula.[34]

For most regimental officers high rank was – at best – a distant dream, quite irrelevant to their daily lives. If an officer serving in a regiment was interested in purchasing his next step, he either had to wait for a vacancy within his own regiment or look outside it. When an officer wished to sell his commission, either because he had been promoted or because he had decided to leave the army, it was generally offered to his juniors in the regiment in order of seniority, and only if they all refused was it made available to officers outside the regiment. So if Major Bloggs of the Blankshires purchased promotion to a lieutenant-colonelcy his commission would be offered first to Captain Smith – the most senior captain – then, if Smith was unable or unwilling to purchase it, to Captain Jones, the second most senior, and so on until it found a purchaser. If Captain Partridge, the third most senior captain, took up the offer he would leapfrog Smith and Jones and become the junior major in the regiment. However, the commander-in-chief reserved the right to let a longer-serving officer from outside the regiment purchase the commission. This was usually only done when the Horse Guards believed that the regiment needed an infusion of new blood, or had a poor opinion of the internal candidate who was most likely to purchase the commission.[35]

Promotion by seniority worked in almost exactly the same way, with Captain Smith becoming Major Smith in our example, while Captain Jones now became the most senior captain, and Captain Partridge the second most senior, and so on as every officer in the regiment junior to Major – now Lieutenant-Colonel – Bloggs moved up one step. If an officer transferred into a new regiment he automatically became the most junior officer of his rank in the regiment, even if he had already spent years in this rank in his old regiment. (There was a difference between seniority in the regiment and seniority in the army.) This meant that it made sense for an officer not to move between regiments except when he was gaining a step in rank anyway, so there was no disadvantage in moving for Lieutenant-Colonel Bloggs, who was going to be the junior lieutenant-colonel in any case, while if Captain Smith had grown tired of the Blankshires, the moment to move was *after* he had been promoted Major Smith, not before, when he would go to the bottom of the list in his new regiment.

Seniority within the regiment had practical implications. It determined which company an officer would serve in or command: the senior captain commanded the grenadier company for example, and this meant that officers quite often moved from one company to another. Most infantry regiments had two battalions, and in this case the most senior officers of each rank served in the first battalion, and the junior lieutenants, captains and so forth served in the second battalion. The intention was that the first battalion would be employed actively in the field, while the second battalion would be used mostly for home defence and to train recruits for the first battalion, although this seldom worked quite like this in the Peninsula. The result was that officers were quite often transferred from one battalion to the other, from active service in the Peninsula to home duties and back again, as their position in the regimental pecking order changed, although under pressure from Wellington such changes were generally delayed until the close of the campaigning season.[36]

In the summer of 1811 Peter Le Mesurier returned to Spain to join the first battalion of his regiment (the 9th Foot) with a party of recruits, mostly volunteers from the militia. He saw some active campaigning, but was not engaged with the enemy, and at the end of the year he told his father, 'I find every body about me Stirring their Interest for Promotion, but to little effect. I must own, I should not dislike to have some Person to look up to for their Interest, for if I wait for the common course of Promotion I need not look forward for a Company these Five years'. Nothing came of this, and a year later he remarked 'You will perceive by the Army list I am creeping up; I am now 22^d Lieu^t: [in the regiment] so that, should I escape next Campaign, I may probably look out for a Company in the course of Four or Five years more'. And in November 1813 he outlined the advantages and risks of purchasing his next step – the rank of captain and the command of a company; he was eager to have this next step and dreaded the thought of serving for more years as a subaltern, but was deterred by the risk that if Napoleon was soon defeated and there was peace, the army would be reduced and all the officers in second battalions would probably be placed on half-pay. Better to be a full pay lieutenant in the first battalion than a half-pay captain.[37]

The hardest steps to gain were those from lieutenant to captain, and captain to major, and consequently these were the most frequently purchased: between one quarter and one third of all officers paid to gain these steps at the time of the Peninsular War. In general it took an officer only a year or two to rise from ensign or cornet to lieutenant, but then an average of six years to be promoted captain, and anything from six to sixteen years to be promoted major, so that the typical major would be in his mid to late thirties and would already have spent half his life in the service. It was not a system likely to produce an excess of youthful dash and enterprise in the higher ranks of the army; yet these were the figures for the height of the war years – after Waterloo promotion became much slower and purchase much more important.[38]

Harry Smith joined the 95th Rifles on 5 May 1805, receiving his first commission for free. Three months later he borrowed £550 from his father (a considerable sum for a provincial surgeon with a large family to advance to one of his children) and purchased a lieutenancy. This gave him seniority over only one existing junior officer, but the 95th was about to form a second battalion, and by purchasing this step Smith gained seniority within the regiment over all the lieutenants appointed to it. Nonetheless there were still 26 lieutenants above him in the 95th, so it is not surprising that he remained a lieutenant for six years. During that time, 16 of these lieutenants were promoted captain (14 by seniority, two by purchase), one had purchased a captaincy in another regiment, three had retired or resigned, three had exchanged into other regiments and three had been killed in action. Two lieutenants who were junior to him in the regiment but with longer service in the army, had purchased captaincies ahead of him. On 11 October 1811 he became the senior lieutenant in the 95th. Three months later Captain John Uniacke of the 95th was killed in the storm of Ciudad Rodrigo, and Smith was promoted captain a few weeks later (the promotion was gazetted on 28 February 1812). Further promotion followed when he brought home General Ross's dispatch announcing the capture of Washington in 1814, and again as part of the general promotion of officers who took part in the Battle of Waterloo, so that he ended the war a lieutenant-colonel, having purchased one step along the way, seen a great deal of action in an elite regiment and had some experience on the staff. He was an unusually able, and an unusually fortunate, officer: a more typical officer joining the army at the same time as Smith would have finished the war as no more than a captain, assuming that he had survived.[39]

Life for officers on home service was undemanding but often quite dull. When John Cooke and the 2nd battalion of the 43rd Light Infantry returned from Walcheren in late 1809 they spent some time in Colchester and then at Sudbury where the men began to recover from the fever that had run through their ranks leaving many dead. 'Those officers whose health was sufficiently re-established frequented the balls at Bury St Edmunds, which were extremely well attended by the neighbouring families. These occasional jaunts, and a few private parties, made the time pass pleasantly enough until we were ordered to Weeley Barracks. There, with two other regiments, we spent a sombre winter.' Cooke and a friend, Lieutenant Thomas Wilkinson, used their time that winter to make a careful model of a small baronial castle from wood and some sheet tin. 'Painted glass windows were inserted in the gothic apertures of the keep, and a little gilded silken flag was placed on the summit. We also cut out about 150 little wooden soldiers, and painted them. The officers were ornamented with gold and silver paper according to their respective ranks.' The castle was besieged 'not with a battering-ram, but with [a] small brass cannon, of a calibre which carried swan shot'. And a protracted siege it was, the garrison being reduced to a courageous sergeant who was whisked up the ranks to become a lieutenant-colonel, but who finally fell heroically in the line of duty. Almost 30 years later, after the vicissitudes of his eventful life, Cooke still kept a few of the model soldiers he had made then. 'In the spring we shifted our quarters to Colchester, being perfectly sick of our rustic amusements of shooting larks and skating, and of pacing up and down a large solitary barrack square. We had been surrounded by a rich grass country without anything worth the appellation of village for a considerable distance.' That summer a detachment of 320 officers and men was sent from the second battalion to reinforce the first battalion serving with Wellington in Portugal. Much to Cooke's dismay he was not sufficiently senior to be included, and nor was Wilkinson or another friend Lieutenant Charles Gore. They pestered their commanding officer with entreaties and arguments and finally, at his suggestion, sent a memorial containing a plea to be allowed to serve to the Horse Guards. Rather surprisingly the Commander-in-Chief granted their request and they were given special permission to accompany the detachment. 'What a moment! Gore and myself rubbed our hands, and [Wilkinson] fell on his knees and returned thanks to Heaven for his good fortune. Our heavy baggage was crammed into the store, and that evening, with light hearts, we proceeded to London.' It was not prudent or rational thus to seek out the dangers and privations of active service, but Cooke was only 20 and his friends scarcely if at all older, and it is not hard to understand why they were eager for adventure, activity and some purpose in their lives compared to the tedium of life at home.[40]

Not everyone disliked home service however, and Ralph Heathcote paints a most attractive picture of his life in the Royal Dragoons in Scotland in 1806:

> I can most sincerely assure you that the situation in which I am placed is . . . pleasant . . . All the officers of our regiment are perfectly well bred, polite and gentlemanly men, some indeed far superior to most people I have yet seen [in Britain]. The manner in which I was received astonished me. The style in which we live is very elegant, though not expensive . . .

He was pleased that 'There are no hard drinkers in the regiment, and the greatest regularity is preserved', and added that the 'only part I dislike is the looking on at punishments; though they are not so cruel as abroad, it is still very disagreeable'. Heathcote's duties were not onerous:

> Our sergeants drill the men, etc. etc., and do the greater part of the duty of a German officer. Officers never attend the foot drills of the regiment when the whole is commanded by the sergeants. We only attend on parades (they last about a quarter hour) and on field days when the regiment is mounted and exercises on horseback: the fatigue then is nothing.

Nor did he find that much subordination was required:

> Except on parade, every officer is perfectly equal; and if a man were mad enough even then to refuse to march to the right, because his colonel commanded it, let him put up his sword, go home, and sell his commission, and then he will be as free as ever. English officers are not to be compared with German ones. It is not the King who has given us our rank. We have bought it – from the cornet up to the colonel. That makes a most essential difference.

He spent much of his time 'reading (there is a very good circulating library near our barracks), drawing, music, etc. Captain Radcliff and I have a musical society, and play quartettes two or three times a week. I generally go to bed at my old hour, ten, and get up at eight. In short, I amuse myself so well, that time passes away without my scarcely knowing how.' And when there were exercises, they were a pleasure rather than an imposition:

> If a field-day is ordered (we have about four a week) there is neither riding school nor foot-drill. By field-day is meant exercising – the whole regiment on horseback. As we exercise on the sands of the seashore we must regulate our time according to the tides of the ocean, and then I leave you to judge how fine it must be riding on the hard sand, having a most beautiful sea view before you, adorned by the shores of Fife. I have heard the Firth of Forth (Bay of Edinburgh) compared with the Bay of Naples, and am certain it is the most picturesque country I ever saw. At five the trumpet sounds for dinner (for the officers I mean, the privates dine at twelve). We generally sit down twelve of us, married officers not belonging to the mess. Our dinner is excellent; our knives and forks and spoons are silver, with the cypher of the regiment upon them; this is upon all the plates, glasses, decanters, etc., and forms a most elegant effect.

However, Heathcote was still very new to the life, and it was summer: these pleasures, along with the society of his fellow officers, might begin to pall as months and then years slipped by.[41]

Life in most colonial garrisons was less appealing, for local society was much more limited and the climate was often unhealthy. The West Indies in particular was notorious for encouraging a combination of indolence, self-indulgence and excessive drinking, which was not helped by the constant threat of disease and the limited prospect of active service. The Canadian provinces and the Cape of Good Hope were much more attractive, but still often dull, while India had its own particular challenges. These problems were all compounded by the fact that regiments were often left in a single colony for many years without any regular system for granting home leave to the officers – let alone the men – who might as a result feel marooned and cut off from their families and friends at home, without the consoling sense of purpose provided by active operations.[42]

Even at the height of the Peninsular War Wellington had no more than one quarter of the entire British army under his command, although as units came and went it is probable that something like one half of the junior officers in the army served in the Peninsula at one time or another. Much of their time was spent in cantonments, often in the remote uplands of the Portuguese–Spanish border near Ciudad Rodrigo, where the main army spent the spring and summer of 1810 and the winters of 1811–12 and 1812–13. Life in cantonments was seldom particularly comfortable or interesting. William Swabey wrote in his diary on 4 March 1813, 'I feel myself so constantly engaged in the pursuits of infantry officers in England, viz: watching fishes swim under the bridge, throwing stones at pigs, etc. I am ashamed of it, but have nothing else to do'. And a newcomer noted that

[t]he indolent & inactive life of an officer, when not actually engaged in the field was to be seen in great perfection – *Roderic[k] Random* (an odd volume) was the only book in the possession of the corps – this passed thro' hands from the colonel [to] the ensign. The first days of my arrival in consequence of the rain gave me almost disgust of the military character – I visited several – some I found lounging in chairs others asleep on their beds & in that most elegant of attitudes elbows placed upon the windows the hands supporting the head – the person watching the dirty stream running down the street carrying with it every species of filth.[43]

When engaged in active operations regimental officers were just as exposed to the weather, shortages of food and other hardships as their men, and many a young subaltern – or even an experienced captain – was grateful to accept a leg of mutton or hatful of beans which his men had happened to find on their march and not to enquire too closely about its provenance, for the army often outpaced its supplies. Rank brought some privileges: when the quartermaster was allocating billets the most senior officer naturally got the best, and in 1812 Peter Le Mesurier told his sister 'I enjoy marching more than being in Quarters because I am too young a Sub[altern] to ever have a good Quarters'. Some officers loved the life: George Simmons in the 95th wrote that 'it is quite immaterial to me whether I roll myself in a blanket and sleep upon the ground . . . to be living in England after this wild, romantic existence would not give me half so much satisfaction'. For others there was a balance between suffering and satisfaction:

> This is a terrible life, but the sweets of the Army are to come when we get to old England, at present we have the bitters of it. I assure you I like this much better than if I was receiving the same pay in the Militia and doing nothing. I have when sitting with my friends in England something to say for myself, but were I doing nothing I should be obliged to hold my tongue. I am rejoiced beyond measure at being ordered to join my Regt. instead of living in idleness in the Depôt while they are suffering in Portugal.

A few actually quit the army and turned to other careers. Joseph Dornford had joined the 95th Rifles rather than the Church, but it did not take him long to realize his mistake and he told his fellows: 'I am astonished how you can joke and pass off so lightly scenes of misery and woe such as we have gone through . . . God knows how I repent ever turning soldier.' He left the army, took holy orders and was elected a Fellow of Oriel before receiving a living in Northamptonshire.[44]

Officers occasionally reflected on their choice of profession. John Aitchison wrote in his diary in May 1811:

> Were any misfortune to deprive my worthy parent of the means of supporting me . . . how could I live? Not by my pay for that is barely sufficient for my cloth[e]s! . . . Do not imagine from this that I abso-lutely hate my profession – by no means – the profession of arms

always has been and ever will be respectable – I rejoice in contributing in any way my assistance to add to the renown of my country, and I glory in having acted in deeds which have immortalized my regiment [the 3rd Foot Guards] and have enhanced the character of the army – but how dearly purchased! – at two and twenty I find myself unequal to extraordinary exertion, and I am compelled to live as *cautiously* abstemious as a ruined *debauchee* and what is worse, I am left in doubt whether I shall ever be restored to my former health, but I am galled most at *the want of independence* which I can never gain.[45]

And Peter Le Mesurier told his sister that he hoped that her son 'may never be a Soldier but chuse some other profession where he may acquire a decent fortune without exposing himself to the hardships inseperable [*sic*] from a Soldier's life'. Yet his own feelings were ambivalent, as he expressed in another letter:

> If a Man wishes to lead an unsettled life, let him enter the Army. He will not want variety and at the same time do some good, and gain credit for fighting for his Country. Who would not brave any Danger to have such Compliments paid him as Major Gen[l]: Sir James Leith has, in one of the last Gazettes, for his Bravery at Badajoz and the ever memorable Action of Salamanca when he led the Fifth Division to Victory. This sounds so very beautiful that I am inclined to belive [*sic*] that, had I an opportunity I would not leave the Army, in hopes of having praises bestowed on me at some future time.[46]

And while old soldiers often grew sentimental there was some truth as well as a good deal of nostalgia in John Kincaid's retrospect on his life in the Rifles:

> No officer during that time had one fraction to rub against another; and when I add that our paunches were nearly as empty as our pockets, it will appear almost a libel upon common-sense to say that we enjoyed it; yet so it was – our very privations were a subject of pride and boast

to us, and there still continued to be an esprit de corps – a buoyancy of feeling animating all, which nothing could quell; we were alike ready for the field or for frolic, and when not engaged in one, went headlong into the other.

Ah me! when I call to mind that our chief support in those days of trial was the anticipated delight in recounting those tales in after years, to wondering and admiring groups around our domestic hearths, in merry England; and when I find that so many of these after years have already passed, and that the folks who people these present years, care no more about these dear-bought tales of former ones than if they were spinning-wheel stories of some 'auld wife ayont the fire'; I say it is not only enough to make me inflict them with a book, as I have done, but it makes me wish that I had it all over to do again; and I think it would be very odd if I would not do exactly as I have done, for I knew no happier times, and they were their own reward![47]

One of the main disadvantages of life as a soldier was that it made it difficult to marry. The pay was not adequate to support a wife and it afforded almost no hope of a settled and comfortable home in which husband and wife could live and bring up a family. At the outset of his career Peter Le Mesurier expressed the common view that it was unreasonable for an officer to expect his wife to accompany him on active service:

Capt[n]: Louzern kept me company last night till past 11 o'Clock. He is a very pleasant man. He is a married man with four Children and has left both Wife and children behind. He has been right, for I think women endure many hardships in transports therefore please to tell my good Sister Ann that I do not intend to Marry before I am totally unfit for His Majesty's service.

By 1811 this had extended to a feeling that officers should be slow to marry at all, at least in wartime:

I must beg of you or some of my sisters, when they see my newly married cousin, to congratulate her on my part & to wish her many happy years as M[rs] Thomson. I am affraid [*sic*], however, a soldier's life will not be the hapiest [*sic*] she could have chosen. I must own, it would not give me much pleasure to hear of my Dear Sisters being engaged to an Off[ice][r]: From what I have seen & heard it would by no means suit them. It makes both the Husband & Wife wretched. When the Regiment is under orders for Service she is affraid [*sic*] of loosing [*sic*] him & he dreads the consequences, should he have the misfortune to lose his life, of leaving a beloved wife and family with perhaps a wretched pitance [*sic*] of Forty or Fifty pounds a year. These are my reasons against a Soldier's [*sic*] marrying, which I hope will be approved of by my D[ea][r] Sisters.

Not that he had any objection to the idea of marriage in general, indeed at the end of 1812 he joked that, 'As I think it probable that we shall have peace ere long, I intend, should I be placed on half-pay, to offer myself in Matrimony to any Lady with a decent fortune and retire to live quietly in some little cottage. My Sisters may be able to give me advice on the subject.' Unfortunately his sisters informed him that the disadvantages of being a soldier's wife had become too well known, and that belles were less inclined than before to be captivated by the sight of a red jacket:

I am excessively sorry to find by Anne's letter that, instead of raising in the estimation of the Ladies, we have fallen so much. This unfortunate war in the Peninsula has, I suppose, been the cause of this great falling off, for instead of a Blooming Fresh countenance that Off[ice][rs]: have on leaving the Home Station for service, they return with a Tanny, Emaciated face, some wanting legs, others Arms & Eyes, &[c]:, &[c]:, which, I suppose, is the cause of their dislike to Soldiers. If, at some future time, our Duty consisted only of Field Days in Guernsey for their amusement, perhaps we may become favourites again.[48]

Nonetheless some officers did marry and a few of their wives even came out to the Peninsula with them, although most then stayed in

Lisbon. A rare exception was Susannah Dalbiac, the wife of Lieutenant-Colonel Charles Dalbiac of the 4th Dragoons. A slight, delicate woman, she endured all the privations of the campaign, sleeping out in all weathers and searching the battlefield of Salamanca in the dark for her husband, who was fortunately unharmed. Her behaviour was exceptional and was much admired in the army, with the commander of the brigade writing home to his sister, 'I am surprised how she has been able to stand the trial without injury to her health . . . Sincerely do I wish them both a safe return to their own fireside to enjoy as they ought the inestimable reward of such fidelity and attachment!' And, in the most famous love story of the Peninsular War, Harry Smith found his Juana in the ruins and chaos of Badajoz after it had been stormed and was being sacked by the victorious British troops. Juana accompanied Harry through all the campaigns that followed and, as he wrote with less reticence than was common among English gentlemen, 'inspired me with a maddening love which, from that period to this (now thirty-three years), has never abated under many and the most trying circumstances'.[49]

It was easier when a regiment was at home, although most officers would still need something more than their pay to support a wife and family in comfort. Ralph Heathcote dined with Lieutenant-Colonel Grey, his commanding officer, 'who lives a mile from our barracks at Porto Bello, a beautiful little town close to the sea. He is a man of great fortune, married to a very handsome woman, who did the honours of her table in a superior manner. He himself is a very pleasant, polite man, who has seen very much of the world, both Europe and the Indies.' Yet even for such fortunate couples there was the ever present prospect of separation if the regiment was ordered overseas, and it seems likely that many officers left the army and looked for another occupation when they wanted to marry. Not that finding another occupation was easy, with John Aitchison admitting to his brother that 'I really regretted having entered the army' but that he felt that he should 'persevere . . . and endeavour to overcome all difficulties . . . for I am quite unacquainted with business, and now weaned from the necessary habits'. His view may have been coloured by the fact that he was recovering from malaria at the time and feeling particularly downcast, but it would not be surprising if a number of officers felt trapped in their profession, unhappy where they were but unable to discover an alternative.[50]

⪼⫸⪻

In 1813, the most costly year of the war, 168 British officers were killed in action or died of their wounds, and a further 258 died of disease or misadventure, making a total of 426 deaths, or less than one in thirty officers in the service at that time. In most years the proportion of those killed in action was considerably lower, with illness generally accounting for twice as many deaths as battle. Making some heroic assumptions and a good deal of plain guesswork we can estimate that over the course of the war about one officer in ten died, either from illness or enemy action, and that one in every six or seven officers was wounded. This applies to all the officers who served in the regular army at some point between 1803 and 1815; and the odds of being killed or wounded were higher for those serving in the later years of the war than in the years before 1809. In addition there were many officers who survived, but whose health was permanently damaged by wounds, illness or the hardships they suffered while campaigning.[51]

The rewards seem hardly commensurate with these risks or with the demands of active service. A few senior officers gained fortunes, most obviously the Duke of Wellington with his multiple peerages and parliamentary grants amounting to £700,000. Lieutenant-General George Harris, who commanded the army that captured Seringapatam in 1799 received £130,000 in prize money, but even his principal subordinates got much less: Sir David Baird was disappointed with his £11,000, and Wellington got just over £4,000 on that occasion, while a British subaltern received £432: a pleasant windfall, but not life-changing. Yet Seringapatam was the greatest prize of the whole war, and the army generally had far fewer opportunities of securing prize money than the navy, and when it did the fruits almost invariably went to a very senior officer: there was no equivalent position to the fortunate or favoured frigate captain becoming a rich man as the result of a single cruise.[52]

In November 1812 there were 518 generals in the army (including major-generals and lieutenant-generals), but only 200 of these were employed, including only 3 of the 77 full generals. Promotion over the rank of lieutenant-colonel was entirely by seniority, so the senior ranks of the army were filled by aged men of no great ability; however, generals were not paid except when they were employed. Most generals derived some income from a regimental rank (usually the half-pay of a major or a lieutenant-colonel), and some also held a sinecure which was bestowed by the commander-in-chief as a reward for service, or as a pension, or as a piece of patronage. Being appointed colonel of a regiment was a valuable sinecure, with pay and other perquisites usually amounting to between £400 and £1,000 or a little more, although when Henry Torrens congratulated Wellington on being appointed Colonel of the Royal Horse Guards in 1813 he assured him that the position was worth around £3,000 a year. However, the Royal Horse Guards was known to be the most valuable regiment in the army, and it is not unlikely that Torrens was exaggerating a little. In general cavalry regiments were more lucrative than infantry regiments; and single battalion regiments were worth less than those with two or even three battalions. There were not enough regiments to go around, even when all the colonial and veteran units were included, but about one third of the generals in the army (168 of the 518) were regimental colonels, almost always holding the position for life except when they were moved to a more valuable vacancy. The second common means of financially rewarding generals was to appoint them governor of a fortress or colony. Some of these appointments were active, even onerous, full-time positions, but many others had few or no duties. Their pay ranged equally widely: Lord Chatham received £3,500 a year as Governor of Jersey without ever needing to give it much, if any, attention; while the governorship of Scarborough Castle yielded a mere £15 a year. The governorship of Quebec was probably more typical of the sinecures, producing nearly £350 a year and not requiring residence. An admiral ashore with his guaranteed half-pay was in a much better position than a general who had to depend on the favour of the Horse Guards to receive anything.[53]

Generals employed at home or in some colonies might do quite well financially, but those in the Peninsula often found that their pay and allowances did not cover their costs. In 1813 Wellington wrote home on behalf of two of his principal subordinates, Lieutenant-General Sir Rowland Hill and Lieutenant-General Sir John Hope: 'They, each of them, command a large corps, and great expenses must be incurred by them; and I know the former, and I believe the latter, has not the means of defraying those expenses.' Neither man was independently wealthy, but both had their pay and allowances as a lieutenant-general on service, supplemented with colonelcies (Hill of the 94th, Hope of the 92th Foot), and Hill was also Governor of Blackness Castle (worth £283 a year). Yet when Hope took over his command from Sir Thomas Graham he found that his pay amounted to £1,861 and his expenses would be not less than £2,140. Good horses were essential and expensive, but generals were also expected to feed their aides-de-camp, staff and visitors to their head-quarters including newly arrived officers and those coming on business.[54]

The career of Galbraith Lowry Cole, one of Wellington's most successful divisional commanders, illustrates the limitations of the army as a career from a worldly point of view. Cole was born in 1772, three years after Wellington, and was one of the fortunate generation who joined the army before the outbreak of the war in 1793. He rose from cornet in the 12th Dragoons in 1787 to lieutenant-colonel in 1794, and held a number of important staff positions in the early years of the war, serving in the West Indies, Ireland, the Mediterranean and Egypt. He was well connected both in the army and in society: he was the second son of the Earl of Enniskillen, and sat in both the Irish and British Parliaments. In 1808 he was promoted major-general, and in 1813 lieutenant-general a few months after receiving the Order of the Bath. His division was one of the best managed in the army, he played a prominent part in numerous battles and sieges, he was thanked by Parliament, and he was twice wounded: slightly at Albuera and more severely at Salamanca. Few men in Wellington's army played a larger part in the war or achieved more fame, yet when he returned to England in the autumn of 1814 he was discontented and unhappy with his prospects. He told his sister a few months later that 'Every feeling in me of honourable ambition is crushed by what I feel unmerited neglect. It is foolish, I believe, to give way to these feelings, but they get the better of me in spite of myself. Had I the means of retiring from public life, I would not hesitate in doing so . . .'. In June 1815 he married Lady Frances Harris, the 32-year-old daughter of the Earl of Malmesbury, whom he had first met years before. He missed Waterloo as a result, but held an important position in the Army of Occupation of France, yet even then he remained troubled by his comparative poverty and lack of prospects. At the end of the occupation he was offered a peerage, but declined because he did not feel that he had the means to support the honour, and in 1822 he accepted the governorship of Mauritius 'from a sense of duty towards my children', hoping to make substantial savings from his (admittedly generous) salary. Cole and his wife spent the next decade first in Mauritius and then at the Cape of Good Hope. Their life was comfortable and not unpleasant, but it is striking that such a successful soldier should have been forced to spend his fifties in distant exile as a reward for his services.[55]

The regimental officers who formed the great bulk of the army were naturally much worse off. With the coming of peace the army was drastically reduced and large numbers of young men found themselves on half-pay with little prospect of further advancement. The rate of half-pay was increased in 1814 but remained low: a captain in an ordinary infantry regiment received seven shillings a day, and a lieutenant-colonel 11 shillings (£128 and £200 respectively per annum). An army captain thus received a little more than a naval lieutenant but less than a commander; while a lieutenant-colonel was at the lower end of the scale of a naval captain. In most cases this was a meagre reward for hard service, but the system could be abused, and in February 1814 John Orrok secured a commission in the 78th Foot for his brother-in-law with an eye firmly on peace and half-pay. 'All the second Battalions will be reduced and if Jamie is not within eight of the top of the Ensigns, he will be sent on half pay. He can then become a Nurseryman again and have an annuity of £40 a Year for life.' In the event Jamie took a liking to soldiering and managed to avoid going on half-pay, so that the plan worked out rather differently than Orrok intended. The Horse Guards would certainly not have approved of a half-pay officer working as a nurseryman, or in any position not suitable for a gentleman, but there were probably many cases of officers being forced into menial positions without the knowledge of the army authorities.[56]

A career in the army took a considerably different shape to a career in the navy. Young men joined the army later but then usually served continuously so long as the country was at war, while even at the height of the conflict with Napoleon naval officers spent much time ashore and on half-pay. Neither career was well rewarded, but there was a greater chance of a financial windfall for officers in the navy. The navy was also much more competitive, while the ability of officers in the army to purchase promotion gave them greater independence. A naval officer depended on the support and patronage of superior officers in the early stages of his career and then on influence with the Admiralty for his employment in an attractive position as a captain, commodore or admiral. An army officer's progress through the ranks was much smoother, oiled by purchase if necessary, and it was only when he had been promoted a colonel or a major-general and was looking for employment on the staff that he needed the support of a superior officer or the Horse Guards. (Not that being employed as the ADC to a general, or as a staff officer, would do anything other than help in his advancement, but it was less necessary than in the navy.) On the other hand, a naval captain – even a naval commander – had much more autonomy than even a lieutenant-colonel or major commanding a battalion in the army. He was responsible for the safety of his ship and his crew and would often be employed on an independent operation detached from the main fleet. Except in the colonies, where junior army officers were sometimes expected to act far from their superiors, it was rare for even a major-general to be allowed much initiative or room to decide even how to deploy his own units.

The wastage rate in both services was high: only a small proportion of the young men who joined attained the rank of naval captain or lieutenant-colonel in the army. Naval officers seem to have found it a little easier to marry, although the position of a wife of an officer in either service was far from enviable. It was probably easier for officers in the army to find a new career after the war, if only because they had joined at a later age and so had a slightly greater experience of civilian life, but it is likely that many officers in both services felt trapped in a career without means of escape. Some men, like Henry Austen, made valuable connections in the army (or, in his case, the militia) which laid the foundations for a subsequent career, but for many, like John Aitchison, it proved a cul-de-sac.

Harry Smith remained in the army, and went on to serve in Africa and India winning fresh honours, notably at Aliwal in 1846. In 1852 he was a standard bearer at the funeral of the Duke of Wellington, and two years later was finally promoted lieutenant-general, 49 years after he joined the army. He died in 1860 and was buried at Whittlesey. His wife, Juana, after whom Ladysmith is named, survived until 1872, a full 60 years after the storming of Badajoz. She was passionately devoted to her husband's memory, often telling her young relatives stories of '"Your uncle Harry", pronouncing the name with the full Continental *a* and a strongly trilled *r*.'[57]

Felix Calvert sailed to join Wellington's army just a week before Waterloo. On 23 June his mother, who was staying at Brighton, wrote in her journal,

> I went at four o'clock to the Library, and soon after the papers arrived, giving an account of the Duke of Wellington's great victory of the 18th . . . I returned home in great anxiety. But a few minutes after I received by the coach a letter from Mr C[alvert], saying that Sir James and Mr. Holmes had searched through the list of killed and wounded at the Foreign Office, and Felix's name was certainly not among them. I am always fearing that there may be some mistake.

On the next day: 'No fresh news, except that prisoners were coming fast . . . I feel very unhappy at not getting a letter from Felix. What can be the reason? Bonaparte has abdicated in favour of his son . . . The Duke of Wellington is at Compiègne – within forty miles of Paris. But I care for nothing till I hear from my beloved boy.' Finally, a week after hearing of the battle,

I am the happiest creature imaginable! This morning brought me, thank God! a letter from my Felix dated June 22nd, safe and well, though he had been in the whole of the actions of the 16th [Battle of Quatre Bras] and 18th [Battle of Waterloo]. On the 16th a piece of his boot was torn away by a shell, and on the 18th his horse was killed under him and four or five shots went through his coat.

Felix Calvert survived for another forty years and died in London in 1857.[58]

Mrs Le Mesurier was not as fortunate as Mrs Calvert. Her son Peter was killed at the Battle of the Nive on 10 December 1813. His last letter home ended:

Remember me also to my D[ea]r Father, Julia, Abr[aha]m, Car[l] and my Kind Friends, particularly Uncle & Aunt W[illia]m & Doct. If things turn out as I wish, I hope to pass my Easter Holidays with you. Till then, [that] God bless you and grant you Health and Happiness is the sincere prayer of, Dear Mother, your most Affectionate Son, P. Le Mesurier.

He was 24 years old.[59]

CHAPTER TWELVE

INDIA

SIR WALTER SCOTT, IN one of his lesser works, published in 1827, has a character advise a budding novelist to send his hero to India:

> That is the true place for a Scot to thrive in; and if you carry your story fifty years back . . . you will find as much shooting and stabbing there as ever was in the wild Highlands. If you want rogues, as they are so much in fashion with you, you have that gallant caste of adventurers, who laid down their consciences at the Cape of Good Hope as they went out to India, and forgot to take them up again when they returned.

The advice is taken, and in the story within the story, one of the characters muses on the romantic appeal of India and its promise of great wealth:

> 'Oh, Delhi! oh, Golconda! have your names no power to conjure down idle recollections? India, where gold is won by steel; where a brave man cannot pitch his desire of fame and wealth so high but that he may realize it if he have fortune for his friend? Is it possible that the bold adventurer can fix his thoughts on you, and still be dejected . . .?'[1]

India – at least the India of the 1760s and '70s – was seen as a land where unscrupulous European adventurers might win extraordinary riches by daring, courage and good luck, or perish in the attempt.

However, as the advice to set the story half a century in the past recognized, British rule in India had changed character since the first days of wild exploitation. Resentment and alarm at the effect that such fortunes would have in Britain, as well as the damage done in India, led to a reaction, symbolized by the recall and impeachment of Warren Hastings. Pitt's government appointed Lord Cornwallis as Governor-General in 1786, with instructions to reduce corruption and raise the standard of behaviour in public office to something more closely aligned with that prevailing at home. It took time, but Cornwallis's reforms and the change in attitudes they reflected gradually permeated the British community in India, with strong support of subsequent Governors-General including Lord Wellesley. More emphasis was placed on expanding British political influence and hegemony than on trade or the enrichment of individual British officers or officials, and empire began to take on incongruous overtones of moral rectitude. Great fortunes were still made, and not always without some sacrifice of integrity, but there was diminishing tolerance of flagrant abuses. At the same time the British became more insular – there were more of them in India, they mixed more with each other, and were less open to adopting Indian ways (including some of the forms of corruption that Cornwallis was trying to reduce). The generation of British officers who lived openly with Indian women, dressed in Indian clothes, smoked hookahs and had little expectation or even wish to return home, persisted, but became old-fashioned and were even the object of mockery to young men arriving fresh from England in the first decades of the nineteenth century. British officers still often learned Indian languages, but they became much more aloof and foreign – although, of course, there were many exceptions to these generalizations, with some officers of the old school never having attempted to understand the country in which they were living, and some later officers throwing themselves into Indian culture with enthusiasm.[2]

Although India in the late eighteenth and early nineteenth centuries was no longer quite the El Dorado it had appeared a generation before, it still appealed as a land of opportunity, especially for men who lacked first-rate connections or money at home, or who had already been disappointed in their first endeavours, or who had damaged their reputation by their imprudence. It was dangerous: most of the young men who sailed from Britain to take up positions in the service of the East India Company in the decades around 1800 never returned home, and of those who did, only a minority came home with a fortune. Nonetheless there was no shortage of applicants for positions in India, and the Company divided its patronage carefully between its directors, with the chairman and deputy chairman each receiving a double share, and the President of the Board of Control (the politician with oversight of British interests in India) given four times the quota of an ordinary director. For many years this politician was Henry Dundas, and he gave many positions to young Scots, some of whom did very well in India, and whose appointment helped consolidate Dundas's immense political influence in Scotland.[3]

The easiest way to secure an appointment to a position in India was through a personal connection to one of the directors of the Company. William Hickey's father had sufficient influence to secure his appointment as a cadet in the Madras army, although not enough to gain the more prized position of a civilian official – or writer – on the Bengal establishment, which was generally supposed to promise an easier path to riches.

A few days after our return to town my father took me to visit Sir George Colebrooke, the director who had nominated me a cadet. The Baronet received us with politeness, telling my father it afforded him pleasure to have had it in his power to comply with his request. He said he had appointed me for Madras in preference to Bengal, which was by many considered the most advantageous for a military man, because the coast of Coromandel was then the seat of an active war with Hyder Ali, and consequently more likely to give promotion to a young soldier, and that instead of remaining a cadet two, three, or four years, as would probably happen to those who went the ensuing season to Bengal, I should obtain a commission in the Madras army upon landing.

From Sir George Colebrooke's, we went to Mr. Laurence Sullivan's, then a man of great influence and a leading Director. He likewise was very kind, and promised to give letters that would be of essential service to me. He recommended my father to lose no time in securing a passage for me, as the ships would all be much crowded. From Mr. Sullivan's we went to the India house, where I was introduced to Mr. Coggan, one of the Company's principal officers, who . . . gave me a printed list of necessaries for a writer, observing that most of the articles therein specified would be equally useful to a military man, only I must recollect in addition to take a few yards of scarlet, blue, green, and yellow cloths, in order to make up regimentals according to the corps to which I should be attached . . .

A formal interview at India House followed, in which Hickey admitted to having no military experience and expressed satisfaction with the terms which he was being offered, and that was all. His appointment was issued and he was given 20 guineas towards the cost of his equipment and supplies for the long voyage. He had already secured his passage with Captain Waddell on board the *Plassey*, for which he paid 50 guineas for a seat at the captain's table.[4]

It was less easy for those without such personal connections. In 1818 Sydney Smith unwisely thought that India might suit his sensitive, rather frail eldest son, Douglas, who was then only 13. He wrote to Lord Holland reminding him of an earlier promise to ask Alexander Baring to secure a writership, adding, 'I am aware of the greater facility of procuring a Cadetship, but I cannot find it in my heart to doom him to such a lot . . . I am aware it is a great thing to ask'. Either the chain of obligation contained one too many links to reel in as large a prize as a writership or Smith had better second thoughts, for Douglas was not condemned to India, but sent to Westminster School (where he was badly bullied) and then on to Christ Church before his health finally collapsed and he died at the age of 24. Political influence was probably more efficacious in securing an appointment to India than a promotion in the navy, for the large number of directors meant that anyone who was well connected would usually know someone who might be inclined to help, but good standing in the City was more useful, for the directors were primarily men of commerce, not politics or society.[5]

At least Smith had a powerful and influential patron to act on his behalf; for those without such connections it could be a hard struggle to find a good place. In 1802 the newly married John Orrok was in London desperately looking for a position which would enable him to support his wife Betsy. After meeting a succession of disappointments he placed an advertisement in a newspaper offering 300 guineas to anyone who could provide him with a situation with an adequate salary. He received a response from an agent who 'in an underhand way is acquainted with People of Interest, gives them sums of money for to procure [sic] different situations under Government and charges the person so appointed 40 or 50 guineas more than he pays to the Persons who have obtained them thro their Interest'. The agent offered him a cadetship in the Indian army for 300 guineas 'and began to expatiate on the vast promotion, Luxury, etc., that I would meet with there and that he would get me a letter to the Commander-in-Chief who he said would *immediately* provide for me'. However, Orrok cut him short by announcing that he had already served in India in a British regiment and that his father was a senior officer in the Company's army, and he 'knew the Information that he gave me was very *incorrect*'. The disconcerted agent beat his retreat, but it is likely that he found other young men – and their fathers – who were more receptive to his promises.[6]

In 1809 a parliamentary inquiry received evidence that there was an illicit trade in Indian appointments. It recorded details of two dozen cases in which an appointment had actually been made – three writerships and 21 cadetships – and there were other cases where the transaction had fallen through or where there was insufficient evidence. In none of these cases was there any evidence of the personal involvement or knowledge of any of the directors of the Company: it was always done indirectly, and the committee professed itself satisfied that none of the directors knew what was going on. An example shows how the scheme worked: in 1806–7 Edward James Smith was nominated as a writer to Bengal by George Thellusson, one of the directors. Thellusson and his two brothers were MPs, and successful merchants and businessmen, although their reputation for stability and integrity was far below that of Baring. George Thellusson had appointed Smith to the position simply to oblige his cousin, Mr Woodford. Woodford admitted to the committee that he had received £3,500 from Mr Tahourdin, an attorney who had introduced Smith to him, but positively declared that Thellusson had known nothing of this and had received nothing. He had grown up with his cousin and they had always been close. He told the committee:

> you will not wonder perhaps that he should be naturally inclined to do what I wished, without any very minute inquiry into those things; he could not suppose I made any improper use of it, however I might have been culpable in so doing. I should have thought caution on his part would have shewn a suspicion that he must have thought me undeserving, and that I should have thought myself in some degree injured. Mr. George Thellusson and I were the earliest friends, and he could have no reason till now in supposing I abused his confidence in any of those transactions.[7]

This was not the only position that Woodford obtained from his cousin and sold through Tahourdin. Another writership in Bengal was sold for 3,500 guineas of which Mr Woodford received £3,000, Mr Tahourdin £150, and the remainder was divided between a Mr Donovan and a Mr Garrat. Cadetships were worth much less, generally between £200 and £300, sometimes going for even less, so that the agent who approached Orrok was pitching his bid high. Several other directors were involved in other appointments, and even Lord Castlereagh was implicated in one transaction, although this involved several intermediaries and there was no suggestion that Castlereagh knew that money had changed hands at any point, let alone that he personally benefited.[8]

Henry Austen's bank and agency business was also implicated in the illicit trade in the appointments, and specifically in the dealings between Woodford, Tahourdin and Jeremiah Donovan. Indeed, they introduced Donovan to Tahourdin stating him to be a friend of theirs and a gentleman of great respectability. This was not a view widely shared, for Woodford told the inquiry that he had no direct knowledge of Mr Donovan but had known his reputation for years, and that 'if I had had any idea that such a man as Mr Donovan could have been connected with the transaction, I certainly should not [have had anything to do with it]'. But the transaction was completed at Austen & Co. with Henry Austen supervising the deposit of the money. This was the unsavoury end of agency business and Henry was clearly not only going beyond strict legality, but also beyond what was generally regarded as acceptable practice. The actual morality of the question is rather less clear: after all, this was an age in which the seats in Parliament and church livings were freely sold, and there is no reason to suppose that the young men who paid for their positions in India were any less capable or more rapacious than those who obtained them through private influence and personal friendship. The greater risk was that such transactions encouraged the belief that this was how all appointments were made, that the whole system was more corrupt than was actually the case, and that this in turn led to the exploitation of the credulous and unwary who paid agents like Donovan large sums for things, such as a commission in the army, that might be obtained without cost.[9]

Mountstuart Elphinstone, the fourth son of the soldier and Scottish peer Lord Elphinstone, was still at school in London in March 1795 when he learned that his uncle, one of the directors of the Company, had secured his appointment as a writer in Bengal. He dutifully wrote home telling his mother that he was 'very much obliged to my uncle, and very happy to be appointed', although he had previously wanted to join the army. He only admitted to regretting that 'I will not be able to return to Scotland for want of time, and so have no possibility of seeing you and my sisters. If that were possible (which it is not), I should like it of all things.' The fleet sailed a few weeks later, and the 15-year-old Elphinstone did not enjoy his passage, writing home after a month at sea that the captain's

> manners have made him disliked by every one of his passengers. He seems to have the most thorough contempt for them all, us poor dogs in particular . . . I cannot express my dislike to the voyage. Give my love to my sisters and Curly. Oh! how happy I would be to be even at Kensington, in the same island with you, and where I had letters every four days, while here I cannot hear oftener than once in the six months!

He reached Calcutta on 26 February 1796 after a voyage of almost eight months, including six weeks at Rio de Janeiro and almost as long at Madras.[10]

John Shore made the same passage a generation earlier and was dismayed to find his fellow passengers, and especially the dozen other young writers and cadets heading to India for the first time, a rough and disorderly set who managed to fight two duels even before they left Portsmouth and three or four more at subsequent landfalls. 'You cannot guess how truly mean and despicable some of them appear; contriving and hatching up every scheme to pick up a little money which their present poverty or future prospect of indigence can suggest.' The captain was uncouth and irreligious, something which troubled Shore, who was a serious young man, and who was even missing his younger brother, 'When I was with him, I little knew how I loved him; but an absence, such as this, confirms my affection, and teaches me how dear he is to me'. Fortunately the second mate treated Shore well, and one of the older passenge , a Mr Hancock, proved a good friend, 'a gentleman of real merit an real worth, and an exceeding good scholar', who gave Shore the run of his travelling library. The young man spent a good deal of his time reading, writing and practising the German flute, and he assured his mother 'I do not in the least repent the choice of life I have made: on the contrary, I am more pleased with my condition every day. I never had any objection to this way of life, but to the distance by which we are separated, and by the pains of parting'.[11]

Not everyone disliked the journey, and in 1814 John Orrok scouted objections when proposing that his unmarried sister-in-law go out to India in search of a husband.

With regard to her not standing the voyage, I am not the least afraid of that. A fine large Indiaman is not to be compared with an Aberdeen Smack, the motion is very different. She may be sick for the first eight or ten days, as most people are, but after that she will enjoy the passage amazingly as they generally dance every Evening on the quarter Deck and live like Princes (or Princesses).

In the end the plan was abandoned as too expensive: the passage (one way) would cost £233 whereas Orrok's wife Betsy had paid only £100 in 1803 when she had accompanied him to India. The 'fishing fleet' as it came to be known, was still in its infancy, a costly and dangerous recourse for young women with limited prospects at home and driven either by desperation or a strong sense of adventure.[12]

After months at sea the end of the journey was naturally a moment of high excitement for all on board. William Hickey remembered that on the night before they were expected to land,

I went to my cot, but the thoughts of being so near the place of our destination entirely banished sleep, and finding all my efforts were in vain, I put on my clothes and went upon deck. Just as I got my head above the Companion ladder, I felt an indescribably unpleasant sensation, suddenly, as it were, losing the power of breathing, which alarmed me much, for I supposed it to be the forerunner of one of those horrid Indian fevers of which I had heard so much during our voyage. Whilst worried by this idea, my friend Rogers, whose watch it was, said to me, 'Well, Bill, what do you think of this? How do you like the delightful breeze you are doomed to spend your life in?' Enquiring what he meant, I found that what had so surprised and alarmed me was nothing more than the common land wind blowing as usual at that hour directly off shore, and so intensely hot that I could compare it only to standing within the oppressive influence of the steam of a furnace.

The ship's carpenter was suddenly taken ill and died within an hour. 'This quick death, added to the horrid land wind, gave me a very unfavourable opinion of the East Indies.'[13]

According to James Welsh, who arrived in Calcutta in July 1790 as a young cadet,

> every thing the stranger meets on landing, differs so widely from all that he had been accustomed to in Europe, that the mind is lost in surprise: a surprise, not a little increased, on finding that *here* no European uses his own legs; but that all ranks and ages must bend to the custom of the place, and be carried. Here, then, the poor Griffin [newcomer], once landed, finds himself a man of some consequence; surrounded by hundreds of natives of various castes and costumes, all eagerly pressing on him their proffered services, he is hurried into a palanquin, and borne away as it were in triumph, he knows not whither.

Welsh goes on to say that a new arrival will be greeted with kindness and hospitality by relations or friends, housed and fed well, but will suffer immensely from the heat and the terrible mosquitoes. After a restless night he will emerge, covered with sores from the mosquito bites – for he will not have been able to tolerate the closed curtains that would keep them out – to find 'the sun in a clear unclouded sky, for all the world like a red-hot cannon ball'. Half a dozen servants attend him, dressing him in fine linen and he sits down to breakfast in a strange dreamlike state, 'and the spell is not soon broken; unless indeed he should be ordered out for morning drill, when *Brown Bess* and the *Goose Step* soon dispel his airy visions'.[14]

Welsh was fortunate. He belonged to the Madras army (the Company had three separate armies in India, based at Bengal, Madras and Bombay) and was greeted warmly by Lieutenant Ridgeway Mealy, the adjutant of his regiment, who 'received me into his own house, and became to me, in every sense of the word, a second parent'. Mealy taught him his duty as a soldier and encouraged him to learn Persian and Hindustani – the languages most useful to an officer in the Madras army – and by his example protected Welsh from the influence of some of the other officers, who were not, at that time, renowned for 'industry, morals, or sobriety'.[15]

A few years later a Military Academy was established at Trippasore to provide some months of basic training for newly arrived officers. Edmund Goodbehere attended the Academy in 1803 and gives a favourable account of it:

Our time here is well and fully employed. We rise at daybreak or rather before, as soon as the reveille begins to beat, and before it be finished we must all appear on the parade for drill, which lasts about two hours or better, leaving off about seven o'clock. We then run to our quarters and dress for guard-mounting at half-past seven, which is over by eight. We then breakfast. At 10 we repair to the mess house and study the language three days in the week, and the other three copying military manoeuvres, reading the regulations of the service, copying General Orders and reading Martial Law. We then dress for dinner at two, which is over about half-past three. We then have the remainder of the day to ourselves unless when on guard . . . We go through every gradation here: private, corporal, sergeant, ensign, in which last three stations no cadet is to act for more than 15 days, that all may have an equal chance of learning their duty. I assure you I am very happy and comfortable and quite satisfied with my situation. We have a good mess, of which Captain Box, our commander, is president. We are allowed at dinner half a pint of Madeira. At breakfast we have eggs, cold meat and tea.[16]

Two years later John Orrok evidently thought it an admirable institution, but Henry Bevan, who attended it in 1809 when it had been moved to Cuddalore, was less impressed. He described his fellow cadets as 'a wild set, composed of nearly one hundred and forty young men, whose exuberant and ardent spirits were constantly employed in all manner of mad pranks' and who would persecute anyone who refused to join in. 'Some of the tricks played by the cadets were merely the pardonable follies of young men; such as stealing out by night to indulge in strong potations at the house of a native, who found it his profit to aid in their gratifications.' Others were rather more serious, and one cadet who was suspected of telling tales to the authorities at the college was dragged out of bed and nearly drowned in a nearby pond of dirty water, and continued to be persecuted until he was removed from the college. Nor were the Indian teachers exempt:

> The *Moonshees*, who were sent to instruct the young men in the native languages, were never failing butts; their gravity of demeanour, their sallow complexions, rendered more dark by the contrast of their long cotton dresses, and the mixture of servility with magisterial authority in their manners, naturally provoked our ridicule. On one occasion gunpowder was introduced under a chair on which a grave *Moonshee* was sitting, and the train fired. He was terribly frightened by the explosion but sustained no injury save in his dress . . .

Another account describes the young men as in 'a continual uproar, blowing coach-horns and bugles, baiting jackals with pariah-dogs, fighting cocks, shooting kites and crows', and claims that all they learned was 'drinking, coarse language, vulgar amusements and gaming'. Soon afterwards the Academy was abolished, mostly due to pressure from home to economize, but Bevan regarded it as 'a wise act, as the establishment was productive of more harm than good'.[17]

Bevan also commented that

> A great error, committed by young officers on first joining the Indian army, is to affect contempt for the soldiers whom they are to command, calling them 'black fellows,' 'niggers,' etc. A residence of a few months at a Mofussil [up country] station soon clears the head of all that nonsense; the sepoy has many opportunities of obliging his officer, and he never neglects them if his heart be won by kindness.

According to Bevan, Indian troops usually treated not only British officers but also ordinary British soldiers well: 'The sepoy finding a British soldier drunk in the roads or fields is always ready to help him to his rooms, and assist in hiding his delinquency.' Native officers kept apart, more from their own religious scruples than from the reluctance of English officers to mix with them, but were jealous of their dignity and 'especially anxious to be the sole medium of communication between the European officer and the privates'. Bevan believed that few things fostered good relations more than subscriptions from the European officers towards the cost of religious processions and festivals – both Hindu and Muslim – celebrated by their men, and strongly defended this against criticism that it encouraged idolatry. 'I cannot disguise my opinion, that as we have taken the place of the native rulers of Hindustan, we are bound to make our government as little offensive to the prejudices of our subjects as possible.'[18]

Not all British officers took this view, and racial prejudices hardened considerably between the late eighteenth century and the middle of the nineteenth, but it is notable that sweeping prejudice was most likely to be expressed by those who were newly arrived in India, or who had spent their time in the relatively closed, Anglicized society of Calcutta, Madras or Bombay. Five months after landing in Bengal Arthur Wellesley – the future Duke of Wellington – wrote home that 'I have not yet met with a Hindoo who had one good quality, even for the state of society for his own country, and the Mussulmans are worse than they are'. But when he left India eight years later, after working closely with many Indians in positions of power and independence, he asked a friend to 'remember me most kindly to Purneah, Bistnapah, and all my friends, black, white and grey at Seringapatam and elsewhere within your reach'.[19]

⋙◆⋘

At the beginning of the nineteenth century the East India Company had around 4,500 British employees in India: roughly 3,500 officers in its armies and about 1,000 writers and other civilian officials. In addition there were several thousand rank and file white soldiers in the Company's European regiments; a substantial presence of the British regular army; and a number of British civilians pursuing independent activities ranging from lawyers to bakers, dancing masters to artists. Yet even in the late 1820s, when the British community had increased substantially, there were only 41,000 Europeans of all sorts in India.[20]

The Company's armies had grown remarkably rapidly in the second half of the eighteenth century. In 1763 the total strength of the three armies was less than 20,000; by 1805, at the close of the Maratha War, it was over 150,000 men, and this despite continual pressure from the directors in London to reduce, not increase, military spending. The number of senior officers in the army was not increased to take account of this expansion: by 1784, when the total strength of the Company's armies was well over 100,000 men there were only 10 colonels and 30 lieutenant-colonels in the whole service. This unsatisfactory situation was perpetuated simply to save money, and it led to a good deal of discontent among the officers of the Indian armies. The problem was made even worse by the rule – imposed by Parliament – that an officer in the regular British army always outranked an officer of the same rank in the Company's service. This meant that the higher and more lucrative positions commanding armies and large detachments were mostly held by regular army officers, denying the Company's officers some of the best plums in view and possibly encouraging them to concentrate their ambitions on making money rather than winning glory. It also caused much irritation lower down the chain of command, where a major or even a captain in the Company's army, who might have 15 or 20 years' experience of warfare in India, was subordinated to a young man fresh from home who was woefully ignorant of Indian conditions.[21]

Promotion for officers was entirely by seniority within each of the three armies, and because there was so little room at the top it was exceedingly slow. By the 1780s it took about 30 years of service to reach the rank of colonel, and very few officers – perhaps only one in one hundred – survived and stayed the course for that long. British officials sometimes objected to the reliance on seniority, with Lord Cornwallis declaring that 'no system for military promotion can so effectually tend to destroy all spirit of energy and attention to discipline, as that of a regular succession of the mass of Officers, according to seniority, from the lowest to the highest, throughout a whole army'. And the modern historian who has paid most attention to the subject admits that '[t]he whole system often produced aged incompetence at the top and frustration below, and only by subterfuges were its worst consequences avoided'. Nonetheless, when reforms were proposed, they were met with a storm of protest from the officers themselves, who declared that '[w]e are not generally speaking, men of interest, else we should not have preferred a service in which seniority gives command'. And they argued against any change which 'may transform the soldier into the Courtier; and make a Campaign at St. James' more desirable and advantageous than arduous exertions in the Field'. They took for granted that any element of selection or promotion on 'merit' would open the door to patronage and favouritism and that they would suffer as a result. The feeling was so strong that the authorities in India and in England were forced to back down and retain seniority as the sole means of promotion.[22]

Officers in the Company's armies in India were paid poorly, but this mattered little for they looked to their allowances and their perquisites, not their salary, for the great bulk of their income. These allowances were higher in the Bengal army, where the cost of living was relatively low, and lowest in the Bombay army, where living was also expensive; something which largely explains the preference most cadets had for the Bengal service. The most important of the allowances was 'batta', an additional payment that was meant to reflect the hardships of active service, but which had gradually spread to become almost universal, and which was paid at a rate which did not reflect any actual hardship but rather the wealth of the Company's government in that part of India. 'Batta' was paid to all officers and even to their men, with double batta being common in Bengal, and the amount naturally increasing sharply with rank. The second most important allowance was the bazaar fund, a perquisite of the senior officer commanding a unit or a station, who would receive a portion of the duties levied on the bazaar that accompanied his unit to supply it with luxuries and some necessities. Cornwallis regarded it as one of the worst abuses in the army, because it gave commanding officers a financial incentive to encourage their troops to drink and consume opium – the most profitable products sold in the bazaar – but its value and the fact that it was relatively senior officers who benefited from it, made it impossible to abolish. Officers of the rank of captain and above (and in the Company's service a captain was a relatively senior officer) also received 'revenue money', which was paid out of a fund that originally represented 2.5 per cent of the total revenue collected in Bengal.[23]

There were many other, smaller, allowances that contributed to an officer's finances, although they were less important than the ways in which an alert and not-too-scrupulous officer might make a profit. For example, none of the three armies had its own transport service, and every campaign – or even a peaceful change of quarters – required the hiring of a large number of draft animals: mostly bullocks, but sometimes also camels and elephants. These were invariably supplied by an officer or civil official of the Company, who would pass on the contract – less a very handsome commission – to an Indian contractor. The position of paymaster, or any other official having temporary custody of large sums of public money, gave a perfect opportunity to benefit from the extremely high rates of interest prevailing in India. But direct exploitation of Indian rulers and large landowners through usurious loans, while still continuing to a degree, was largely a legacy of the days before Cornwallis's new approach.[24]

Attempts to reform the system of allowances met strenuous and in the end successful resistance, with the officers arguing that they amounted to a breach of contract. 'In our early youth we exiled ourselves from our Native Country, we bade adieu to our friends and every gratification, not for the mere receipt of the present pay of our respective Ranks, but from the chance of obtaining at one period or another, those High emoluments.' It was the success of the lucky few who survived and in the end gained great wealth that had provided the incentive for the vast majority of the officers to enter the Company's service in the first place. Faced with something that fell very little short of mutiny the Company not only abandoned the proposed reforms, but was forced to make other concessions that improved the position of officers and which are said to have cost some £350,000 a year.[25]

Despite all these sources of income and the multitude of servants, most junior British officers in the Company's armies were far from prosperous. Thomas Munro, at the time a young officer in the Madras Army, wrote home to his sister in 1789 wishing that she could

> be transported for a few hours to my room, to be cured of your Western notions of Eastern luxury, to witness the forlorn condition of old bachelor Indian officers . . . walking in an old coat, and a ragged shirt, in the noonday sun, instead of looking down from my elephant, invested in my royal garments . . . I never experienced hunger or thirst, fatigue or poverty, till I came to India – that since then, I have frequently met with the first three, and that the last has been my constant companion.[26]

The problem, at least in most cases, was that when a young officer arrived in India he began to encounter expenses that he could not avoid, but it would be some time before he received any income, even his pay. Unless he had private means, this left him little alternative than to borrow, and there were numerous Indian money lenders who were happy to oblige him. Once in debt it was easy to borrow more, and with such a high mortality rate the arguments for postponing present pleasures in order to have greater resources later were not especially compelling. The interest rate on this debt was high, and the officer was forced to take out life insurance to ensure that it would be repaid in the event of his death. Consequently it would be many years before an officer's income had reached the point where it could even cover his expenses and the accumulated cost of his debt, let alone begin to pay off the capital. When John Orrok's father died in 1810 he was a senior officer in the Company's service – a lieutenant-colonel – who had been in India for more than 30 years, yet his total estate was only worth about £12,000, and this was far more typical than the wealthy nabob who returned home with a fortune after a few years in India.[27]

In February 1804, eight months after he arrived in India, Edmund Goodbehere graduated from the military academy at Trippasore and was appointed lieutenant in the 2nd battalion of the 18th Madras Native Infantry, then stationed at Poona, nearly seven hundred miles away. He wrote home to his uncle describing how he had purchased a horse and a tent (for which he received a tent allowance) and employed a lascar to manage them. 'The bullocks here are about the size of asses in England. In India no man will perform two offices, which necessarily obliges us to have a number of attendants.' He was about to make his way to Poona with another newly appointed officer in the same regiment, and they would be accompanied for part of their way by two other officers going to another unit. The four officers would have more than 20 attendants between them, but this was the bare minimum in India. Purchasing all the necessary equipment had cost more than he could afford, but Mr Tulloch in Madras had kindly lent him the money he needed and would charge him only the official, legal rate of interest of 12 per cent. He hoped to pay off this loan within a year, and did not want to draw on his uncle unless it was absolutely necessary and had been arranged in advance.[28]

Two and a half years later Goodbehere was in temporary command of a detachment of four companies of the battalion stationed at Nundydroog in Mysore, and had hopes of being appointed adjutant. 'Should I succeed it will be a very good thing for me, the pay and allowances being but little less than a captain's and the situation being a sort of introduction to other appointments on the staff.' His hopes were realized, but two years later, in October 1808, he explained to his brother that his high income was matched by equally high expenses.

> You were no doubt pleased to hear of my late appointment, which places me in the receipt of nearly £500 sterling a year. This appears at first sight a tolerable sum, though I assure you from the manner in which we are obliged to live it does not go near so far as you may imagine. On succeeding to my situation I purchased an Arab horse for something more than 70 guineas, which was accounted very cheap.

Whether Goodbehere ever got clear of his early debt is not known, but in the end it did not matter very much, for he died after a long and painful illness on 12 November 1810 at the age of 26.[29]

The news of Goodbehere's death was announced to his uncle by Lieutenant Robert Murcott of the same regiment who wrote that 'Every attention that could be paid him was shown by his brother officers, whose affections he had completely gained . . . where he was known he was respected and beloved'. The death notice in the Madras *Gazette* made the same point, that he was 'endeared by every tie of friendship' to his fellow officers. Beneath the conventional phrasing lies the reality that an officer's happiness and even his survival in India were largely dependent on his relations with the other European officers in his battalion who provided him with society, friendship and even a sense of family. Henry Bevan explicitly acknowledges this:

> European society is so limited at a Mofussil station, that unless mutual kindness and mutual forbearance were practised the place would be worse than a prison. I have often observed that officers who displayed anything but friendly and social dispositions when quartered in large cantonments, became most pleasant and agreeable companions when sent to a country station. This more especially the case when a station is occupied by a single regiment; the *esprit de corps* then comes into full exercise under the most favourable circumstances, and the phrase, 'brother-officers', instead of being a mere cant, really expresses fraternal affection.[30]

Of course things did not always go this well, and Bevan is equally eloquent on the way that an officious, fidgety commanding officer, obsessed with 'all the petty points of military etiquette' could make life a misery for the unfortunate officers under his command. Bevan's own greatest pleasures seem to have been in spending time on survey work, getting to know new country, its people and its game, for he was a keen sportsman who wrote enthusiastically about the different sorts of hunting and shooting he was able to pursue while away from his cantonments. He also enjoyed talking to local people, inviting the leading men of any nearby village to his tent, learning about the immediate locality and providing hospitality in the form of a Nautch or performance by dancing girls for which he would pay.

> Some persons have represented the Nantch [*sic*] as an improper exhi- bition which it is disgraceful to countenance; they must either have seen it under very unfavourable circumstances, or have given scope to their own perverted imaginations. There is no doubt that any species of dance may be represented by the performers so as to suggest licen- tious ideas, but there is just as little reason for denying that a dance may be perfectly innocent, and confined to a simple exhibition of graceful motion and flexibility of limb . . . so far as my experience goes, there is more for the rigid moralist to condemn in one Italian ballet, than in all the Nantches [*sic*] I ever witnessed in India.[31]

Relatively few junior officers married, although many established relationships with Indian women. Edmund Goodbehere wrote to his brother in 1808, 'I fancy I need not tell you marriage has no place in my thoughts, and it is doubtful if it ever will, though as a soldier you will not suppose me insensible to female charms.' When he died he left behind him a young child, for whose benefit Lieutenant Murcott proposed to appropriate the small sum realized by the sale of Goodbehere's clothes and other possessions amounting to about £200. Henry Bevan is quite open about the prevalence of such connections, and remarks that 'Offspring [are] anxiously desired by the mothers, as it establishes a kind of claim to continued protection, but this often proves a source of great anxiety and regret to the fathers in after-life.' On the whole his view is sympathetic, although his underlying attitudes are distinctly dated:

> The traits of character in these mistresses are of course very various, but in general their conduct depends on the treatment which they receive. Many of them regard the interests of their protector as iden- tified with their own, and exert the utmost vigilance to save him from

the impositions and peculations of his servants: in the hour of sickness and sorrow they endeavour to allay his pains by most soothing cares, and no attendant can exhibit more affectionate watchfulness over a suffering invalid than an Indian female. Jealousy is their dangerous passion; under its influence they administer deleterious drugs, either to ensure revenge, or as is more frequently the case, with the superstitious hope of retaining their master's affections. But this jealousy is exhibited only when their rival is another native woman; I never knew an instance of a Hindu woman attempting to take revenge for the marriage of her master to a European wife; on the contrary I have known them, years after all intercourse had been abandoned, exhibit the most respectful attachment to the wife and children of their former master.

The picture, however, must sometimes be reversed; the debts under which several officers of the Indian army have been crushed to the very earth, may too often be traced to the capricious extravagance of a mistress, though not so frequently as to the pernicious habits of gambling.[32]

Life for an officer in the Company's armies had some advantages compared to the life of an officer in the regular army at home. There were fewer opportunities to mix in educated European society, but some officers such as Henry Bevan relished the chance to explore unfamiliar, exotic country and to learn to appreciate at least a little of its culture. Officers in the Company's service were also more likely to exercise responsibility and be forced to use their independent judgement when they were still quite young, for India in this period was never completely peaceful and small units were constantly engaged in minor operations. As one veteran wrote, junior officers in India were

habituated to act in an emergency with a facility that few subordinate officers in Europe have a prospect of obtaining. Before an officer attains the rank of Captain, he must unavoidably have been in command of parties on distant marches, in the conveyance of stores, in the guard of posts and strongholds, in the business of collecting and menacing refractory chiefs . . . and in every other species of duty which can occur.

Even Cornwallis acknowledged that 'In the Company's Service . . . they have been more in the practice of judging and acting for themselves, than officers who have served in a less extensive field'. Esprit de corps, a love of India and a sense of professional pride offered a better chance of happiness than the dream of returning home a wealthy man.[33]

⇒·⇐

Writers, the civilian officials serving the East India Company, faced many of the same challenges as officers in the Company's armies. The difficulty of the climate, the threat of disease, the discomforts of the local fauna, especially insects, and the sense of isolation from home and family, all amounted to a severe test of stamina, health and character. New arrivals were usually assigned to a department of government at Calcutta, Madras or Bombay for their first year. Here they could make a start on learning the local languages and begin to adjust to the climate and the different mores of society. They were often able to choose between belonging to the judicial and the revenue departments, with one old India hand declaring that 'the latter affords the wider field for the exercise of ability, and the active energies of mind; the duties of the judicial functionaries are of a sedentary nature, and chiefly suited to persons of studious habits'.[34]

There is a vivid account of the life of a writer in India in the early nineteenth century in a sketch written by Henry Roberdeau in about 1805, six years after he had arrived in India. Roberdeau belonged to the judicial department, and held the position of Registrar at Mymensingh, a provincial town in Bengal. His district was about the size of an English county, with a population of just under two million. The land revenue was permanently set at £90,000, which he regarded as too low. There should have been six British officials in the town, but there was no doctor at the time and Roberdeau had no assistant, so that there were only four:

himself, the Magistrate, the collector and the collector's assistant. 'I get up between five and six,' he wrote, describing his daily routine, 'mount my Horse for a Ride, return about seven, bathe and dress for breakfast, to which I sit down about nine o'clock. This meal is soon despatched and then comes my Hookah, I smoke and read or write until eleven when the "Nazir" of the Court informs me that business is ready.' He stayed in court from eleven till

> four, five or six according to the season of the year. On leaving Court I take a Ride or drive or walk or lounge until the light begins to fade, when I dress for Dinner. I get into my Tonjon [a kind of palanquin] and go wherever Dinner may be and get to Bed again by eleven o'clock. This is literally my life, with exception to changes made by little sporting excursions.[35]

As registrar, Roberdeau administered both Hindu and Muslim law. He had a pundit and a qadi to guide him, but responsibility for the decision rested with him, although he took only the less serious cases, leaving the others to the magistrate. All these cases were subject to appeal to one of the six provincial Courts of Appeal, while Courts of Circuit, like assizes, visited each district twice a year to hear the most serious criminal cases. 'The Circuit Judge is helped by a Muslim Law Officer, who gives a written opinion, both as to guilt and punishment; if the Judge of Circuit agrees with his Law Officer he gives orders for the sentence to be carried out; if he disagrees he refers the whole case to a superior Court in Calcutta.' Unfortunately there was, as yet, no properly organized police force, and Roberdeau describes those that did exist as 'a worthless undisciplined set of Scoundrels very different from the Regular Troops which are brave, honourable and obedient'.

The British officials were well paid: the head of a district receiving more than £2,000 a year, tax free, and the collector about the same, depending on the wealth of the district. Commercial Residents were paid less but were allowed the opportunity of private trade which could be very lucrative. And there were some valuable appointments to aspire to, such as the Collector of Customs, the Secretaries to the Government and secretaries to various boards, 'all of them capital appointments'.

There was little social interaction with the local Indian population, and this was not driven entirely by reluctance on the British side. 'You are aware that the Natives will not eat or drink with us of anything from our Tables; do not therefore imagine black faces at our Dinners.' And:

The natives of every cast[e], are in their manners and customs so totally different from us that beyond what duty and business compells [sic] we can have no association. I believe they privately look on us with a great deal of contempt and generally believe us to be wanting in Religion, merely I suppose because we have not the idle and super-stitious outward forms of worship which they so much pride them-selves in.

Roberdeau acknowledged that this left the handful of British officials entirely dependent upon each other for society. 'You will wonder how we can find conversation, considering the smallness of our Party, but our Evenings are, I assure you, very cheerful.' During the heat and the wet season – about eight months of the year – there was nothing to be done apart from conversation and other quiet amusements.

We are for two-thirds of the year in a kind of vacuum . . . A Billiard Table affords occasional relaxation and beyond that I have nothing further to mention save Books and the Pen. This dearth of Recreation is not however much felt because all Civil Servants in the country have business to perform and that business must be done . . . However to speak generally, a Country life in India is dull gloomy spiritless and solitary, and a Man doomed to it is much to be pitied if he has not lasting amusements and resources within himself.

The cooler dry season was much pleasanter and afforded all sorts of diversions, with hunting and similar sport high on the list. The officials lived in fairly basic housing, in

Bungalows, a word I know not how to render unless by a Cottage. These are always thatched with straw on the roof and the walls are sometimes of Bricks and often of matts. Some have glass windows besides the Venetians but this is not very common . . . To hide the sloping Roofs we put up a kind of artificial ceiling made of white cloth . . .

There are 'curtains over the doorways to keep out the wind and . . . I have two Bungalows near to each other, in one of which I sleep and dress and in the other sit and eat'. 'Bed in the hot weather is dreadful, sometimes not a breath of air and we are obliged by the musquitoes, to sleep behind curtains.' 'Another plague is a small Red Ant, which bites very sharp'; they were kept at bay by standing the bedposts in pans of water.

Water is 'the universal drink', and Roberdeau has milk and water instead of tea for breakfast. Concern for health necessitates a degree of abstemiousness: when they drink wine it is always claret, for 'a pint of port would throw a man into a fever and Madeira is too strong to be drunk freely'. There is no way to preserve meat, and the servants will not eat anything that has been served on a European's table, so that a great deal of waste in unavoidable. Bread and butter were both made by the servants, but animals could be bought cheaply and slaughtered for the table.

Roberdeau ends his account with a sketch of the general character of his fellow servants of the Company.

An Englishman in India is proud and tenacious, he feels himself a Conqueror amongst a vanquished people and looks down with some degree of superiority on all below him. Indolence, the disease of the climate, affects him with its torpid influence . . . A cool apathy, listless inattention and an improvident carelessness generally accompanies most of his actions; secure of today, he thinks not of tomorrow. Ambitious of splendor, he expends freely . . . Generosity is a feature in the Character too prominent to be overlooked, but as it sometimes borders on extravagance it loses some of its virtue. Bring distress before his eyes and he bestows with a liberality that is nowhere surpassed . . . In the public Character, whatever Calumny and Detraction may say to the Contrary, he is minutely just, inflexibly upright and I believe no public Service in the whole world can evince more integrity.

It is interesting that after admitting so many flaws he lays such emphasis on the claims to justice and integrity, just those virtues which had, in an earlier generation, been so conspicuous by their absence and which, while clearly gaining ground, were still far from universal.[36]

<hr />

When John Shore finally reached Calcutta in 1769 he was so ill that he had to be carried ashore and his shipmates had doubted that he would live long enough to make landfall. But he recovered from this first illness, and was appointed to the Secret Political Department of the Bengal government where he spent a year copying documents and living in cramped, miserable quarters for which he paid more in rent than his entire meagre annual salary. His health continued to be poor, he slept badly and his admiring and pious biographer (his son) admits that he 'indulged in the same behaviour as other young men', while retaining an unusual reputation for honesty and integrity. At the age of 19 he was appointed an assistant magistrate to a large district and the bulk of the work, some six hundred cases in a single year, fell on his young shoulders. He studied all the languages used locally, not just Hindustani but Persian, Arabic and Bengali, formed a lasting friendship with his moonshee or teacher, and laid the foundations for the considerable scholarship he would develop in later years. Gradually he came to understand more about the district in which he was living, the habits of the people, the nature of their land tenure and the structure of society. In April 1772 he wrote home telling his mother that he was living in a comfortable house four miles from the town of Moorshedabad, with healthy air, 'cooing doves, whistling blackbirds, and a purling stream'. But he felt very isolated, not seeing another European more than once a week, and finding even the educated Indians narrow-minded and pedantic. He doubted that the local population were any happier under British rule than they had been before, even though it considerably eased the burden on the poor and protected them from the ravages of marauders.

Above all Shore was homesick, writing to his mother, 'Three years, and almost four, have elapsed, since I had the happiness of seeing you. How many more must revolve before we meet again, is a reflection which leaves behind it a melancholy uncertainty.' He found solace in religion, and admitted that he felt some pangs when he heard that his brother had decided to become a clergyman. 'I almost envy my brother in the choice he has made; and now think I should have been happier had I fixed upon the same.' A year later he told an old friend,

Notwithstanding I have met with as much success and countenance as most adventurers who settled in this country at the early period of life I did, I cannot but regret that I ever left England . . . Not that I lament the loss of the diversions in Europe: it is the frequency of dissipation in this place that I complain of, and the unsettled mode of life I am in. The die is, however, now cast; and I must extend my views to futurity, banishing all retrospect on the past. These are sentiments which I wish to be concealed from my mother, as they will necessarily make her uneasy.[37]

The reward for this exile and labour? In the first five years of his service Shore never earned as much as £500 in a year, and at the end of 10 years in India he had saved nothing. He survived and persevered, rising to the very summit of British India, being appointed Governor-General, the only servant of the Company to be entrusted with that supreme position after Warren Hastings, and at the end of 30 years service he returned home with a modest fortune of £25,000.[38]

Shore was unusually honest and some much larger fortunes were made: Warren Hastings is thought to have sent home between £200,000 and £250,000; Lieutenant-Colonel Mark Wood, who had clearly benefited handsomely from his five years as Chief Engineer in Bengal, brought home £200,000; and William Hollond died as late as 1836, leaving over £1 million which he had acquired in mysterious circumstances while serving in the Bengal Civil Service. But far more men died in obscurity and often debt in India than returned home with fortunes. According to one contemporary study, between 1796 and 1820 only 201 officers of the Bengal army retired to Europe, while 1,243 died in India. Another report tells us that between 1762 and 1783 there were 508 men appointed as writers in Bengal. Of these 150 or almost one third had died in India by 1784: 321 were still there and only 37 had returned home, and not all of those had made a fortune. Of 1,200 British officers who served in the Bengal army over the same period, only five had returned home with fortunes of £20,000 or more by 1784 and at least 30 were dependent for their subsistence on Lord Clive's charitable fund. Similar figures exist for the Bombay service, although clearly some of those who were still in India would, like John Shore, have survived and prospered.[39]

Most officers and officials in the Company's service in the second half of the eighteenth century knew that they would never make enough money to go home, and accepted their exile. 'I can live here very genteelly [sic] on my means,' one wrote in 1776 'and as I shall probably never more visit England, will make everything as agreeable to myself as possible. Nothing but an extraordinary gust of fortune can ever procure a soldier one in these iron days, and to be dependent at home will not agree with my constitution; consequently I shall never leave India . . .' Over the next few decades the chances of survival increased, although the time an officer needed to stay in India before reaching high rank also lengthened. Conditions slowly improved and gradually India became less of a wild lottery and something a little closer to a normal career, yet for a young man in 1790 or 1800 joining the Company's service still represented a gamble where the odds of gaining even a modest competency were far outweighed by the likelihood of an early grave far from home. 'Here people die one day, and are buried the next,' Lucretia West, the wife of the Recorder of Bombay wrote in her journal in 1826. 'Their furniture is sold the third. They are forgotten the fourth.' Three years later both she and her husband died of cholera.[40]

CONCLUSION

ANY COMPARISON OF THE different careers open to the younger sons of good families in the late eighteenth and early nineteenth centuries gives different results depending on the criteria used. For some parents, the priority was placing their son in a career at as young an age as possible and at the least cost. In these cases the navy and India had clear advantages for neither required the payment of a premium and both accepted boys while they were still very young. A position of clerk in a government office or a merchant's business might also sometimes be had without cost, although not at such a young age. Parents might apprentice their son to an attorney or a surgeon-apothecary when the boy was still in his early or mid teens, but unless there was some close connection this usually required the payment of a fairly substantial premium – several hundred pounds – which might prove a real obstacle to the father of a large family. The army was generally both more expensive and required boys to be a little older again – 17 or 18 generally for their first commission – although at the height of the Peninsular War, first commissions could be obtained quite readily without payment. The least attractive careers for parents with these priorities were the Church, the law and medicine, for each generally (although not always) needed a university degree, and most young men pursuing these careers needed considerable support from their family until they were well into their twenties.

However, parents who were in less of a hurry and who gave greater weight to the chances of their son achieving a comfortable independence, with little risk, would view the choice of career in a different light. For them, the role of a surgeon-apothecary, an attorney or government clerk was a fairly safe choice, with the Church also being worth consideration. They were less likely to want their son to become a barrister or physician, where the chances of success were more doubtful; while commerce, the army, the navy and India were all clearly unattractive, especially the last. But if surgeon-apothecaries, attorneys and government clerks were a good choice for the prudent, they were careers that were most unlikely to lead to great heights, and ambitious parents – or young men of ambition – were more likely to look to the Bar (and sometimes through it, to politics), the navy and, less confidently, the army and India, as the careers which gave the greatest hope of gaining exceptional fame and fortune. Business may have been a better bet in this regard, though its appeal seemed more mercenary, at least to outsiders.

The careers that attracted the greatest social prestige, and which were most favoured by the sons of the nobility and the well connected, were, first and foremost, the more attractive government offices, followed by the navy and the army, and then, at a little distance, the Church and the Bar. Very few young men from the most privileged backgrounds pursued careers in medicine, as attorneys, in the lower branches of government, in business or in India. But for the sons of 'the middling sort' – shopkeepers, farmers and the like – the army and the navy appeared to offer a particularly attractive way to rise above their origins and make good their claim to being a gentleman.

Some careers were particularly unsuited to a young man who found it difficult to tolerate authority and who craved his independence. The army and the navy obviously required considerable subordination, and so, less obviously, did the position of attorney or physician. Clergymen had a large degree of practical autonomy, and were sometimes the leading figure in their district, but they might also have a resident patron to whom they needed to defer. Barristers and businessmen had to make their own way, but lived and worked in a tight-knit community of their peers and often needed their respect, if not their friendship, if they were to prosper.

If the spirit of adventure and the search for glory were the leading motives, the army, the navy and India were the most obvious choices, although all three involved a great deal of tedium and humdrum routine even in wartime, while they were often stultifying when the country was at peace. Still, they at least offered the prospect of travel abroad, which was an expensive – often too expensive – luxury for those who pursued other occupations. But for those who valued their health and their comfort the scales were inverted, with India clearly at the bottom, followed by the navy and then the army; while the roles of a clergyman, an attorney or the holder of some civil office, looked the most appealing. And for those who wanted to grow rich, business (sometimes beginning in an attorney's office) was the most likely path, although even here the odds were heavily stacked against success.

In reality few if any parents or young men viewed the choice of career in such an abstract manner: what counted most, and with good reason, was a connection which brought the prospect of some patronage to help in the entry and early stages of the career, and to a lesser extent the character and abilities of the young man and his personal preferences as well as those of his parents.

For all their diversity, there was much that these careers had in common. They all had a high rate of failure, although this failure took different forms. Many men who took holy orders were never appointed to a living and spent their lives either as curates or schoolteachers or in some other poorly paid role. And even some of those who did get a living did not receive enough income to educate and bring up their children in the manner befitting the children of a gentleman. Equally, many young men who served their years as an attorney's clerk never succeeded in establishing a practice of their own; while many clerks in government offices were stuck in backwaters from which they could not escape. An ill-timed peace stranded thousands of midshipmen and naval lieutenants in limbo, the former needing to find another career for their subsistence, the latter struggling on grossly inadequate half-pay, where their only real hope was a fresh war as soon as possible. Army officers were equally at risk of having their careers cut short; while in both services – and even more in India – premature death (more from disease than enemy action) brought many careers to an abrupt halt. Bankruptcy ended the careers of many merchants and bankers, while many barristers never succeeded in establishing the reputation that would lead attorneys to trust them with their cases. Even physicians and surgeons quite often failed to make an impression and either abandoned the profession altogether or struggled along without much in the way of prosperity or respect.

Although it is impossible to accurately quantify the numbers who failed in these various ways, they were certainly significant and much greater than the numbers who achieved outstanding success. For the tiny handful who did rise to the very pinnacle of their profession, success in one career was often quite similar to success in another. Wealth, a landed estate, a knighthood or even a peerage, and entrée into high society, were the fruits of success, whether you were a naval officer or a banker, a physician or a nabob. Lord Eldon did not achieve the fame or glory of a Nelson or a Wellington, but he did much better than Admiral Collingwood or Galbraith Lowry Cole, who were themselves relatively successful. But for most men success did not extend much beyond a comfortable competence, enough money to marry and bring up their children and launch them, in their turn, on a career in the gentlemanly professions. Francis Austen, not the Duke of Wellington, is typical of a successful younger son.

All these careers recruited both from the younger sons of gentlemen and from those a little further down the social scale – the sons of respectable tradesmen, shopkeepers, farmers and the like. A good family background gave some advantages, including confidence, but in most careers it counted for relatively little compared to connections within the profession and, at least in some cases, wealth. These careers formed the tidal zone where lower reaches of the gentry – indeed, of the upper classes generally – overlapped and merged with the upper reaches of the bourgeoisie, or 'the middling sort'. Many – most – of the younger sons of good families joining these careers were on their way down the social scale; while the sons of the bourgeoisie who entered them were attempting to gain and hold a position higher (socially if not always financially) than their father had attained. Often this produced friction, snobbery and petulance among individuals; but there was also a great deal of camaraderie, and a sense of collective identity whether as naval officers, surgeons, barristers or whatever, which transcended differences in family background.

In most, if not all these careers, success was rather easier to achieve during the French wars than in the decade or two after Waterloo. The war had seen an immense expansion of the army and navy, with honourable, if not often very rewarding places for thousands of younger sons; but with the peace came immediate and sharp reductions which stranded many young men in the early stages of their career, and left their younger brothers looking for any suitable opportunity. In 1823 John Wilson Croker acknowledged the problem:

> the distress to which the middle classes in England are just now exposed is very great, the Army and Navy shut up – the Church over-loaded – Law producing less than ever it did – young Gentlemen have the greatest difficulty in finding the means of livelihood and the number of Half Pay Officers who look for civil employment and whose services give them a kind of claim increase that difficulty.

Nor, according to Edward Gibbon Wakefield, had the position improved a decade later:

> The very high prizes of the bar and the church have always led to a keen competition in these professions so that at all times there has been a large proportion of barristers without briefs, and of clergymen eager to obtain a miserable curacy; but at this time, the proportion of briefless barristers is greater than ever, as well as the number of clergymen eager to be curates. And, at this time, not only the bar and the established church are crowded with hungry competitors, but also

every dissenting church, the attorney's branch and all the branches of the medical and surgical professions. Nay, full, overflowing, as are all these professions, the number of young people who hope to live by them is far greater than ever: witness the crowds of students in the inns of court, of young men every year admitted to practice as attorneys, of clerical students in the universities and dissenting schools, and of students in the schools of medicine and surgery. It seems impossible that a third of them should ever live by the pursuits which they intend to follow . . .[1]

On the other hand, it should be noted that the mortality rate in the army, the navy and even in India was much higher during the war years than in the long peace which followed. 'A bloody war or a sickly season' made room for promotions, but only at the cost of the abrupt termination of many careers at a point far short of any normal definition of success.

It is rather surprising that the large number of well-educated young men, brought up in comfort if not affluence, only to be faced with such limited and bleak prospects, did not develop a greater sense of collective identity and grievance, and turn to radical politics to remedy the flagrant injustices of a society that could treat them in this manner. Presumably they retained a sufficiently strong sense of belonging to the privileged classes and were not sufficiently alienated to want to upend the applecart, but revolutions have been fuelled by less reasonable complaints, and Britain in the years immediately after Waterloo was seething with discontent. At that time, however, most half-pay officers and other young gentlemen in a similar position probably imagined that some fresh war would soon break out, or some other opportunity would arise, that would rescue them from the doldrums and carry them forward in their career. Like the proverbial frog boiling in water, their disillusionment was gradual and they slowly adjusted to their altered circumstances and diminished prospects.

Most of the gentlemanly professions reacted to the reduction of opportunities after the war by closing ranks and becoming more exclusive. With the army and navy stagnating, purchase in the former and patronage in the latter became much more important in securing promotion and employment. In the law a surplus of barristers made success more elusive, while the increased number of gentlemen – including retired officers – seeking a new career in the Church tested existing patronage networks to the limit, and probably encouraged the tide of opinion against clergymen holding multiple livings. Some young men from relatively modest backgrounds, who might during the war have gained a commission in the army or the navy, turned to different branches of commerce. Others looked to a future in the colonies, as did some whose career in the services had ground to a halt. More young men of good family than ever before were willing to contemplate a career – and actually doing the work – as a clerk in a government department in the decades after Waterloo. The government also extended its reach into many other areas of the economy and society in the decades after 1815, and this eventually created a host of new positions for younger sons and middle-aged junior officers on half-pay. Other innovations, such as the telegraph and the railways, created additional opportunities, and businesses grew larger and so produced more senior positions, although this took many years. Teaching also gradually became a profession in its own right and not just a sideline for clergymen. Few of these new opportunities were equal in prestige to the traditional gentlemanly professions, but they were often at least as well paid and offered as good a life.

Even in the relatively prosperous years before Waterloo most younger sons struggled to succeed in their chosen profession. Each of the careers open to them had its own shape and trajectory, and required a different mixture of ingredients, although there were some common elements. Of these the most important was luck and timing: the good fortune to enter a career at a point when opportunities favoured a young man, and to be well established, and so be able to dispense rather than require patronage, when opportunities became scarce. It was simply impossible for a man born in the 1780s or 1790s to replicate the career of Nelson or Wellington: the long peace after Waterloo left them stranded on the lower rungs of the ladder without any opportunity to distinguish themselves. Luck was equally necessary at every subsequent stage in their career, both in ensuring that they were in the right place at the right time – able to take part in a campaign or a battle – and in preserving their lives. Other careers were almost equally influenced by timing and chance: a merchant or banker might be ruined by an economic depression that came before he was properly established, but he might also benefit enormously from the opportunity of purchasing the assets of bankrupt rivals. John Scott's career turned on the unexpected illness of a senior barrister which gave him the chance to take the lead in his first important case; while Sydney Smith would probably never have become the darling of Whig society if he had gone with his pupil to Heidelberg rather than Edinburgh.

Good health was almost as important as luck: not all successful men were robust, but a man needed a great deal more good fortune if he was to overcome illness as well as all the other obstacles in his path, and the careers of a large number of young men, especially in India and the army, were terminated by illness. A man could suffer from chronic ill-health and still be a capable and successful clergyman, providing that his ailment was not too debilitating, and there were many government offices for which illness was no great bar. He could be a sleeping partner in a bank, but would struggle to be the active partner, and frequent or severe illness might throw doubt on his creditworthiness as a merchant. A soldier or sailor needed to time his illnesses well if they were not to prevent his taking part in important campaigns, and he needed to have the under-lying toughness to recover from the wounds and fevers from which he was likely to suffer.

Patronage was important in all careers: but it had to be the right sort of patronage to be useful. A title alone carried little weight: to have an uncle, or even a father, who was an earl or a viscount, did not in itself help a young clergyman secure a living or a midshipman get his first appointment as a lieutenant in the navy. The best form of patronage was frequently within the profession: the warm support of an influential officer in the navy would help guide a young man through his early promotions and then ensure that he received active and lucrative commands. In the army a well-disposed general could take a junior officer onto his staff, introduce him to other senior officers and possibly even send him home with dispatches. This would not enable him to break the speed limits on promotion, but it would help ensure that he stayed close to the action and was given every opportunity of distinguishing himself compatible with his rank. Similarly a senior barrister might smooth the path for a protégé, and even judges were known to show favour on occasion, although the law was a profession where patronage could only do so much, and where a considerable degree of competence was generally necessary to ensure success. In many cases patronage was essential in achieving an initial appointment but then lost its influence. The owner of an advowson could appoint a young clergyman to a living, but unless he had a second living to bestow, or could influence someone else who did, his subsequent support would matter little to the clergyman's career – although good relations with the local landowner would greatly affect the comfort of the clergyman's life.

Political patronage was relatively limited in comparison. A Member of Parliament could secure a young man a commission in the army or a position as a midshipman; and if he supported the government he might be able to obtain a clerical living from the Lord Chancellor or Prime Minister, but it was unlikely to be a good one. A local landowner or MP might get a position as a customs officer or excise man for a young protégé, or possibly the position of a clerk in a government office, but to obtain anything more desirable it was usually necessary to be in a position to reciprocate: the Archbishop of Canterbury probably had more chance of securing a naval promotion than a junior Lord of the Admiralty. A powerful political figure like Lord Lonsdale was given a great deal of patronage to dispense within his locality, and this in turn added to his influence with other sources of patronage within the government: if he asked the Lord Chancellor to give a young clergyman a living in the south of England, the Lord Chancellor would know that he could repay the favour in kind at a later date. But political office in itself, even a position in cabinet, did not necessarily bestow much patronage power on its holder.

Money could also be extremely helpful in some careers, but was not a universal solvent. It could be used to purchase a living for a clergyman or a commission and subsequent promotions in the army. It was essential in establishing a business as a merchant or banker, and it was necessary to support a young man at university or studying the law. In most gentlemanly professions beginners required an allowance from home in the early years to make life comfortable, for pay was seldom sufficient to do more than cover the most basic essentials if it did that much. But it was not helpful in promotion for a naval officer, it was irrelevant to the bestowal of most clerical livings, or to progress at the Bar or success as an attorney. Nor was it always a good investment: a lieutenant-colonel in a cavalry regiment who had purchased his position would have spent almost £5,000 which his family would lose completely if he fell ill and died.

Ability also counted for more in some circumstances than others. An inspiring and devoted clergyman who took great care of his parishioners was not much more likely to secure an additional living or other preferment in the Church than one who was often absent and who never did more than the bare minimum – unless, of course, the parish was in a fashionable part of London, or somewhere else where the work of the good clergyman could be noticed by people who mattered. Similarly, a good regimental officer might be admired by his fellow officers and by the men under his command, and this might help preserve his life on campaign, but it was most unlikely to lead to his being promoted any more rapidly than his less attentive colleagues. Diligence, care and honesty rather than brilliance were the qualities most needed by an attorney or most bankers. On the whole, the navy, the Bar and commerce seem to have been the most competitive careers, where ability really did count for much, although even here ability without luck was profitless.

A second type of ability counted for less in determining success, but a great deal more in the happiness of an individual. This was the ability to enjoy an imperfect life, to get along with a small circle of fellows, many of whom were not particularly compatible; to put up with the physical discomforts of life on board ship, or on active service, or in an old fashioned and poorly repaired vicarage. It was the ability to make and retain friends even with years of separation; to hold onto religious faith in times of trouble, or to let it go without serious regret or doubts; to tolerate boredom, not drink too much, and to find satisfying outlets for physical and mental energy. It was the ability to prevent disappointed hopes and ambitions from curdling, to accept patronage with gratitude and not to resent the better fortune of an older brother, and to count blessings as well as misfortunes. Hearty good humour, cheeriness, and not too much pride, refinement or delicacy of feeling were all valuable qualities for most members of these professions; while a sharp intellect and independent mind, a strong sense of justice and a reforming spirit were all decided disadvantages in most circumstances, just as they are today in many large organizations. Like most abilities, these advantageous qualities were largely a gift of nature, but they could also be improved by diligence and attention, just as unhelpful characteristics could be suppressed and would gradually atrophy.

To return to our original question: what careers would the Bennet sisters have pursued if they had all been boys? The answer for the masculine counterpart of Jane Bennet is obvious. As the eldest he would have inherited the estate when his father died, and if he had been the true equivalent of Jane, he would have provided generously for his mother and been a good and helpful brother to his siblings, much as Edward Knight was for the Austen family. But he would also have married and had a family of his own, and would have expected his younger brothers to make their own way in the world once they were fairly launched.

If Lydia had been a boy he would surely have joined the army, for 'scarlet fever' infected adolescents of both genders. He would probably have enjoyed life in the army, at least at first, for there were plenty of outlets for his boisterous high spirits in the mess and there is no reason to suppose that Lydia was devoid of courage. Still, the outlook for a young man joining the army was not especially good, and he was quite likely to die in some foreign country of a foul disease, or grow old and disappointed in the service before being placed on half-pay. It is easy to imagine him in middle-age, a shabby, rather disreputable retired captain or major, living cheaply in lodgings in some seaside town and frequently touching one of his more successful brothers for a loan, which he never repaid.

The fate of the male version of Catherine, the second youngest of the Bennet children, is less clear. He might have followed Lydia's counterpart into the army and shared his fate, but family tradition has it that Jane Austen imagined Catherine being improved by the marriages of her two oldest sisters and the society she met through them, and ultimately marrying a clergyman with a living near Pemberley. In our alternative universe it is possible that he himself became a clergyman and, like Mr Collins, was fortunate enough to find as generous and attentive a patron as Lady Catherine de Bourg.

The career of Mary's counterpart is as obvious as that of Lydia's – he would have become an attorney, having been articled to Uncle Philips. Indeed, family tradition again says that Austen indicated that Mary herself would 'obtain nothing higher than one of her Uncle Philip's [*sic*] clerks'. Mary's outlook and character – her pedantry and self-importance – transfer without difficulty onto a young attorney, and would ripen fully into pomposity and dullness with years and success. In middle age Mary's counterpart would be prosperous, self-satisfied and a great bore – in other words a stalwart of local society.[2]

And what of Elizabeth – what career would her male equivalent pursue? Probably not the army, the navy or India: Mr Bennet was unlikely to want to exile his favourite child so far from home, while Elizabeth appears to have been immune to scarlet fever and was already too old for the navy. Assuming that the young man shared Elizabeth's intelligence and ready wit, it is possible to imagine him doing well in court, and a barrister's career is a possible answer; but there is nothing in *Pride and Prejudice* to suggest an appetite for the years of grinding study needed to qualify. The Church then? Perhaps. It is not hard to imagine a male version of Elizabeth Bennet as a clergyman in the mould of Sydney Smith, but there is no hint that the Bennets had any connections with the Church or knew anyone with a living at their disposal. Elizabeth did, however have a much loved uncle and aunt who were well established in business in London, and what could have been more natural than that they would take their favourite nephew and introduce him into the mercantile world? With their support he might do very well, and find a good deal of interest and satisfaction as well as prosperity in commerce. It was not as safe or as prestigious as the Church, but there was more room for ambition and for independence, and the rewards might be far greater. Still, it was very unlikely that a young man brought up in the business by the Gardiners would even make the acquaintance of Georgiana Darcy, and virtually impossible that he would propose and be accepted. But it was not really much more likely that a young clergyman, surgeon or barrister, army or naval officer, without some fortune behind them, would be any more successful as her suitor, especially as she had only just escaped Wickham's unscrupulous advances.

In some respects younger sons were less well off than their sisters. Each sister – whether oldest or youngest – had a chance of marrying well, and there was little for them to envy in the early years of their brothers' careers, except, perhaps, for those who went to university. But a woman's life had equal or greater perils of its own: the first wives of all of Jane Austen's brothers who married predeceased them, and four of the brothers went on to marry a second time. These five men had 33 children between them, with two of the wives having 11 children each before they died, worn out. Such fecundity, and such spousal mortality, were not the norm, but they were not so very unusual either. For all the obvious privilege of their lives compared to the great mass of the population, the daughters and younger sons of good families did not generally have a particularly easy life.

Our lives today are much safer: death in childbirth is now very rare and even our most dangerous professions have a much lower mortality rate than the army, the navy or going to India in the early nineteenth century. Except among the aristocracy, eldest sons have lost their pre-eminence and privilege; young women no less than young men are expected to have a career, and parents are presumed to treat all their children equally. We have a much greater array of professional careers from which to choose, ranging from air traffic controller to zoologist. The old distinction of the gentlemanly professions has become blurred, but there are still 'good jobs' whose quality is not entirely related to the income they produce. Bridget Jones's Mark Darcy is not just a lawyer, but a barrister, and not just a barrister, but a human rights' lawyer; and he is, of course, the acme of a modern gentleman. Our expectations are far higher than they were in Jane

Austen's day: we want a career that will be financially rewarding and personally fulfilling, that will interest us and enable us to feel that we have made the world a better place. Inevitably this often means that we are disappointed, but our careers are even more important today than they were in 1800 in defining our place in the world, shaping our identity and proving our value, not least to ourselves. Whether work should be so important in our lives is quite another question.

Inflation in the Late Eighteenth and Early Nineteenth Centuries

Long-term inflation was low during the eighteenth century with some fluctuations, usually in wartime. According to the Bank of England Inflation Calculator £100 in 1700 was worth only £138.08 in 1784, a cumulative annual rate of 0.4 per cent. It increased greatly during the long war with France when Britain went off the gold standard, and this was followed by a period of sharp deflation after the war as Britain returned to the gold standard. Prices did not fall all the way to their prewar level, but the increase from 1784 to 1830 was only just over 30 per cent. The fluctuations can be seen below, the figures coming from the Bank of England Inflation Calculator.

£100 in 1784 was worth

£ 98.68 in 1790
£177.63 in 1800
£189.47 in 1810
£167.11 in 1815
£153.95 in 1820
£125.00 in 1823
£130.26 in 1830
and £14,615.79 in 2018 (or 146 x)

Equally, £100 in 1800 was worth   £ 73.33 in 1830
and £8,228.15 in 2018 (or 82 x)

So it really does matter where you start from.

(Source: https://www.bankofengland.co.uk/monetary-policy/inflation/
inflation-calculator accessed 26 February 2019)

Some Numbers

Unfortunately the surviving information does not allow for a comprehensive, statistical comparison of the different careers open to young gentlemen. It is partial and incomplete even on the basic question of the numbers of men in each profession at any one time, let alone their income, life expectancy, wealth at death or social background.

The following figures, gleaned from a variety of sources, are offered as no more than helpful pointers and should be treated with considerable caution. It is important to remember that membership of these professions was not restricted to the sons of gentlemen and men in the gentlemanly professions, and in some cases younger sons of good families only made up a minority of these professions.

The population of England and Wales in 1801 was just over nine million; while by 1851 it had risen to just under 18 million. Over the same period the population of Scotland rose from 1.6 million to 2.9 million, and that of Ireland from 5.2 million to 6.5 million (Mitchell & Deane, *Abstract of British Historical Statistics*, pp. 8–9).

THE CHURCH

It is thought that there were about 7,500 Anglican clergymen holding one or more livings in 1815; however, many more than this took holy orders (Virgin, *Church in an Age of Negligence*, p. 202). In the 60 years from the beginning of the 1780s to the end of the 1830s, 21,867 men were ordained as deacons of the Church, although not all of them went on to become ordained as priests (Slinn, *Education of the Anglican Clergy*, p. 21). This supports the common estimate of there being about 10,000 ordained clergymen of the Church of England at the beginning of the nineteenth century. By 1851 this figure had risen to 17,463 Anglican clergy in England and Wales (Corfield, *Power and the Professions*, p. 128).

MEDICINE

Simmons's *Medical Register for the Year 1783* lists 3,166 practitioners in England outside London. We know that there were a further 960 practitioners in London at about this time, and that Simmons's list is not quite complete, so that the total number of practitioners in England in the 1780s was probably between 4,000 and 4,500. Of these rather more than 500 were physicians and most of the remainder were surgeon-apothecaries, the forerunner of the modern general practitioner (Lane, 'The Medical Practitioners of Provincial England in 1783', p. 355; Bynum, 'Physicians, Hospitals and Career Structures . . .', pp. 106–7). These figures exclude surgeons and physicians serving with the army and navy or in the colonies.

THE LAW

There were only 379 barristers listed in the *Law List* in 1785 (the figure is probably not complete) but this rose steadily and inexorably:

1790	424
1800	577
1810	708
1820	840

1830   1,129
1840   1,835

(Duman, 'Pathway to Professionalism: The English Bar in the Eighteenth and Nineteenth Centuries', p. 619).

In 1805 it is thought that there were at least 5,200 attorneys in practice, and this total rose to 11,350 by 1851, so that the ratio of barristers to attorneys rose sharply over the period (Corfield, *Power and the Professions*, p. 91).

CIVIL OFFICE

The total number of officers employed by the national government in the civil administration (including Ireland) was:

1797   17,640
1810   24,930
1815   24,598
1829   22,367

(Chester, *English Administrative System*, p. 166).

However, only a small minority of these positions would have been regarded as suitable for the sons of gentlemen.

THE NAVY

In 1794 the Royal Navy had a total of some 420 ships of war, and had active employment for just over 1,400 naval officers (Southam, *Jane Austen and the Navy*, p. 76). The number of officers on the active list rose during the course of the war, reaching 4,873 on 1 September 1813, of whom 2,448 were actually employed, afloat or onshore. The total number of officers continued to rise immediately after the war, reaching 5,937 on 1 January 1816, and then dwindled very slowly: to 5,664 on 1 January 1820. However, active employment for these officers became scarce: only 1,004 officers were actively employed on 1 January 1816, and 597 on 1

January 1818 (or little more than one officer in ten). The remainder were put on half-pay (Lewis, *The Navy in Transition*, pp. 64–9). These figures do not include officers of the marines.

THE ARMY

There were 3,107 officers in the British regular army in 1792, a figure which rose to 10,590 in 1814 – excluding those on half-pay and serving in veteran and foreign regiments. In addition the number of officers in the separate Ordnance arm (the artillery and engineers) rose from 361 to 912 over the same period. In the final years of the war the army needed to find approximately 1,000 new officers every year to replace those who left the service (Glover, *Wellington's Army*, p. 36). The British and Irish militia employed a further 3,908 officers according to a return of 1808 (Cookson, *The British Armed Nation*, p. 224n).

INDIA

In the early nineteenth century there were approximately 1,000 British civilian officials, writers and the like, employed by the East India Company in India, and about 3,500 British officers serving in its armies. Given the high death rate suffered by these men, there must have been a high level of recruitment to sustain these numbers (Embree, *Charles Grant and the British Rule in India*, p. 126; see also Malcolm, *Malcolm*, p. 554).

NOTES

ONE – YOUNGER SONS AND THEIR FAMILIES

1. Chamberlain, *Lord Aberdeen*, pp. 25–6.
2. The correspondence between the brothers has been published: Gordon, *At Wellington's Right Hand*. See in particular p. 101 (the merinos), pp. 88–9 (the silver plate), p. 57 (the port wine), p. 364 (Aberdeen scorns the statues at Merida) and p. 328 (Aberdeen on art).
3. Gordon, *At Wellington's Right Hand*, pp. 293–4, 332 (the allowance); p. 253 (Aberdeen criticizes Alexander's extravagance); Chamberlain, *Lord Aberdeen*, pp. 56–7 for Aberdeen's spending.
4. Thirsk, 'Younger Sons in the Seventeenth Century' *passim* provides a fascinating comparison with the late eighteenth and early nineteenth centuries.
5. Rothery, 'The Reproductive Behaviour of the English Landed Gentry in the Nineteenth and Early Twentieth Centuries', p. 674; Harris, *Siblinghood and Social Relations in Georgian England*, p. 15.
6. Stone and Stone in their seminal work *An Open Elite?*, pp. 5–6, acknowledge the way that 'younger sons were left to trickle downwards', but having done so, they turn their attention to the main subject of their study: the entry of new families into local elites and the ways in which older families endeavoured to preserve their predominance.
7. Austen-Leigh and Austen-Leigh, *Jane Austen: A Family Record*, pp. 67, 76–7, 84, 182–3, 244–5; Lane, *Jane Austen's Family: Through Five Generations*, pp. 94–5, 216–17. Jane Austen's mother, Cassandra, also had ducal connections: her grandmother, Mary Brydges, was a sister of the 1st Duke of Chandos. Austen-Leigh and Austen-Leigh, *Jane Austen: A Family Record*, p. 7.
8. In fact the 2nd Duke of Ancaster had four daughters and two sons. The elder son became a soldier and inherited the title at the age of 28; his brother became a Member of Parliament, until, at the age of 50, he succeeded his nephew as the 5th Duke of Ancaster in 1779. He was predeceased by his only child – a daughter – and when he died in 1809 the dukedom became extinct.
9. Some sources hyphenate the name Leigh-Perrot and some do not, but I have followed Deirdre Le Faye in using the hyphen (in her edition of *Jane Austen's Letters*, in *Jane Austen: A Family Record*, and her *Chronology of Jane Austen*) rather than Maggie Lane in *Jane Austen's Family*, who does not. According to Joan Austen-Leigh, in 'Jane Austen's Favourite Nephew', the

Leigh-Perrots did not use the hyphen in the nineteenth century (p. 144); however, spelling even of proper names was often inconsistent and irregular at that time.

10. Lane, *Jane Austen's Family: Through Five Generations*, pp. 199, 203–4, 208–13, 217–18 (quote on p. 217). The gift may actually have been rather more than £10,000, for Le Faye, *Chronology of Jane Austen*, p. 641 mentions a further £1,600 'to his building'.

11. Le Faye, *Chronology of Jane Austen*, p. 654, gives the dates, and lists individual bequests totalling £28,600; Lane, *Jane Austen's Family through Five Generations*, pp. 243–4; Austen-Leigh, 'Jane Austen's Favourite Nephew', pp. 144–53.

12. Austen-Leigh and Austen-Leigh, *Jane Austen: A Family Record*, pp. 40–1, 51–2. Edward's adoption is a little odd, for Catherine Knight was only 29 in 1783 and her husband Thomas 48, rather too young, one would have thought, to despair of having children. And even if there was some medical or other reason why this was unlikely, there was the possibility of Catherine dying suddenly and Thomas remarrying. Fortunately this did not happen, but Edward's position may not have been as assured as hindsight makes it appear.

13. Austen-Leigh and Austen-Leigh, *Jane Austen: A Family Record*, pp. 81, 98, 148; Tomalin, *Jane Austen*. pp. 131–2 for the allowance Mrs Knight may have paid Jane.

14. Thorne, *History of Parliament. The Commons 1790–1820*, vol. 5, p. 511. The only detailed account of William Wellesley-Pole's life is 'The Forgotten Brother', an unpublished MA thesis by Greg Roberts (Queen Mary University of London, 2009).

15. Super, *The Chronicler of Barsetshire*, pp. 2–5.

16. Hickey, *Memoirs of William Hickey*, vol. 1, pp. 23–6.

17. Stone and Stone, *An Open Elite?*, p. 111.

18. Aitchison, *Ensign in the Peninsular War*, p. 12; Southam, *Jane Austen and the Navy*, pp. 67–8.

19. Southam, *Jane Austen and the Navy*, p. 20; Scott, *The Life of Captain Matthew Flinders*, pp. 11–17; Estensen, *The Life of Matthew Flinders*, pp. 5–7; Muir, *Wellington: The Path to Victory*, p. 9; Thomas Hood, quoted in Robson, *The Attorney in Eighteenth Century-England*, pp. 62–3. See also Calvert, '"What a Wonderful Change Have I Undergone . . . So Altered in Stature, Knowledge & Ideas!"', p. 13.

20. Campbell, quoted in Miles, '"A Haven for the Privileged"', p. 202.

21. Lewis, *A Social History of the Navy*, pp. 214–15; Sir David Baird to Sir Arthur Wellesley, 2 April 1809 printed in Gordon, *At Wellington's Right Hand*, p. 42.

22. Hickey, *Memoirs of William Hickey*, vol. 1, p. 41.

23. Virgin, *The Church in an Age of Negligence*, pp. 91, 180.

24. Cicero, quoted in Beard, *SPQR*, pp. 440–1.

25. Lt-Col. Arthur Gore to Capt. John Orrok, 4 Oct 1812, quoted in Orrok, *Letters of Captain John Orrok*, pp. 117–18; Mornington to Pitt, 27 Jan. 1793, quoted in Thorne, *History of Parliament. The Commons 1790–1820*, vol. 5, p. 511; Hickey, *Memoirs of William Hickey*, vol. 1, p ix.

26. Austen, *Northanger Abbey*, p. 176 (vol. 2, ch. 7).

27. Austen, *Sense and Sensibility*, pp. 102–3 (vol. 1, ch. 19).

28. For Lord Wellesley's jealousy of Wellington see the conversation recorded in 'The Political Notebook of Richard Wellesley II', Carver Manuscripts 54, University of Southampton (partly quoted in Muir, *Britain and the Defeat of Napoleon 1807–1815*, p. 209 and Muir, *Wellington, Waterloo and the Fortunes of Peace 1814–1852*, pp. 8–9.

TWO – MONEY AND SOCIETY

1. The Bank of England's useful 'Inflation Calculator' suggests that this is a reasonable as well as a convenient figure: it is a bit too low for the years up until the Suspension of Cash Payments in 1797, then a bit too high for the next 20 years when the value of money was lowered by wartime inflation; and quite close to accurate for the 1820s after the postwar deflation. See Appendix 1 for more details. However, as I hope that this chapter will show, *any* single figure is no more than a crude guide. A multiplier of one hundred works quite well for the incomes of younger sons, but much less well for other classes in society.

2. Austen, *Sense and Sensibility*, pp. 4–5, 24, 26 (vol. 1, chs 1, 4 and 5); Virgin, *The Church in an Age of Negligence*, p. 96. Other sources give rather higher wages for servants, with even a kitchen maid receiving £10 a year, and a footman more than £20 (Mahony, *Wealth or Poverty*, pp. 90–5), but there was much variation between one part of the country and another.

3. Austen, *Sense and Sensibility*, pp. 26, 40, 58 (Willoughby's offer of a horse), pp. 110, 153–5, 279 (vol. 1, chs 5, 9, 12, 20; vol. 2, ch. 3; vol. 3, ch. 3).

4. Austen-Leigh and Austen-Leigh, *Jane Austen: A Family Record*, pp. 94, 130–1.

5. Tomalin, *Jane Austen*, pp. 219–20, 242, 247, 258, 274.

6. Austen, *Sense and Sensibility*, p. 91 (vol. 1, ch.17); Anon., *A New System of Practical Domestic Economy*, pp. 438–43.

7. Austen, *Pride and Prejudice*, pp. 28, 301, 371 (vol. 1, ch. 7; vol. 3, chs 7 and 16); Austen, *Sense and Sensibility*, pp. 196–7 (vol. 2, ch. 8). Stewponds were artificial lakes or ponds which provided fish for the table.

8. Colquhoun in Porter, *English Society in the Eighteenth Century*, pp. 388–9; Sir A. Wellesley to Sir John Cradock, 15 Jan. 1805, WP 1/160, see Muir, *Wellington: The Path to Victory*, pp. 163–4 for the context.

9. Austen, *Pride and Prejudice*, p. 15 (Bingley and his sisters), p. 10 (Darcy), p. 202 (Miss Darcy), p. 378 (Mrs Bennet) (vol. 1, chs 4, 3; vol. 2, ch. 12; vol. 3, ch. 17); Colquhoun in Porter, *English Society in the Eighteenth Century*, pp. 388–9.

10. Romilly, *Memoirs*, vol. 1, p. 45; Melikan, *John Scott, Lord Eldon*, pp. 5–6, 8; Sir Arthur Wellesley's salary as Chief Secretary for Ireland is given in *Parliamentary Debates*, vol. XI, col. clxiii 'Third Report of the Committee of Finance'; Gray, *Spencer Perceval*, pp. 121, 463.

11. Creevey to Miss Ord, 13 Sept. 1821 and 15 June 1827, *Creevey Papers*, pp. 374 and 462 (for Lambton); Thorne, *History of Parliament. The Commons 1790–1820*, vol. 1, pp. 288–9; Rubinstein, *Who Were the Rich?*, vol. 1, pp. 318–19, 433; £14 billion is the reported wealth of David and Simon Reuben, who hold fourth position on the 2018 *Sunday Times* list of the richest people in the UK, giving them a roughly similar, if less prominent, position to Rothschild in the early nineteenth century.

12. Marshall, 'The Personal Fortune of Warren Hastings in Retirement', pp. 540–52.

13. Reiter, *The Late Lord*, p. 175. Chatham had two pensions, but both were heavily committed to pay off old debts, many of them inherited from other members of his family.

14. Calvert, *An Irish Beauty of the Regency*, p. 23; Orrok, *The Letters of Captain John Orrok*, pp. 127, 150–1.

15. Flinders, *'Gratefull to Providence'*, vol. 2, p. 30; Collins, *Jane Austen and the Clergy*, p. 58; Orrok, *The Letters of Captain John Orrok*, p. 129; Thompson, *English Landed Society in the Nineteenth Century*, p. 84.

16. Quoted in John Harding-Edgar, *Next to Wellington*, p. 343.

17. Austen, *Sense and Sensibility*, p. 71 (vol. 1, ch. 14); Sweetman, *Raglan*, p. 49; Burghersh, *Correspondence of Lady Burghersh with the Duke of Wellington*, p. 217.

18. Austen, *Sense and Sensibility*, pp. 284, 369 (vol. 3, chs 3, 13); Austen, *Mansfield Park*, pp. 388–92, 413, 439 (vol. 3, chs 8, 11, 15). The statement that the Prices had an income of £400 depends on the assumption that on her marriage Mrs Price had the same capital as her sister, Lady Bertram, i.e. £7,000 yielding £350 a year, and that the half-pay of her husband, Lieutenant Price of the Marines, was approximately £50.

19. Austen, *Sense and Sensibility*, pp. 276–7 (vol. 3, ch. 2).

20. Colquhoun in Porter, *English Society in the Eighteenth Century*, pp. 388–9; Lucas, *The Life of Charles Lamb*, vol.1, p. 73; vol. 2, p. 140.

21. John, 'Farming in Wartime, 1793–1815', in *Land, Labour and Population in the Industrial Revolution*, ed. Jones and Mingay, p. 33; Thompson, *English Landed Society in the Nineteenth Century*, pp. 193–5 (servants); Gérin, *Anne Brontë*, p. 121; Gérin, *Charlotte Brontë*, p. 170.

22. Rubinstein, *Who Were the Rich?*, pp. 13, 377–8.

23. Rubinstein, *Who Were the Rich?*, p. 29; Reiter, *The Late Lord*, pp. 16, 179–81, 207–8; Fisher, *The History of Parliament: The Commons 1820–1832*, vol. 4, p. 566–7.
24. Thorne, *History of Parliament: The Commons, 1790–1820*, vol.1, pp. 306–17; Wellington to John Malcolm, 26 June 1813, in Kaye, *The Life and Correspondence of Major-General Sir John Malcolm*, vol. 2, p. 91.
25. Austen, *Emma*, p. 181 (vol. 2, ch. 4).
26. Muir, *Wellington: The Path to Victory*, pp. 7–8; Bell, *Sydney Smith*, p. 5; Austen-Leigh, *Memoir of Jane Austen*, p. 9 reports that the neighbouring squire on one occasion appealed to Mr Austen to settle a dispute over the relative locations of Paris and France.
27. Austen, *Emma*, pp. 92–3, 111–12 (vol.1, chs 11, 13).
28. Austen, *Emma*, pp. 32–3 (vol.1, ch. 4); Dr Johnson famously condemned Lord Chesterfield's *Letters to His Son* as teaching 'the morals of a whore and the manners of a dancing master', Boswell, *The Life of Samuel Johnson*, vol.1, p. 177.
29. Austen, *Emma*, pp. 50–1 (vol.1, ch. 7).
30. Austen, *Emma*, p. 29 (vol.1, ch. 4).
31. Austen, *Emma*, pp. 207–9 (vol. 2, ch. 7).

THREE – THE CHURCH

1. Bell, *Sydney Smith*, pp. 8–9; Virgin, *Sydney Smith*, p. 34–8.
2. Bell, *Sydney Smith*, pp. 8–10; Virgin, *Sydney Smith*, pp. 34–8.
3. Bell, *Sydney Smith*, pp. 8–10.
4. Bell, *Sydney Smith*, pp. 2–3, 141.
5. Virgin, *Church in an Age of Negligence*, pp. 110–12; Jacob, *The Clerical Profession in the Long Eighteenth Century*, pp. 39–41.
6. Bell, *Sydney Smith*, p. 7.
7. Virgin, *Church in an Age of Negligence* p. 135; Collins, *Jane Austen and the Clergy*, pp. 39–41.
8. Virgin, *Church in an Age of Negligence*, pp. 132–3; Jacob, *Clerical Profession in the Long Eighteenth Century*, pp. 56, 59. The whole subject of nongraduate clergy is explored in detail and with authority by Sara Slinn in her *The Education of the Anglican Clergy 1780–1839* which appeared after this chapter was written.
9. Corfield, *Power and the Professions*, p. 126; Virgin, *Church in an Age of Negligence*, pp. 132–3; Jacob, *Clerical Profession in the Long Eighteenth Century*, pp. 31–6.
10. Austen-Leigh, *Jane Austen: A Family Record*, p. 212; Jacob, *Clerical Profession in the Long Eighteenth Century*, p. 37 re college silver.
11. Bell, *Sydney Smith*, pp. 7–8; Virgin, *Sydney Smith*, pp. 33–4.
12. Virgin, *Church in an Age of Negligence*, pp. 53–4; value of the Netheravon living from the Clergy of the Church of England Database.
13. Virgin, *Church in an Age of Negligence*, pp. 34, 47, 90. The figures given by Virgin are not entirely consistent but this does not affect the overall picture.
14. Collins, *Jane Austen and the Clergy*, p. 86; Cass, 'In Defence of George Austen', pp. 55–62.
15. Corfield, *Power and the Professions*, p. 126; Virgin, *Church in an Age of Negligence*, p. 151; Jacob, *Clerical Profession in the Long Eighteenth Century*, p. 70; Collins, *Jane Austen and the Clergy*, p. 31.
16. Virgin, *Church in an Age of Negligence*, pp. 173, 179; Anon., *The Private Patronage of the Church of England*, p. 9. See Melikan, *John Scott, Lord Eldon*, p. 211 for a different calculation of the breakdown of church patronage.
17. Austen, *Mansfield Park*, pp. 23–4 (vol.1, ch. 3); Austen, *Sense and Sensibility*, p. 295 (vol.3, ch. 5).
18. Treitel, 'Legal Puzzles in Jane Austen's Works', pp. 53–4.
19. *The Times*, 14 April 1817, p. 2.
20. Austen-Leigh and Austen-Leigh, *Jane Austen: A Family Record*, pp. 6, 67, 78–9.
21. Le Faye, *Chronology of Jane Austen*, 5 and 6 April 1792, 7 Jan. 1805 and 14 Feb. 1805, pp. 141, 305.
22. Outhwaite, *Scandal in the Church*, pp. 5–12; cf. Collins, *Jane Austen and the Clergy*, pp. 24–5.

23. Quoted in Virgin, *Church in an Age of Negligence*, pp. 179–80.
24. Virgin, *Church in an Age of Negligence*, p. 91; Collins, *Jane Austen and the Clergy*, pp. 14, 58.
25. Melikan, *John Scott, Lord Eldon*, pp. 193–6.
26. Muir, *Wellington: The Path to Victory*, p. 550; Muir, *Wellington: Waterloo and the Fortunes of Peace*, pp. 100, 239–40; Gash, *Lord Liverpool*, pp. 202–3.
27. Gibson, 'The Tories and Church Patronage', pp. 266–74; Gibson, '"Unreasonable and Unbecoming"', pp. 48–53.
28. Virgin, *Church in an Age of Negligence*, p. 140 for the figure of one in five, which he says was virtually unchanged from 1805 to 1835 despite the increase in the number of clergy being ordained in the early nineteenth century. Jones quoted in Collins, *Jane Austen and the Clergy*, p. 30. Smith's remark about curates is well known and is said to have originally appeared in an article in the *Edinburgh Review* of 1822 headed 'Persecuting Bishops'. Strangely neither Bell nor Virgin appears to quote it in their biographies of Smith.
29. Jacob, *Clerical Profession in the Long Eighteenth Century*, pp. 66–7; Cass, 'In Defence of George Austen', p. 59.
30. Jacob, *Clerical Profession in the Long Eighteenth Century*, p. 61.
31. Woodforde quoted in Jacob, *Clerical Profession in the Long Eighteenth Century*, pp. 70–1.
32. Virgin, *Church in an Age of Negligence*, pp. 136, 153–4.
33. Roberts, *Mary Russell Mitford*, pp. 179–80. Twenty-four letters possibly referring to the Greek alphabet, although it is still odd.
34. Bell, *Sydney Smith*, pp. 11–15, 18–22, 30–3; Virgin, *Sydney Smith*, pp. 42–55, 61–8.
35. Thompson, *English Landed Society in the Nineteenth Century*, pp. 82–4, although Tomline was Pitt's university tutor and later private secretary, not his childhood tutor. For more on the Duchess of Leinster and Mr Ogilvie see Tillyard, *Aristocrats*, pp. 245ff.; however, Mr Ogilvie was not a clergyman.
36. Bell, *Sydney Smith*, pp. 24–6; Virgin, *Sydney Smith*, p. 58.
37. Bell, *Sydney Smith*, p. 49.
38. Virgin, *Sydney Smith*, p. 130.
39. Bell, *Sydney Smith*, pp. 73–4; Virgin, *Sydney Smith*, pp. 149–51.
40. Virgin, *Sydney Smith*, pp. 173, 191–2, 202–3.
41. Collins, *Jane Austen and the Clergy*, pp. 95–6; Jacob, *Clerical Profession in the Long Eighteenth Century*, pp. 176–7; McKellar, 'Attending Divine Service in the Revd. George Austen's Day', p. 7.
42. Virgin, *Sydney Smith*, p. 152.
43. Virgin, *Sydney Smith*, pp. 151, 178–80; Bell, *Sydney Smith*, pp. 106–7.
44. Bell, *Sydney Smith*, pp. 115–18.
45. Virgin, *Sydney Smith*, pp. 179–81.
46. On clothing: Collins, 'The Rev. Henry Tilney', p. 159; Austen, *Mansfield Park*, p. 416 (vol.3, ch. 12). On clergy in society: Jacob, *Clerical Profession in the Long Eighteenth Century*, pp. 165–6; Collins, *Jane Austen and the Clergy*, pp. 109–15; Austen, *Pride and Prejudice*, p. 169 (vol. 2, ch. 7) for Mr Collins.
47. Virgin, *Sydney Smith*, pp. 154–5; Bell, *Sydney Smith*, pp. 93–5, 99–101, 142, 198–9.
48. Virgin, *Church in an Age of Negligence*, p. 143; Austen, *Mansfield Park*, pp. 110–11 (vol.1, ch. 11).
49. Smith quoted in Bell, *Sydney Smith*, p. 102; Jacob, *Clerical Profession in the Long Eighteenth Century*, p. 167.
50. Collins, *Jane Austen and the Clergy*, pp. 46–7, 54–5, 86; Bell, *Sydney Smith*, p. 214.
51. Chesterfield quoted in Hughes, 'The Professions in the Eighteenth Century', pp. 186–7.

FOUR – MEDICINE

1. Crosse, *A Surgeon in the Early Nineteenth Century*, pp. 4–5; Thomson-Walker, 'John Green Crosse, of Norwich', p. 9. Both sources often quote the same passage of Crosse's journal with minor variations; in these cases I have followed *A Surgeon in the Early Nineteenth Century*, but Thomson-Walker includes occasional details not in the larger work.

2. Crosse, *A Surgeon in the Early Nineteenth Century*, pp. 5–6; Thomson-Walker, 'John Green Crosse, of Norwich', pp. 9–10.

3. Lane, 'The Medical Practitioners of Provincial England', pp. 354–5; Bynum, 'Physicians, Hospitals and Career Structures . . .', p. 107. In contemporary Western societies such as the USA, UK and Australia the ratio of doctors to patients is between two and three doctors per thousand people, or between four and six times the figure for England in 1783; although Bynum remarks that the figure for London (slightly over one per thousand) was actually higher than the figure regarded as 'about right' in 1985 when he was writing.

4. Loudon, *Medical Care and the General Practitioner*, pp. 35ff.; Thomson-Walker, 'John Green Crosse, of Norwich', p. 12.

5. Thomson-Walker, 'John Green Crosse, of Norwich', pp. 10–11; Crosse, *A Surgeon in the Early Nineteenth Century*, pp. 14–23; see also Digby, *Making a Medical Living*, p. 52 for Crosse's warm praise of Bayly: 'He was made up of affection and kindness . . . my old, my earliest, my best instructor.'

6. William Chamberlaine, *Tirocinium Medicum: Or a Dissertation on the Duties of Youth Apprenticed to the Medical Profession* (1813), quoted in Loudon, *Medical Care and the General Practitioner*, p. 47 and in general pp. 39–48.

7. Chamberlaine quoted in Loudon, *Medical Care and the General Practitioner*, p. 47.

8. Chamberlaine quoted in Loudon, *Medical Care and the General Practitioner*, p. 46.

9. Loudon, *Medical Care and the General Practitioner*, pp. 40–2, 105.

10. Thomson-Walker, 'John Green Crosse, of Norwich', pp. 11–12; Crosse, *A Surgeon in the Early Nineteenth Century*, pp. 31–51.

11. Adams in Loudon, *Medical Care and the General Practitioner*, p. 51; Thomson-Walker, 'John Green Crosse, of Norwich', p. 11.

12. Weekes's letters quoted in Loudon, *Medical Care and the General Practitioner*, pp. 50–1.

13. Loudon, *Medical Care and the General Practitioner*, pp. 51–2; Thomson-Walker, 'John Green Crosse, of Norwich', p. 11.

14. Flinders, *Gratefull to Providence*, vol. 2, pp. 239–40n. As Flinders died only a few weeks later it seems unlikely that he succeeded in selling the practice. For the percentage of practitioners who worked alone see Lane, 'Medical Practitioners of Provincial England', p. 364. The purchaser of a practice would also commonly advertise the fact: for an example of such an advertisement see Marland, *Medicine and Society in Wakefield and Huddersfield, 1789–1870*, p. 263.

15. Lane, 'Medical Practitioners of Provincial England', p. 363.

16. Darwin quoted in Lane, 'Medical Practitioners of Provincial England', p. 362.

17. Thomson-Walker, 'John Green Crosse, of Norwich', pp. 11–15; numbers of births from Loudon, *Medical Care and the General Practitioner*, pp. 97–8.

18. Loudon, 'The Nature of Provincial Medical Practice in Eighteenth-Century England', p. 12.

19. William Chamberlaine quoted in Loudon, 'The Nature of Provincial Medical Practice in Eighteenth-Century England', p. 12.

20. Loudon, *Medical Care and the General Practitioner*, pp. 102, 114; Loudon, 'The Nature of Provincial Medical Practice in Eighteenth-Century England', pp. 8–9, 17; Marland, *Medicine and Society in Wakefield and Huddersfield, 1789–1870*, p. 262 (for Marshall).

21. Smith quoted in Nixon, 'Thomas Baynton, 1761–1820', p. 100. On the importance of bedside manner to success in general see Digby, *Making a Medical Living*, pp. 7, 77–8.

22. Scott, *The Surgeon's Daughter*, pp. 2–3; Loudon, *Medical Care and the General Practitioner*, pp. 117–25. Thomas Bayly would sometimes travel more than 20 miles to treat a patient: Crosse, *A Surgeon in the Early Nineteenth Century*, p. 14.

23. Loudon, *Medical Care and the General Practitioner*, pp. 109–13; Smith quoted in Loudon, 'The Nature of Provincial Medical Practice in Eighteenth-Century England', p. 25.

24. Flinders, *Gratefull to Providence*, passim esp. vol. 1. pp. xxi–xxii, vol. 2. pp. 172–3. Loudon, *Medical Care and the General Practitioner*, pp. 103–9.

25. Loudon, *Medical Care and the General Practitioner*, p. 123.

26. Loudon, *Medical Care and the General Practitioner*, p. 132 ('virtually moribund'); Lane, 'Medical Practitioners of Provincial England', p. 366 (numbers); Hamilton, 'The Medical Professions in the Eighteenth Century', pp. 142–3, 147 (the Royal College and the Licentiates).

27. Loudon, *Medical Care and the General Practitioner*, pp. 8, 19–20, 27 (Barr), 38–9 (Jenner); Bynum, 'Physicians, Hospitals and Career Structures . . .', p. 116 (*accoucheurs*); *ODNB* (Jenner, confirming Loudon's account of how Jenner obtained his MD).

28. Gregory quoted in Loudon, *Medical Care and the General Practitioner*, p. 25; Abernethy quoted in Crosse, *A Surgeon in the Early Nineteenth Century*, p. 38.

29. Lane, 'Medical Practitioners of Provincial England', p. 361 and *ODNB* for quote.

30. Loudon, *Medical Care and the General Practitioner*, pp. 268–9; Marland, *Medicine and Society in Wakefield and Huddersfield, 1789–1870*, pp. 261–2, see also p. 266.

31. Lane, 'Medical Practitioners of Provincial England', pp. 368–9, quoting a report in the *Coventry Mercury* for 9 December 1782.

32. Bynum, 'Physicians, Hospitals and Career Structures . . .', pp. 119–20.

33. Bynum, 'Physicians, Hospitals and Career Structures . . .', pp. 120–1.

34. Wells quoted in Hamilton, 'The Medical Professions in the Eighteenth Century', p. 148; Loudon, *Medical Care and the General Practitioner*, pp. 30–4; Marland, *Medicine and Society in Wakefield and Huddersfield, 1789–1870*, pp. 293–7. See also Ackroyd et al., *Advancing with the Army*, pp. 66–78, which shows that army surgeons came, as we might expect, from a little further down the social scale: fewer had fathers in the gentlemanly professions and more had fathers who were tradesmen, shopkeepers and the like.

35. Scott, 'The Surgeon's Daughter', pp. 2–3, 42; Jane Austen to Anna Austen, 10–18 August 1814, *Jane Austen's Letters*, no. 104, p. 280; Austen, *The Watsons*, p. 30. See also Mr Hoggins, the surgeon in Elizabeth Gaskell's *Cranford* who was esteemed as a surgeon, but whose manners were deplored by the ladies of Cranford, pp. 190, 212–13.

36. Thorne, *History of Parliament. The Commons, 1790–1820*, vol. 1, pp. 305–8, 313–14; on Knighton see Liverpool to Wellington, 16 July 1823, Wellington, *New Despatches*, vol. 2, p. 103 and discussion of the subject 'The King, Knighton and Lord Liverpool', Muir, life-ofwellington.co.uk, the online commentary to Muir, *Wellington: Waterloo and the Fortunes of Peace*.

FIVE – THE LAW: BARRISTERS

1. *The Life of a Lawyer Written by Himself* (1830) quoted in Corfield, *Power and the Professions*, p. 71; George Jackson to his mother, 24 August 1808, *Diaries and Letters of Sir George Jackson* vol. 2 pp. 259–60. For the ceremonies around the assizes see also Duman, *The Judicial Bench in England*, p. 23.

2. Twiss, *Life of Lord Eldon*, vol.1, pp. 23–39.

3. Twiss, *Life of Lord Eldon*, vol.1, pp. 48–58.

4. Twiss, *Life of Lord Eldon*, vol. 1, pp. 66–82.

5. Twiss *Life of Lord Eldon*, vol. 1, pp. 83–95; Melikan, *John Scott, Lord Eldon*, p. 2, see also pp. 140–2.

6. Twiss, *Life of Lord Eldon*, vol. 1, pp. 84, 97–100.

7. Twiss, *Life of Lord Eldon*, vol.1, pp. 101–6, 113, 121.

8. Twiss, *Life of Lord Eldon*, vol.1, pp. 116–24.

9. Twiss, *Life of Lord Eldon*, vol.1, pp. 127–8.

10. Duman, 'Pathway to Professionalism', p. 619; Lucas, 'A Collective Biography of Students and Barristers of Lincoln's Inn', pp. 245–6, 249. Lucas gives figures showing that rather more than half of the students admitted to the Inns of Court were eldest or only sons, and argues that this means that 'It is time that we dismissed the notion that the bar constituted a provision for younger sons' (pp. 240–1). However, the fact that such a high proportion of students were not called to the Bar makes it dangerous to draw conclusions about those who were called to

the Bar on the basis of those enrolled in the Inns of Court. Moreover, we know that only one third of all the barristers who were appointed to the judicial bench between 1727 and 1875 were eldest or only sons, which suggests that younger sons were well represented in the profession (Duman, *Judicial Bench in England*, p. 53).

11. Lucas, 'Collective Biography of Students and Barristers of Lincoln's Inn', pp. 233–4; Lemmings, *Professors of the Law*, pp. 67–8; Austen, *Sense and Sensibility*, pp. 102–3 (vol.1, ch. 19). See also Phillips, *The Profligate Son*, p. 24 for an instance of a father avowedly wanting his son to study law 'more with a view to direct your mind to laudable pursuits, than that you should depend upon the profession of law for your maintenance and support'.

12. Quoted in Duman, *The English and Colonial Bars in the Nineteenth Century*, pp. 81–2. See also Surtees, *Handley Cross*, ch. XXIV for a wonderfully vivid description of his experiences as a law student in the 1820s, lightly dressed as fiction.

13. Pugsley, 'The Western Circuit', pp. 43–4; Duman, *The English and Colonial Bars in the Nineteenth Century*, p. 90; Thorne, *The History of Parliament. The Commons 1790–1820*, vol. 4, pp. 21–2.

14. Duman, *Judicial Bench in England*, p. 59. Duman's figures add up to only 89 per cent; presumably the remainder were those whose age could not be ascertained, but this is not stated.

15. Campbell, *Life of John, Lord Campbell*, vol. 1, p. 48 (letter dated 16 January 1800); see also Duman, *The English and Colonial Bar in the Nineteenth Century*, p. 83 and Romilly, *Memoirs*, vol. 1, p. 93.

16. Campbell, *Life of John, Lord Campbell*, vol. 1, p. 193 (letter dated January 1807).

17. Campbell, *Life of John, Lord Campbell*, vol. 1, p. 193 (letter dated December 1806); on devilling see Corfield, *Power and the Professions*, p. 90.

18. Duman, *Judicial Bench in England*, pp. 59–62.

19. Duman, *Judicial Bench in England*, pp. 55–7.

20. Duman, *Judicial Bench in England*, p. 24; George Eden quoted in Thorne, *History of Parliament. The Commons 1790–1820*, vol. 3, p. 660–1 'more bugs . . .'; Campbell, *Life of John, Lord Campbell*, vol. 1, p. 278 (letter dated 1 April 1812).

21. Gray, *Spencer Perceval*, pp. 8–9, 11; Romilly, *Memoirs*, vol. 1, pp. 71–4, 76–7, 91–4; see also Campbell, *Life of John, Lord Campbell*, vol. 1, p. 279 (letter dated 1 April 1812) for his dislike of life on circuit: 'Our men talk of little else but of the business done in the court, and who is getting on and who is falling off, abusing and backbiting one another.'

22. Coleridge diary quoted in Pugsley, 'The Western Circuit', pp. 47–8.

23. Coleridge diary quoted in Pugsley, 'The Western Circuit', pp. 44–8.

24. Melikan, *John Scott, Lord Eldon*, pp. 190–209, see also Duman, *Judicial Bench in England*, pp. 72–104.

25. Duman, *Judicial Bench in England*, pp. 3, 17–18, 22. For Eldon's fortune see above p. 27.

26. Duman, *English and Colonial Bars*, p. 96 including the quote.

27. Quoted in Lane, *Jane Austen's Family Through Five Generations*, pp. 224–5.

SIX – THE LAW: ATTORNEYS AND SOLICITORS

1. Figures from Corfield, *Power and the Professions*, p. 82; Robson, *The Attorney in Eighteenth-Century England*, pp. 166–7.

2. Trollope, *The Vicar of Bullhampton*, ch. 9, pp. 60–1; Boswell, *The Life of Samuel Johnson*, vol. 1, p. 420 (1770).

3. Austen, *The Watsons*, pp. 76–7; Austen, *Emma*, pp. 137, 248, 183 (vol. 1, ch. 16; vol. 2, chs 11, 4).

4. Miles, '"A Haven for the Privileged"' pp. 198–201.

5. Robson, *The Attorney in Eighteenth-Century England*, p. 57.

6. Quoted in Robson, *The Attorney in Eighteenth-Century England*, pp. 157–8.

7. Robson, *The Attorney in Eighteenth-Century England*, p. 158.

8. Hickey, *Memoirs of William Hickey*, vol. 1, pp. 68–9.

9. Robson, *The Attorney in Eighteenth-Century England*, pp. 61–6.

10. Pattisson quoted in Corfield, *Power and the Professions*, p. 71; Stow's 1755 *Survey of London* quoted in Robson, *The Attorney in Eighteenth-Century England*, pp. 59–60.

NOTES to pp. 120–52

11. Hickey, *Memoirs of William Hickey*, vol. 1, pp. 69–70.
12. Hickey, *Memoirs of William Hickey*, vol. 1, pp. 89–90, 97–8.
13. Miles, '"A Haven for the Privileged"', p. 206.
14. Hickey, *Memoirs of William Hickey*, vol. 1, pp. 330–2.
15. Corfield, *Power and the Professions*, pp. 80, 82; Schmidt, 'The Country Attorney in Late Eighteenth-Century England', p. 240; Miles, '"A Haven for the Privileged"', pp. 204–5.
16. Miles, '"A Haven for the Privileged"', p. 206.
17. Miles, '"A Haven for the Privileged"', p. 207.
18. Miles, '"A Haven for the Privileged"', pp. 201, 205; Day quoted in Robson, *The Attorney in Eighteenth-Century England*, p. 59n.
19. Schmidt, 'The Country Attorney in Late Eighteenth-Century England', pp. 239–43, 255.
20. Schmidt, 'The Country Attorney in Late Eighteenth-Century England', pp. 246–52.
21. Schmidt, 'The Country Attorney in Late Eighteenth-Century England', pp. 253–4, 269; Schmidt, 'The Smiths of Horbling', p. 159.
22. Edward Yescombe, '"Hazardous and Scanty Securitys"', pp. 97–8; details of Edward Yescombe's career from the Clergy of the Church of England Database.
23. Edward Yescombe, '"Hazardous and Scanty Securitys"', pp. 98–111.
24. Edward Yescombe '"Hazardous and Scanty Securitys"', pp. 99–100, 111–16.
25. Edward Yescombe, '"Hazardous and Scanty Securitys"', pp. 116–17.

SEVEN – BANKING AND COMMERCE

1. Austen, *Pride and Prejudice*, pp. 15, 139, 388 (vol. 1 ch. 4; vol. 2, ch. 2; vol. 3, ch. 19).
2. Thirsk, 'Younger Sons in the Seventeenth Century', pp. 363, 367–8; Chesterfield quoted in Hughes, 'The Professions in the Eighteenth Century', pp. 186–7.
3. Thorne, *History of Parliament. The Commons 1790–1820*, vol. 1, pp. 318–23.
4. Thorne, *History of Parliament. The Commons 1790–1820*, vol. 2, pp. 195–6, vol. 4, pp. 844–5; Fisher, *History of Parliament. The Commons, 1820–1832*, vol. 2, pp. 461–3, vol. 6, p. 814.
5. Lodge, *The Peerage and Baronetage of the British Empire* (1873), p. 810; Colby, *The Waterloo Despatch*, pp. 26, 38–9; see also Stone and Stone, *An Open Elite?*, p. 52.
6. Kynaston, *The City of London*, vol. 1, p. 22; Bell, *Sydney Smith*, p. 47.
7. Thorne, *History of Parliament. The Commons 1790–1820*, vol. 1, p. 318.
8. Kynaston, *The City of London*, vol. 1, pp. 10–11, 26.
9. Tann, 'James Tappenden, Town Clerk of Faversham . . .', pp. 213–22, 225–6.
10. For Henry Hickey see above, p. 11 and Hickey, *Memoirs of William Hickey*, vol. 1, pp. 23–6; for two Eton boys apprenticed in 1755 see Hughes, 'The Professions in the Eighteenth Century', p. 186.
11. Romilly, *Memoirs of Sir Samuel Romilly*, vol. 1, pp. 19–20.
12. Jerdan, *Autobiography of William Jerdan*, vol. 1, pp. 27–9.
13. Quoted in Kynaston, *The City of London*, vol. 1, p. 47.
14. Kynaston, *The City of London*, vol. 1 p. 30; Tann, 'James Tappenden', pp. 221–2; Uglow, *In These Times*, p. 96; Austen, *Lady Susan* in *Minor Works*, p. 250 (letter 5).
15. Uglow, *In These Times*, pp. 91, 96–7; Kynaston, *The City of London*, vol. 1, pp. 60, 89–90.
16. Quoted in Kynaston, *The City of London*, vol. 1, p. 80.
17. Mahony, *Wealth or Poverty*, pp. 115–17 (including quote from Charles Hales, the contemporary authority).
18. Kynaston, *The City of London*, vol. 1, pp. 19, 75–7.
19. Anon., 'The Nineteenth Century Banker's Clerk', pp. 37–40.
20. Uglow, *In These Times*, pp. 88–90.
21. Anon., 'A Bolton Banking Partnership' (extracts from the memoirs of Robert Barlow), pp. 31–41.
22. Caplan, 'Jane Austen's Soldier Brother', pp. 122–43; Kaplan, 'Henry Austen and John Rawston Papillon', pp. 11–15; Clery, *Jane Austen: The Banker's Sister*, pp. 40–3, 55–7, 64.
23. Caplan, 'Jane Austen's Banker Brother', pp. 69–71; Clery, *Jane Austen: The Banker's Sister*, pp. 67–8.

24. Jones, 'Richard Cox, Army Agent and Banker', pp. 178–81; Jones, 'Cox and Co.: Army Agents Craig's Court: the Nineteenth Century', pp. 178–81; Clery, *Jane Austen: The Banker's Sister*, p. 83.

25. Caplan, 'Jane Austen's Banker Brother', pp. 71–4; Clery, *Jane Austen: The Banker's Sister*, pp. 83, 88–91, 94–6; Hurst, 'Henry Thomas Austen – "Being a Hampshire Man" ', pp. 135–8.

26. Bennett, 'Lord Moira and the Austens', pp. 129–52; Clery, *Jane Austen: The Banker's Sister*, p. 186. Court proceedings referred to £3,400 lent at this time on notes of hand with a face value of £4,000; it is possible that a further £2,000 was lent, but Moira's total debt to Austen & Co., including earlier loans, was never said to be more than £6,500.

27. Caplan, 'Jane Austen's Banker Brother', pp. 74–9; Jane Austen to Cassandra Austen, 11 January 1809, *Jane Austen's Letters* no. 64, p. 171. Deidre Le Faye, the scrupulous editor of Austen's letters, suggests that High-diddle was a riding horse; Caplan thinks it refers to a clerk.

28. Tomalin, *Jane Austen*, pp. 133–4, 188–9; Clery, *Jane Austen: The Banker's Sister*, pp. 181–5; Jane Austen to Francis Austen, 3–6 July 1813, *Jane Austen's Letters*, no. 86, p. 224.

29. Caplan, 'Jane Austen's Banker Brother', pp. 79–81.

30. Caplan 'Jane Austen's Banker Brother', p. 84; Austen-Leigh and Austen-Leigh, *Jane Austen: A Family Record*, pp. 190–1; Jane Austen to Cassandra Austen, 23 June 1814, *Jane Austen's Letters*, no. 102, pp. 276–7. Unfortunately this was not the famous masked ball held at Burlington House a week later (on 1 July 1814) attended by the Duke of Wellington, just back from the Continent after five years hard campaigning, as well as Byron, dressed as a monk, John Cam Hobhouse in his Albanian costume and all high society and some of the more daring *demi-monde* as well.

31. Caplan, 'Jane Austen's Banker Brother', pp. 84–8; Corley, 'Jane Austen and her brother Henry's bank failure', pp. 114–18; Clery, *Jane Austen: The Banker's Sister*, p. 261; Le Faye, *Chronology of Jane Austen*, p. 532, cf. Austen-Leigh and Austen-Leigh, *Jane Austen: A Family Record*, p. 191 where the details differ. Although Caplan denies that the sureties were called upon, Corley's evidence appears to show that they were, and that the losses of Edward Knight and James Leigh Perrot were greater than the £30,000 in total often mentioned. Clery (p. 283) states that each guarantor was required to pay £21,000 by instalments.

32. Caplan, 'Jane Austen's Banker Brother', pp. 87–8; Caroline Austen quoted in Lane, *Jane Austen's Family*, p. 178; Jane Austen to James Edward Austen, 16–17 December 1816, *Jane Austen's Letters*, no. 146, p. 337.

33. Meacham, *Henry Thornton of Clapham*, pp. 30–1; Thorne, *History of Parliament. The Commons, 1790–1820*, vol. 5, pp. 370–3; entry on Henry Thornton in the *ODNB*.

34. Marianne Thornton to Hannah More, 7 December 1825, Forster, *Marianne Thornton*, pp. 107–8. Forster was Marianne Thornton's great-nephew and a bequest from her when he was still a child gave him financial independence, enabling him to become one of the most significant English novelists of his generation.

35. Marianne Thornton to Hannah More, 7 December 1825, Forster, *Marianne Thornton*, pp. 108–13. Fisher, *History of Parliament. The Commons, 1820–1832*, vol. 6, p. 814 states that the Governor was not involved due to his close ties with the bank, and that the amount lent was £300,000 not £400,000, but confirms much of the rest of Marianne's account.

36. Marianne Thornton to Hannah More, 12 and 29 December 1825, Forster, *Marianne Thornton*, pp. 114–17. For another, quite similar, account of the stress and anxiety for the family of the partners of a bank on the brink of failure see Darwin, *Emma Darwin: A Century of Family Letters, 1792–1896*, edited by her daughter Henrietta Litchfield, vol. 1, pp. 99–102.

37. RBS Heritage Hub-People-Henry Sykes Thornton; Boase, *Modern British Biography*, vol. 3, p. 961.

38. Thorne, *History of Parliament. The Commons, 1790–1820*, vol. 1, p. 318, vol. 4, pp. 540–3; Fisher, *History of Parliament. The Commons 1820–1832*, vol. 6, p. 342; Kynaston, *The City of London*, vol. 1, pp. 82–3; Colby, *The Waterloo Despatch*, pp. 31, 38–9. William Manning's son was Henry, later Cardinal, Manning.

EIGHT – CIVIL OFFICE

1. Muir, *Wellington: The Path to Victory*, pp. 37–9; Wesley's letter to Camden of 25 June 1795 is printed in Brialmont and Gleig, *Life of Wellington*, vol. 1, pp. 22–3 and is reproduced in the online commentary to Muir's biography at lifeofwellington.co.uk. Lord Mornington changed the spelling of the family surname from Wesley to Wellesley in 1797 and his younger brothers, including Arthur, had little choice but to follow suit. He was granted a peerage as Viscount Wellington in 1809, rising to Duke of Wellington in 1814.
2. Muir, *Wellington: The Path to Victory*, p. 19; Gash, *Mr Secretary Peel*, pp. 124–5. In 1804 and 1805, Lord Nelson, at the high point of his career, proved equally unsuccessful in procuring a civil office for his brother-in-law Thomas Bolton, whose business and farming ventures had not flourished. Knight, *The Pursuit of Victory*, pp. 623–4.
3. Sir Arthur Wellesley to Lady Anne Smith, Dublin Castle, 10 June 1807, Wellington, *Supplementary Despatches*, vol. 5, p. 82; Anne, Countess of Mornington to AW, 22 May 1807, WP 1/168/40/1; see also Muir, *Wellington: The Path to Victory*, pp. 193–6 and online commentary at lifeofwellington.co.uk.
4. Memorandum by Sir Arthur Wellesley n.d. [1809], printed in Aspinall and Smith, *English Historical Documents*, vol. 11, pp. 265–71.
5. For Sir Arthur Wellesley on William Wellesley-Pole's position in Queen's County see Memorandum by Sir Arthur Wellesley n.d. [1809] printed in Aspinall and Smith, *English Historical Documents*, vol. 11, p. 270; for the way the Duke of York and Wellington carefully avoided politicizing the army see Muir, 'Politics and the Peninsular Army', pp. 72–93: there were some exceptions such as the treatment of the radical soldier-politician Major-General Ronald Ferguson by the Horse Guards, but they remained untypical. For naval officers and Indian patronage see chapters 10 and 12 above.
6. Hamilton, 'John Wilson Croker', pp. 53–5.
7. Hamilton, 'John Wilson Croker', p. 61.
8. Croker to Horatio Smith, 6 November 1811, quoted in Hamilton 'John Wilson Croker', p. 57.
9. Croker to Lord Exmouth, 25 April 1824, quoted in Hamilton, 'John Wilson Croker', pp. 57–8. Croker introduced promotion by merit to the Admiralty office in 1816 (*ibid.*). 'Barrow' was John Barrow, Croker's colleague, Second Secretary to the Admiralty from 1807 to 1845. Where Croker's position was a political appointment, Barrow's was permanent, although the distinction between the two was still forming and was sometimes contested.
10. Figures from Chester, *English Administrative System*, pp. 148, 166–7; Cohen, *The Growth of the British Civil Service*, pp. 34–5. See also Holmes, *Augustan England*, pp. 239–61, who argues that the bureaucracy of the early eighteenth century laid the foundation for a professional civil service (esp. p. 242), and Parris, 'The Origins of the Permanent Civil Service' who lays greater emphasis on the ways in which it fell short of later norms.
11. Chester, *English Administrative System*, p. 224.
12. Brewer, 'Servants of the Public – Servants of the Crown', pp. 130–1 (social origins of recruits); Hoon, *The Organization of the English Customs Service*, pp. 206–8.
13. Brewer, 'Servants of the Public – Servants of the Crown', pp. 128–36, 141–5; Cohen, *Growth of the British Civil Service*, p. 33 (for their pay).
14. Patrick Murray's journal quoted in Harding-Edgar, *Next to Wellington*, p. 26; Aberdeen to Alexander Gordon, 25 July 1810 and 13 February 1811 in Gordon, *At Wellington's Right Hand*, pp. 101, 162; Pückler-Muskau, *A Regency Visitor*, p. 37.
15. Virgin, *Sydney Smith*, pp. 264–5.
16. Cohen, *Growth of the British Civil Service*, pp. 24–25; Holmes, *Augustan England*, p. 252; Hamilton, 'John Wilson Croker', p. 57. Little information appears to have survived about the position and lives of the supernumerary clerks.
17. Austen, *Mansfield Park*, p. 381 (vol. 3, ch. 7); Knight, *Pursuit of Victory*, pp. 8–9, 21, 80, 127, 657, 671. Nelson's father was a clergyman, as was his maternal grandfather, the father of Maurice Suckling. For the social background of clerks in general see Murphy, '"Writes a Fair Hand and Appears Well Qualified"', pp. 28–33.

18. Cohen, *Growth of the British Civil Service*, p. 30; Middleton, *Administration of British Foreign Policy*, pp. 157–8.
19. Murphy, '"Writes a Fair Hand and Appears Well Qualified"', pp. 21–8, 36–7; Brewer, *The Sinews of Power*, p. 68 for supernumerary clerks including women.
20. Cohen, *Growth of the British Civil Service*, pp. 25–8, 39–41; Chester, *English Administrative System*, pp. 147–9.
21. Cohen, *Growth of the British Civil Service*, p. 28, cf. Chester, *English Administrative System*, pp. 145–7.
22. Holmes, *Augustan England*, pp. 249–50, 252; Ward, 'Some Eighteenth-Century Civil Servants', pp. 53–4; Gray, *Spencer Perceval*, pp. 311–13.
23. Cohen, *Growth of the British Civil Service*, pp. 29–30; Middleton, *Administration of British Foreign Policy*, p. 283, cf. pp. 169–70 where the size of the pensions to Hay's sisters is given at £175 each.
24. Taylor, *The Taylor Papers*, pp. 2–19 (esp. 12, 17–18); Middleton, *Administration of British Foreign Policy*, pp. 88–9, 313; *ODNB*; Fisher, *History of Parliament: The Commons, 1820–32*, vol. 7, pp. 369–73 (includes quote from Brougham).
25. Gash, *Lord Liverpool*, pp. 67, 131–2; Muir, lifeofwellington.co.uk, 'Lord Warden of the Cinque Ports'; Sack, *The Grenvillites*, pp. 34–7.
26. Greville, *The Greville Memoirs*, vol.1, pp. xiii–xvii, vol. 3, p. 207 (14 June 1835) and vol. 4, pp. 54–5 (7 May 1838).
27. See above p. 155.
28. Hoon, *Organization of the English Customs System*, pp. 130–1 and n; Cohen, *Growth of the British Civil Service*, pp. 24–6, 38–9.
29. Beckett, *The Rise and Fall of the Grenvilles*, p. 69 (Buckingham's Irish salary); Middleton, *Administration of British Foreign Policy*, pp. 103, 144–8, 326; Lee, *George Canning and Liberal Toryism*, pp. 78–81 (Canning's constituency duties as Member for Liverpool).
30. Gray, *Spencer Perceval*, pp. 308–10.
31. Priscilla's father, William Wellesley-Pole, was also a member of the cabinet, although much less influential than Wellington. See *ODNB* entries for Francis and George Jackson. Strictly speaking, Carmarthen introduced Francis into the service and Francis then introduced George, but it was Carmarthen's influence and patronage that underlay the entry of both men into the service. For their subsequent careers see George Jackson's excellent diary and correspondence published as *Diaries and Letters* and *The Bath Archives*.
32. Jones, *The British Diplomatic Service*, pp. 12–18.
33. Hoon, *Organization of the English Customs System*, p. 78 (quote 'Without exception . . .'), p. 59 (salary); Ward, 'Some Eighteenth-Century Civil Servants: The English Revenue Commissioners, 1754–98', pp. 46–9; Chester, *English Administrative System*, p. 224 (60 in 1800).
34. Ward, 'Some Eighteenth-Century Civil Servants', pp. 28–30, 42–4, 48–9.
35. Welbourne, 'Bankruptcy before the Era of Victorian Reform', p. 51; Robson, *The Attorney in Eighteenth-Century England*, pp. 104–5.
36. Moorman, *William Wordsworth*, pp. 240–3.
37. Moorman, *William Wordsworth*, pp. 244–6.
38. Moorman, *William Wordsworth*, pp. 247–50.
39. Moorman, *William Wordsworth*, pp. 246–53. On Hume, see Muir, *Wellington: Waterloo and the Fortunes of Peace*, pp. 251–2.

NINE – THE NAVY: YOUNG GENTLEMEN AT SEA

1. Rodger, *Wooden World*, pp. 253–5; Scott, *Life of Matthew Flinders*, pp. 11–14; Dundonald, *Autobiography of a Seaman*, vol. 1, pp. 45–9; Southam, *Jane Austen and the Navy*, p. 20; Dutton and Elder, *Colonel William Light*, pp. 28–9; Marryat, *Life and Letters of Captain Marryat*, vol. 1, pp. 13–15.
2. For the parents' perspective: Southam, *Jane Austen and the Navy*, p. 19; Rodger, *Wooden World*, pp. 253–4; and, more broadly, Lewis, *Social History of the Navy*, pp. 288–92. For the age of boys

joining, see Wilson, *A Social History of British Naval Officers*, pp. 17–19 and Consolvo 'Prospects and Promotion', p. 142; for their need for an allowance see Lewis, *Social History of the Navy*, p. 38.

3. Wilson, *Social History of British Naval Officers*, pp. 16–17, 84–92. Wilson's conclusions are based on detailed research into the background of 556 randomly selected officers, and are therefore more convincing than the previous studies by Lewis, *Social History of the Navy*, pp. 27–59 and Cavell, *Midshipmen and Quarterdeck Boys*, pp. 2–5, 37–48 which rely excessively on self-reporting or incomplete data, which is liable to introduce distortions that tend to raise the social status of the fathers of the officers. However, even Wilson's work cannot tell us what proportion of naval officers were the sons of gentlemen: many, but not all, of the fathers who were in the professions, and some but a lower proportion of those in commerce, would have regarded themselves, and been generally accepted, as gentlemen, but with no clear definition of the term it is impossible to quantify the proportion.

4. Cavell, *Midshipmen and Quarterdeck Boys*, pp. 7–10, 39; Knight, *William IV*, p. 29; Southam, *Jane Austen and the Navy*, pp. 20–1.

5. Scott, *Life of Matthew Flinders*, pp. 17–18; Dutton and Elder, *Colonel William Light*, p. 29; Rodger, *Wooden World*, p. 267.

6. Southam, *Jane Austen and the Navy*, pp. 13–14, 21–9, 36–7; Cavell, *Midshipmen and Quarterdeck Boys*, pp. 26–30.

7. [William Nugent Glascock] *Naval Sketch-Book; or, the Service Afloat and Ashore* 'by an Officer of Rank', vol. 1, pp. 3–4.

8. Gardner, *Above and Under Hatches*, p. 12; Rodger, *Wooden World*, p. 37.

9. Although the name of the author is given on the title page as Alfred Burton, *The Adventures of Johnny Newcome in the Navy* is attributed to John Mitford in many library catalogues, the ODNB and Wikipedia. However, in 2017 the antiquarian bookseller David Brass Rare Books listed a copy of a different book: *Adventures of Johnny Newcome in the Navy*, with John Mitford's name printed on the title page and illustrations by Charles Williams (another contemporary carica-turist). This was first published in 1819 in eight monthly parts and then went into at least three editions as a book, but has since been generally forgotten and the two books are conflated. David Brass cites Martin Hardie, *English Coloured Books* (1906 reprinted 1990), p. 173 which discusses both books and states that Mitford's was 'an open imitation' of Burton's.

10. Burton, *Adventures of Johnny Newcome in the Navy*, pp. 39–44.

11. Burton, *Adventures of Johnny Newcome in the Navy*, pp. 45–52.

12. Marryat, *Life and Letters of Captain Marryat*, vol. 1, pp. 229–30 quoting Marryat's fragmentary recollections.

13. Burton, *Adventures of Johnny Newcome in the Navy*, pp. 68–77. Marryat describes similar punishments in his novel *Frank Mildmay*, pp. 31–2, and Gardner alludes to them in *Above and Under Hatches*, pp. 23–4.

14. Burg, *Boys at Sea, passim* esp. pp. 71, 77–8, 94–7 (for Captain Allen); Rodger, *Wooden World*, pp. 80–1. Churchill is said to have told his personal assistant Anthony Montague-Browne, 'I never said it. I wish I had.'

15. Lewis, *Social History of the Navy*, p. 262; Cavell, *Midshipmen and Quarterdeck Boys*, pp. 11–13.

16. Cavell, *Midshipmen and Quarterdeck Boys*, pp. 11–13; Lewis, *Social History of the Navy*, pp. 262, 267–9.

17. Cavell, *Midshipmen and Quarterdeck Boys*, pp. 12–14; Burton, *The Adventures of Johnny Newcome in the Navy*, p. 106.

18. Rodger, *Wooden World*, pp. 39–40, 46, 62, 69–71.

19. Rodger, *Command of the Ocean*, p. 508; Wareham, *The Star Captains*, p. 53; Cavell, *Midshipmen and Quarterdeck Boys*, pp. 14–15, 25; Lewis, *Social History of the Navy*, pp. 260–1 (for schoolmasters).

20. See Burton, *Adventures of Johnny Newcome in the Navy*, pp. 104–6, 119–20 for example.

21. Gardner, *Above and Under Hatches*, p. 29; Burton, *Adventures of Johnny Newcome in the Navy*, pp. 198–235.

22. Nicolas's account was first published in the *Bijou* in 1829 and reproduced as an appendix in Allen, *Memoir of the Life and Services of Admiral Sir William Hargood*, pp. 278–92 (quote from p. 281).

23. Rodger, *Wooden World*, pp. 37–8; Gardner, *Above and Under Hatches*, pp. 52–3, 82; Rodger, *Command of the Ocean*, p. 382; Wilson, *Social History of British Naval Officers*, p. 29.

24. Gardner, *Above and Under Hatches*, pp. 90–1, see also pp. 71–2.

25. Knight, *The Pursuit of Victory*, pp. 28–32; Austen, *Persuasion*, pp. 50–1 (vol. 1, ch. 6).

26. Nelson to Charles Connor, n.d. [*c*. 1804] in Nelson, *The Dispatches and Letters of . . . Lord Nelson*, vol. 7, p. ccxiv; see also Knight, *Pursuit of Victory*, p. 619 who states that Charles Connors (surname with an 's') was a midshipman on the *Victory* from May to October 1804.

27. Nelson quoted in Knight, *Pursuit of Victory*, p. 17; Pocock, *Remember Nelson*, p. 42 (for Hoste); Rainier's letter to his nephew is printed in Parkinson, *War in Eastern Seas*, pp. 432–6; Cathcart quoted in Wilson, *Social History of British Naval Officers*, p. 111; see also Rodger, *Command of the Ocean*, pp. 386–8 and 509.

28. Cavell, *Midshipmen and Quarterdeck Boys*, pp. 2–3, 35–6. Despite the claims of Nelson and St Vincent any influx of the nobility into the navy during the French wars was limited, and the vast majority of officers continued to come from the same background as before: see Wilson, *Social History of British Naval Officers*, pp. 91–2.

29. Austen, *Mansfield Park*, p. 236 (vol. 2, ch 6).

TEN – THE NAVY: PROMOTION AND EMPLOYMENT

1. Southam, *Jane Austen and the Navy*, pp. 28–9, 39–41, 44. Mr Austen's letter to Francis is printed in full on pp. 30–3. I have accepted Southam's argument that while his immediate family knew Francis as Frank, the more formal name is more appropriate for us to use 'coming to him from the outside . . . across so many years . . . especially for an officer of such formality and punctiliousness' (p. xii).

2. Southam, *Jane Austen and the Navy*, pp. 45–7. As a child, Hastings had known Mrs Austen's family, and he sent his young son George (1757–64) home from India to be brought up in the Austen household; although unfortunately George died while still young. Hastings was also the godfather of Eliza Hancock, the daughter of his friend and business partner Tysoe-Saul Hancock and his wife Philadelphia, who was Mr Austen's sister. Hastings made Eliza a generous financial settlement, and she went on to marry first Jean Capot de Feuillide (inaccurately known as the Comte de Feuillide) and second Henry Austen. *Jane Austen's Letters*, pp. 533, 485.

3. Southam, *Jane Austen and the Navy*, pp. 13–14, 43–7; Le Faye, *Chronology of Jane Austen*, pp. 137, 152.

4. According to Slope, 'Serving in Nelson's Navy', pp. 354–5, 359 only about half of midshipmen were ever made lieutenant. Some of the others died, others left the navy, while there were others who never had any expectation of gaining commissioned rank, but who went on to be made warrant and petty officers.

5. Consolvo, 'Prospects and Promotion', pp. 140–3; Southam, *Jane Austen and the Navy*, pp. 42–3; Cavell, *Midshipmen and Quarterdeck Boys*, pp. 22–4; Lewis, *Social History of the Navy*, p. 203. Wilson, *Social History of British Naval Officers*, pp. 11–12 has evidence that a higher proportion of officers were under age than was previously thought: more than one third by the early years of the nineteenth century.

6. Consolvo, 'Prospects and Promotion', p. 143; Southam, *Jane Austen and the Navy*, pp. 42–3, 188, 298–302; Austen, *Mansfield Park*, pp. 298–302 (vol. 2, ch 13); see also Rodger, *Command of the Ocean*, pp. 380–2.

7. Manwaring, *My Friend the Admiral*, pp. 9–14; Rodger, *Wooden World*, pp. 269–70; Consolvo, 'Prospects and Promotion', pp. 144–5. Nelson's first voyage was in a West India merchantman while still officially in the navy – this was organized by his uncle Captain Maurice Suckling, to spare him the dull routine of life on a guard ship. See Knight, *Pursuit of Victory*, p. 26.

8. Lewis, *Social History of the Navy*, pp. 233–7, quoting Edward Mangin, chaplain of the *Gloucester* on both hammocks and wine. Sugar of lead is another name for lead acetate, a sweetener that is also toxic.

9. Lewis, *Social History of the Navy*, pp. 237–8.

10. For details of all these ships and Francis's time in them see Caplan, 'The Ships of Frank Austen', pp. 75–8.
11. Lewis, *Social History of the Navy*, pp. 212–15. This was not the famous Thomas Cochrane, Lord Dundonald, but his cousin. Wilson, *Social History of the Navy*, pp. 87–8 states that 'two thirds of officers were never actively employed at a rank higher than lieutenant'.
12. Austen, *Mansfield Park*, p. 368 (vol. 3, ch 6); see Southam, *Jane Austen and the Navy*, p. 206n for background about the introduction of the lieutenant's uniform in 1812.
13. Consolvo, 'Prospects and Promotion', p. 156: these figures are actually lower than those Consolvo gives on p. 149 which are distorted by the presence on the 'active' list of a number of elderly lieutenants who did not receive promotion until after 1823 when it was employed as a step to induce them to retire. See also Southam, *Jane Austen and the Navy*, pp. 105–13 and Le Faye, *Chronology of Jane Austen*, pp. 219 and 239 for dates of Francis's promotions.
14. Southam, *Jane Austen and the Navy*, pp. 75–6.
15. Southam, *Jane Austen and the Navy*, pp. 77–8; Collingwood quoted in Lewis, *Social History of the Navy*, pp. 223–6.
16. Southam, *Jane Austen and the Navy*, pp. 83–4; Sydney quoted in Reiter, *The Late Lord*, p. 30; Austen, *Mansfield Park*, pp. 298–9 (vol. 2, ch. 13).
17. Southam, *Jane Austen and the Navy*, pp. 84–9.
18. Bennett, 'Lord Moira and the Austens', pp. 139–41; Southam, *Jane Austen and the Navy*, pp. 93–5; see also Wareham, *The Star Captains*, pp. 32–41, 47–51 for an excellent discussion of the reasons why the command of a frigate was so desirable.
19. Bennett, 'Lord Moira and the Austens', pp. 135–8; cf. Southam, *Jane Austen and the Navy*, p. 53 who gives an alternative but less plausible explanation for Charles's promotion.
20. Southam, *Jane Austen and the Navy*, pp. 89–93, quoting Francis Austen's memoir (which was written in the third person); Jane Austen to Cassandra, 24–26 December 1798, *Jane Austen's Letters*, no. 15, p. 29.
21. Lewis, *Social History of the Navy*, pp. 183–4, see also pp. 216–19; Consolvo, 'Prospects and Promotion', p. 149
22. Hindmarsh, *From Powder Monkey to Governor*, *passim* and p. 29 and the entry on Hindmarsh in the *ODNB*.
23. Consolvo, 'Prospects and Promotion', pp. 151–2.
24. O'Byrne, *A Naval Biographical Dictionary*, vol. 1, pp. 27–8; see also Hubback and Hubback, *Jane Austen's Sailor Brothers*, pp. 60–90, 98–109, which includes many extracts from the log of the *Peterel*; Caplan, 'Ships of Frank Austen', p. 78 for his return to England.
25. Lewis, *Social History of the Navy*, pp. 191–5, 296–7; Rodger, *Command of the Ocean*, pp. 518–19.
26. Rodger, *Command of the Ocean*, p. 518.
27. Francis Austen's letter quoted in Southam, *Jane Austen and the Navy*, pp. 98–100; the full text of the letter is printed in Hubback, *Jane Austen's Sailor Brothers*, pp. 148–61, although Southam uses 'a more accurate transcript in the possession of the late Mr Alwyn Austen'.
28. Southam, *Jane Austen and the Navy*, pp. 100–2; Caplan, 'Ships of Frank Austen', pp. 79–80.
29. Jane to Cassandra Austen, 20–22 February 1807, *Jane Austen's Letters* no. 51, p. 128; Caplan, 'Ships of Frank Austen', pp. 80–1; Southam, *Jane Austen and the Navy*, pp. 102–3.
30. Caplan, 'Ships of Frank Austen', pp. 81–2; Southam, *Jane Austen and the Navy*, pp. 103–4, 288–90.
31. Lewis, *Social History of the Navy*, pp. 229–33.
32. Lewis, *Social History of the Navy*, pp. 229–30; Rodger, *Wooden World*, pp. 65–8; Southam, *Jane Austen and the Navy*, pp. 281–6, 328–9. Southam (p. 328) states that Cassandra Austen, Francis's daughter, was 40 at the time of the voyage, but she was born in 1814 and so was only 30.
33. Austen, *Persuasion*, pp. 70–1 (vol. 1, ch. 8), cf. Rodger, *Command of the Ocean*, pp. 526–7 for real examples. Charles Austen's wife Fanny travelled with him from her home in Bermuda on his ship the *Cleopatra* with their two infant children in 1811 and she subsequently lived with him on the *Namur*, a guardship anchored off Sheerness, Southam, *Jane Austen and the Navy*, p. 54. (In a most untypical slip Rodger confuses Fanny Austen with Francis's wife Martha and states that she was with him in the Baltic in 1812.)

34. Lewis, *Social History of the Navy*, pp. 293–311.
35. Lewis, *Social History of the Navy*, pp. 196–8, 313; Lewis, *Navy in Transition*, p. 67; Austen, *Persuasion*, pp. 97–9 (vol. 1, ch. 11). There were precedents for the extensive promotion at the end of the war: see Wareham, *The Star Captains*, pp. 18–19.
36. Perceval quoted in Gill, 'Children of the Service', p. 155; Dundonald, *Autobiography of a Seaman*, vol. 1, p. 53; Southam, *Jane Austen and the Navy*, pp. 127–30; Ward and Gooch, *The Cambridge History of British Foreign Policy*, vol. 1, p. 257n.
37. *ODNB* entries on Keith and Rainier; Southam, *Jane Austen and the Navy*, p. 135 for Pellew; and Lewis, *Social History of the Navy*, p. 321 for Collingwood.
38. Southam, *Jane Austen and the Navy*, pp. 115–18, 123–6.
39. Consolvo, 'Prospects and Promotion', p. 153; Wareham, *The Star Captains*, p. 46; Southam, *Jane Austen and the Navy*, pp. 127, 136; Caplan, 'Jane Austen's Banker Brother', p. 73.
40. Consolvo, 'Prospects and Promotion', p. 146–7; see also Lewis, *Social History of the Navy*, pp. 390–1, 419–21; Wareham, *The Star Captains*, pp. 29 and 98 (one in four of his sample died during the war) and Southam, *Jane Austen and the Navy*, p. 71.
41. Lewis, *Social History of the Navy*, pp. 146–7; see also Consolvo, 'Prospects and Promotion', p. 148.
42. Consolvo, 'Prospects and Promotion', p. 156.
43. Lewis, *Navy in Transition*, pp. 64–71, 79–81, 88–92. For a fictional counterpart to Lieutenant Price, albeit from the army not the navy, think of Captain Brown in *Cranford* by Elizabeth Gaskell.
44. *ODNB*.

ELEVEN – THE ARMY

1. Smith, *The Autobiography of Sir Harry Smith*, pp. 158–9.
2. Calvert, *An Irish Beauty of the Regency*, pp. 91–8.
3. Glover, *Wellington's Army in the Peninsula*, p. 36. These figures do not include the Engineers and Artillery which increased from 361 officers in 1792 to 912 in 1814 (*ibid.*, p. 36).
4. Glover, *Wellington's Army*, pp. 43–4; Burnham and McGuigan, *The British Army Against Napoleon*, pp. 151–2.
5. Glover, *Wellington's Army*, p. 44; Smith, *Autobiography of Harry Smith*, pp. 1–3; Greenwood, *Through Spain with Wellington*, pp. 3–5. A commission that was granted in this way could not normally be sold.
6. Glover, *Wellington's Army*, p. 36; Haythornthwaite, *The Armies of Wellington*, p. 23.
7. John Orrok to William Reid [snr], Hydrabad, 29 September 1806, Orrok, *Letters of Captain John Orrok*, pp. 78–9; Greenwood, *Through Spain with Wellington*, p. 36n; Glover, *Wellington's Army*, p. 38.
8. Glover, *Wellington's Army*, pp. 39–40; Geike, *Life of Sir Roderick I. Murchison*, vol. 1, pp. 16–17.
9. Breihan and Caplan, 'Jane Austen and the Militia', pp. 18–21; Heathcote, *Letters of a Young Diplomatist*, p. 128; Chambers, *Memoir of William and Robert Chambers*, p. 60; Cooke, *A True Soldier Gentleman*, pp. 29–48; Glover, *Wellington's Army*, p. 40.
10. Jane Austen to Cassandra, 9–10 January 1796, *Jane Austen's Letters*, no. 1, p. 2.
11. Cooke, *A True Soldier Gentleman*, p. 49.
12. Heathcote, *Letters of a Young Diplomatist*, pp. 123–4.
13. Heathcote, *Letters of a Young Diplomatist*, p. 131.
14. Bunbury, *Reminiscences of a Veteran*, vol. 1, p. 54; Gronow, *The Reminiscences and Recollections of Captain Gronow*, p. 1; Greenwood, *Through Spain with Wellington*, pp. 7–9.
15. Greenwood, *Through Spain with Wellington*, p. 27; '*de bonnes aventures*', literally 'some good adventures', has clear overtones of roistering and sexual indulgence; 'Esprits forts' meaning 'strong spirits' – probably with the connotation of 'thick headed' and quarrelsome.
16. Greenwood, *Through Spain with Wellington*, pp. 34–5.
17. Greenwood, *Through Spain with Wellington*, p. 35; Hennell, *A Gentleman Volunteer*, p. 103.
18. Bunbury, *Reminiscences of a Veteran*, vol. 1, pp. 7–8.
19. Kincaid, *Adventures in the Rifle Brigade*, p. 265; Clark-Kennedy, *Attack the Colour!*, p. 64.

20. According to Glover, *Wellington's Army*, p. 44 of 140 members of peerage families serving in the army on full pay, 79 were in the cavalry or the Guards, and half of those in the cavalry were in five fashionable regiments. Burnham and McGuigan show that in 1812 there were five royal princes, 59 other peers, and 167 sons of peers holding commissions in the army, or 227 officers out of a total of more than 10,000, *The British Army Against Napoleon*, p. 17. And some of these peers – such as Lord Harris – were officers who had been ennobled as a reward for their victories. Existing discussions of the social origins of the vast majority of army officers who were not members of the peerage are impressionistic rather than rigorous or statistical; however, it is unlikely that the evidence is sufficiently robust or precise to permit a comprehensive analysis. On Thomas Bradford (senior) see Coote, 'William Lindley', pp. 11–12.

21. Glover, *Wellington's Army*, p. 37; Wellington and Macdonald quoted in Strachan, *Wellington's Legacy*, p. 111.

22. Glover, *Wellington's Army*, pp. 38–9; Torrens to Wellington, 23 May 1810, WO 3/596, pp. 374–5: this letter was written in response to a complaint from Wellington that Sergeant John Clarke of the Guards had not received a commission in the 52nd Light Infantry that Wellington had recommended him for, but in a West India regiment. See also Divall, *Inside the Regiment*, pp. 115–17.

23. Shipp quoted in Spiers, *Army and Society*, p. 3; Haythornthwaite, *Armies of Wellington*, p. 29.

24. Hennell, *A Gentleman Volunteer*, p. 1 and *passim*; Crowe, *An Eloquent Soldier*, p. 82.

25. Glover, *Wellington's Army*, p 38; Nenadic, 'The Impact of the Military Profession on Highland Gentry Families', *passim*; Dutton and Elder, *Colonel William Light*, pp. 7–11. It is probably significant that there was little in Light's appearance to suggest the non-European part of his ethnic heritage: he was described as 'of medium height, sallow complexion, alert and hand-some, with face clean shaven except closely cut side whiskers, black curly hair, brown eyes, straight nose, small mouth, and shapely chin' (*ibid.*, p. 39). See also John Perkins who was born into slavery in Jamaica – probably with a white father, certainly a black mother. He rose eventually to be a post-captain in the navy in 1800. His career is detailed in *ODNB* and by Wilson, *Social History of British Naval Officers*, p. 123. However, Wilson adds (p. 124) that so far as we know Perkins was the only black naval officer.

26. Burnham and McGuigan, *The British Army Against Napoleon*, p. 144.

27. Sir John Moore to John Spottiswood, 18 January [1804], Brownrigg, *Life and Letters of Sir John Moore*, pp. 146–7; Glover, *Wellington's Army*, p. 43.

28. Greenwood, *Through Spain with Wellington*, pp. 44, 62–3. To make clothes last they were often turned inside out and remade when they began to grow shabby.

29. Grattan, *Adventures with the Connaught Rangers*, pp. 54–5. 'Cocker' refers to a popular arith-metic textbook of the day.

30. Glover, *Wellington's Army*, p. 43; Tomkinson, *The Diary of a Cavalry Officer*, p. 3; Cairnes to Maj.-Gen. W. Cuppage, 19 August 1813, Dickson, *Dickson Manuscripts*, vol. 5, pp. 1023–4; cf. the similar reaction of Captain Francis Beaufort RN to the offer of money from Lloyd's Patriotic Fund to officers in Southam, *Jane Austen and the Navy*, p. 125.

31. Glover, *Wellington's Army*, p. 76.

32. Glover, *Wellington's Army*, p. 76; Haythornthwaite, *Armies of Wellington*, pp. 31–2; Glover, 'Purchase, Patronage and Promotion', p. 359.

33. Muir, *Britain and the Defeat of Napoleon*, pp. 46, 86; the King to Castlereagh, 27 March 1809, George III, *Later Correspondence*, vol. 5, p. 247.

34. Anglesey, *One-Leg*, p. 67. Henry William Paget was Edward Paget's eldest brother and in time became Earl of Uxbridge and then Marquess of Anglesey.

35. Glover, *Wellington's Army*, pp. 76–7.

36. Hennell, *A Gentleman Volunteer*, p. 132 and note; Crowe, *An Eloquent Soldier*, p. 130.

37. Greenwood, *Through Spain with Wellington*, pp. 86, 153, 206.

38. Glover, 'Purchase, Patronage and Promotion', pp. 356, 358; Divall, *Inside the Regiment*, p. 111.

39. Glover, 'Purchase, Patronage and Promotion', p. 360. Smith's majority and lieutenant-colonelcy were both his rank *in the army*; his *regimental* rank in the 95th remained captain.

40. Cooke, *True Soldier Gentleman*, pp. 63–5, 68.

41. Heathcote, *Letters of a Young Diplomatist*, pp. 122–5, 129–33. Officers in the Prussian and other German armies were expected to live more closely with their men, and pay them more attention, than in the British army at this time.

42. For some interesting if highly coloured details of the life of British officers serving in the West Indies see Buckley, *The British Army in the West Indies*, pp. 339–47.

43. Swabey, *Diary of Campaigns in the Peninsula*, p. 182; Smith, 'Journal in Spain . . .', pp. 278, 281.

44. Greenwood, *Through Spain with Wellington*, p. 98; Simmons and Dornford both quoted in Haythornthwaite, *Armies of Wellington*, p. 26; 'terrible life' from a letter from Lt W. H. Hare to his parents, 23 January 1812, [Hare], 'Letters from the Front', p. 270. For a rich and well-informed account of the experience of the war in the Peninsula see Brett-James, *Life in Wellington's Army, passim*.

45. Aitchison, *An Ensign in the Peninsular War*, p. 11.

46. Greenwood, *Through Spain with Wellington*, pp. 154, 164.

47. Kincaid, *Adventures in the Rifle Brigade*, p. 271.

48. Greenwood, *Through Spain with Wellington*, pp. 10, 58, 147, 150; see also Mahony, *Wealth or Poverty*, p. 164 for a quote from Southey which supports Anne Le Mesurier's view, although it predates the Peninsular War.

49. On Mrs Dalbiac see Long, *Peninsular Cavalry General*, p. 93 and Brett James, *Life in Wellington's Army*, pp. 273–6; Smith, *The Autobiography of Sir Harry Smith*, pp. 71–2.

50. Heathcote, *Letters of a Young Diplomatist*, p. 126; Aitchison, *An Ensign in the Peninsular War*, p. 11. Aitchison remained in the army even after the war and rose to command the Scots Guards and serve as a major-general in India between 1845 and 1851. He decided that he would not marry until he was no longer actively employed, and delayed the nuptials until he was 68 years old. Even so he and his wife had three children, two of whom unfortunately drowned while still very young (*ibid.*, p. 12).

51. These are my calculations based on a variety of sources including a return in the War Office, WO 79/50, 'Return of the Numbers of killed and wounded under the command of Lord . . . Wellington'; Glover, *Wellington's Army*, p. 36; Burnham and McGuigan, *British Army Against Napoleon*, p. 212; and Hodge, 'On the Mortality arising from Military Operations', *passim* and especially p. 266.

52. Muir, *Wellington: The Path to Victory*, pp. 89, 595–6; Muir, *Wellington: Waterloo and the Fortunes of Peace*, pp. 10, 90; 'Scale of the Prize-Money for the Capture of Seringapatam' in Wellington, *Supplementary Despatches*, vol. 1, p. 223; Burnham and McGuigan, *British Army Against Napoleon*, pp. 170–1 gives the prize money distributed to the army for its services in the Peninsula: the short campaign of 1814 was by far the most lucrative, but even for that a captain received only £50. A subaltern who served in all the campaigns from 1809 to the end of 1813 would receive only just over £22 in prize money.

53. Glover, *Wellington's Army*, pp. 19, 147–9; Torrens to Wellington, 'Private', 13 January 1813, WO 3/604, pp. 60–2; Reiter, *The Late Lord*, pp. 72, 89.

54. Glover, *Wellington's Army*, p. 149.

55. Cole, *Memoirs of Sir Lowry Cole*, pp. 109, 134–5, 182, 202; Thorne, *History of Parliament. The Commons, 1790–1820*, vol. 3, pp. 482–3; Fisher, *History of Parliament. The Commons, 1820–1832*, vol. 4, pp. 712–13 (includes the second quote); entry on Cole in the *ODNB*.

56. Burnham and McGuigan, *The British Army Against Napoleon*, pp. 173–4; Orrok, *Letters of Captain John Orrok*, pp. 130–1, 143–4; Wellington to Robert Peel, 26 June 1824, WP 1/795/15 expresses his views on the impropriety of a half-pay officer acting in any position not 'that of a gentleman'.

57. Smith, *Autobiography of Lieutenant-General Sir Harry Smith* (1902 edition), vol. 2, p. 327: the one-volume abridged edition of 1910 generally cited here does not include this reminiscence by the editor.

58. Calvert, *An Irish Beauty of the Regency*, pp. 250–1; Boase, *Modern English Biography*, vol. 1, p. 519.

59. Greenwood, *Through Spain with Wellington*, p. 211.

TWELVE – INDIA

1. Scott, 'The Surgeon's Daughter', pp. xxii–xxiii and p. 53.
2. Mason, *A Matter of Honour*, pp. 174–75, cf Dalrymple, *White Mughals*, *passim*.
3. Callahan, *The East India Company and Army Reform*, pp. 16–17, 25.
4. Hickey, *Memoirs of William Hickey*, vol. 1, pp. 117–18, 124–5, cf Malcolm, *Malcolm*, pp. 15–16 for a more difficult interview at India House. However, as John Malcolm was still only 12 years old at the time, it is not surprising that the directors had doubts about accepting him as a cadet; and yet they did so, albeit after some hesitation.
5. Sydney Smith to Lord Holland, 28 February and 9 March 1818, *Letters of Sydney Smith*, vol. 1, pp. 285–6; Virgin, *Sydney Smith*, pp. 196–8.
6. Orrok, *The Letters of Captain John Orrok*, p. 25.
7. 'Report from the Committee appointed to Inquire into the Existence of any Abuses in the Disposal of the Patronage of the East India Company', ordered to be printed 23 March 1809, *Parliamentary Debates*, vol. 13, col. cxxv–clxxviii, quote on col. cxlvii. For Thellusson's background see Thorne, *History of Parliament. The Commons 1790–1820*, vol. 5, pp. 361–2 and the adjacent entries on his brothers. Woodford's full name was Emperor John Alexander Woodford and he has another modest claim to fame as an important bibliophile and book collector.
8. 'Report from the Committee appointed to Inquire into the Existence of any Abuses in the Disposal of the Patronage of the East India Company', cols cxxvii, cxxi–cxxx, clxxii–clxxiv.
9. Caplan, 'The Missteps and Misdeeds of Henry Austen's Bank', pp. 106–7; Caplan, 'Austen & Co. and the Mary Anne Clarke Scandal of 1809', p. 221; 'Report from the Committee appointed to Inquire into the Existence of any Abuses in the Disposal of the Patronage of the East India Company', cols. cxliv–cxlv.
10. Colebrooke, *Life of the Honourable Mountstuart Elphinstone*, vol. 1, pp. 9–11.
11. Teignmouth, *Memoir of the Life and Correspondence of John, Lord Teignmouth*, vol. 1, pp. 11–18. It is possible that 'Mr Hancock' was Tysoe Saul Hancock, a surgeon and friend of Warren Hastings and the father of Jane Austen's cousin Eliza de Feuillide, who became Mrs Henry Austen.
12. Orrok, *The Letters of Captain John Orrok*, pp. 145–6.
13. Hickey, *Memoirs of William Hickey*, vol. 1, pp. 163–4.
14. Welsh, *Military Reminiscences*, vol. 1, pp. 1–4.
15. Welsh, *Military Reminiscences*, vol. 1, pp. 8–9.
16. Goodbehere, 'Letters of Lieutenant Edmund Goodbehere', p. 6.
17. Orrok, *The Letters of Captain John Orrok*, p. 68; Bevan, *Thirty Years in India*, vol. 1, pp. 28–30, 42; Mason, *A Matter of Honour*, p. 179; Mount, *The Tears of the Rajas*, pp. 26–8.
18. Bevan, *Thirty Years in India*, vol. 1, pp. 89–93, 100.
19. Arthur Wellesley to Lord Mornington, 12 July 1797 and to John Malcolm, 3 July 1805, *Wellington Supplementary Despatches*, vol. 1, pp. 12–17, vol. 4, pp. 509–12.
20. Embree, *Charles Grant and the British Rule in India*, p. 126; Furber, *John Company at Work*, pp. 23–5; Malcolm, *Malcolm*, p. 554.
21. Callahan, *The East India Company and Army Reform*, pp. 6, 21–2, 38.
22. Callahan, *The East India Company and Army Reform*, *passim*, quotes on p. 205 (Cornwallis), pp. 23–4 (Callahan's own criticism of the system), pp. 25 and 192 (the officer's protests). Callahan's study is a model of an academic monograph, taking an obscure and apparently dry subject and showing it to be intrinsically interesting and with much wider implications.
23. Callahan, *The East India Company and Army Reform*, pp. 27–33.
24. Furber, *John Company at Work*, pp. 21–2; Callahan, *The East India Company and Army Reform*, pp. 11, 33–6.
25. Callahan, *The East India Company and Army Reform*, pp. 193–5, 206 (quote on p. 193). In 1809 the white officers of the Madras army did mutiny in the face of proposed cuts to their allowances, and John Orrok gives an interesting account of these events as a well-informed bystander. Orrok, *The Letters of Captain John Orrok*, pp. 86–90.
26. Munro quoted in Malcolm, *Malcolm*, p. 26.

27. Mason, *A Matter of Honour*, pp. 190–1; Malcolm, *Malcolm*, pp. 26–7; Orrok, *The Letters of Captain John Orrok*, pp. 2, 91–3.
28. Goodbehere, 'Letters of Lieutenant Edmund Goodbehere', pp. 8–10.
29. Goodbehere, 'Letters of Lieutenant Edmund Goodbehere', pp. 11–12, 15, 18–19.
30. Goodbehere, 'Letters of Lieutenant Edmund Goodbehere', pp. 18–19; Bevan, *Thirty Years in India*, vol. 1, pp. 88–9.
31. Bevan, *Thirty Years in India*, vol. 1, pp. 85–8, 36–7.
32. Goodbehere, 'Letters of Lieutenant Edmund Goodbehere', p. 16; Bevan, *Thirty Years in India*, vol. 1, pp. 19–20.
33. J. H. Stocqueler quoted in Mason, *A Matter of Honour*, pp. 189–90; Cornwallis quoted in Callahan, *The East India Company and Army Reform*, p. 35.
34. Bevan, *Thirty Years in India*, vol. 1, p. 26.
35. Roberdeau's account in Woodruff, *The Men who Ruled India*, vol. 1, pp. 163–71.
36. Roberdeau's account, which was written *c.* 1805, is printed in Woodruff, *The Men who Ruled India*, vol. 1, pp. 163–71.
37. Teignmouth, *Memoir of the Life and Correspondence of John, Lord Teignmouth*, vol. 1, pp. 25–49.
38. Woodruff, *The Men who Ruled India*, vol. 1, p. 144. Several servants of the Company acted as governor-general after Shore, most notably Sir George Barlow, but they were not formally appointed to the position and occupied it for only an interim period, generally not more than a few months.
39. Marshall, 'Private Fortune of Warren Hastings', p. 541; Callahan, *The East India Company and Army Reform*, pp. 34–5 (for Lt-Col Mark Wood); Rubinstein, *Who Were the Rich?*, vol. 1, pp. 428–9 (for Hollond); Mason, *A Matter of Honour*, p. 174 for Walter Badenach's figures of officers between 1796 and 1820; Furber, *John Company at Work*, pp. 27–8 for figures of officers appointed between 1762 and 1783.
40. West quoted in Finn, 'Colonial Gifts', p. 208; date and details of her death from *Debrett's Baronetage of England*, 7th edition, 1839, p. 202.

CONCLUSION

1. Croker quoted in Hamilton, 'John Wilson Croker', p. 57; [Edward Gibbon Wakefield], *England and America*, vol. 1, pp. 94–5.
2. For the later lives of both Catherine and Mary see Austen-Leigh and Austen-Leigh, *Memoir of Jane Austen*, p. 158; Austen, *Pride and Prejudice*, pp. 385–6 (vol. 3, ch 19).

BIBLIOGRAPHY

THE NATIONAL ARCHIVES

WO 3/596 Correspondence of the Military Secretary of the Commander-in-Chief, 1810.
WO 3/604 Correspondence of the Military Secretary of the Commander-in-Chief, 1813.
WO 79/50 'Return of the Numbers of killed and wounded under the command of Lord . . . Wellington'.

ONLINE RESOURCES

Bank of England Inflation Calculator: https://www.bankofengland.co.uk/monetary-policy/inflation/inflation-calculator
British Museum: britishmuseum.org which, among other things, reproduces caricatures of the period with the descriptions from Dorothy George's invaluable catalogue.
Clergy of the Church of England Database: CCEd http://theclergydatabase.org.uk/
Life of Wellington: online commentary and supporting material to Muir, *Wellington* (see below) at lifeofwellington.co.uk
Oxford Dictionary of National Biography (cited as *ODNB*) at http://www.oxforddnb.com/
RBS Heritage Hub-People-Henry Sykes Thornton at https://www.rbs.com/heritage/people/henry-sykes-thornton.html

UNIVERSITY OF SOUTHAMPTON

Carver Manuscripts 54, The Political Notebook of Richard Wellesley II
Wellington Papers:
Anne, Countess of Mornington to AW, 22 May 1807, WP 1/168/40/1.
Wellington to Robert Peel, 26 June 1824, WP 1/795/15.

PRINTED SOURCES

Ackroyd, Marcus, Laurence Brockliss, Michael Moss, Kate Retford and John Stevenson, *Advancing with the Army. Medicine, the Professions, and Social Mobility in the British Isles 1790–1850* (Oxford, Oxford University Press, 2006).

Aitchison, John, *An Ensign in the Peninsular War. The Letters of John Aitchison*, ed. W.F.K. Thompson (London, Michael Joseph, 1981).

Allen, John, *Memoir of the Life and Services of Admiral Sir William Hargood* (Greenwich, privately printed, 1842).

Anglesey, Marquess of, *One-Leg. The Life and Letters of Henry William Paget, First Marquess of Anglesey, K.G., 1768–1854* (London, Reprint Society, 1962).

Anon. 'The Banker M.P.', *Three Banks Review*, no. 32, Dec. 1956, pp. 33–42.

Anon. 'A Bolton Banking Partnership. The First Thirty Years', *The Three Banks Review*, no. 25, March 1955, pp. 31–41.

Anon. *A New System of Practical Domestic Economy founded on Modern Discoveries, and the Private Communications of Persons of Experience*, 'new edition' (London, Henry Colburn, 1827).

Anon. 'The Nineteenth Century Banker's Clerk', *Three Banks Review*, no. 36, Dec. 1957, pp. 37–50.

Anon. *The Private Patronage of the Church of England. A Guide to All Ecclesiastical Patronage in the Hands of the Nobility and Gentry, Corporations, Hospitals and Trusts*, 'published annually' (London, George Cox, 1855).

Anon. 'Ships and Ships' Husbands', *The Three Banks Review*, no. 28, Dec. 1955, pp. 38–48.

Aspinall, A. and E. A. Smith, *English Historical Documents*, vol. XI, *1783–1832* (London, Eyre & Spottiswoode, 1969).

Austen, Jane, *The Watsons* (London, Leonard Parsons, 1923).

Austen, Jane, *Emma*, ed. R. W. Chapman (Oxford, Clarendon Press, 1926).

Austen, Jane, *Mansfield Park*, ed. R. W. Chapman (Oxford, Clarendon Press, 1926).

Austen, Jane, *Northanger Abbey*, ed. R. W. Chapman (Oxford, Clarendon Press, 1926).

Austen, Jane *Persuasion*, ed. R. W. Chapman (Oxford, Clarendon Press, 1926). (*Northanger Abbey* and *Persuasion* are bound together as volume 5 of the Oxford edition of the Novels of Jane Austen, but the pagination for *Persuasion* begins afresh.)

Austen, Jane, *Pride and Prejudice*, ed. R. W. Chapman (Oxford, Clarendon Press, 1926).

Austen, Jane, *Sense and Sensibility*, ed. R. W. Chapman (Oxford, Clarendon Press, 1926).

Austen, Jane, *Lady Susan*, in *Minor Works*, ed. R. W. Chapman (Oxford, Oxford University Press, 1954).

Austen, Jane, *Sanditon*, in *Minor Works*, ed. R. W. Chapman (Oxford University Press, 1954).

Austen, Jane, *Jane Austen's Letters*, ed. Deirdre Le Faye, 4th edn (Oxford University Press, 2011). (Also the heavily annotated edition of the novels edited by David M. Shapard (New York, Anchor Books, 2010–17); and the lavishly produced Belknap Press edition, full of interesting comments and fascinating illustrations.)

Austen-Leigh, James Edward, *Memoir of Jane Austen*, ed. R. W. Chapman (Oxford, Clarendon Press, 1926).

Austen-Leigh, Joan, 'Jane Austen's Favourite Nephew', *Persuasions*, no. 18, 1996, pp. 144–53.

Austen-Leigh, William and Richard Arthur Austen-Leigh, *Jane Austen: A Family Record*, revised and enlarged by Deidre Le Faye (London, The British Library, 1989).

Aylmer, G. E., 'From Office-Holding to Civil Service: The Genesis of Modern Bureaucracy', *Transactions of the Royal Historical Society*, vol. 30, 1980, pp. 91–108.

Bailey, Martha, 'The Marriage Law of Jane Austen's World', *Persuasions On-Line*, vol. 36, no. 1, Winter 2015 (http://www.jasna.org/persuasions/on-line/vol36no1/bailey.html).

Beard, Mary, *SPQR: A History of Ancient Rome* (London, Profile Books, 2015).

Bearman, Robert, 'Henry Austen and the Cubbington Living', *Persuasions*, no. 10, 1988, pp. 22–6.

Beckett, John, *The Rise and Fall of the Grenvilles. Dukes of Buckingham and Chandos, 1710 to 1921* (Manchester, Manchester University Press, 1994).

Bell, Alan, *Sydney Smith* (Oxford, Clarendon Press, 1980).

Bennett, Stuart, 'Lord Moira and the Austens', *Persuasions*, vol. 35, 2013, pp. 129–52.

Benzaquén, Adriana, 'Educational Designs: The Education and Training of Younger Sons at the Turn of the Eighteenth Century', *Journal of Family History*, vol. 40, no. 4, 2015, pp. 462–84.

Bevan, Major H., *Thirty Years in India: or, A Soldier's Reminiscences of Native and European Life . . . from 1808 to 1838*, 2 vols (London, Pelham Richardson, 1839).

Boase, Frederic, *Modern British Biography*, 6 vols (London, Frank Cass, 1965 – first published 1901).

Boswell, James, *The Life of Samuel Johnson, LL.D.*, 2 vols (Oxford, Oxford University Press, 1922 with title given as *Boswell's Life of Johnson*).

Breihan, John and Clive Caplan, 'Jane Austen and the Militia', *Persuasions*, no. 14, 1992, pp. 16–26.

Brett-James, Antony, *Life in Wellington's Army* (London, Allen & Unwin, 1972).

Brewer, John, *The Sinews of Power: War, Money and the English State, 1688–1783* (New York, Alfred A. Knopf, 1989).

Brewer, John, 'Servants of the Public – Servants of the Crown. Officialdom of Eighteenth-Century English Central Government', in *Rethinking Leviathan. The Eighteenth-Century State in Britain and Germany*, ed. John Brewer and Eckhart Hellmuth (London, Oxford University Press for the German Historical Institute, 1999), pp. 127–48.

Brialmont, A. and G. R. Gleig, *History of the Life of Arthur, Duke of Wellington*, 4 vols (London, Longman, Brown, Green, Longmans and Roberts, 1858).

Bright, Pamela, *Dr Richard Bright (1789–1858)* (London, Bodley Head, 1983).

Brownrigg, Beatrice, *The Life and Letters of Sir John Moore* (New York, Appleton, 1923).

Bruce, Anthony, *The Purchase System in the British Army, 1660–1871* (London, Royal Historical Society, 1980).

Buckley, Roger Norman, *The British Army in the West Indies. Society and the Military in the Revolutionary Age* (Gainesville, University Press of Florida, 1998).

Bunbury, Major Thomas, *Reminiscences of a Veteran*, 3 vols (Uckfield, Naval and Military Press, n.d. – first published 1861).

Burg, B. R., *Boys at Sea. Sodomy, Indecency and Courts Martial in Nelson's Navy* (Basingstoke, Palgrave Macmillan, 2007).

Burghersh, Lady [Priscilla Fane, née Wellesley-Pole], *Correspondence of Lady Burghersh with the Duke of Wellington*, ed. by her daughter Lady Rose Weigall (London, John Murray, 1903).

Burnham, Robert and McGuigan, Ron, *The British Army Against Napoleon* (Barnsley, Frontline, 2010).

Burns, Arthur, Kenneth Fincham and Stephen Taylor, 'Reconstructing Clerical Careers: The Experience of the Clergy of the Church of England Database', *Journal of Ecclesiastical History*, vol. 55, no. 4, Oct. 2004, pp. 726–37.

Burton, Alfred, *The Adventures of Johnny Newcome in the Navy. A Poem in Four Cantos* with sixteen coloured plates by T. Rowlandson from the author's designs (first published, London, Simpkin and Marshall, 1818; this reprint London, Methuen 1904).

Bynum, W. F., 'Physicians, Hospitals and Career Structures in Eighteenth-Century London', in *William Hunter and the Eighteenth-Century Medical World*, ed. W. F. Bynum and Roy Porter (Cambridge, Cambridge University Press, 1985), pp. 105–28.

Callahan, Raymond, *The East India Company and Army Reform, 1783–1798* (Cambridge, MA, Harvard University Press – Harvard Historical Monographs no. LXVII – 1972).

Calvert, [Frances], *An Irish Beauty of the Regency*, ed. Mrs Warrenne Blake (London, John Lane, the Bodley Head, 1911).

Calvert, Leanne, ' "What a Wonderful Change Have I Undergone . . . So Altered in Stature, Knowledge & Ideas!": Apprenticeship, Adolescence and Growing Up in Eighteenth- and Nineteenth-Century Ulster', *Irish Economic and Social History*, vol. 20, 2018, pp. 1–20.

Campbell, John, *Life of John, Lord Campbell, Lord High Chancellor of Great Britain*, ed. by his daughter, Mrs Hardcastle, 2 vols (London, John Murray, 1881).

Caplan, Clive, 'Jane Austen's Soldier Brother: The Military Career of Captain Henry Austen of the Oxfordshire Regiment of Militia, 1793–1801', *Persuasions*, no. 18, 1996, pp. 122–43.

Caplan, Clive, 'Jane Austen's Banker Brother: Henry Thomas Austen of Austen & Co., 1801–1816', *Persuasions*, no. 29, 1998, pp. 69–90.

Caplan, Clive, 'Austen & Co. and the Mary Anne Clarke Scandal of 1809', *Jane Austen Society Collected Reports 2001–2005*, pp. 219–24.

Caplan, Clive, 'The Ships of Frank Austen', *Jane Austen Society Report*, 2008, pp. 74–85.

Caplan, Clive, ' "We Suppose the Trial is to Take Place This Week" ', *Jane Austen Society Report*, 2008, pp. 152–9.

Caplan, Clive, '"The Brewery Scheme is Quite at an End"', *Jane Austen Society Report*, 2010, pp. 92–6.

Caplan, Clive, 'The Missteps and Misdeeds of Henry Austen's Bank', *Jane Austen Society Report*, 2010, pp. 103–9.

Cass, Jocelyn Creigh, 'In Defence of George Austen', *Persuasions*, no. 16, 1994, pp. 55–62.

Cavell, S. A., *Midshipmen and Quarterdeck Boys in the British Navy, 1771–1831* (Woodbridge, Boydell Press, 2012).

Chalus, Elaine, '"My Dearest Tussy": Coping with Separation in the Napoleonic Wars (the Fremantle Papers, 1800–14)', in *A New Naval History*, ed. Quintin Colville and James Davey (Manchester, Manchester University Press, 2018), ch. 2.

Chamberlain, Muriel E., *Lord Aberdeen. A Political Biography* (London and New York, Longman, 1983).

Chambers, William, *Memoir of William and Robert Chambers*, 12th edn (Edinburgh, W. & R. Chambers, 1883).

Chester, Sir Norman, *The English Administrative System 1780–1870* (Oxford, Clarendon Press, 1981).

Clark-Kennedy, A. E., *Attack the Colour! The Royal Dragoons in the Peninsula and at Waterloo* (London, Research Publishing, 1975).

Clay, Christopher, 'Property Settlements, Financial Provision for the Family and the Sale of Land by the Greater Landowners, 1660–1790', *Journal of British Studies*, vol. 21, no. 1, Autumn 1981, pp. 18–38.

Clery, E. J., 'Austen and Masculinity', in *A Companion to Jane Austen*, ed. Claudia L. Johnson and Clara Tuite (Oxford, Blackwell, 2009) pp. 332–42.

Clery, E. J., *Jane Austen – The Banker's Sister* (London, Biteback, 2017).

Cochrane, Thomas – see Dundonald

Cock, Raymond, 'The Bar at Assizes: Barristers on Three Nineteenth Century Circuits', *Kingston Law Review*, vol. 6, 1976, pp. 36–52.

Cohen, Emmeline W., *The Growth of the British Civil Service, 1780–1939* (London, Frank Cass & Co., 1965 – first published 1941).

Colby, Reginald, *The Waterloo Despatch* (London, HMSO, 1965).

Cole, G. L., *Memoirs of Sir Lowry Cole*, ed. Maud Lowry Cole and Stephen Gwynn (London, Macmillan, 1934).

Colebrooke, Sir T. E., *Life of the Honourable Mountstuart Elphinstone*, 2 vols (London, John Murray, 1884).

Collinge, J. M., *Foreign Office Officials, 1782–1870* (London, University of London, Institute of Historical Research, 1979).

Collins, Irene, *Jane Austen and the Clergy* (London and New York, Hambledon and London, 2002).

Collins, Irene, 'The Rev. Henry Tilney, Rector of Woodston', *Persuasions*, no. 20, 1998, pp. 154–64.

Consolvo, Charles, 'The Prospects and Promotion of British Naval Officers, 1793–1815', *Mariner's Mirror*, vol. 91, no. 2, pp. 137–59.

Cooke, Lt John, *A True Soldier Gentleman. The Memoirs of Lt. John Cooke, 1791–1813*, ed. Eileen Hathaway (Swanage, Shinglepicker, 2000).

Cookson, J. E., *The British Armed Nation 1793–1815* (Oxford, Clarendon Press, 1997).

Coote, Peter, 'William Lindley: Country Houses of the Doncaster Area', *Trust Topics: Doncaster Civic Trust Newsletter*, 43, May 2011, pp. 9–14.

Copeland, Edward, '*Persuasion*: The Jane Austen Consumer's Guide', *Persuasions*, no. 15, 1993, pp. 111–23.

Copeland, Edward (ed.), *The Cambridge Companion to Jane Austen* (Cambridge, Cambridge University Press, 1997).

Corfield, Penelope J., *Power and the Professions in Britain, 1700–1850* (London and New York, Routledge, 1995).

Corfield, Penelope J., 'The Rivals: Landed and Other Gentlemen', in *Land and Society in Britain, 1700–1914. Essays in Honour of F. M. L. Thompson*, ed. Negley Harte and Roland Quinault (Manchester, Manchester University Press, 1996), pp. 1–33.

Corley, T. A. B., 'Jane Austen and her Brother Henry's Bank Failure 1815–16', *Jane Austen Society Collected Reports*, 1996–2000, pp. 139–50.

Cotton, Sir Evan, *East Indiamen. The East India Company's Maritime Service*, ed. Sir Charles Fawcett (London, The Batchworth Press, 1949).

Creevey, Thomas, *The Creevey Papers*, ed. Sir Herbert Maxwell (London, John Murray, 1923).

Crosse, V. Mary, *A Surgeon in the Early Nineteenth Century: The Life and Times of John Green Crosse . . . 1790–1850* (Edinburgh, E. & S. Livingstone, 1968).

Crowe, Charles, *An Eloquent Soldier. The Peninsular War Journals of Lieutenant Charles Crowe of the Inniskillings, 1812–1814*, ed. Gareth Glover (Barnsley, Frontline, 2011).

Dalrymple, William, *White Mughals. Love and Betrayal in Eighteenth-Century India* (London, HarperCollins, 2002).

Darwin, Emma, *Emma Darwin: A Century of Family Letters, 1792–1896*, ed. by her daughter Henrietta Litchfield, 2 vols (London, John Murray, 1915).

Debrett's Baronetage of England, ed. William Courthope, 7th edn (London, Rivington, 1839).

Dickson, Lt-Col Sir Alexander, *The Dickson Manuscripts*, ed. Maj. John H. Leslie, 5 vols (Cambridge, Trotman, 1987–91 – first published 1908 in two volumes).

Digby, Anne, *Making a Medical Living. Doctors and Patients in the English Market for Medicine, 1720–1911* (Cambridge, Cambridge University Press, 1994).

Divall, Carole, *Inside the Regiment. The Officers and Men of the 30th Regiment during the Revolutionary and Napoleonic Wars* (Barnsley, Pen & Sword Military, 2011).

Duman, Daniel, 'Pathway to Professionalism: The English Bar in the Eighteenth and Nineteenth Centuries', *Journal of Social History*, vol. 13, 1980, pp. 615–28.

Duman, Daniel, *The Judicial Bench in England, 1727–1875. The Reshaping of a Professional Elite* (London, Royal Historical Society, 1982).

Duman, Daniel, *The English and Colonial Bars in the Nineteenth Century* (London & Canberra, Croom Helm, 1983).

Dundonald, Thomas, Earl of [Thomas Cochrane], *Autobiography of a Seaman*, 2 vols, 2nd edn (London, Richard Bentley, 1861).

Dutton, Geoffrey and David Elder, *Colonel William Light – Founder of a City* (Melbourne, Melbourne University Press, 1991).

Edgeworth, R. L., *Essays on Professional Education*, 2nd edn (London, J. Johnson, 1812).

Ellis, Kenneth, *The Post Office in the Eighteenth Century. A Study in Administrative History* (London, Oxford University Press, 1958).

Embree, Ainslie Thomas, *Charles Grant and the British Rule in India* (London, George Allen & Unwin, 1962).

Estensen, Miriam, *The Life of Matthew Flinders* (Sydney, Allen & Unwin, 2002).

Finn, Margot C., 'Colonial Gifts: Family Politics and the Exchange of Goods in British India, c.1780–1820', *Modern Asian Studies*, vol. 40, no. 1, 2006, pp. 203–31.

Fisher, D. R. (ed.), *The History of Parliament. The House of Commons 1820–1832*, 7 vols (Cambridge, Cambridge University Press for the History of Parliament Trust, 2009).

Flinders, Matthew, *'Gratefull to Providence': The Diary and Accounts of Matthew Flinders, 1775–1802*, ed. M. Beardsley and N. Bennett, 2 vols (Woodbridge, Boydell Press, Lincoln Record Society, vols 95 and 97, 2007 and 2009).

Forster, E. M., *Marianne Thornton 1797–1887. A Domestic Biography* (London, Edward Arnold, 1956).

[Foster, William], 'Mr Charles Lamb of the India House', *Macmillan's Magazine*, vol. 75, 1896–7, pp. 192–200.

French, Henry and Mark Rothery, '"Upon Your Entry into the World": Masculine Values and the Threshold of Adulthood among Landed Elites in England 1680–1800', *Social History*, vol. 33, no. 4, Nov. 2008, pp. 402–22.

French, Henry and Mark Rothery, *Making Men. The Formation of Elite Male Identities in England, c.1660–1900. A Sourcebook* (Basingstoke, Palgrave Macmillan, 2012).

French, Henry and Mark Rothery, *Man's Estate. Landed Gentry Masculinities, c.1660–c.1900* (Oxford, Oxford University Press, 2012).

French, Henry and Mark Rothery, 'Male Anxiety among Younger Sons of the English Landed Gentry, 1700–1900', *Historical Journal*, forthcoming and online doi:10.1017/S0018246X18000420.

Furber, Holden, *John Company at Work. A Study of European Expansion in India in the late Eighteenth Century*, Harvard Historical Studies vol. 55 (Cambridge, MA, Harvard University Press, 1951).

Gardner, James Anthony, *Above and Under Hatches, Being Naval Recollections in Shreds and Patches . . .* , ed. Christopher Lloyd (London, Batchworth Press, 1955).

Gash, Norman, *Mr Secretary Peel. The Life of Sir Robert Peel to 1830* (London, Longmans and Co., 1961).

Gash, Norman, *Lord Liverpool* (London, Weidenfeld & Nicolson, 1984).

Gash, Norman, *Robert Surtees and Early Victorian Society* (Oxford, Clarendon Press, 1993).

Gaskell, Elizabeth, *Cranford* (London, Macmillan, 1924).

Geike, Archibald, *Life of Sir Roderick I. Murchison*, 2 vols (London, John Murray, 1875).

George III, *The Later Correspondence of George III*, ed. A. Aspinall, 5 vols (Cambridge, Cambridge University Press, 1962–70).

Gérin, Winifred, *Anne Brontë* (London, Thomas Nelson, 1959).

Gérin, Winifred, *Charlotte Brontë. The Evolution of Genius* (Oxford, Oxford University Press, 1987).

Gibson, William, 'The Tories and Church Patronage: 1812–1830', *Journal of Ecclesiastical History*, vol. 41, April 1990, pp. 266–74.

Gibson, William, *The Achievement of the Anglican Church, 1689–1800. The Confessional State in Eighteenth Century England* (Lampeter, Edwin Mellen Press, 1995).

Gibson, W. T., ' "Unreasonable and Unbecoming": Self-Recommendation and Place-Seeking in the Church of England, 1700–1900', *Albion*, vol. 27, no. 1, Spring 1995, pp. 43–63.

Gill, Ellen, ' "Children of the Service": Paternalism, Patronage and Friendship in the Georgian Navy', *Journal of Maritime Research*, vol. 15, no. 2, 2013, pp. 149–65.

[Glascock, William Nugent], *Naval Sketch-Book; or, the Service Afloat and Ashore* 'by an Officer of Rank', 2 vols (London, for the author, 1826).

Glover, Michael, *Wellington's Army in the Peninsula, 1808–1814* (Newton Abbot, David & Charles, 1977).

Glover, Michael, 'Purchase, Patronage and Promotion in the Army at the Time of the Peninsular War', *Army Quarterly*, vol. 103, 1972–73, pp. 211–15, 355–62.

Glover, Michael, 'The Purchase of Commissions: A Reappraisal', *Journal of the Society for Army Historical Research*, vol. 58, no. 236, Winter 1980, pp. 223–35.

Goodbehere, Lt Edmund, 'The Letters of Lieutenant Edmund Goodbehere, 18th Madras N.I., 1803–1809', ed. S. G. P. Ward, *Journal of the Society for Army Historical Research*, vol. 57, no. 229, Spring 1979, pp. 3–19.

Gordon, Alexander, *At Wellington's Right Hand. The Letters of Lieutenant-Colonel Sir Alexander Gordon, 1808–1815*, ed. Rory Muir (Stroud, Sutton Publishing for the Army Records Society, 2003).

Grattan, William, *Adventures with the Connaught Rangers, 1809–1814*, ed. Charles Oman (London, Greenhill, 2003).

Gray, Denis, *Spencer Perceval. The Evangelical Prime Minister, 1762–1812* (Manchester, Manchester University Press, 1963).

Greenwood, Adrian (ed.), *Through Spain with Wellington: The Letters of Lieutenant Peter Le Mesurier of the 'Fighting Ninth'* (Stroud, Amberley, 2016).

Greville, Charles, *The Greville Memoirs, 1814–1860*, ed. Lytton Strachey and Roger Fulford, 8 vols (London, Macmillan, 1938).

Gronow, Capt. Rees Howell, *The Reminiscences and Recollections of Captain Gronow* (Nunney, R. S. Surtees Society, 1984).

Hamilton, Bernice, 'The Medical Professions in the Eighteenth Century', *Economic History Review*, 2nd series, vol. 4, no. 2, 1951, pp. 141–69.

Hamilton, C. I., 'John Wilson Croker: Patronage and Clientage at the Admiralty, 1809–1857', *Historical Journal*, vol. 43, no. 1, 2000, pp. 49–77.

Hansard, *The Parliamentary Debates from the Year 1803 to the Present Time*, published under the superintendence of T. C. Hansard.

  vol. XI 11 April-4 July 1808 including 'Third Report on the Committee of Finance' (London, R. Bagshaw, 1808).

  vol. XIII 8–30 March 1809 (London, Longman, Hurst, Rees, Orme and Brown et al., 1812) Appendix IV 'Report from the Committee Appointed to Inquire into the Existence of any Abuses in the Disposal of the Patronage of the East India Company' ordered to be printed 23 March 1809, cols. cxxv–clxxviii.

  House of Lords Sessional Papers vol. 191 (1825): evidence given to the Lords Select Committee into the State of Ireland.

Harding-Edgar, John, *Next to Wellington. General Sir George Murray* (Warwick, Helion, 2018).

[Hare, Lt W. H.], 'Letters from the Front, 1812 and 1942', *Blackwood's Magazine*, April 1943, pp. 269–72.

Harris, Amy, *Siblinghood and Social Relations in Georgian England. Share and Share Alike* (Manchester, Manchester University Press, 2012).

Haythornthwaite, Philip J., *The Armies of Wellington* (London, Arms and Armour, 1994).

Heathcote, Ralph, *Ralph Heathcote. Letters of a Young Diplomatist and Soldier During the Time of Napoleon*, ed. Countess Gröben (London, John Lane, the Bodley Head, 1907).

Hendy, Graham, ' "A Pretty Easy Way of Dawdling Away One's Time": The Canons of Winchester in the Long Eighteenth Century', *Hampshire Studies: Proceedings of the Hampshire Field Club Archaeological Society*, vol. 63, 2008, pp. 37–57.

Hennell, George, *A Gentleman Volunteer. The Letters of George Hennell from the Peninsular War*, ed. Michael Glover (London, Heinemann, 1979).

Hickey, William, *Memoirs of William Hickey*, ed. Alfred Spencer, 4 vols, 8th edn (London, Hurst & Blackett, n.d. [1920s]).

Hillan, Sophia, *May, Lou & Cass. Jane Austen's Nieces in Ireland* (Belfast, Blackstaff Press, 2011).

Hindmarsh, F. Stewart, *From Powder Monkey to Governor. The Life of Rear Admiral Sir John Hindmarsh* (Northbridge, WA, Access Press, 1995).

Hodge, W. B., 'On the Mortality Arising from Military Operations', *Quarterly Journal of the Statistical Society*, vol. 19, Sept. 1856, pp. 219–71.

Holmes, Geoffrey, *Augustan England. Professions, State and Society, 1680–1730* (London, George Allen & Unwin, 1982).

Hoon, Elizabeth E., *The Organization of the English Customs System 1696–1786* (Newton Abbot, David & Charles, 1968 – first published 1938).

Horn, D. B., *The British Diplomatic Service, 1689–1789* (Oxford, Clarendon Press, 1961).

Howell, David W., *Patriarchs and Parasites. The Gentry in South-West Wales in the Eighteenth Century* (Cardiff, University of Wales Press, 1986).

Hubback, J. H. and Edith C. Hubback, *Jane Austen's Sailor Brothers: Being the Adventures of Sir Francis Austen G.C.B. and Rear-Admiral Charles Austen* (London, John Lane, 1906).

Hughes, Edward, 'The Professions in the Eighteenth Century', in *Aristocratic Government and Society in Eighteenth-Century England*, ed. Daniel A. Baugh (New York, New Viewpoints, 1975), pp. 184–203.

Hume, Robert D., 'Money and Rank', in *The Cambridge Companion to Emma*, ed. Peter Sabor (Cambridge, Cambridge University Press, 2015), pp. 52–67.

Hurst, Jane, 'Henry Thomas Austen – "Being a Hampshire man"', *Collected Reports of the Jane Austen Society 2001–2005*, pp. 135–8.

Jackson, George, *The Diaries and Letters of Sir George Jackson, K.C.H. from the Peace of Amiens to the Battle of Talavera*, ed. Lady Jackson, 2 vols (London, Richard Bentley, 1872).

Jackson, George, *The Bath Archives. A Further Selection from the Diaries and Letters of Sir George Jackson, K.C.H. from 1809 to 1816*, ed. Lady Jackson, 2 vols (London, Richard Bentley, 1873).

Jacob, W. M., *The Clerical Profession in the Long Eighteenth Century, 1680–1840* (Oxford, Oxford University Press, 2007).

Jenkins, Hester and D. Caradog Jones, 'Social Class of Cambridge University Alumni of the 18th and 19th Centuries', *British Journal of Sociology*, vol. 1, no. 2, June 1950, pp. 93–116.

Jerdan, William, *The Autobiography of William Jerdan*, 4 vols (London, Arthur Hall, Virtue & Co., 1852).

John, A. H., 'Farming in Wartime, 1793–1815', in *Land, Labour and Population in the Industrial Revolution. Essays Presented to J. D. Chambers*, ed. E. L. Jones and G. E. Mingay (London, Edward Arnold, 1967), pp. 28–47.

Jones, Hazel, *Jane Austen and Marriage* (London, Continuum, 2009).

Jones, K. R., 'Richard Cox, Army Agent and Banker', *Journal of the Society for Army Historical Research*, vol. xxxiv, no. 140, Dec. 1956, pp. 178–81.

Jones, K. R., 'Cox and Co.: Army Agents. Craig's Court: The Nineteenth Century', *Journal of the Society for Army Historical Research*, vol. xl, no. 164, Dec. 1962, pp. 178–86.

Jones, Raymond A., *The British Diplomatic Service, 1815–1914* (Waterloo, ON, Wilfrid Laurier University Press, 1983).

Kaplan, Deborah, 'Henry Austen and John Rawston Papillon', *Jane Austen Society Report*, 1987, pp. 11–15.

Kaye, Sir John, *The Life and Correspondence of Major-General Sir John Malcolm . . .* , 2 vols (London, Smith Elder, 1856).

Kincaid, Capt. Sir John, *Adventures in the Rifle Brigade and Random Shots from a Rifleman* (Glasgow, Richard Drew, 1981 – reprint of the 1909 edition).

Kindred, Sheila J., 'Charles Austen: Prize Chaser and Prize Taker on the North American Station, 1805–1808', *Persuasions*, no. 26, 2004, pp. 188–94.

Knight, Roger, *The Pursuit of Victory. The Life and Achievements of Horatio Nelson* (London, Allen Lane, 2005).

Knight, Roger, *William IV. A King at Sea* (London, Allen Lane, 2015).

Kynaston, David, *The City of London*, vol. 1, *A World of Its Own, 1815–1890* (London, Pimlico, 1995).

Lampard, K. J., 'Country Banks and Economic Development in the late Eighteenth and Early Nineteenth Centuries: The Case of the Margate Bank', *Archaeologia Cantiana*, vol. 112, 1993, pp. 77–92.

Lane, Joan, 'The Medical Practitioners of Provincial England in 1783', *Medical History*, vol. 28, no. 4, 1984, pp. 353–71.

Lane, Maggie, *Jane Austen's Family through Five Generations* (London, Robert Hale, 1984).

Lane, Maggie, 'Brothers of the More Famous Jane: The Literary Aspirations, Achievements, and Influence of James and Henry Austen', *Persuasions*, no. 31, 2009, pp. 13–32.

Lee, Stephen M., *George Canning and Liberal Toryism, 1801–1827* (Woodbridge, Boydell Press for the Royal Historical Society, 2008).

Le Faye, Deirdre, 'James Austen – Army Chaplain', *Jane Austen Society*, Report for 1994, pp. 8–11.

Le Faye, Deirdre, *A Chronology of Jane Austen and Her Family, 1600–2000*, 2nd rev. edn (Cambridge, Cambridge University Press, 2013).

Lefroy, Thomas, *Memoir of Chief Justice Lefroy* (Dublin, Hodges, Foster & Co., 1871).

Le Mesurier – see Greenwood

Lemmings, David, *Professors of the Law: Barristers and English Legal Culture in the Eighteenth Century* (Oxford, Oxford University Press, 2000).

Lewis, Michael, *A Social History of the Navy, 1793–1815* (London, George Allen & Unwin, 1960).

Lewis, Michael, *The Navy in Transition. A Social History, 1814–1864* (London, Hodder & Stoughton, 1965).

Lodge, Edmund, *The Peerage and Baronetage of the British Empire* (London, Hurst & Blackett, 1873).

Long, R. B., *Peninsular Cavalry General (1811–1813). The Correspondence of Lieutenant-General Robert Ballard Long*, ed. T. H. McGuffie (London, Harrap, 1951).

Loudon, Irvine, 'The Nature of Provincial Medical Practice in Eighteenth-Century England', *Medical History*, vol. 29, 1985, pp. 1–32.

Loudon, Irvine, *Medical Care and the General Practitioner, 1750–1850* (Oxford, Clarendon Press, 1986).

Lucas, E. V., *The Life of Charles Lamb*, 2 vols (London, Methuen, 1905).

Lucas, Paul, 'A Collective Biography of Students and Barristers of Lincoln's Inn, 1680–1804: A Study in the "Aristocratic Resurgence" of the Eighteenth Century', *Journal of Modern History*, vol. 46, no. 2, June 1974, pp. 227–61.

BIBLIOGRAPHY

McKellar, Hugh D., 'Attending Divine Service in the Revd. George Austen's Day', *Persuasions*, no. 6, 1984, pp. 7–9.

McKellar, Hugh D., '"The Profession of a Clergyman"', *Persuasions*, no. 7, 1985, pp. 28–34.

Madan, Spencer, *Spencer and Waterloo. The Letters of Spencer Madan, 1814–1816*, ed. Beatrice Madan (London, Literary Services and Production, 1970).

Mahony, Stephen, *Wealth or Poverty. Jane Austen's Novels Explored* (London, Robert Hale, 2015).

Malcolm, John, *Malcolm. Soldier, Diplomat, Ideologue of British India. The Life of Sir John Malcolm (1769–1833)* (Edinburgh, John Donald, 2014).

Manwaring, G. E., *My Friend the Admiral. The Life, Letters and Journals of Rear-Admiral James Burney* (London, George Routledge & Sons, 1931).

Marland, Hilary, *Medicine and Society in Wakefield and Huddersfield, 1780–1870* (Cambridge, Cambridge University Press, 1987).

Marryat, Florence, *Life and Letters of Captain Marryat*, 2 vols (London, Richard Bentley, 1872).

Marryat, Captain Frederick, *Frank Mildmay; or the Naval Officer*, 'new edition' (London, Routledge, Warne and Routledge, 1863 – first published 1829).

Marshall, P. J., 'The Personal Fortune of Warren Hastings in Retirement', *Bulletin of the School of Oriental and African Studies*, 1965, vol. 28, no. 3, pp. 540–52.

Mason, Philip, *A Matter of Honour. An Account of the Indian Army, its Officers and Men* (London, Book Club Edition, 1974).

Mathew, W. M., 'The Origins and Occupations of Glasgow Students, 1740–1839', *Past & Present*, no. 33, April 1966, pp. 74–94.

Mathias, Peter, 'The Lawyer as Businessman in Eighteenth-Century England', in *Enterprise and History. Essays in Honour of Charles Wilson*, ed. D. C. Coleman and Peter Mathias (Cambridge, Cambridge University Press, 1984), pp. 151–67.

Meacham, Standish, *Henry Thornton of Clapham, 1760–1815* (Cambridge, MA, Harvard University Press, 1964).

Melikan, R. A., *John Scott, Lord Eldon, 1751–1838. The Duty of Loyalty* (Cambridge, Cambridge University Press, 1999).

Middleton, C. R., *The Administration of British Foreign Policy, 1782–1846* (Durham, NC, Duke University Press, 1977).

Miles, Michael, '"A Haven for the Privileged": Recruitment into the Profession of Attorney in England, 1709–1792', *Social History*, vol. 11, no. 2, May 1986, pp. 197–210.

Mingay, G. E., 'The Eighteenth-Century Land Steward', in *Land, Labour and Population in the Industrial Revolution. Essays Presented to J. D. Chambers*, ed. E. L. Jones and G. E. Mingay (London, Edward Arnold, 1967), pp. 3–27.

Mingay, G. E., *The Gentry. The Rise and Fall of a Ruling Class* (London and New York, Longman, 1976).

Mitchell, B. R. and Phyllis Deane, *Abstract of British Historical Statistics* (Cambridge, Cambridge University Press, 1962).

Moorman, Mary, *William Wordsworth. A Biography. The Later Years 1803–1850* (Oxford, Clarendon Press, 1965).

Mori, Jennifer, *The Culture of Diplomacy. Britain in Europe, c. 1750–1830* (Manchester, Manchester University Press, 2010).

Morley, Edith J., *The Life and Times of Henry Crabb Robinson* (London, J.M. Dent and Sons, 1935).

Mount, Ferdinand, *The Tears of the Rajas. Mutiny, Money and Marriage in India, 1805–1905* (London, Simon & Schuster, 2015).

Muir, Rory, *Britain and the Defeat of Napoleon, 1807–1815* (New Haven and London, Yale University Press, 1996).

Muir, Rory, 'Politics and the Peninsular Army', *Wellington Studies*, IV, 2008, pp. 72–93.

Muir, Rory, *Wellington: The Path to Victory, 1769–1814* (New Haven and London, Yale University Press, 2013).

Muir, Rory, *Wellington Waterloo and the Fortunes of Peace, 1814–1852* (New Haven and London, Yale University Press, 2015).

Murphy, Anne L., '"Writes a Fair Hand and Appears to be Well Qualified": The Recruitment of Bank of England Clerks, 1800–1815', *Financial History Review*, vol. 22, no. 1, 2015, pp. 19–44.

Nelson, Horatio, Lord, *The Dispatches and Letters of Vice-Admiral Lord Viscount Nelson*, ed. Sir Nicholas Nicolas, 7 vols (London, Chatham, 1998 – first published 1844–47).

Nenadic, Stana, 'The Impact of the Military Profession on Highland Gentry Families, *c.* 1730–1830', *Scottish Historical Review*, vol. 85, no. 219, April 2006, pp. 75–99.

Nixon, J. A., 'Thomas Baynton, 1761–1820', *Proceedings of the Royal Society of Medicine: The History of Medicine*, vol. 8, 1915, pp. 95–102.

O'Byrne, William R., *A Naval Biographical Dictionary*, 2 vols (Polstead, Hayward, 1990 – first published 1849).

Orrok, John, *The Letters of Captain John Orrok*, ed. Alison McBrayne (Leicester, Matador, 2008).

Outhwaite, R. B., *Scandal in the Church. Dr Edward Drax Free, 1764–1843* (London and Rio Grande, Hambledon Press, 1997).

Parkinson, C. Northcote, *War in Eastern Seas, 1793–1815* (London, George Allen & Unwin, 1954).

Parris, Henry, 'The Origins of the Permanent Civil Service, 1780–1830', *Public Administration*, vol. 46, Summer 1968, pp. 143–66.

Perry, Ruth, 'Brotherly Love in Eighteenth-Century Literature', *Persuasions On-Line*, vol. 30, no. 1, Winter 2009 (http://www.jasna.org/persuasions/on-line/vol30no1/perry.html).

Phillips, Nicola, *The Profligate Son, Or, a True Story of Family Conflict, Fashionable Vice, and Financial Ruin in Regency England* (Oxford, Oxford University Press, 2013).

Pocock, Tom, *Remember Nelson. The Life of Captain Sir William Hoste* (Newton Abbot, Readers Union, 1978).

Porter, Roy, *English Society in the Eighteenth Century* (Harmondsworth, Penguin, 1986).

Pressnell, L. S., *Country Banking in the Industrial Revolution* (Oxford, Clarendon Press, 1956).

Prest, Wilfred (ed.), *The Professions in Early Modern England* (London, Croom Helm, 1987).

Pücker-Muskau, Hermann von, *A Regency Visitor. The English Tour of Prince Pückler-Muskau Described in his Letters, 1826–1828*, ed. E. M. Butler (London, Collins, 1957).

Pugsley, David, 'The Western Circuit, 1817–1844', *Bracton Law Journal*, vol. 26, 1994, pp. 43–54.

Razzell, P. E., 'Social Origins of Officers in the Indian and British Home Army: 1758–1962', *British Journal of Sociology*, vol. 14, 1962, pp. 248–60.

Reiter, Jacqueline, *The Late Lord: The Life of John Pitt, 2nd Earl of Chatham* (Barnsley, Pen & Sword History, 2017).

[Roberts, David], *The Military Adventures of Johnny Newcome With an Account of his Campaign on the Peninsula and in Pall Mall* with fifteen coloured sketches by T. Rowlandson (London, Methuen, 1904).

Roberts, Greg, 'The Forgotten Brother' [William Wellesley-Pole] (unpublished MA thesis, Queen Mary University of London, 2009).

Roberts, W. J., *Mary Russell Mitford. The Tragedy of a Blue Stocking* (London, Andrew Melrose, 1913).

Robson, Robert, *The Attorney in Eighteenth-Century England* (Cambridge, Cambridge University Press, 1959).

Rodger, N.A.M., *The Wooden World. An Anatomy of the Georgian Navy* (London, Collins, 1986).

Rodger, N. A. M., *The Command of the Ocean. A Naval History of Britain, 1649–1815* (London, Allen Lane, 2004).

Romilly, Samuel, *Memoirs of the Life of Sir Samuel Romilly, Written by Himself*, ed. by his sons, 3 vols (London, John Murray, 1840).

Rothery, Mark, 'The Reproductive Behaviour of the English Landed Gentry in the Nineteenth and Early Twentieth Centuries', *Journal of British Studies*, vol. 48, July 2009, pp. 674–94.

Rothery, Mark and Jon Stobart,'Inheritance Events and Spending Patterns in the English Country House: The Leigh Family of Stoneleigh Abbey, 1738–1806', *Continuity and Change*, vol. 27, no. 3, 2012, pp. 379–407.

Rubinstein, William D., *Who Were the Rich? A Biographical Directory of British Wealth-Holders*, vol. 1, *1809–1839* (London, Social Affairs Unit, 2000).

Sack, James J., *The Grenvillites, 1801–1829. Party Politics and Factionalism in the Age of Pitt and Liverpool* (Urbana, University of Illinois Press, 1979).

Schmidt, Albert J., 'The Country Attorney in Late Eighteenth-Century England: Benjamin Smith of Horbling', *Law and History Review*, vol. 8, no. 2, Fall 1990, pp. 237–71.

Schmidt, Albert J., 'The Smiths of Horbling: Country Attorneys', *Huntington Library Quarterly*, vol. 54, no. 2, Spring 1991, pp. 143–76.

Scott, Ernest, *The Life of Captain Matthew Flinders, R.N.* (Sydney, Angus & Robertson, 1914).

Scott, Sir Walter, 'The Surgeon's Daughter', in *Chronicles of the Cannongate*, 1st series (Henry Frowde, Oxford University Press, 1912 – first published 1827).

Slinn, Sara, *The Education of the Anglican Clergy, 1780–1839* (Woodbridge, Boydell Press, 2017).

Slope, Nick, 'Serving in Nelson's Navy. A Social History of Three Amazon Class Frigates' (unpublished, PhD thesis, Thames Valley University, 2005).

Slothuber, Linda, '"The Holders of Hay & the Masters of Meadows": Farmers in Jane Austen's World', *Persuasions*, no. 37, 2015, pp. 29–42.

Smith, Harry, *The Autobiography of Lieutenant-General Sir Harry Smith*, ed. G. C. Moore Smith, 2 vols (London, John Murray, 1902).

Smith, Harry, *The Autobiography of Sir Harry Smith*, ed. G. C. Moore Smith (London, John Murray, 1910) (unless otherwise stated, this is the edition cited in the notes).

Smith, Henry, 'Journal in Spain, England, Scotland, Portugal, Spain and England, 1809–1810', unpublished transcription of a manuscript in the University of Kansas Library: Spencer Collection, MS C214.

Smith, Sydney, *The Letters of Sydney Smith*, ed. Nowell C. Smith, 2 vols (Oxford, Clarendon Press, 1953).

Southam, Brian, *Jane Austen and the Navy* (Greenwich, National Maritime Museum, 2005).

Spiers, Edward M., *The Army and Society, 1815–1914* (London, Longman, 1980).

Staves, Susan, 'Resentment or Resignation? Dividing the Spoils among Daughters and Younger Sons', in *Early Modern Conceptions of Property*, ed. John Brewer and Susan Staves (London and New York, Routledge, 1995), pp. 194–218.

Stone, Lawrence and Jeanne C. Fawtier Stone, *An Open Elite? England 1540–1880* (Oxford, Clarendon Press, 1984).

Strachan, Hew, *Wellington's Legacy. The Reform of the British Army, 1830–1854* (Manchester, Manchester University Press, 1984).

Super, R. H., *The Chronicler of Barsetshire. A Life of Anthony Trollope* (Ann Arbor, University of Michigan Press, 1988).

Surtees, Robert, *Handley Cross* (London, Bradbury Agnew, n.d.).

Swabey, Lt William, *Diary of Campaigns in the Peninsula for the Years 1811, 1812 and 1813*, ed. Col. F. A. Whinyates (London, Trotman, 1984).

Sweetman, John, *Raglan. From the Peninsula to the Crimea* (London, Arms & Armour, 1993).

Tann, Peter, 'James Tappenden, Town Clerk of Faversham, Attorney, Banker, Industrialist and Bankrupt, 1742–1841', *Archaeologia Cantiana*, vol. 115, 1995, pp. 213–29.

Taylor, Sir Herbert, *The Taylor Papers, Being a Record of Certain Reminiscences, Letters and Journals in the Life of Lieut-Gen. Sir Herbert Taylor* (London, Longmans, Green, and Co., 1913).

Teignmouth, Lord, *Memoir of the Life and Correspondence of John, Lord Teignmouth by his Son*, 2 vols (London, Hatchard and Son, 1843).

Thirsk, Joan, 'Younger Sons in the Seventeenth Century', *History*, vol. 54, 1969, pp. 358–77.

Thomas, David, 'The Social Origins of Marriage Partners of the British Peerage in the Eighteenth and Nineteenth Centuries', *Population Studies*, vol. 26, no. 1 1972, pp. 99–111.

Thompson, F. M. L., *English Landed Society in the Nineteenth Century* (London, Routledge & Kegan Paul, 1963).

Thomson-Walker, Sir John, 'John Green Crosse, of Norwich', *Proceedings of the Royal Society of Medicine: The History of Medicine*, vol. 26, no. 4, 1933, pp. 9–16 (pp. 391–8).

Thorne, R. G., *The History of Parliament. The House of Commons, 1790–1820*, 5 vols (London, Secker & Warburg for the History of Parliament Trust, 1986).

Tillyard, Stella, *Aristocrats. Caroline, Emily, Louisa and Sarah Lennox 1740–1832* (London, Chatto & Windus, 1994).

The Times, classified advertisements from *The Times* at various dates, specified in the references.

BIBLIOGRAPHY

Tomalin, Claire, *Jane Austen. A Life* (London, Viking, 1997).

Tomkins, Alannah, 'Who Were His Peers? The Social and Professional Milieu of the Provincial Surgeon-Apothecary in the Late Eighteenth Century', *Journal of Social History*, vol. 44, no. 3, 2011, pp. 915–35.

Tomkinson, Lt-Col William, *The Diary of a Cavalry Officer* (London, Swan Sonnenschein, 1895).

Treitel, G. H., 'Legal Puzzles in Jane Austen's Works', *Jane Austen Society Report* for 1986, pp. 45–59.

Trollope, Anthony, *The Vicar of Bullhampton* (Oxford, Oxford University Press, 1988).

Twiss, Horace, *The Public and Private Life of Lord Chancellor Eldon*, 3 vols (London, John Murray, 1844).

Uglow, Jenny, *In These Times. Living in Britain Through Napoleon's Wars, 1793–1815* (London, Faber & Faber, 2014).

Virgin, Peter, *The Church in an Age of Negligence. Ecclesiastical Structure and Problems of Church Reform, 1700–1840* (Cambridge, James Clarke & Co., 1989).

Virgin, Peter, *Sydney Smith* (London, HarperCollins, 1994).

[Wakefield, Edward Gibbon], *England and America. A Comparison of the Social and Political State of Both Nations*, 2 vols (London, Richard Bentley, 1833).

Wallis, Patrick and Cliff Webb, 'The Education and Training of Gentry Sons in Early Modern England', *Social History*, vol. 36, no. 1, February 2011, pp. 36–53.

Walpole, Spencer, *The Life of the Rt. Hon. Spencer Perceval*, 2 vols (London, Hurst and Blackett, 1874).

Ward, Sir A. W. and G. P. Gooch, *The Cambridge History of British Foreign Policy, 1783–1919*, vol. 1, 1783–1815 (Cambridge, Cambridge University Press, 1922).

Ward, S. G. P., *Wellington's Headquarters* (London, Oxford University Press,1957).

Ward, W. R., 'Some Eighteenth-Century Civil Servants: The English Revenue Commissioners, 1754–98', *English Historical Review*, vol. 70, no. 274, Jan. 1955, pp. 25–54.

Wareham, Tom, *The Star Captains. Frigate Command in the French Wars* (London, Chatham Publishing, 2001).

Welbourne, E., 'Bankruptcy before the Era of Victorian Reform', *Cambridge Historical Journal*, vol. 4, no. 1, 1932, pp. 51–62.

Wellington, Duke of, *Despatches, Correspondence, and Memoranda of Field Marshal Arthur Duke of Wellington, K.G.*, ed. by his son the Duke of Wellington 'in continuation of the former series', 8 vols (London, John Murray, 1857–1880) (cited as Wellington *New Despatches*, these volumes cover 1819–32).

Wellington, Duke of, *Supplementary Despatches, Correspondence and Memoranda of Field Marshal Arthur, Duke of Wellington, K.G.*, ed. by his son, the Duke of Wellington, 15 vols (London, John Murray, 1858–72).

Welsh, Col. James, *Military Reminiscences Extracted from a Journal of Nearly Forty Years' Active Service in the East Indies*, 2 vols (London, Smith, Elder and Co. 1830).

Wilson, Evan, *A Social History of British Naval Officers, 1775–1815* (Woodbridge, Boydell Press, 2017).

Wood, Andrew B., 'The Limits of Social Mobility: Social Origins and Career Patterns of British Generals, 1688–1815' (unpublished PhD thesis, London School of Economics and Political Science, 2011).

Woodruff, Philip, *The Men who Ruled India*, vol. 1, *The Founders* (London, Jonathan Cape, 1965).

Wordsworth, John, *The Letters of John Wordsworth*, ed. Carl H. Ketcham (Ithaca, NY, Cornell University Press, 1969).

Wright, Christine, *Wellington's Men in Australia. Peninsular War Veterans and the Making of Empire c. 1820–40* (Basingstoke, Palgrave Macmillan, 2011).

Yescombe, Edward, '"Hazardous and Scanty Securities". The Career of William Yescombe, Bath Attorney, 1760–1774', *Bath History*, vol. 10, 2005, pp. 97–120.

INDEX